TROLLRÚN: A Discourse on Trolldom and Runes in the Northern Tradition
Copyright © 2021 Nicholaj de Mattos Frisvold
Cover images and interior artwork on pages 1, 42, and 46 by Childerico.
'A Presentation of Trollrún' by Claude Lecouteux was translated by Estelliane Kermagoret.

All Rights Reserved.

ISBN 978-1-907881-95-4 (Hardcover)
ISBN 978-1-907881-96-1 (Paperback)

A catalogue for this title is available from the British Library.
10 9 8 7 6 5 4 3 2 1

Except in the case of quotations embedded in critical articles or reviews, no part of this book may be reproduced or transmitted in any form or by any means, electronic or mechanical, including photocopying, recording, or by any information storage and retrieval system, without permission in writing from the publisher.

Nicholaj de Mattos Frisvold has asserted his moral right to be identified as the author of this work.

Hardcover edition printed by Biddles, Norfolk.

First published in 2021
Hadean Press
West Yorkshire
England

www.hadeanpress.com

TROLLRÚN

A Discourse on Trolldom and Runes
in the Northern Tradition

NICHOLAJ DE MATTOS FRISVOLD

Acknowledgments

I would like to extend thanks and appreciation to my wife Katy, my parents Thor, Grethe and Inga, my good friends and colleagues like Rune Flaten, Rune Ødegaard, Gustav Holberg, Mari Högberg, Dr Johannes Gårdbäck and Claude Lecouteux for having influenced this book in various ways. Appreciation is also due to the many fine people making up the Nath community in Norway and to all of you who wished to remain nameless, I give my gratitude. I would also like to give a hat tip to Jim Yahazim and Stephen Grasso for hints and help with grammar, and as always, great gratitude to the wonderful visionaries Erze and Dis at Hadean for making this work manifest.

Finally, thanks to Line Esborg and the University of Oslo and the helpful people working at the Trolldoms archives, also thanks to Gidlunds förlag in helping out with source material.

A Linguistic note

In this book, I have for the large part decided to maintain modern Anglican and Nordic spelling of words, save for those times I have replicated the original Old Norse texts. At large I have ended on more contemporary spellings of names and concepts and favored the expressions used in contemporary Norway, yet with a sense of finding a middle ground between the Norse vernacular and the contemporary international standards and uses. The translations in this book were made using a synoptic method, i.e. looking at all available translations in Norwegian, Danish, Swedish and English compared to the Old Norse original text and basically re-translating everything, leading to the translations being my own.

Contents

Introduction by Johannes Gårdbäck ... 11

A Presentation of Trollrún by Claude Lecouteux ... 13

Part I: TROLLATÁL

Chapter One: The Northern Tradition ... 17

Chapter Two: Old Norse Cosmology ... 29

Chapter Three: Trolldom ... 59

Chapter Four: Magical Beings of the North ... 97

Chapter Five: A Genealogy of Trolls ... 119

Chapter Six: The Northern Observance ... 143

Chapter Seven: The Stars and Wells of Yggdrasil ... 167

Chapter Eight: The Way of *Seidr* ... 189

Chapter Nine: The Black Books of the North ... 215

Part II: RUNATÁL

Chapter Ten: Origin of the Runes ... 229

Chapter Eleven: Magical Runes and Runic Magic ... 239

Chapter Twelve: Runic Cryptology ... 253

Chapter Thirteen: The Secret of the Runes ... 255

Chapter Fourteen: Bureus and the Noble Runes ... 303

Appendix A: On the Symbolism of the Rune-drum ... 317

Appendix B: The *vargulf* and Lycanthropy in the North ... 323

Appendix C: Correspondences between runes and Trees of the North ... 331

Bibliography ... 333

Index ... 337

Introduction

Nicholaj de Mattos Frisvold first became known to me through the vast and deep network of Norwegian traditional witches. Over the years I have come to respect his great knowledge and abilities concerning traditions far away from the snowy mountains of the North and followed his work with interest.

In this book Frisvold, being a Norwegian by birth, finally returns to his roots, and in doing so not only sheds a welcome native light on the internationally well-known aspects of our tradition but also serves to bring forth some more unknown gems from the treasure house of Northern magic.

This book can be likened to a concert of old Norse music in which Frisvold takes us on a journey through time and landscape. He plays all of our common magical instruments of the tradition such as the Runes, *Seidr*, Mythology, Norse Gods and Goddesses but also instruments practically unknown to outsiders like Trollblót, Starlore, nature spirits and Nordic herbal associations.

All along Frisvold is narrating the concert with in-depth historical facts and his personal views.

If you've only seen the instruments of Trolldom but never heard them played by a native practitioner, this book will give you a sense of the tunes passed down by Nordic ancestry.

Frisvold belongs to the world of witchcraft, which has a slightly different fretting than that of my own realm of pure folk magic, but the songs that come out all speak of our tradition and the melodies have the same acoustics. It is music shaped by deep fjords, big forests and long winters.

The North may have changed in modern times but know that the music of Trolldom presented in this book can still be heard all over Scandinavia if you put your ear to the ground. It is played in counties still called "The realm of Ran", in villages still named "The Grove of Frey", "The mountain of Ull" or "The field of Frigga", heard near "The well of Thor" or "The Stones of Odin" and next to mounds of ancient kings named Gandalf, Ragnar or Harald. It is music still played by people named "Bear", "Wolf", "Oak" and "Linden". It is so common and normal to us natives that we rarely reflect upon it and even more rarely talk about it.

The trolls are still here in great abundance. Frisvold does not exaggerate when he sums it up by this excellent reflection:

"The earth with its mounds, groves, dark woods and graves was populated with death and beings from the other side in such richness that it is difficult to arrive at a conclusion of where the dead end and the mysterious beings dwelling in the moldy nightside of the world begin."

So to all of you who heard the songs of the North call from afar and felt a longing across great oceans and vast plains, it is my pleasure to welcome you in and take part of the magical music of *Trollrún*.

Johannes B. Gårdbäck
2018

A Presentation of Trollrún

In this inspired study, Nicholaj de Mattos Frisvold explores magic/spellcraft (trolldom), divination and the runes in the Norse tradition, starting from the old Norse cosmology, then presenting to us fantastic creatures, especially trolls, before switching to rituals and the ancients' practices, in particular the siðr, which rely on beliefs deeply anchored in mentalities which are still prevalent today, like in Iceland for example. Thanks to numerous authors from the Middle Ages and the 16th century – Adam of Bremen, Snorri Sturluson, Olaus Magnus – Frisvold allows us to discover the background of the Pagan world, with its sacrifices (blót) to the many gods (Óðinn, Freyr), to the Dísar, small Fate divinities, and the use of Þórr's hammer. He doesn't forget to talk about the local spirits of the land (vættir) or Yggdrasil, the cosmic tree whose name means "Óðinn's Steed." Frisvold also strives to present Scandinavian grimoires, the *svarteboken* – Vinjeboka, Cyprianus, Kvamsboka…

The second installment of this study is entitled Rúnatal – "speech on runes", a title borrowed from a part in the *Hávamál* (*Sayings from the Very High One*), and begins by discoursing on the origin of this alphabet, the Futhark, and the current state of the research; indeed, several theories compete with one another about its origins (Etruscan or not, etc.). Then, they are followed by the magical runes (*sigrúnar, ölrunar, bjargrúnar, brimrúnar, limrúnar, málrunar, hugrúnar*), for which Nicholaj de Mattos Frisvold supplies some explanations, and the runic magic which uses runes, plants (mistletoe, wolfsbane…), locks of hair, nails, eggs, apples.

Then, Frisvold studies runic cryptology and gives the reader the means to understand how some data were coded, and he commentates on each rune.

This book is a great way to access old Norse culture. Very well documented, it is highly readable, the original texts are translated, and the paintings and illustrations make some analyses more concrete.

Claude Lecouteux
Professeur émérite à la Sorbonne

Part I

TROLLATÁL

Chapter One

The Northern Tradition

Magic practiced by the common people in pre-Christian times was part of everyday culture. It was embedded in the practical skills of everyday living. – Nigel Pennick[1]

The Northern Tradition defines the spirituality and magic of the people in the northern parts of Europe, and in particular Scandinavia, the region the Romans referred to as Thule, meaning "the borders of the known world". The Northern Tradition is bound to its given geography with its climate, vegetation, culture and history encoded in its inhabitants and ancestry, and it generates a unique worldview and outlook upon the world. There are many ways of defining the geographical district of what constitutes the north, and for the purposes of this book, Thule was used as the compass and hence, the Northern Tradition is predominantly limited to present-day Scandinavia.

Besides folk tales, fairy tales and oral traditions, the primordial sources for knowledge about *trolldom* in Scandinavia are from what is called the Poetic Edda and the Prose Edda. The meaning of the word "Edda" is disputed; some say it means "great grandmother" and others think the word means "inspiration" or simply "writing". Nevertheless, the written Edda is an attempt to preserve the Northern inheritance for future generations. While the Poetic Edda consists of 29 poems, the Prose Edda is written in the form of a saga by the politician and historian Snorre Sturlasson (1179-1241). Both texts were written down in the middle of the 13th century. The Prose Edda is a saga of the history of the Norse families and political movements, but it is also a handbook of poetry and presents a survey of Norse mythology. It is also important to understand that the Edda is a historic-poetic work, with poetry taking the lead in the text. Hence, the Edda can be seen to fall nicely into the tradition starting with Homer's *Odyssey* and Vergil's *Aeneid*. The form of Snorre's Prose Edda seems the common format for presenting wisdom in Scandinavia. It is arranged as a dialogue of wisdom-competition, similar to what we find in Kalevala and in the writings of Aristotle and some of Plato's dialogues.

---

1 2005:2.

The folklore and mythology of the Northern Tradition saw an increase in interest due to the works of Jacob Grimm (1785-1863) and Victor Rydberg (1828-1895) and the compositions of Richard Wagner (1813-1883). This revival that occurred during the German *Sturm und Drang* era celebrated the heroic and glorious aspects of the Northern Tradition, as much as it did its qualities of existential dread and sense of the marvelous. This period also coincided with the peak of interest in theosophy, and through the speculations of Rudolf Johan Gorsleben (1883-1930) in his magnum opus *Hoch-Zeit der Menschheit* (*The Wedding of Humanity*), the heroic greatness of the Northern Tradition was presented as fundamental and true for the unification of the world through the principles of what can perhaps be defined as a theosophical Odinism. These esoteric and occult musings were continued by Guido von List (1848-1919), Karl Maria Wiligut (1866-1946) and Siegfried Adolf Kummer (1899-?),[2] all of them focusing in particular on the runes. These texts were also important for Nazi SS Commander Heinrich Himmler and inspired his interest in the runes, which the world got to know through the esoteric propaganda and occult interest of the Nazis.

There was also a great desire to revive the *forn sidr*, or the old ways, in Scandinavia during the early parts of the 20th century, often in the shape of "new heathenism". These movements somehow concluded in the establishment of Àsatrulaget (Fellowship of Æsir faith), where the public cult of the Æsir was revived with the use of memory, will and text under the wise guidance of Sveinbjørn Beinteinsson in 1972, and spread out into the world, preserving and safeguarding the memory of the public cult of the Æsir.

This book will not particularly focus on the parts of the Northern Tradition that are concerned with religion and mythology; rather the emphasis will be on trolldom and runes, predominantly from a pre-modern or at least magical perspective. Stephen Mitchell[3] is occupied with the shift in perception of the world that occurred during the transition from the late Middle Ages to the era of Enlightenment – this shift from an enchanted to a dis-enchanted worldview is important to keep in mind when we strive to understand the perception of the world that made trolldom possible. We are always faced with the dilemma of perception when we re-appraise arcane material as we attempt to see the world through the pre-modern and enchanted lenses of medieval man instead of through the eyes of contemporary society.

---

2 Since Kummer simply disappeared at some point, the date for his death is not stated with certainty.

3 2011.

Besides trolldom, *seidr, gandr, blót* and runes, the Black Books should be considered an integral part of the Northern Tradition; to understand the variety of these practices it is equally important to understand what kind of nature spirits practitioners were interacting with, and also what the relationship between the "cunning ones" and the Æsir, Vanir and Jotun might have been. If we want to gain insight into the Scandinavian pre-modern worldview, this means that the genealogy of the Æsir becomes important, as well as the concept of the soul and what role the stars would have played for a practitioner. This focus on worldview is essential, because the revival of Nordic mythology that has influenced the world since the 19th century has held a dis-enchanted perspective on the Northern Tradition, and largely discarded the folk magic and trolldom traditions that were passed on in sagas, annotations and legends. The 19th century revival gave primary focus to the Æsir, and everything else became rudimentary, curious shadows within the great Æsir panorama. The Northern Tradition appraised from the perspective of a cunning one will paint quite a different picture, and it is from this cunning point of view that the traditions will be treated in *Trollrún*.

In order to understand a given tradition, it is crucial to understand the people who kept the tradition, the land they lived on, the way the seasons turned, and their mentality, struggles and influences. Trolldom, like any sorcerous art born from the customs of the land, will necessarily be rooted in the needs of the people and understood from the perspective of their landscape, language, geography and perception of the world.

I also believe it is vital to make a distinction between the way the tradition was handled in its own time and what it became following the tides of transformation. A living tradition will always find itself in a constant state of change and renewal, like a serpent shedding its skin as maturity, need and opportunity present itself. One example of this is how the runes in modern days are used as a divinatory oracle modeled on tarot and astrology, which was certainly not how they were used by medieval practitioners of these mysteries in the Scandinavian mountains. Another is how the ecclesiastical impulse, Catholic and Protestant, shaped the cunning arts and the worldview of its practitioners. This doesn't mean that there is anything wrong with using tarot correspondences in understanding the runes, for example, but it is important to understand where this comparative idea came from.

In terms of the Northern Tradition, the ecclesiastical influence is of great importance and is not something that should be objected to for the sake of shaking out any Christian remains in the tradition. Rather, it would be more beneficial to take into account this influence, as we would any other influence that had an impact on the culture in question. If we look at the time of Christening in Scandinavia, we find that as Olav spread the Catholic faith across the land of Skade, the Gulating law[4] that remained in effect until 1273 stated explicitly that the heathen customs could continue as private cults and practices, and there were no penalties involved in maintaining the old customs despite Catholicism being the official religion.

The consequences of a new, official faith adopted by the Chieftains allowing people to continue to practice their old ways was perhaps to invite an immediate sympathy due to the absence of threat. Instead of resistance, a curiosity about why a new religion would allow the customs of the land to remain would encourage investigation of what this new religion was about, and likely make the field of correlation between heathen and Christian ideas friendlier.

The transition from Catholic to Lutheran Christianity in Scandinavia began in 1521; due to the dissolution of the Kalmar Union, we are speaking of a territory that counted Denmark and Norway, as well as the Duchies of Schleswig (a Danish district) and Holstein (a German district) – Denmark extended over today's Denmark, Iceland, Greenland, Faroe Islands, Skåneland and Gotland in Sweden as well as Øsel (Saaremaa) in Estonia. By 1528, under the reign of Christian III, this geographical location was deemed Lutheran.

In 1587 we see the first of the famous Faustbooks, the publication of the little tract *The History of Dr. Johann Fausten*, later made famous by Goethe's theatre play and mirroring the Black Books and Cyprians in Scandinavia. As for Black Books, the oldest so far dates back to 1480 and was published by Mary Rustad as *Vinjeboka* – but the majority of Cyprians date from the 16th to the 18th centuries and gained a renewed popularity with the cheap paperback prints of several grammars of the art in France in the 18th and 19th century. These *Bibliothèque bleue* editions were printed in great number; at this time, French as well as German was often spoken by the Scandinavian intellectuals who in turn translated several of these grimoires for private use or public circulation in small circles.

It is with the Cyprians that we see the ecclesiastical magic coloring northern magic and craft but this coloring would only

---

4   This was the law code dating back to around the 8th century largely focusing on regulations concerning farms and agriculture. It was replaced, yet in large parts also continued by the Magnus Lagabötes Land-law that was in effect until 1688.

be admissible if there was some form of resonance between Catholic Christianity and the heathen customs. I believe this resonance is well explained in Emma Wilby's thesis[5] where she concludes that the term "the old religion" was indeed a reference to Catholic Christianity, as this term is used in the transition period from Catholicism to Anglican and Lutheran movements. Catholicism with its enchanted prayers, barbarous language of Latin, transubstantiation, the cult of the dead through saints, and appeal to the senses and emotions through its Mass would for sure be in greater harmony with magical thinking than Lutheranism and its iconoclasm and demonization of the emotions in favor of reason.

Catholic Christianity, due to the consequences of Reformation, became vilified and was turned into the scapegoat of the Lutherans. It was referred to by Martin Luther as "the synagogue of Satan", and we must ask why he saw the Vatican in this way. For sure, the greed and political involvement of the Vatican in the late Middle Ages and the Renaissance explains parts of it, but we need to go to its doctrine to see the complete picture. Luther made a doctrinal reformation, about faith and, in the end, about what would constitute Christian dogma and creed, and in this Luther found the Roman Catholic Church to be the synagogue of Satan. The facets he attacked the most were superstition, the allowance of rightful "magic", the veneration of saints and the veneration of the dead. The Roman Catholic Church was, in turn, a Christian interpretation of Roman customs, and so we are speaking of understanding spirits of land, air and water, deities and venerated ancestors in a specific way.

The Roman interpretation was actively used when the Romans conquered new territories and saw in the existing deities variations of their own gods. They gave to them praise names or epitaphs which referred to a deity already known by them, and thereby recognized the new territory under the rulership of a force they already knew to be the same, yet different. In this, a desire to understand and find common ground was always present, which I believe can explain a part of the success of the Roman Empire to expand in such magnitude as it did.

The Roman interpretation was also vividly used when Roman Catholic Christianity started to spread out, and so heathen temples were destroyed and a saint was appointed to oversee the renewal on old grounds. In this way, saints were used to interpret the forces that were already present. Hence, in substituting a saint or a planetary deity, what the god was replaced by would also represent a succession of the same power and idea, a similar force dressed in a different

---

5   2006.

language. This would explain the use of saints and other Biblical figures in spells and enchantments.

The word trolldom has been used as a collective term for the witchcraft, magic and sorcery of the healing and harming kind that was practiced in Scandinavia. Until the 16th century, the practice of trolldom was not necessarily seen as malicious, and the cunning folk were not considered the servants of the Devil. This is because the acts of cunning folk, like helping with childbirth and bestowing remedies and cures and also prophetic gifts were not considered something one did for personal gain, nor was there any malice connected to such practices. It was not until the late Middle Ages, when the world was sailing into the more intellectual magic of the Renaissance, that the fusion between cunning folks' practices and diabolism occurred, due to the continental obsession with *malefica* or black magic and by extension what was grouped under the labels "witchcraft" and "sorcery".

When we go through the Nordic sagas, we are presented with a conglomerate that speaks of the social structure and the collective beliefs of a culture. The mythologies presented together with popular beliefs expressed just as much the norms and values of the society revealed in metaphors and symbols. Trolldom is usually presented as something of an underground phenomenon, as a hidden lore that only a few possessed, something feared and respected. Trolldom was instead an integral part of the culture in Scandinavia. In Gretti's saga, which was written down in the early 14th century, we have one example of how the magical climate appeared in the 11th and 12th centuries where trolldom and seidr are translated into black magic and sorcery. It is the mother of Grettir who tells her son the following:

> Be on your guard against treachery. You will not be killed by weapons; I have had strange dreams, be wary of sorcery; few things are mightier than black magic.

We see from this short account that trolldom was associated with treachery, that trolldom and seidr were viewed as something real and effective, and we see the importance of dreams and omens. Dreams and omens were the collective field where magic was done, and also discovered. A raven dwelling at your window for no good reason would always be an ominous sign, as would sudden strange behavior amongst domesticated animals. Omens were taken, and if negative consequences were witnessed, specialists were called upon to interpret the omens or the bad dreams. It follows that the

Northern Tradition is rich in material speaking about interpreting dreams and omens, as demonstrated in Carl Herman Tillhagen's book *Folklig Spådomskonst* from 1968, which can be translated into "Rustic peoples forms of divination". Divination by clover and ox-eye daisy (*Leucanthemum vulgare*), and by throwing shoes and pointed objects over the left shoulder, were popular ways to gain simple answers, as were taking in signs from everything: embers, wind, birds in flight and anything unusual happening in given routines or gatherings. These could all be subject to interpretation, such as the popular superstition that dressing with your shirt inside out means gifts or good news will arrive that day.

The distinction between "black" and "white" magic in the Northern Tradition is linked to the principles found in Utgard, the outer realm where Jotun lives, and Midgard, where humans live, which represents the cosmic center. This division is necessary in order to understand the Old Norse idea of magic. We see in the Edda how Utgard is both a place of danger as well as a place of wisdom. Thor goes there to fight; Odin goes there to talk. Utgard also represents the abode of chaos, the place within the world created by Odin and the Æsir that is a constant threat to the temporary order they made from the body of the slain giant Ymir.

Troll has a strong connotation with Jotun, and so trolldom, the art of trolls, often gained a dubious reputation, yet it comprised a reality that no one could escape. It was woven into the fabric of society and imagination. Hence, we can see in this that the idea of black magic stems originally from a perception of the chaos that lives beyond the hedge of the orderly. Seidr, on the other hand, was usually seen as something positive, a respected art. The aim of seidr was primarily focused on gaining insight into the past or discovering causes for misfortune in a farmstead or village, aiming towards rectifying what had fallen into chaos and destruction. But since seidr was, after all, a form of trolldom, it inspired a certain awe, since it could also be used to gain control over a specific situation and in matters of influence. While seidr was subject to an ambiguity that usually was more positive than negative, it was not so with trolldom. Whenever trolldom is mentioned in the sagas it is always in the pursuits of gaining power or the ability to influence man, beast and nature. This skill or power could either be learned, passed on, or be inherited or given in a number of ways.

As elsewhere in the world, witches could be blamed for failing crops and misfortunes. From what we see in sagas and in folktales it was usually wizards, or male practitioners, more than "witches", who were respected as men of *kunning* – wise or cunning men.

These people were also considered quite gentlemen-like since they were often versed in how to behave properly, compose poetry and song, and were somehow less feared than female practitioners. This might be related to the strong connection between trolldom and the troubadour tradition that was a male pursuit and well-respected.

We can find some traces of the terms used to describe male/female practitioners of trolldom, especially in the sagas where women tend to be described in less favorable and more dangerous terms than men. Still today in Norway, a word like *trollkone* or *trollkjerring* (trollmaiden) holds a negative flavor, but in medieval times this was a term used for a cunning and wise woman.

The terms used for wizards and witches were for men words like *galdramadr, trollmadr, vitki* and *skratte*, while women were called *gýgr, seidkone, trollkone* or *volve*. It is interesting to see that these labels were often interchangeable with names for nature spirits, especially *vaettir*. Vaettir and Jotun were closely connected under the commonality of both being trolls, just like a *trollmann* was often described as a troll himself, as much as a *seidkone* would be one.

Other terms used to describe these trollish people of the north were the terms *fródr* and *fornfraedi*, words used to describe people who had access to old knowledge; old knowledge always somehow stemmed from the Jotun and was considered a form of knowledge that had been passed down in clandestine and secret ways. These also included the more magical dimensions such as spell-casting and divination, together with a general knowledge of the many aspects of the old tradition. So we see how, in one term, a lot of other terms are deeply connected.

If a person possessed the knowledge of the past, he or she was automatically an authority and an advisor, and often knowing too much came with some form of fearfulness. If one could see back in time and understand what was *forn* (past), one assumedly also possessed the power to look into the future; the fear was most likely evoked due to the connection such a person had with the Norns, the three Fates that dictated the destiny of all living things. With the exception of seidr, no practice was more connected to trolldom than the art of carving runes with the aim of cursing or healing. Our most precious source for understanding the importance of the runes, and also what a deep secret they were, can be found in *Hávamál* where Odin says the following about the runes in stanza 142:

The Northern Tradition

Rúnar munt þú finna
ok ráðna stafi,
mjök stóra stafi,
mjök stinna stafi,
er fáði fimbulþulr
ok gerðu ginnregin
ok reist hroftr rögna.

The runes you must find and the meaningful letter,
A very great letter
A very powerful letter
Which the mighty sage stained
And the powers magnanimous made
And the runemaster of the ruling ones carved out

    The act of uttering words was considered almost as powerful as was words spoken in the spirit of hate or love, which were assumed to have physical form and could not be taken back. The verbs used in these instances were *gala* and *galdra*, which refer to a song or chant in the sense of a charm or a spell. *Galdr* could be performed as a powerful poetic song as much as it could a murmuring, or in the form of *lokkur*, which is both an instrument and a way of singing that would attract animals. Of interest is that the word *galdra* is etymologically related to the word *galen*, mad or insane, which might be indicative of the trance or state of mind of the person uttering these galdrs. This state of mind is often ascribed to troubadours, those who function as the "memory" of the culture. In Sturlasson's handbook for poets, he writes about certain meters used for galdr called *ljódahattr* and *galdralag.*

    We find many instances where both witches and gods are told to sing over wounds to heal, or to sing over runes that have been carved. One of the most fearsome forms of galdr and runemagic is what is known as *níd*. Originally this word spoke about ridicule and harm, and was often very vulgar in its imagery. A *niding* one, deserving of harmful ridicule, is described as a person lacking honor or shame, a vile and sordid person. Some of the famous people connected to this art were called Kveld-Ulfr (evening wolf) and Egil Skallagrímsson, who was said to be half-troll. We will return to this particular form of seidr in more detail, but for now, this account from *Egil's saga* will demonstrate the power and magnitude ascribed to trolldom when used by a true cunning one:

Egil went up onto the island. He took a hazel pole in his hand and went to the edge of a rock facing inland. Then he took a horse's head and put it on the end of the pole. Afterwards he made an invocation, saying "Here I set up this scornpole and turn its scorn upon King Eirík and Queen Gunnhild" – then he turned the horse's head to face land – "and I turn its scorn upon the nature spirits [*landvaettir*] that inhabit this land, sending them astray so that none of them shall find its resting-place by chance or design until they have driven King Eirík and Queen Gunnhild from this land!" Then he drove the pole into a cleft in the rock and left it to stand there. He turned the head towards the land and carved the whole invocation in runes on the pole.

At the root of the Northern Tradition we find the Norns, the three Jotun women that commanded the Fate of every living being and carved its Fate into Yggdrasil. Fate was considered a part of the soul, and was commonly viewed as something threatening. For a people that lived in darkness, snow, and ice for large parts of the year, Fate was by extension often unkind, and even Odin in *Hávamál* complains about the cruelty of Fate and how even the Æsir were powerless in front of it. Fate was unavoidable, as was the chaotic darkness in the months of winter, and in this the importance of turning what was grim into something joyous was important. Trolldom and runes, in the sense of "secrets" at large, could be used to temporarily turn this ill Fate and manipulate it.

This was a world populated with benign and hostile beings where everything could bring omens and predictions. It was a world of darkness celebrating summer, ale and daylight. Perhaps a poem by the Swedish cunning man Keeron Ögren[6] can summarize the temperament of the Northern Tradition as the next chapter will trace the Old Norse Cosmology.

> Of all things that is found in the world
> Most of it is hidden
> For man's small minds it is hidden
> Greater in the world is what is invisible
> More profound than we can imagine
> The world is always bigger
> Here lives little people and vaettir
> Rulers and trolls

---

6   2005.

Ghosts and beings
A world bounty of beings
Large and small
Call them
If you will
Because the invisible ones
They are found in this world
Even though it seems like
They are living in another place
As it was in another room
In the same house
They are here
We just do not always notice
Because we are only human

We are weaving a web that makes sense
We are weaving a curtain
To cover the truth
And that makes the world sensible
Ah, if we only knew what was hidden in the web
If it was taken away
The world would shatter and end
Don't curse the curtain
Which without nothing would show itself
Truth before the curtain
Was nothing
But a fall in the abyss
We are men
And we barely manage to live
In a world of men
But don't believe for a second
That the world is human
Sometimes we sense something
Through the rifts in the web
That is not mystery
We are weaving our web
The curtain in front of the abyss
Live with the curtain
Make sure it doesn't blow away
But do not be perplexed
To know that there are things
Behind the curtain

Chapter Two

Old Norse Cosmology

It appears to me that in the same way the Sami's have in their original heathenism fused it with Christian imageries – in the same way as we find in the Theology of the old Norsemen traces of Christian teachings. – Thomas von Westen, 1723

Investigating a culture's cosmology and worldview is always a complex undertaking, and it is crucial to lay down some premises for such investigations. When we speak of the Northern Tradition, we need to be aware of the religious shifts that marked the worldview, first in the 10th century with the advent of Catholicism, and then in the 15th century with the advent of Lutheranism. There is also the paradigm shaped by the ever-changing zeitgeist that is perhaps the most complicating factor as it frequently leads us to look at the past with the perception of the present.

The most detailed account of Nordic cosmology is found in Snorre Sturlasson's Prose Edda. His presentation has frequently suffered critique due to the similarities between his cosmology and Christian myths and theology, which raises questions about the level of Christian bias involved in his understanding of the Old Norse cosmology. It is questionable whether the Christian factor was truly anything of concern, not only because 12th century Catholicism in the Northern hemisphere was quite different from contemporary Catholicism, but also because Iceland was not formally brought under the jurisdiction of Norway until 1262. The Icelandic laws prior to this were very lenient regarding heathenism and its practice. Penalties and punishments could in theory happen, but rarely did because in Iceland there was a boundary in law between public cult (Christendom) and private cult (heathenism). This law insisted on the social position and function of the private and official cults, yet the old ways were in no way forbidden to practice. The law was only concerned with keeping what was supposedly private in the realm of the farmstead, and so the restrictions surrounding the old ways were principally concerned with how public you could and should be with your private rituals and ceremonies. If we look at the practices of blót on a public and private level it might appear that the law was not about favoring Christianity at all, but rather ensuring that everything was done in its right place. The larger communal blót was done for the sake of the larger community, but the types of blót that were benign and important for the family were of a private and intimate character. Dealing with your ancestors and your vaettir pertained to the private sphere and was respected as such. What was private was supposed to be kept private, and what was public stayed in the public sphere. This lack of prohibition, combined with Snorre's preservation work, led to his Prose Edda being the first written account of the Nordic Tradition and its cosmology.

Attempting to understand Snorre in relationship to the history, culture, religion, and philosophy of his time will enable us to understand better the depth and nuances that shaped his background and the context from which he was presenting the Nordic Tradition and custom. Snorre was an aristocrat, well-traveled and from a family of troubadours. He was himself interested in history and politics as much as poetry, theology, and mythology. Like Herodotus, Diodorus or Pliny, he wanted to secure the legacy of his people for the generations to come, and in this Christianity, with its intense interest in writing everything down, might have been a most welcome inspiration for Snorre, the troubadour-historian.

The Nordic historian-poets were known as *Skalds*, and it was their legacy Snorre was preserving in his work, both the Eddaic poetry and the Skaldic poetry. Actually, Snorre was quite critical of the tradition of bards and troubadours on the continent, judging them both as bad historians and mediocre poets. Concerning the latter, the text *Ynglingatal* is perhaps one of the more famous examples of Skaldic poetry, yet it is also one of the most simple in the use of poetic meters. Its detailed syntax and rich sentences are bound together by ever-changing *heiti*[7] and *kennings*[8] that turn Skaldic poetry into art and memory, history and words that copulate like a nest of serpents, bringing variations of the same stories, songs and legends into remembered history perceived as art in progress. The Skalds were artists as well as historians and journalists and were, for instance, present at the battle at Stiklestad in 1030, where Olav Haraldsson, in spite of his defeat, saw it as a triumph for his "White Christ", and documented the event for generations to come. At least since the year 800[9] they were present in courts to document proceedings,

---

7   Names.

8   Synonyms.

9   Interesting to note is that the troubadour tradition originated in Occitania, present day southern France in the early 12th century, but the Nordic Skald tradition that has much in common with it dates back

and their services could be hired for journalistic, historical, or artistic purposes. Snorre was occupied with preserving various Nordic forms of poetry, including the Eddaic poetry that was signified by meters that were more magical in effect,[10] and also the type of memory that was conveyed using "charming meters" that were of a different kind, namely wisdom, myth, folklore and magic. There was a specific meter used for any given purpose.

Snorre, being a Skald and a nobleman and living in a place and a time where the Old Customs co-existed with the New Religion, would naturally present his work as a synthesis of historical accounts, poetic interpretations, and artistic and philosophical renderings. His account was concerned with honoring both the memory of the land, his own vision, and the shifting world in which he was living and experiencing. We need to take into account all of these influences in order to understand his presentation of the Northern Tradition.

We should also keep in mind that from the Viking attacks in England in 789, through to the defeat of King Harold at the Battle of Hastings in 1066, the Scandinavians traveled frequently and made contact with several different cultures. The connection with present-day France, Germany and Belgium was strong, and even Spanish, Moorish and Italian influences were brought back to Scandinavia from the 900s and onwards, which would contribute to a richness of cultural sensibility being spread across Scandinavia in the form of songs, tales, and poetry.

Scandinavia was deemed Christian from around 1020, at least in terms of its acceptance as an official religion. We also know that until the 15th century, a distinction was made between private devotion and the public cult/religion. Heathenry was not immediately forbidden with the advent of Catholic Christianity; the notion of heathenism as forbidden or wicked came to prominence later with Protestant Christianity when Scandinavia was caught up in the continental "witch craze" during the 16th century.

It is common to differentiate between paganism/heathenism and Christianity as a means to aid us in making sense of the old customs of the North. Andreas Nordberg in his article on "Continuity of the Old Norse Religion"[11] questions if we are not better off abolishing the term "religion" altogether when we are speaking of the Old Nordic Tradition. Such distinction would perhaps be useful because

---

to 800. Given the intense 300 years of traveling in the Viking era from 800 onwards, perhaps the Scandinavian Skalds somehow inspired, at least partly, the troubadour tradition.

10 Especially the meter known as Ljóðaháttr.
11 In Raudvere & Schjødt (eds), *More than Mythology*, 2012: 119.

heathen Scandinavians were not really doing religion in the sense we understand it today. This is a matter that will be discussed in more detail in the sixth chapter when the Nordic observance will be presented, but for now, we should just mark the difference in worldviews on a mere theological level.

In Christendom we find an elevated and untouchable creative force distant from the world of men, while in the Nordic worldview gods walk amongst men. A factor like this should give cause to pause and realize that Christian ideas infused in such a worldview would find a different reflection and understanding in terms of what was already present in the Nordic mythology. Hence, the similarities between Balder's resurrection and the resurrection of Jesus Christ are not necessarily speaking of Balder becoming Christian, but that Balder was already subject to this theme prior to Christianity's influence and a correlative realization took place. This is certainly a valid hypothesis given how Christian mythology was inspired from foreign mythologies and legends itself.

Another important factor is that when we are speaking of Christianity in the 11th and 12th century, we need to realize that Christianity in the high Middle Ages was quite different from the Roman Catholic Church we see today. It was a period of theological restlessness, dissent, and heresy as well as political frustration on the continent, and that includes Scandinavia. One factor that ties Norway to the greater ecclesiastical mission, in terms of politics, peace, heresy and theological confusion, is found in the crusade of King Sigurd and the dramatic events in medieval Europe that followed.

In the year 1107, King Sigurd I of Norway joined a Crusade and went to Jerusalem through Iberia. In 1119, the Order of the Knights Templar was founded and its cause was sanctioned and blessed by the Pope. In 1130, Sigurd I died, starting a 100-year period of civil war between his potential successors. In 1130-1138, the world experienced the papal schism with a pope and an antipope. In 1162, Genghis Khan was born, and 45 years later the Mongols spread fear across Eastern Europe. By 1243, we have seen seven years of papal war, and it is only after the papal war in 1265 that some theological order started to take early shape with the publication of Thomas Aquinas' *Summa Theologica*, which was used as the base for what Catholicism really was. This means that the idea of Christianity held by Snorre was a pre-Thomist Christianity, focused on the importance of the Church and the teachings of particular monastic orders (most likely without really having any truly unified theological understanding given the theological disarray at the time), the consequences of the crucifixion, the miracle of the Eucharist, the life of Jesus and the saints. Beyond that, little else in Catholicism was fixed as such.

The 12th and 13th centuries were dominated by the Crusades, Mongols and schisms, and it is almost natural that we see the first Episcopal Inquisition established in this theological chaos, more precisely in 1184 in Languedoc. This first Inquisition was established to combat heresy within the Church; it was later established under the jurisdiction of the Dominicans in 1229 in Rome as a Papal Inquisition investigating all baptized members of the congregation. The Episcopal Inquisition targeted the Cathars and Waldensians in France, while the Papal Inquisition targeted heretics at large and, in particular, heretics among the clergy. Confessions could, from this point on, be extracted with the help of torture.

The 13th century was the time of Snorre, but he shared this period with people like Albertus Magnus, Dante, Marco Polo, Roger Bacon, Thomas Aquinas and Francis of Assisi. We are speaking of a time when Christianity was in flux and, besides the Crusades, was dominated by monastic reform and a large increase in monastic orders. Anselm, Bernhard of Clairvaux and Hildegard of Bingen are a few of the notable names that come to mind when thinking of this period when friars made great advances in wine and beer making, calligraphy and translations of philosophy, theology, and literature in general.

In 1260 we see the appearance of *The Golden Legend*, the compilation of the lives of the saints, which describes them in a similar fashion as Herodotus and Homer spoke of heroes and gods, entirely embraced in a worldview enchanted and filled with marvels. Also, here we get an idea of vital elements in Christianity, namely its radical dualism, that opens a world of intense contrast between the angelic and demonic, and thus, a world of magic, sin, penitence, virtue and heroism finds its shape in imagination, art, poetry, theology and philosophy along with the introduction of Purgatory.

In the 13th century, it was still possible to do magic and marvels as long as it was effectuated by God and his angels and not by some false idol or demon. Clearly Snorre was influenced by Christianity, but the kind of Christianity that was as enchanted and contradictory to theology as was any other philosophical theology playing itself out in the minds of the 13th century learned aristocrats.

The historian Jacques Le Goff and the philosopher Charles Taylor, in different ways, both address the pre-modern perspective and its marvelous content in their description of the ensouled and enchanted worldview that dominated continental thinking until the Industrial Revolution made the Cartesian premises a disenchanted material reality – a world free from superstition, ghosts and living ancestors. This focus on the shift in worldview from the pre-modern and modern, first established by Weber, is crucial to use as a cosmological reference if we seek a better idea of how the pre-modern Norsemen actually perceived the world. The greatest difference between us and them is this shift from an enchanted worldview to a disenchanted worldview which became dominant as the western world entered the age of Enlightenment.

Weber saw religion in an evolutionist and progressive frame of development from superstition to science, where Protestantism was viewed as the form of religion that would eliminate magic. His perceived vision of modernity bringing with it disenchantment rings true, as modernity invited in a larger field for atheism and scientific doubt. This was somehow rooted in the impact Lord Byron and the romantics had upon the world, culminating with Nietzsche and how he took the pulse of the world with his philosophy. Ironically through *sturm und drang*, pessimism and industrial revolution, we find that science and religion have become more dogmatic and narrow as a consequence of the disenchantment of the world. Now, not only God is dead, but any spiritual substance can be relocated to a field of primitivism and superstition in the name of calculus and scientific measurement. Gordon White in his *Star Ships*[12] discusses this field between disenchantment and magic in relation to how the status quo of science presents a paradigm born from its own dogmatic conviction, which leads scientists to employ deliberately misleading data and to manipulate conclusions. White quotes Wendy Doninger, in reference to Martin Buber, in how the range of exploration has become narrower and science more dogmatic in the following way:

> All positive religion rests on an enormous simplification of the manifold and wildly engulfing forces that invade us: it is the subduing of the fullness of existence. All myth, in contrast, is the expression of the fullness of existence, its image, its sign; it drinks incessantly from the gushing fountain of life. Hence, religion fights myth where it cannot absorb and incorporate it…[13]

This observation is important because in attempting to establish a pre-modern cosmology it is vital that we understand the history, culture, geography, and forces at play in the culture or society we

---

12 Scarlet Imprint, 2016.
13 White, 2016: 220.

seek to form an idea of. In other words, it is crucial that we take as a nucleus the imagination of the people we want to understand. Imagination, as used by clerics in the 12th century, defined a quality born from sensibility. This sensibility was mediated between the internal and external world, and within it nature was animated and alive, populated with invisible denizens like wind and as tangible as wine and bread.

As Charles Taylor comments in *A Secular Age*,[14] unbelief was not an option for pre-modern man; unbelief became an option in tandem with the secular society and in particular with the rise of Modernity. In this, Lord Byron (1788-1824) and the Romantic Movement, but also Percy B. Shelley (1792-1922) and his thesis *The Necessity of Atheism* published in 1811, took the pulse of the time as well as moved its zeitgeist onward into the beginning of Modernity where atheism or unbelief was clearly an option.

This means that in order to arrive at an understanding of the worldview of the Norsemen in the 13th century, and onward through the full impact of Protestantism and folk religiosity into the Modern era, we need to allow myth to speak loudly in an enchanted world where history itself is subject to an artistic deconstruction mediated by the importance of imagination, memory and worldview. As Le Goff wrote:

> History is a matter of transformation and memory, memory of a past that continues to live and to change as one society succeeds another.[15]

Not only this, the variations at global and local levels, as well as within fraternities and disparate groups, generate a great diversity, even in geographical regions of presumed "sameness".[16] This leads to enormous problems in generalizing the belief, customs and theology of the heathen Scandinavians, as people on the west coast would probably hold different sets of beliefs and customs from people in the far north, while being bound by commonality and similarity. It is this commonality that must be uncovered in order to understand the cosmology that lies at the root of the old heathen customs, pre-Christian as well as those transformed through the influence or presence of Christianity.

Given all these factors it is highly plausible that Snorre may have been influenced by Christian mythology as much as any other

---

14 2007.
15 1988: 11.
16 See Kjeldstadli, 1999, Raudvere & Schjødt (eds), 2012.

mythology, local and foreign, in his presentation of Nordic cosmology, and yet these are just a few salient elements instrumental in shaping his understanding of Nordic cosmology. In Snorre's time, it was the Ptolemaic earth-centered cosmology derived from Aristotle that was in vogue. Copernicus' heliocentric model and Bruno's pantheism is still 300 years ahead of Snorre, hence the focus was on earth as the center of the world, and this naturally infused the worldview in specific ways.

A Crossroad of Fire and Ice made from Nothing

For the Nordic people, the two contrasts in the world were ice and fire, and naturally by mere observation it was the interaction of these two forces which was considered to hold the potential for creation. Snorre does not say where the fire and the ice originally came from, but gives them directions of south and north. Hence the Nordic cosmology, as presented by Snorre, starts with how fire and ice, as active and passive principles, took shape in Ginnungagap, the great void. The fire and the ice are described as two homesteads: Nifelheimen, foggy and cold in the north, and Muspellheimen, fiery and hot in the south. Rivers go out from both of these homesteads or worlds, with the northern river filling up Ginnungagap with snow, cold and ice, as the southern river brings heat and fire.

From this, the first giant Ymir took shape. As he was sleeping in the void, male and female *rimtusser*, what are commonly known as frost-giants, were born from his left armpit, and from his legs he gave birth to a son. Out of this same process came another being called Audhumla, the cosmic cow, that feeds the giant Ymir with milk. Audhumla, by licking the stones formed in Ginnungagap, revealed from the ice the first Jotun, Buri, which in turn begot a son called Borr that married Bestla, daughter of the giant Bolthorn. Bestla and Borr became the parents of Odin, Vile and Ve. Odin and his brothers killed Ymir and exterminated all the frost giants, except for Berghjelmir and his wife, who continued to give birth to more frost giants.

After killing Ymir, Odin and his brothers then took the body of Ymir and from it created the earth, made the heavens from his skull, and placed four dwarves to support the four corners of the heavens. Then they took sparks and fire from Muspellheimen and spread stars across the heavens. Outside the eclipse of the earth we find the ocean, and at the coast, the Jotun were given their dwelling which was called Utgard.

In the far north they placed the Jotun Raesvelg,[17] who looked like an eagle, and was responsible for natural disasters like storms and tsunamis. From the maggots generated from Ymir's putrid flesh they created more dwarves and spread them out across the earth, making their dwelling under stones and under the earth. At the center of Asgard they planted Yggdrasil, the cosmic tree (which will be discussed in detail in the seventh chapter). At the center of the earth they made Midgard and secured it using the eyelids of Ymir to make a natural barricade against the Jotun.

In Midgard, they placed Ask and Embla, the two first humans, whom they created from driftwood. In the center of Midgard they made Asgard, the homestead of the Æsir, as well as the rainbow-bridge named Bifrost to connect heaven and earth. As this cycle of temporal time comes to an end, Bifrost will start to shake and collapse at the apocalyptic event known as Ragnarök, which will announce the end of the world as we know it, and the sons of Surt from Muspellheimen will flow over the world bringing destruction and death to the majority of the Æsir, ending their reign.

In the way it is described, we might conclude that Asgard is considered a parallel reality in the world of men, not much different from the ideas of the fairy realm and other realities not normally perceived by the human sight. It corresponds to "the other side" and is in harmony with the enchanted worldview of the Middle Ages.

At this point, it would be helpful to look in more detail at the semantics of this cosmogony. If we look at Ginnungagap, it is usually translated as "gaping void" or "wide void", but it appears composed of three words: *ginn*, *unga* and *gap*. *Ginn* is a predicate and is also the root for the subject *ginnar*, which means "attractor", "mover" or "gatherer"; while as a predicate, it always holds the meaning of "expanse", "might" and "power". *Unga* means "young", and refers to what is in expanse, what is not yet mature, and which is still in growth; while *gap* refers to a "wide open mouth",[18] or a cavity, which gives us the idea of Ginnungagap as a void in constant growth, and that its nature and direction is to constantly become something along a scale of immature potential into mature possibilities and realities in various degrees of manifestation.

Nifelheimen means "foggy home" or "hidden home", while Muspellheimen means "place of resistance" or "home of opposition". It is interesting that it is here in the fiery south, the home

---

17 "Eater of Corpses".
18 Clive Tolley argues in his D.Phil thesis (1993) a reference to the wolf in relation to Ginnungagap, suggesting that the world ended by wolves was also begun by wolves.

of Surt, we find the ongoing construction of Naglfare,[19] the ship made from the fingernails of dead people, which, together with the collapse of Bifrost, will play a vital role in Ragnarök. This would indicate that fire and the south was perceived as the home of chaos, typified by Loke, whose name means to do something in a chaotic and unpredictable manner, as well as signifying the steady flame and heat coming from a fire. Hence, fire is the creative potential rising from the chaos to work upon the ice and fog in Nifelheimen, and Bifrost is what connects the North and the South, the horizontal axis of the ever-turning solstices, as much as it does the visible and invisible realms.

The name Ymir is most likely derived from *im* that can mean both "glowing embers" and "hot vapors" and would perhaps suggest what happens when hot embers are thrown into cold waters, which, in turn, becomes a metaphor for creation. Also, it would be worthy to mention that this play between fire and water is frequently used in trolldom for sorcerous ends, such as divination and healing. Divination or medicine can be made from pouring hot lead into water, or by introducing nine pieces of glowing embers from nine different woods to water or ale, producing a magical liquid.

What is interesting about Ymir is that he simply appears from Ginnungagap, and then, as he is sleeping, more beings suddenly appear from under his armpit and from the rubbing of his legs. Ymir is also called Aurgjelmir, a word that refers back to both "earth" and "origin" but also *gjelme* which means "to sound" or "to make a noise". This might refer to the importance of sound in the process of creation and how sound would enable matter to take a given shape. We also find in Ginnungagap the cosmic cow Audhumla, which refers to "wealth" and "richness" and might mean simply "rich in milk". As she feeds Ymir, she also reveals Buri from the work of her hot tongue on the ice. Buri is the first settler or farmer who stepped out from the fog and mist and gave birth to Bor, which holds the additional meaning of being something supportive and a covering. Hence, Buri represents the first farmer while Bor is the first homestead or farmhouse.

On the other hand, we have the offspring from Ymir such as Trudgjelmir and Berghjelmir, both holding names associated with making noise or great sounds, as well as Bestla, which means "to scream", and who, with Buri, gave birth to Odin and his brothers, Vile and Ve. Odin and his brothers murdered and dismembered Ymir and gave rise to a creation of their own. In this way, it seems that the

---

19 Naglfare is also the name of a Jotun that together with Nátt (Night) begot Audr, or abundance.

worlds are destroyed and renewed, each world using the same matter but put together in different ways, mediated by the forces taking charge of the creative process that give creation a unique imprint and direction.

As we see, the Nordic cosmology is cyclic, and we do find several references to other mythologies in its presentation, revealing a common traditional or perennial theme. We find Greek, Indian, Egyptian and Christian similarities bound together in the cold and icy reality of the Norsemen where, naturally, fire was the great awakener of life, the force of revelation that could reveal what ice and snow kept hidden. There can be many explanations for this, but explanations that follow a historical or mythological linear path of reference might not deepen our understanding of the cosmology as would addressing the themes in a traditional perspective.

Apparently, the element of fire is considered vital as the agent of revelation, such as in the case of Audhumla's tongue that reveals what is hidden. Fire, in its own right, is the element that brings life from the cold, icy matter resting in the Great Void. Fire is also the element of creation for Heraclitus and the element constituting djinns and angels. Fire is associated with the life-giving breath, and, at the beginning and the end of the world, fire was also the element that ensured that you would stay alive in Scandinavia and not freeze to death. Creation appears caused *ex nihilo*, but there are no musings found concerning the beginning of creation, which perhaps is logical for a cyclical cosmology that gives its prime focus to the present cycle and how it came to be.

We also find the concept of a giant, cosmic being subject to dismemberment, as we find in the myths of Purusha in the Vedas. In this phase of creation, we see the absence of a creative God. The idea of the godhead seems to suggest a mass of matter, the potential of which is activated by fire, while creation itself is made by beings that adopted the name Æsir, the "shining ones", who became creator principles because of the dismemberment of the cosmic giant.

The Greek relationship between titans as the elder race, and giants and monsters in the eyes of the Olympic gods, is difficult to escape here, namely, how creation and time is generated by spiritual forces that are the children and grandchildren of the cosmic giant. This theology is radically different from what we find in Christendom and is perhaps more akin to Valentinian Gnosticism and its concept of the demiurge than anything else.

There are several factors we should take into account in order to arrive at an understanding of this cosmogony. First, it looks like the old Norsemen held ideas similar to the Greek *protogenos*, meaning, self-generated spiritual denizens that appear from a chaotic substance who establish a path and direction of a given cycle of unfolding at its primordial genesis, setting the standards for the type of world they would naturally uphold. Second, it might look like they held beliefs similar to Anaximander's (610-546 BCE) theories on natural selection in competitive environments, better known through the work of Charles Darwin's *On the Origin of Species* (1859), but which actually rested on a rich history of similar thoughts. In this sense, even the Platonic *golden chain of being* incorporates ideas and principles we today ascribe to Darwin, where from the *confusum* and chaos a variety of animal, mineral and vegetable shows itself in the *prima materia* due to the sub-lunar influences and mysterious occult laws determined by environment and geography.

In *Rigveda*, the Purusha Sukta describes the establishment of the *varnas*, the castes. We also find the same motif in the Eddic poem *Rigstula*. Here, the Norse god Rig/Heimdal establishes the three castes of people in society, revealing the traditional triad of peasant, warrior and priest which constitute the social fabric that unfolds around the cosmic axis represented by kingship.[20] In this triad, we find the organization of the worlds of the cosmos, three upon three, and also among the Æsir themselves where they all have particular functions that aim towards preservation of one of these castes or social roles. This means that creation as we know it was made from something preexistent, a remodeling of something prior, and the Æsir were a force both regulating and creating cosmological possibility. They had no power to totally thwart what was already there; however, they could regulate and place borders and connections where they wanted proximity and distance.

As we see in *Voluspá*, this order was always considered temporary, and as such, bound by the laws of time and temporality. The Fate of the world was to always return to a chaotic state in which reorganization would again be possible. It is interesting to note how this idea of energy (fire) and matter that contains the potential for creation is not much different from suggestions made by quantum physics. This similarity could lead to interesting investigations into the ideas of worlds and dimensions understood by the heathens of the 12th century, but I will leave aside such speculations in favor of the traditional themes that we find in the old Nordic cosmology.

As the world was organized in the best way the Æsir could manage, Snorre tells us that three Jotun women came to Asgard,

---

20 This subject will end slightly on the side of the topic of this work, so for a deeper understanding of this subject matter and the Nordic triad I would refer to Dumézil, 1973.

representing the presence of the seed of the Æsir's downfall. This event was followed by the war between Æsir and Vanir, which eventually, as the Æsir and Vanir joined forces, resulted in a truce that culminated in the brewing of a special ale that held the power of inspiration, poetry, and memory. There are many theories about where the Vanir came from, but where they came from is perhaps less important than what they came to represent, and that with the arrival of Jotun in Asgard, the original Æsir were expanded and came to include both Jotun and Vanir.

As we see from several stories, especially where Thor is concerned, elements deemed chaotic must constantly be held at bay, and no matter how powerful the Æsir might be, any attempt at annihilation of Jotun, trolls and other forces considered intrusive to the Æsir order always end up being unsuccessful. Not only this, but the Jotun are always considered a species that possesses knowledge, and whenever the Æsir are in need of something they can't do themselves, they turn to Jotun and trolls for aid, or they simply steal what they want by resorting to trickery. The presence of Jotun is necessary for the existence of the Æsir; it is as though they affirm one another in mystical and needful ways – the one is by virtue of the other.

Three Worlds and Nine Farms

Níu man ek heima, níu íviðjur, mjötvið mæran, fyr mold neðan.
I remember nine farms, nine homesteads in the Tree, the entire youth of the Tree under the Earth
Voluspá 2

Hel kastaði hann í Niflheim ok gaf henni vald yfir níu heimum.
He (Odin) threw Hel in Nifelheimen and gave to her to do as she wanted with nine worlds
Gylfaginning 33

The Old Nordic perception of the world was heliocentric and geocentric, depending on from where in space and place it was observed. This means that the world was perceived to emanate from a center that was considered fixed and upright, that would then flow out into the world, generating a vast landscape where the boundaries were marked by something mysterious or chaotic.

The number 3 recurs with constancy, and this shows itself in the tripartite distinction between the world of the Æsir, men and Jotun, illustrated by the three concentric circles representing the world as it was arranged and ordered by Odin and the Æsir. In this organization of the world, we find Yggdrasil, the world tree, at the center of the dwelling of the Æsir (Asgard), followed by the dwelling of humans (Midgard) and outside this the dwelling of trolls and giants (Utgard or Jotunheimen).[21]

Beneath Midgard we find Midgardsormen, also known as Jormundgandr, the child of Loke with Angrboda, a dragon-serpent that bites its own tail to support Midgard as a "giant marine magical ring", as one of its heiti or poetic synonymous defines it. This means that the world as we know it is supported by a serpent-dragon, the world of men by Jormundgandr, while the center of the world is beneath the roots of the axis mundi and supported by Nidhöggr which gnaws away on the roots of the cosmic tree and drinks from its subterranean wells and springs.

We see already from this what themes stand out in the Nordic perception of the world as its founding blocks or vital elements, namely: trees, circumference, farmsteads, serpent-dragons, a cosmic center balanced by an outlandish boundary of threat, chaos and mystery.

From the axis mundi represented by Yggdrasil, we see that we have farmsteads both in the tree and below it, generating a cosmic crossroad where the axis mundi stretches out vertically and horizontally as it embraces nine farmsteads, or worlds, in total. Svartalfheim, Nifelheimen and Helheimen are beneath the earth, and four other worlds are conceived as being spread out to the heavenly quarters that spin around Asgard, Vanaheim, Midgard and Utgard. Yet no matter how many farmsteads and worlds there might actually be, they will always add up to the mystical nine in total with Yggdrasil itself, a commonality shared with the Pythagorean tetractys.

The mystical number nine is especially encountered in relation to Helheimen. *Voluspá* clearly states that Hel, or Hella, was given nine worlds. But the various presentations of how many worlds we actually find in her realm vary. What we know is that there are two central realms under the earth, beneath the World Tree, which are the realm of Hel and the realm of the black elves. This would suggest a deep connection between the dwarves or pixies residing in Svartalfheim and the realm of Hella. We should also mention that Vanaheim is sometimes described as a realm under the earth as well, but this is not a rule, therefore it is important to invite in the idea that the worlds represent liminal places or "magical" realms, not much different from the ideas of mythical kingdoms filled with

---

21   Steinsland, 2005: 98.

treasures, such as El Dorado, Agartha, Arcadia, Avalon, Shangri-La, Atlantis or Lemuria – realms that would appear in magical and mystical ways, perhaps much like the Irish Anwnn, or those for which conquistadors in the 15th and 16th century set out in the world to explore and search .

What we can extract from Snorre's presentation of Nordic cosmology is that not only did he favor *Grimnismál*, and by consequence, discard the parts in *Voluspá* that contradicted the cosmology in *Grimnismál*, but he also took the Greek model as a pattern and tried to fit everything into it. This explains why we find several contradictions in terms of where farmsteads or realms really are, as well as in the nature and the essence of divinities and spiritual beings of the North. If we accept that the Greek model is not really a perfect fit, and invite the discrepancies in the worldview presented in *Voluspá*, we will end up with a cosmology that is not so much about the dualistic battle between order and chaos, which mimics the Christian theme of an antagonism between good and evil, but a world bound to end in a renewal by the dictate of Fate, a serpentine fabric of creation that severely challenges the dualism Snorre attempted to establish in his presentation of the Nordic cosmology.

The medieval Norsemen were using the material world as a reference for understanding the other side and other realms. Reading the accounts in Snorre, it is almost like the nine worlds and the many realms that spread across the cosmic cross, in the branches of the World Tree and under the earth, were an enormous hall of mirrors with everything reflecting back on everything else in similarity yet with great difference. This difference was caused by geography, by the temperament, genealogy and pedigree of the inhabitants, and by the topology and cosmology that made up the material and spiritual dimensions of these realms. Further, physical places, like the mountainous Jotunheimen on the Nordic west coast, could most likely serve as a crossroads where worlds would meet and where the physical and the immaterial were lodged together in places of power, reflecting back on one another in a mystical triad.[22]

If so, we might perceive these worlds as places to possibly visit through *hamferd*[23] more than by traveling physically (although this could also happen, especially when people were taken by the mound-dwelling huldre-people and other subterranean beings to other realms

---

22 In Nanna Løkka. *Steder og landskap i norrøn mytologi*. PhD. Dissertation. 2010. UiO

23 *Hamferd*, literally "skinflying", meaning to travel out of the body in an altered state and/or to other realms in a different shape, like bear, salmon, wolf, bird, fly and so forth.

and places). This harmonizes more with the Old Nordic concept of the soul,[24] and in this we see deer, wolves, bear, squirrels, boar, cats and horses frequently accompanying the traveler, which gives support for hamferd as the preferred way of traveling to other realms. The realms outside Asgard, Midgard and Utgard are always described as outlandish and frightening. These are places more unusual and different than the three realms connected to the human world, places beyond the known, material world as alternative realities, similar to the many descriptions of the fairy realms in European mythologies where these beings have dwellings, food and drink. There are always some qualitative differences with these places; the normal becomes supranormal and rules and laws are often turned upside down along with the understanding of time itself.

Of all the attempts at mapping the nine worlds, the format that takes into account the vertical and horizontal axis and the four corners of the world might be the best blueprint for understanding the location of the worlds. However, we need to keep in mind that this organization also holds deeper ideas represented by their placement, such as the nature of winds, and what is actually found in terms of quality and nature in these different locations. For instance, the South was always associated with heat and fire, as the North was associated with fog, darkness and danger. Also, we should keep in mind how the nine worlds might be in harmony with the nine celestial spheres, the nine stages on the Platonic Chain, as well as the nine stages in the alchemical process in which chaos is transformed into the Quintessence. One of these cosmological diagrams represents the worlds like in the figure on the following page.

---

24 See Chapter 7 for a full presentation on the Old Nordic concept of the soul.

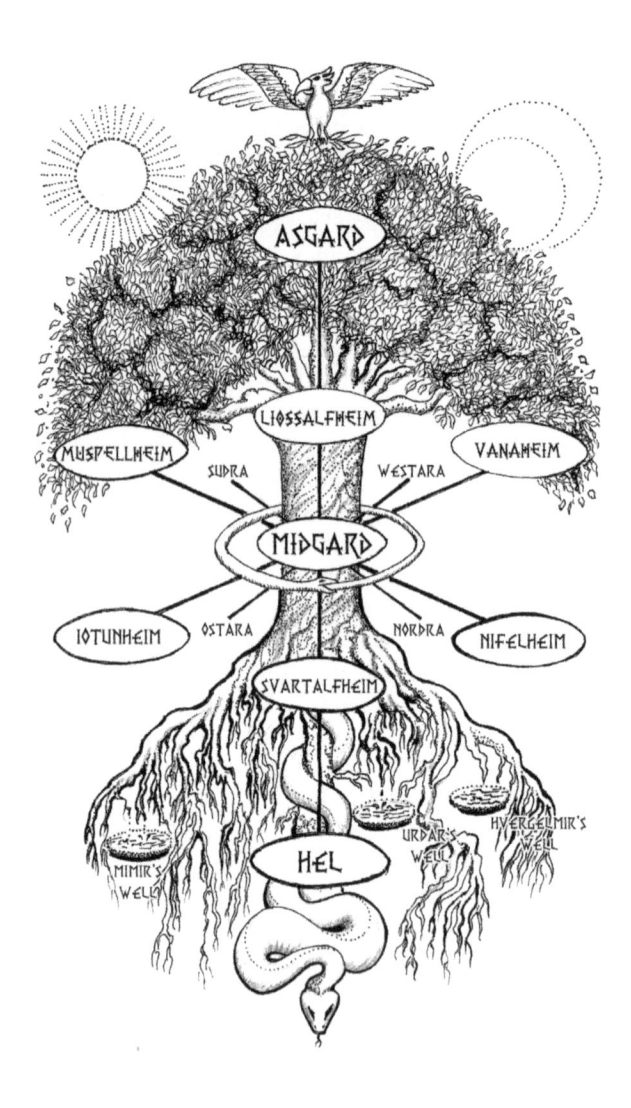

Asgard is the world surrounding Yggdrasil, and here we find the farmsteads of the Æsir like Valhalla, Trudvang, Folkvang, Noatun, Breidablikk and the farms of the other Æsir. Also, we see in this diagram how Asgard is placed higher than the axis mundi in reference to its more "elevated" or central position in the world.

Close to Asgard we find Vanaheim, the realm of the Vanir, that is sometimes described as under the earth and other times on a level with Asgard. Likewise, Alfheim, the home of the bright elves, is in this proximity.

South of Midgard, perhaps where Jotunheimen or Utgard started, we find the dark Ironforest where Heid has her dwelling. Not far away we find the realm of the dwarves, Nidavellir, while the black dwarves live in Svartalfheim. In the outer parts of Midgard, which might be more correctly called Utgard, we find a cave called Gnipahulen, similar to the cave that led to the realm of Hades in Greek mythology, which gives passage to Helheimen, and somehow it is through this same cave that we find the way to Muspellheimen and Nifelheimen.

From this, we see that the world was populated with Æsir, Vanir, dwarves, elves and Jotun. Elves and dwarves were commonly referred to as vaettir, while Jotun were often referred to as trolls, which leaves us with vaettir, troll and Æsir as the dominating categories of spiritual beings. However, revenants and the dead, such as one's ancestors, were also categories of immense importance, so let us give some attention to Hella and her Helheimen.

Helheimen is interesting given the importance of this realm, and in understanding Helheimen we might arrive at a better understanding of how different realms were generally perceived and of their mystical location. Helheimen was ruled by Hel or Hella, described by Snorre as having a blackish blue hue that covered half her face, with her other half the face of death, suggestive of a cranium. Hella is the daughter of Angrboda and Loke, sister of Jormundgandr (Midgard's Serpent) and the wolf Fenrir. From how Angrboda is presented in the Edda, and in particular in *Voluspá*, we can assume that Angrboda is actually the same as Heid. Stanzas 40 and 41 in *Voluspá* describe her in the following way:

Austr sat in aldna	In the East the Old One sat
í Járnviði	in the Ironforest
ok fæddi þar	and there gave birth
Fenris kindir;	to Fenris' offspring
verðr af þeim öllum	amongst the many of them
einna nokkurr	a single one of them
tungls tjúgari	the sorrows of the moon
í trölls hami.	in the shape of a troll.
Fyllisk fjörvi	Taking the fill
feigra manna,	of the lives of the dead ones
rýðr ragna sjöt	the homes of gods
rauðum dreyra;	he makes red with blood;
svört verða sólskin	the sun will become black
um sumur eftir,	and in the summers to come,

veðr öll válynd. all will be burdensome.
Vituð ér enn – eða hvat? Do you want to know more?

Heid/Angrboda is pivotal for the Nordic eschatology, as will be demonstrated shortly. For now, it is important to point out where Hella came from and that her pedigree was birthing a lineage of monsters, she herself a human in shape, whilst her siblings were a wolf and a snake. This speaks of her own essence and quality as the offspring of a troll from Muspellheimen, in the case of her father Loke, and her mother, the one the Æsir tried to kill three times without any success. Hence, the presence of Hella, Fenris and Jormundgandr in the world are also signs announcing the unavoidable collapse of the world.

Therefore, we find Helheimen instrumental in the structure of the world as its role in the cosmic cycle is necessity, by fate and potential. It is the realm holding the memory of the beginning and the potential of creation in the form of the rivers flowing forth from the North and made liquid by the fire from Muspellheimen. Beneath Helheimen we find Nifelheimen, where Hella herself is the child of a troll of fire and the Old One that sizzles and burns.

It is possible to experience a second death in the halls of Hella and end up in the foggy darkness of Nifelheimen. Again we see a Greek motif present in Snorre's presentation, in the realms of forgetfulness, in the rivers of Lethe and Styx, and in how Tartarus is a place beneath Hades, considered a deity and a titan in its own right, much like Hel is a Jotun herself.

Hesiod, in his *Theogony*, states that from the primordial chaos came Gaia (Earth), followed by Ananke (Need/Necessity), and then Tartarus, followed by Eros, and then finally Day and Night followed by Ocean and Heaven. These forces made up the primordial forces rising from the chaos, self-begotten by the enchantment of the Muses.

In the Nordic cosmology, we find an important resonance in the role of the Norns, the Fates that oversee Necessity/Need, Legacy and Birth/Death. Also, even if it is not spoken much of, Gaia/Earth, the goddess Fjörgyn/Jord as she is called in the Edda, is said to be the mother of Thor *and* the father of Frigg. This turns Frigg and Thor into a brother and sister from a most unique pedigree, Earth herself. In adopting Thor as his son and marrying Frigg, Odin must have been making an important pact with Jörd, but Snorre does not write anything about this. Lecouteux suggests that Fjörgyn is a depiction of the relationship between Jörd/Earth and the stormy sky as representative of the importance of thunder and earth in the Nordic cosmology, and that Fjörgyn would be visualized as an oak-clad mountain.[25] If so, Jörd would be like a marshland of birches whilst her name Fjörgyn would denote a specific role of Jörd or Earth when she embraces the role as mother-father.

Helheimen is placed in the North, and we need to understand that "North" refers to the Hyperborean North as well. In other words, North is not only a direction and a wind considered cruel and wild, but it is also an idea and a concept. What comes from "the North" is by definition wicked, dark and cold. Hence, a malicious troll will always be a being of the North even if he is living in the geocentric east. Seeing the discrepancies related to directions, such as how a person can be said to be in Hel, Valhalla and in a given tomb at the same time, would suggest that the concept of death, like the four or eight corners of the world, was understood in quite complex and symbolic ways that can only be explained by reinterpreting the entire idea of the construction of the soul in relation to how it was possible to be dead in three different ways and places at the same time.[26]

Similarly, upon death, it is possible to go to the halls of Ran, to Valhalla or Helgafjell depending on how one died. Valhalla is well known as the homestead of Odin where those fallen in combat go to feast and drink around the fireplace, whereas those who died at sea went to the "Bed of Ran", the spirit of the Ocean, her nine daughters and the waves and maelstroms which are considered a golden hall of riches and sensual pleasures. Helgafjell, or Holy Mountain, is a golden mountain where one's ancestors are said to gather, yet, at the same time, they are in Helheimen and in their grave, so can it be that we are speaking of a collective ancestral memory that is living in Helgafjell?

Memory was of immense importance for the Norsemen of Old. It was, together with *hugr*[27] or "intense thought", one of the qualities that most defined Odin and was constantly related to wisdom, cunning and magic. Ananke, or Necessity, has been mentioned in relation to the Norns, and to the importance of Fate and Necessity in maintaining a Greek reference by virtue of Snorre. In relation to Memory, we find a similar importance in Orphism, exemplified in the Orphic Hymns translated by Robert Taylor where we find hymns not only to gods and heroes, but also to concepts, like Victory, Seasons and to Mnemosyne, the goddess of Memory. Taylor comments on this the following:

---

25 Lecouteux, 2016: 91.
26 See Chapter 7 concerning the anatomy of the soul.
27 This important term will be discussed further ahead in several contexts.

Memory, according to Platonic philosophy, is that power by which the soul is enabled to prosper in some future period, some former energy; and the power of this energy is reminiscence. Now the very essence of intellect is energy, and all its perception are nothing more than visions of itself: but all the energies of the soul are derived from intellectual illumination. Hence we may compare intellect to light, the soul to an eye, and Memory to that power by which the soul is converted to the light, and actually perceives.[28]

Reading through the Eddas and the sagas, there seems to have been four concepts by which everything was moved: these are Need, Fate, Memory and hugr. Hugr is usually translated into "thought", but hugr is more than thought – there is a passion embedded in the idea of hugr that makes it active and effective. We need only to look at the icon of Odin with his two ravens, Hugin (hugr) and Munin (Memory), to realize this importance and how these two concepts were intertwined and intrinsic for continuing tradition, as was done by the poets and troubadours. Odin's ravens fly everywhere, which could be a metaphor for hamferd, and that it is only in the guise of birds and a select gathering of animals that other realms could be visited.

Further, concerning esoteric geography, we should also keep in mind that every realm was similar, yet different, to Midgard, and that it was possible to cross over deliberately or accidentally to these realms, depending on one's cunning and constitution. Just as in Greek mythology, gods could walk the earth and mingle with women to give birth to heroes, so too it was with vaettir, Æsir and Vanir. Huldra could marry humans and have children just as much as Odin could walk the earth in one of his hundred guises.

Distance was measured by how far one could go by foot or on horse, and yet in the moss-clad mound you could find in the forest not far from your farm, you would also find the entrance to the huldre-people and other vaettir. In the same way, the pixies of the farm were not always seen, but you would always be able to see the effects of their presence on your farm by dislocated objects, your offerings placed out to them being consumed and so forth.

What we find is a world of marvels and immense possibilities embracing the human condition of Fate (often unkind), Need, Memory and hugr in all forms. We find a world of gods and ghosts, witches and mythological creatures, a world ensouled and alive

---

28 Taylor, 1981: 214.

everywhere. It is a world released from the ice through the aid of fire, the very same fire that would bring an end to the world as we know it in the cataclysmic event known as Ragnarök, the twilight of the Æsir.

Ragnarök and Gullveig of the Iron Forest

Ragnarök, the cataclysmic event that announces the end of the Æsir-reign and also the world, is supported by an eschatology of fire and cycles, a play between the eternal and the temporal born from the idea that everything born or that has a beginning must also die. This is the Fate of all things; by the dictate of Need, hence by Memory and hugr, tradition is continued and transformed as worlds collapse and resurface. The end of the world is something encoded in the world already from the beginning, with a deed done in the past, namely the attempt to kill Heid/Gullveig in the Ironforest.

The Æsir seem uncannily occupied by killing her – three times they try to kill her, but every time she gives birth. Realizing that the attempts to kill her were to no avail, they accepted defeat and turned their back on the threat that would eventually send them to their death. With the idea of Ragnarök, we see again a Greek reference in how it is a battle between the titanic Jotun and the Æsir, where there are really no winners, yet Balder will rise from the dead and instigate a new Golden era. Of interest are the signs in Midgard that serve as the augurs of Ragnarök arriving, namely: the *finbulvinter*, a harsh winter that never ends and will lead to starvation, war and strife amongst humans; the stars and the moon will fall from the sky; the sun will be eaten by wolves; and the dead will rise and sail in on their ship made from dead men's finger and toenails as the world will be set on fire and sink into the ocean until it again resurfaces in the wake of Balder's resurrection.

This presentation has a reference in Christian mythology, where Balder is conceived as an Æsir in the likeness of the risen and resurrected Christ that will instigate a new kingdom, yet this motif is not Christian *per se*. The idea of cyclical times prefigured by a savior or world redeemer is a concept Christianity borrowed from Gnostic, Greek and perhaps even Vedic sources, and so we find here a traditional theme in the midst of the Christian bias. If we choose to focus on this bias, we might arrive at an even better idea of meaningful elements and ideas in the Old Nordic cosmology.

Let us return to Heid or Angrboda. Heid, which means "bright one", is a name referring to heat of some form and can also be a reference to heiti or "kenning", meaning that her name itself is a reference to something else, namely Gullveig. Gullveig would in contemporary Norse mean "a road of gold", but old Norse gives to *veig* the meaning of "lust" and "drink", so she would be associated with a golden lust or golden drink, something bright and shining yet intoxicating and passionate. Together with Heid/Angrboda we find Loke constantly mentioned as the parents of a special kind of troll, those more monstrous than others and those that would bring the end of the world – and this also includes Thor, who is actually genealogically related to Loke.[29]

In the non-Eddaic poem *Hyndluljoth* (the part known as the shorter *Voluspá*) we read:

40 . Ol vlf Loki	40. Wolf came from Loke
vid Angrbodu	with Angrboda,
enn Sleipni gat	but Sleipnir he sired
vid Suadilfara.	with Svadilfara:
eitt þotti skars	amongst the many trolls
allra feiknazst	one most vile,
þat var brodur fra	from Byleistz's
Byleistz komit.	brother came.
41. Loki af hiarta	41. Loki ate the heart,
lindi brendu	on fire from linden wood,[30]
fann hann haalfsuidinn	half-burnt found
*hugr*stein komu	by hugrstone-wife;[31]
vard Loptr kuidugr	was Lopt[32] sired
af konu illri	by the wicked woman;
þadan er aa folldu	all marvels in the world
flagd huert komit.	were born.

This poem, sung by Freya, is most likely speaking of the inner dimensions of the practice known as seidr. We might see from this a relationship between Freya, Heid and Loke as the patron triad of this form of witchcraft or sorcery connected to possession, various

---

29 https://bladehoner.wordpress.com/2017/11/29/hels-and-thors-family-relations/

30 Linden tree was sacred to wolves and there are several methods describing shapeshifting into wolf by the use of the linden tree.

31 Hugrstone would refer here to a thought or memory born from fire and passion.

32 Lopt is a kenning for Loke.

forms of intoxication, erotic heat and oracles... the art of the *volva*[33] known as seidr.

THE NORTHERN WAY AND THE SUN OF THE ETERNAL NIGHT

Popular folk tales as early as the 15th century conveyed the idea that Norway was, like cranberry, bramble and pine, the creation of the Devil.[34] The tales say that when God had completed creating the world, the Devil got envious of the work, and when God was resting, he went through the leftovers of creative material that consisted of basic stone and moss. Infuriated with the lack of materials, he took what was left and threw it towards the North of the creation, towards the arctic North Pole. In this way Norway, or Scandinavia in some variations of this tale, was created by the Devil.

The symbolism of the North, this place from which Paracelsus said nothing good ever came, constantly associated with darkness and wickedness, is important to look at in some comparative detail as we find these traditional themes will inform our understanding of the Old Nordic worldview and cosmology. Some of these themes related to the North will also expand our understanding not only of the Old Norsemen, but of their magical practices.

Speaking of the North, the first important element is Polaris, the North Star that is commonly symbolized by the lodestone, the axis mundi that is the pole of iron ensuring the attraction between the celestial and mundane. Around the pole we have Ursa Minor and Ursa Major being the two celestial bears marking the oroboros made by the constellation Draco/Nidhöggr, that we also find at the center of the Nordic cosmology in the form of Yggdrasil and its mysteries. Traditionally the North is assigned to Saturn, which the Greek called *Phainon*, "Shining One", and thus the Northern Tradition would possess this quality of "shining" in Saturn as its pole and center, Asgard manifesting the spiritual North, Thule in temporal ways as a Solar city.[35]

Yggdrasil, the ash tree, on the other hand, is Apollonian and solar, hence we see that Yggdrasil planted in the middle of Asgard would be the Apollonian center for the Nordic City of the Sun. The

---

33 Chapter Eight will analyze the practice of *seidr* in depth.
34 In Ronald Grambo, 1990. *Djevelens livshisThorie*. Ex Libris: Oslo.
35 For more details on these traditional themes, Guénon's work is recommended, especially *The Reign of Quantity & the Signs of the Times*. 2001. Sophia Perennis: US.

Æsir themselves are considered shining ones and will serve as fine examples of a solar race that holds the memory of the Saturnian light in the shape of Jotun that marks their origin.

Looking more closely at the commonality in themes, we find that Helios had a chariot drawn by dragons, which he gave to his daughter Medea, who by her witchy ways reclaimed the original light of Saturn. Odin himself, in spite of carrying symbolism leaning towards the Moon and Saturn, such as wolves, ravens, wells and eyes, also possesses a distinctive solar or Apollonian quality, a quality that is, perhaps, properly expressed by the near absence of the Sun during the winter and its eternal presence during the summer the further north you go.

Traditionally, the eyes symbolize the two celestial luminaries, the Sun and the Moon. Odin gave up one of these luminaries, and though it is the left eye, the moon, which is often said to be the one he gave up, what remains of Odin as a lunar and saturnine figure would suggest that he gave up the Sun, hence he became an atypical solar figure. He is reminiscent of Apollo in everything, but with an explicit solar expression that was given up in favor of the wisdom held by the Moon (clairvoyance/wisdom) and the more "titanic" element of Saturn represented by his Jotun heritage. In this form, he represents the two solstices, the summer solstice ruled by Cancer/Moon and the winter solstice by Capricorn/Saturn, yet it is the course of the Sun across the Earth that measures the gates of the solstices.

This gives a worldview represented by North (Nifelheimen) and South (Muspellheimen) in terms of the two solstices, Cancer and Capricorn. The longest night and the longest day are the two moments in the yearly cycle that serve as the hinges of the world as we know it, and it is here the doors are closed and opened so that a new cycle is pushed ahead. The Roman Janus is a great example of this principle, and in Janus might be the deity more in resonance with Odin than any other.

Mistletoe, considered to possess magical potencies, plays an important role in the Nordic eschatology and magic. Mistletoe was an evergreen and attached itself to other trees, and so it was a common belief that the soul of the tree she attached herself to gave up its soul to her. But the mistletoe that grew on oak was considered to have an extremely powerful essence. Mistletoe holds a variety of attributes, typical for plants imbued with much magical virtue. Pliny tells of sacrifices of bulls and cows made in relation to the gathering of mistletoe on the two solstices, suggesting a solar/lunar dynamic involved, where mistletoe itself represents a solar quality with which a lunar sacrifice of white cows or oxen would ensure the turning of the Sun and enable the cosmic cycle to move on. In Dalarne, Sweden, mistletoe was believed born from thunder hitting a tree, just like the essence of Loke was believed born from lightning hitting an oak.

If we look at the events around the death of Balder, we see he is killed by the blind Hönir with an arrow made from mistletoe, the only plant that didn't swear to leave Balder unharmed, all instigated by Loke, Odin made Loke his blood-brother; Odin himself was from the Jotun race and so in the bond between Odin and Loke we might see a bond between the primordial Frost of the North and the Fire of the South temporarily united by blood, yet Fated to end by Need where Balder and the sons of Odin would ensure the memory passed on in the world to come. This theme was instrumental for Bureus and his Noble runes, which will be discussed in the Chapter Fourteen.

Asgard, the abode of immortality, becomes in this fashion the polar mountain, the Olympus, more specifically the mythical Hyperborean center, Thule. Thule is the name the Greeks gave to the center of the spiritual North, most likely associated with the Sanskrit Tula signifying a sacred island of four masters – the spiritual center surging from the meeting of the four corners of the world at the crossroad and axis mundi. Tula in Sanskrit means "balance" or "scales" and refers to the constellation of Libra, which in Chinese astrology is intimately related to Ursa Major, also known as the Scale of Jade, or as we know, the Wagon of Thor. This blessed island, this polar mountain and white shining isle, was conceived of as residing in the most remote regions of the North as the spiritual center of the North Star.

The rainbow and the bridge Bifrost, in the shape of an arch or a line, would replicate the idea of "scales" and represent celestial influence in the terrestrial world and a commingling or exchange of terrestrial and celestial influences. For the Chinese, and also for several West African cultures, the rainbow is considered a serpent, an idea we find in Goethe when he speaks of the serpent that transforms itself into a bridge. The rainbow would then be representative of cosmic cycles, the constant manifestation of the celestial in terrestrial forms, and thus signifies a given cycle. Where we see the rainbow, a beginning and an end is established on a cosmic level with terrestrial eschatological consequences.

Rainbows are composed of six colors, complementary two and two denoting the six directions (E, W, S, N, Up and Down) with the synthesis of colors into the seventh color of whiteness itself, represented by the cosmic axis, Yggdrasil, turning the seventh color/vibration into the cosmic center from whence the shining ones made their dwelling and bound beginning and end into a temporary present.

The bridge between the abode of the immortals and the temporal world will collapse which will also generate a separation between the two realms. The world will gradually break away from the cosmic axis and move farther and farther away from the pole and the cosmic center until the earth, or Midgard, will crash into the oceans and waters of Nidhöggr. It will stay like this until the powers of fire and frost yet again make the world surface from the waters, starting a new cycle, a new Golden Age, ruled by Saturn and announced by Balder, the shining and beautiful one.

Cosmic cycles go through a gradual degeneration after materialization. As the world solidifies it gets stale and the walls built to keep the original forces of chaos away start to erode, creating fissures and cracks where light escapes and darkness enters in, creating an age of dissolution moved by fire and ice, returning everything again to the waters of wisdom through the aid of transformative fire.

It is also interesting to see that, in the Nordic cosmology, we can speak of four ages, similar to the Vedic Yugas, circling in a spiral from cosmic order to social order that spreads from Yggdrasil. The first age is when giants appear in the Void, the second is when the offspring of giants create the world, the third is when Heimdal creates the social order (*trell*/worker, free men and aristocrats), and the fourth age is both an end and a new beginning. This fourth age begins with the death of Balder and the immolation of the reign of the Æsir, but ends as a new golden age, a world ruled by Balder and the children of the Æsir, which reinstalls the City of the Sun with Balder as the immortal King, the end heralding a new beginning.

What happens when an idea becomes materialized is that we are "squaring the circle", hence the immortal becomes temporal and a gradual solidification of the world takes place. In the Vedas, this is represented by Yugas, and in the Nordic Tradition it is represented by the expanse of worlds and cycles that eventually ends in the coming of eternal winter as original forces of chaos and possibility, represented by Jotun of all forms, gradually generate fissures in the walls of the world made by the Æsir, thus bringing an end to one cycle as another begins from the ashes of what once was.

Addressing the traditional themes, we find that Nordic cosmology is resting on a classical eschatology related to manifestation and entropy. Everything from the abode of immortality enters matter and becomes subject to time and decay. We find an idea of cosmic cycles, which move from a golden age towards an age of dissolution that will end the world and open the road for a new golden age. With the solidification of the eternal into a temporal form, we find that as the world becomes more solidified it also starts to break away from its center, as is only natural for the temporal and limited being subject to law, time and matter.

There is naturally much more that can be analyzed in relation to the Nordic cosmology, but in reference to trolldom, the elements discussed and presented here are what are helpful in understanding the philosophy and worldview which we find at the root of the practice, as will be discussed in the subsequent chapter. Here we see the importance of fire, cold, various types of woods, animals and trolls, poetry, memory and hugr utilized within the Old Nordic worldview for magical purposes.

Chapter Three

Trolldom

And his Gandr-art he also uses like a Man. He sends it wherever he desires across the Land.
The Venomous flies of Beelsebub. – Petter Dass, 1696

The sorcerous and magical arts of Scandinavia are known as trolldom. The cunning men and women who possessed knowledge of these arts were known as trollfolk or trollpeople and *trollkunnig* – someone who had the knowledge of trolls. The Icelandic *fjölkunnig* meant the same as trollkunnig, but with a particular emphasis on the use of Black Books, with fjölkunnig being someone that "knew more than they were supposed to know" like the "Black Book priests", with a frequent reference to archaic magical arts and the use of grimoires, "Faustbooks" and "Cyprians". The Sámi *noaids* were said to practice trolldom with their *runa*, which was the name given to their drum in some districts, and those cunning in seidr were also considered in league with trolls.[36]

Gårdbäck, in defining trolldom,[37] gives as synonyms folk magic, sorcery, witchcraft, rootwork, conjure, stregoneria and many others, and if we look at the variety of practices defined as trolldom, such multiple references might be seen as quite correct. Yet I would emphasize the importance of troll in this regard as a common denominator, speaking of the involvement of suprahuman forces and nature spirits of diverse kinds being activated in the human realm through magical and sorcerous means. Trolldom was an ability, power or gift people could either be born with, or given, or it could be taken through rituals and pacts. As such, I would consider trolldom a reference to both what is considered witchcraft in a traditional sense and also the folk-magic used by cunning people. The reference to trolldom as a gift from trolls remains constant. It is spoken of as a particular succession or a set of practices given and solitarily worked.

---

36 Hodne, 2008: 11.
37 Gårdbäck, 2015: 18, 35.

In present day Scandinavia, the word trolldom is the common term used when speaking of the arts: sorcerous, witchy and occult. The idea of the troll would refer to a class of knowledgeable tutelary spirits, to practitioners of sorcery and folk magic, or to people possessing these gifts in a "witchy" way as someone liminal in the society. The wider contemporary association with the word troll is however of some malicious ogre, associated with waters, woods and mountains, solely causing havoc and disruption. Frequently, they have many heads and almost always were seen as living inside mountains guarded by invisible doors and tunnels. This long-nosed ogre type of troll is quite reductive and is to a large extent rooted in Grimm's *Deutsche Mythologie* and the general interest in fairytales and folk tales that were gathered in the 18th century by the brothers Grimm in Germany and by Asbjørnsen and Moe in Norway.[38]

If we look at the decades prior to the collections of Nordic and Germanic fairytales in the 18th century, we find troll being a reference to something more than just a malicious ogre. Old Norse-Icelandic laws categorically stated that it was forbidden to dine with trolls and it was forbidden to "wake them up", given the association they held with possessing destructive powers. Troll was commonly seen as something monstrous, eerie and mysterious, but we find the word troll also used in connection with illness, especially anything that could sting or cause infections, or which generated pus and pain. The word *trülle* is related to the exercise of troll-powers, and it meant both to create a mirage or an illusion, as well as to describe a sexually liberated or lewd woman. The word *trollrida*, or troll-ride, signified both an illness that affected the intestines with infections, and being ridden at night by something monstrous that led to nightmares and sudden pain, especially in vertebrae and joints, which was called troll-shot or witch-shot.

Therefore, when speaking of trolldom, we are speaking of an idea of troll that is far more complex than the fairytale troll of Grimm, and Asbjørnsen & Moe. Àrmann Jakobsson in his article discussing the meaning of troll and *ergi*[39] in medieval Iceland would be a natural place to start reinterpreting the idea of the troll.

One example Jakobsson gives is from the *Eyrbyggja saga*, where we find a woman, Katla, described as an expert in creating optical illusions, calling her opponent Geirridr a troll. Clearly Geirridr is not a long-nosed giantess, rather the idea Katla imposes on troll is that of a *succubi*, and hence we find here an idea more intrinsic to

---

38 The first collection published in 1841.

39 A word usually translated into "unmanly" or perversion, often associated with the practice of *seidr* as will be discussed in Chapter Eight.

witchcraft understood in the concept of trolldom and troll-ridden. In the *Ìslenzk fornrit* series, where the *Eyrbyggja saga* is replicated, we find an interesting footnote stating that troll in its older meaning, prior to the 12th century, used to signify a "magical being", human or non-human.[40]

Also in the Edda, we find troll being used in a variety of different situations, like when Odin goes north to Jotunheimen to visit trolls, whilst Thor goes east to fight trolls, which clearly shows trolls being associated with Jotun and also that some trolls are hostile while others are not. The word troll is used in the Edda in relation to volva in the 39th stanza of *Voluspá* where we find the volva/troll wife/troll woman being described as "a moon-snatcher in troll's shape", giving them an association with the moon and wolves. The trolls live East in the Ironwood and are bound to Fenrir, the moon-chewing wolf that is stronger than the Æsir, and it is Heidr, the three-times burnt one, who represents a possible succession of one form of trolldom through Heidr, Freya and Huldra. This form of trolldom is specifically connected to *myrkrida*, riding the night, the act of changing shape and going out in the form of an animal during given phases of the moon.

This is further supported in the 14th century *Örvar-Odds saga*, where trolldom is tied to Heid, and Heid in turn is seen as the source of seidr. It seems to suggest that Heid is a prototypical *volve*, a prophetess and a medium. In the 15th century *Ketils saga hængs*, we encounter a curious detail where Ketil is awakened by a crack in the woods and follows the sound. Here he sees a *tröllkonu*, a trollwoman/witch, and discovers it is his mother. He asks her where she is going, and she says she is going to *tröllating*, the assembly of trolls. Later that night he saw an enormous amount of *gandreidr* and *myrkaridur*, both words describing the act of riding-out in a different shape, unfolding in the night skies above him, as well as coal dark creatures peeping out from the forest. Here we find trolldom used as a synonym for the art of seidr, and the art of seidr is as we shall see in Chapter Eight more complex than a mere form of Nordic shamanism.

Jakobsson presents a descriptive presentation of thirteen different usages of the word troll, and in listing some of these we might arrive at a better idea of why trolldom is a gift from trolls and what a troll truly is or can be.

- Troll can mean a sort of Jotun, a cruel long-nosed giant as it commonly is understood today.
- It can describe someone possessing supernatural powers, which frequently leads to these people being referred to as

---

40 Jakobsson, 2003: 42.

umenneske, which we can translate into "not-man".
- It can be used to refer to someone large in size or great in strength having trollish characteristics.
- Troll can also refer to beings harmful and nasty, as the wicked spirits encountered in *Örvar-Odds saga*, where Örvar-Odd is constantly plagued by a sorcerer that is said to have the ability to master *"tröll"* and *"óvættr"* (harmful vaettir); here this is directly related to the art of galdr and *forgjörninger* (destructive sorcery). Due to his skills, he is referred to as being more "a spirit" than a man.
- Blámenn were referred to as trollish, warrior spirits, black of hue, who occur in the *Finnboga saga*.
- Animals conjured up could be judged troll, as in the case of *Hrólfs saga kraka* where animals are called trolls.
- *Jómsvíkinga saga* speaks of a class of pagan heroes that appear to have been resuscitated by ritual to help in war, like Thorgerdr, who is referred to as troll.
- In Òlafs saga *Tryggvasonar*, the word troll seems to denote any activity deemed antagonistic to Christianity, and is used both to describe people and the activity itself, and would then count both men and spirits, i.e. demons, ghosts, witches, sorcerers and any allegiance to the old gods be they Æsir, Vanir or vaettir.
- Berserkers and anyone able to shapeshift would be deemed a troll.
- Enemies and strangers could also be referred to as troll.

If we look at the variety of occurrences of the word "troll" we see it is constantly related to a particular attitude and behavior, along with possessing mysterious powers and skills. Troll signifies something "not-man", something from the outside of the confines of man's social structures, something alien, something strong, something fierce, something threatening that possesses a particular kind of knowledge, namely a knowledge and skill that can thwart the order as we know it. In this way perhaps Henrik Ibsen in his play *Peer Gynt* presents trolls in the most correct way as something ambiguous and mysterious, holding a certain dread, though in appearance it is not always possible to see the difference between a troll and a man. A troll can be recognized by its large build and stature sometimes, but more often it is recognized by virtue of its outlandishness and presence. In the Ibsen play, the Old Man in the Mountain states the difference between trolls and men, asserting that while men say: "To thyself be true", the trolls say: "Be true to yourself and to hell with the world", marking a definitive Saturnine division between ordinary men and trolls.

If we allow this short exploration of troll in terms of its usage to take precedence, and also have a look at all the other adjectives and labels given to people practicing trolldom, we find seidr and *fjölkynnig* frequently used. The terms trolldom and seidr were translated by the 11th century German historian Adam of Bremen into *maleficos/* witches and *artis magicae*/trolldom arts.[41] Mitchell ponders this in his presentation of Nordic witchcraft and magic, and questions to what extent trolldom should be translated into the word "magic" and seidr into the word "witchcraft". Even if such translation helps in giving a better idea of what the words refer to, it also includes the particularities of the Nordic Tradition. Hence Mitchell ends on maintaining the Nordic terms in order to avoid erroneous and reductive associations.

Yet, as the prosecution of heretics and practitioners of illicit magic and witchcraft took hold in the Nordic countries, especially from the 16th century with the rise of Luther's Reformation, it came with its own designed and defined demonology, and trolldom became synonymous with all forms of diabolism and malefica ascribed to the practice of "witches" on the continent. In the Nordic countries, this came to include the noaids or Lapp shamans of the northern parts of Scandinavia and the Finns and every nomadic people that were found in Scandinavia. In Christian V's Norwegian Law from 1687, those involved with witchcraft and magic were all mentioned under the general label of "trollfolk". The common medieval translation of troll into German was *teufel*, which means Devil, forging an efficient connection between trolldom and *diablerie* as being completely under the control of the Devil, God's enemy.

Hence, as Lutheranism spread across Germania and Scandinavia with its necessary focus on rightful and wrongful Christendom in its fight against the Synagogue of Satan (the Vatican), the hunt for heresy needed clearer definitions of what was diabolical. The possession rites of seidr, the enchantments and songs of gandr, galdr and *vardlokkur*, rituals and prayers, feeding the dead, communing with vaettir and magical acts of whatever end were judged unlawful, heretical and punishable. Given their heathen nature, all of these practices were considered diabolism.

The 13th to 16th century might be the most significant period of time to examine in order to better understand what trolldom truly was, because in these decades we find a continuous translation and explanation of the customs taking place. Here, the customs

---

41 Mitchell, 2011: 33.

themselves are described to some extent, but also understood and interpreted with a Christian worldview and the demonology and diabolism that was emerging from both Lutheran and Catholic Christian theology at the time. This theology sought to understand Satan and all his works, the force of darkness that was a constant threat to the City of God, and so it had a need for understanding and defining the customs of heathens and heretics. This attempt at a Christian interpretation of heathen practices, which started with Olaus Magnus in the 11th century, somehow culminated with the 16th century idea of the trolldom of the Nordic Tradition as a form of somber diabolism. These practices were believed to have continued the legacy of the Nordic Black Books, of the priests and cunning ones that were working with the Bible in wrongful ways along with many "Bibles written by the Devil". These famous Black Books of the North will be given attention in Chapter Nine.

In this period where Christian interpretation was applied, there is, naturally, room for much bias, but it is important to remind ourselves that Christian elements and ideas were introduced into Scandinavian pagan rituals and customs as much as pagan elements were incorporated into Christian worship and ritual. Hence, this "field of correlation" should be viewed as a place of resonance between the old and the new where a heathen understanding often colored the new customs. We see this in how enchantments and spells, free from Christian influence, maintain their structure and aim, even substituting heathen magical elements and names with Christian magical elements and names.

Amongst the many curiosities of this correlation, one example is a bone-mending charm from the Merseburg Cathedral Library in Germany,[42] dated to the 10th century, which translated from high Germanic reads as follows:

> Phol and Woden were riding in the woods
> And Balder's foal twisted its ankle
> Then Sindgun and Sunna, her sister,
> Chanted a spell over it:
> Then Frija, Volla's sister chanted a spell over it:
> Then Woden chanted a spell over it as well as he could:
> Like the sprain of the bone
> So the sprain of the blood
> So the sprain of the limb
> Bone to bone, blood to blood
> Joint to joint, thus glued together be!

---

42   King, 2016: 111.

This way of creating a mythical magical charm that involved otherworldly beings remained a popular part of the arsenal of practitioners of folk magic, as the many Black Books or Cyprians in Norway and Sweden should testify, where we find saints taking on the roles of Æsir, Vanir and vaettir.

In Bang's collection of trolldom formulas, we find, for instance, the following four enchantments that follow a similar idea as seen in the enchantment quoted above. These two are used to quench fire; the first one is from 1770 and the second one is from 1793:[43]

> Our Lord Jesus Christ
> Went to the river Gideon
> Took water in his right hand
> And quenched the wicked fire that was spreading
> In the name of God, the father, his Son and the Holy Spirit.

> I see you, fire
> I bind you, fire
> With the cord of St. Arents
> With the hand of God
> By the 5 holy powers of wonders
> In the name of God, the father, his son and the Holy Spirit[44]

Likewise, we find two other charms that might have been used in a more heathen context prior to 1800, such as in the following enchantments dated to that time. The first one, in which the wandering motif is used, is about how to quench a fire that has gone out of control, and the second has an enchanting character that is more demanding:

> Jesus and St. Peter were walking the road
> Here they met a fire out of control
> Christ took the fire
> In his right hand
> And then he swallowed the fire

> Jesus ran
> Blood gushing
> Blood
> As the Virgin Mary

---

43 Bang, 2005: 216.
44 Bang, 2005: 564.

In Power stopped!
In the name of the Father, the Son and the Holy Spirit x 3

From the 17th century, it was more common to refer to practitioners of trolldom as "wise ones" or "cunning ones"; amongst the wise ones we find what we would call witches, sorcerers, graveyard wanderers, whispering people, and people who knew how to bless and enchant as well as heretics at large. Some of them used Black Books, others used the Bible, and yet others used spells and techniques they were taught by other cunning ones, ensuring some form of continuity of the gift.

Frequently, we are speaking of a succession of power, some form of transmission taking place. Hence, the idea of the diabolic pact was a natural reference for describing where these people took their powers from. The pact, this alliance with the familiar or fetch, was one part of the spiritual constitution of the wise one, because they were also born with this capacity or gift. Being born with teeth or still within the caul were sure signs of someone inheriting witch powers. Also, the seventh child would be a natural inheritor of powers, as well as those born on Thursday nights,[45] Holy Friday and Christmas Eve. Blacksmiths and priests were believed, by profession, to possess secret power and knowledge, as was everyone named *finn*, in reference to people from Finland, the nomadic Tatars and Roma roaming the *Finnskogen*, the forest of Finns, or the Sámis in Finnmark, the northern state of Norway. Anyone unusual or strange could be considered part of this occult otherness associated with the wise ones. Apparently, the word *finn* was used as early as the year 98 by the Roman Gaius Plinius Secundus who used this word, or rather the more precise *feningi*, to describe whatever people were found north of the Alps. In Scandinavia *finn* referred to Nomadic people and those speaking Finno-Ugric languages, but always with a nomadic connotation, as well as people living in wastelands and woods, continuing the old Norse etymology of finn defining a swamp or marsh.

When we move into the 18th century, it is clear that the Sámi noaid, the woman that cures toothache with an enchantment, the priest that dabbles with the Black Books, or people with the gift of prophecy and healing, were all considered wise, or knowing more than what they were supposed to because they had gained these powers from the Devil.[46]

---

45 Tillhagen, 1962: 48.
46 Ibid., 56.

And therefore, in this presentation of the many facets of trolldom, perhaps starting with the Devil and the pact is a good entrance, because when we look back in time the heathen customs leading to the infernal pact were often rooted in some form of older customs involving exchange with some force, frequently using blood and ale as the medium for exchange, which in time transformed into the wine and bread of the Eucharist. Let us first look at the various ways one could gain suprahuman powers in the form of pacts and trade with the Devil or devilish vaettir.

Taking the Power by Pact, Key and Blood

This pact could be done in various ways. A popular method was to sign a pact with blood from the right pinky and place it in the keyhole of a church at midnight on a Thursday night.

Another method was to walk three times counter-clockwise around a church on Christmas at midnight. At each turn, one should blow through the keyhole of the church as a token of giving up the holy spirit, and on the third round, the doors would open. If one had the courage to go all the way to the altar, he would meet the Devil there. The same procedure is found ascribed to Maundy Thursday, but at the hour prior to the rising of the Sun.

Yet another method is of a more initiatic character where a mentor takes his student to the church for three Thursday nights and walks backwards into the church, while reciting the Lord's Prayer backwards without mentioning the name of Jesus. This being done, one would on the first night see nothing, on the second one would meet trolls dressed in gray with red hats, and then on the third night one would meet the Devil himself. Finally, we find a formula that says at midnight on a Thursday night, preferably Maundy Thursday, take a Bible and a human bone to a crossroad, open the Bible and stand on it whilst beating the bone on the Bible while saying that "this bone is the weight of my soul on Judgment Day". Procedures like this should be repeated for three Thursday nights and could involve other challenges, like placing silver coins in the mouth of a corpse to gain access to the assistance of revenants and various forms of draugr.

The wise ones were considered serious and studious, and were thought to possess knowledge of the entire range of invisible beings, as well as how to cure and how to harm. There was also a belief that the wise ones should never teach their formulas to others, and that if he or she did, they would no longer be able to use them. Also, he or she should never teach or pass on anything to anyone older than him or herself. Teeth falling out were considered a sign of loss of power and the arrival of a more profane station in the life of the wise one. It was usually at this stage that a passing-on of power happened, always in secrecy. What we also find in the descriptions of Tillhagen and Hodne give examples of the level of pragmatism among many of these practitioners. They could often make use of the *Sixth and Seventh Book of Moses* as easily as they could resort to a Psalm or a Cyprian, or make use of their own *fylgja* (fetch), a vaettir, or some Jotun, troll, Æsir, Jesus or a saint. One interesting example of this is found in Finnmark, where among the pietistic congregations known as Laestadians[47] we find a surprising amount of wise ones that effectuate miracles, healing and harming through recitals of passages from the Bible and through other formulas with Biblical content, said to be empowered by breath and whispers.[48]

The notable folklorist Nils Lid[49] comments on many ways of transmission of power or gifts using blood as the agent. Transmission of powers and gifts through blood was common. In the coastal regions the halibut was considered particularly sacred, and to consume its blood while it was still alive was said to give luck in general, but in particular the luck of fishermen. The spike in the inland held the same properties. The blood of bear and moose was said to make the hunter strong and give him clarity in the hunt, but this was also the gift given by the blood of domestic animals, in particular oxen and pigs, where pig's blood would also give one the ability to see in the dark.

To cut someone, to make someone bleed, is a constant sign of ownership and control. This we find in a story from the west of Norway in which a boy accidentally hurt a hulder-girl with his knife and she was declared his by this act. We find similar ideas everywhere in Scandinavia in which men cut women; this is, perhaps, a continuation of the practice of *ganga undir jardarmen*, meaning "to exchange blood to seal pacts and alliances", such as friendships. We see from this that blood held power, that different types of blood possessed different qualities, and that blood was a way to pass on power and be given power, hence we find with great frequency the use of blood as a means to sanctify or empower objects, making them magical or powerful.

---

[47] This movement was started by the Lutheran Sámi preacher Lars Levi Laestadius (1800-1861) originally to deal with the widespread alcoholism amongst the Sámis, but his message was one of fear, hell and brimstone focusing on the awakening to the mercy of Christ through a pietistic and sacrificial lifestyle.

[48] See Kristiansen. 2005. *Samisk religion og læstadianisme*.

[49] Lid, 1935. 48-52.

Eating the heart was an act attributed with great importance; it appears to be an organ better consumed by women, as the virtues of the heart tend to stimulate the particular hugr that was resting in the heart. In *Eiríks saga rauda* it is written that the volva, prior to performing seidr, was searching for a great variety of hearts she could consume as an avenue to increase her magical power.

We also find that a number of items from all kingdoms possess natural[50] magical virtue, such as toads, boar teeth, ravens, woodpeckers, snakes, rowan, oak, acorns, fool's gold, amber and a host of other natural items. Especially important were all things connected to death, such as graveyard dirt or bones. These were considered to possess an inherent magical virtue and served as keys to the other side, either alone or through various forms of manipulation, such as a part of a component in a troll-pouch, along with enchantments, or in anointments of blood, saliva and ale.

In a Black Book from 1790[51] we find two formulas for how to bind favor to you.

1.62 To gain favours and prestige from the mistress of a household.

Before you enter their home loosen up the cord on your stockings on the left foot and tie it again, but loose, say three times, "I bind you, and I don't bind you", place it then back into the stockings. Then you take the cord on the right stocking and you tie it very strong, loosening it up and fasten it strong again while saying three times: "In the name of the Father the Son and the Holy Ghost. May God favor me good fortune in the measure I demand from my mistress." You will then make one more knot on the cord, but this must be done when you are on their land, you will then enter their home.

1.63 A Thursday night go to the gallows where a thief was hung or is still hanging and cut from the main pillar three shavings, cutting upwards on the pillar, and say three times for each shaving: "May God give me great favors with my mistress in the measure I wish", tie up the three shavings and safeguard them. Walk away from the gallows and say as you do this: "Now I walk away from you in the name of God. God will bestow on me so great favors with my

---

50 In part II, Runatal, several items will be given runic correspondences.
51 MS 8:10 in the trolldomsarchive, University of Oslo.

mistress that they will never let me go, rather they will go to the gallows themselves instead of letting me go." Now you leave the gallows ground as you say: "May you hang there forever in the name of the Devil (Fanden)." You will then poke a hole in the sole of your shoes with a fork and in the hole you will place a small piece of the shavings you took and walking with these shoes you will get the necessary aid, so help you God.

Various ways of seeing more (scrying) and animals of second sight

In their 1848 collection of fairytales related to huldre, on page 128, Asbjørnsen & Moe give an account of a wise one called *En Signekjerring*, a woman who knows how to bless, that will be paraphrased here to get an idea of her practice and presence.

The story starts with a wanderer arriving at a cabin in the woods where he meets an elderly woman melting and casting lead in her kitchen to heal a child from rickets. As the wanderer arrives, she gets up from the smoke and fire and states that the child is not suffering from rickets but that it is a changeling. She then goes on to speak about changelings, referring to this one as a trollchild that was just screaming and eating all day long. The child's parents are bewildered because they protected the child using all possible ways. Castoreum[52] was placed in the crib and the child was passed through the fire, crossed and blessed. Also, a silver brooch was pinned to its clothes while an iron knife was lodged in the house just above the door.

The correct method of acquiring lead for the casting was to go seven Thursday nights to seven different churches and scrape the lead from the church windows. Water was gathered at midnight from a river flowing north. She then melted the lead and passed it through a spoon with a hole, allowing the molten lead to flow into the water and take shape while an enchantment was spoken:

> I summon for withering and for weakening
> I command it to leave, I send it away
> I summon it in and I command it out
> I summon the weather and conjure the winds
> I summon in the south, I summon in the east
> I summon in the north, I summon in the west

---

52 The castor sack of a beaver.

I conjure in earth, I conjure in water
I conjure the mountains and I conjure in the sand
I command it down in the root of the Alder
I command it to inhabit the foot of a calf
I conjure it to the fires of Hell
I conjure in the waters running from north
There it will eat, there it will wane away
And never cause lasting harm to the child

Studying the shape created, the wise woman tells the story that the changeling happened because the parents were praying to Jesus when they went over the mountain and then the same across a water, but not when they passed the graveyard before the cock's crow, hence, she ascribes the cause of the situation to provocation of trolls, of the vaettir and finally of the *draugr* at the cemetery. The remedy is to make "a veiled child", which is simply done by tearing up the clothes of the child and sewing them together in the shape of a doll. Inside the doll, silver is placed, preferably silver inherited in the family. In order to distract the otherworldy beings that will come and search for the child, she makes three dolls, and each Thursday night for three weeks she places one doll out in the mountains, one at the water, and one in the cemetery. This doesn't work, so on a Thursday night the wise one takes the changeling out to a dumpster and starts to beat it. While doing this, the changeling changes into a snakelike being that tries to get away from her, but she continues to beat it. This repeats for two more Thursday nights, and on the third night, a woman comes flying out with the human child and asks her to stop hurting it. Apparently, the pain afflicted on the changeling was also harming the child. The "flying woman" accepts an agreement and trades the original child for her troll child, and so the story ends with the changeling returned to its own trollpeople and the human child returned to its family.

It is interesting that in this story are not only the modalities of trolldom like casting, doll making and enchantments, but the importance of the number 3, the direction North, vaettir and *huldre*, mound-dwelling beings of nature living close to lakes, draugr or revenants, the inhabitants of the graveyard, and also how trolls are beings of the mountain.

The familiars of the wise ones were often animals reputed to possess magical powers themselves, like snakes. Of all snakes, albino snakes were considered the most magical, just like the albino reindeer among the Sámis in the northern parts of Scandinavia are considered a vision of "God". The white snake was called the snake of wisdom and seen as the snake that tempted Adam and Eve in Eden. This snake you could catch, boil alive, drink the soup and it would make you forever wise.

Bats, known as the devil's bird, also held supernatural virtues, especially their blood. Three drops of bat blood applied to the eyes would enable you to see in the dark, both literally and in a mystical sense. Bat blood also held the property of making you invincible against attacks and weapons of iron.

Frogs, and even more so toads, were considered to be humans who had been subjected to transmutation due to wickedness they had committed. In some parts of Sweden, like Dalsland, it was as late as the 18th century where killing a toad was considered as vile as it was to kill a human. Toads were also a popular guise for "the other people", especially fairies. We also find rituals similar to the Waters of the Moon, better known as the Toad Bone ritual, where a toad is subject to ritual sacrifice in order to obtain its magical bones. These bones would cause invisibility, attraction and passion, and also serve as a repellent for unwanted passion and erotic interest.

Crows, ravens and magpies have a well-known reputation, being Odin's birds associated with memory and "active thinking", contemplation, and remembering.

All of these animals were subject to interpretation of meaning, given that they served as omens, as extraordinary and unusual behavior among them was often seen as a premonition or an oracle. This idea certainly rests on the idea of a cosmic order and creation that communicates with men. Tillhagen and Grambo give in their respective works a good overview of the various forms of fortunetelling used.

Tillhagen divides the art of divination and fortunetelling into passive and active forms, the latter consisting of interpretation of omens, visions, premonitions and dreams. Within this category, the interpretation of omens and dreams appears to have been most widespread and gave rise to a whole host of occult superstitions related to ominous occurrences. For instance, spilling salt over the table would attract misfortune, breaking a raw egg accidentally would announce that you would injure your leg, and a knife turned towards you on the table, by accident, would announce your death. In general, it appears that this kind of interpretation was based on the perception that what happens to part of a thing will affect it in its totality, and what happens with what symbolizes a given person will affect the person itself. This can be seen in the many blood-stopping enchantments that call upon the memory of some holy person obstructing a river in some way. The memory of this act is then summoned into presence and the force is applied to the bleeding, which would also relate to the importance of hugr and *minne* (memory) in the Old Norse worldview.

At the root of these beliefs, we find the idea of something accidental announcing the arrival of otherworldy or unnatural events that are about to happen, which serve as a warning or omen that the otherworldy intrusion could be avoided or softened. All of these omens were possible to revert; for instance, the salt spilled on the table was neutralized by throwing three pinches of salt over the left shoulder, and the deadly omen given by a knife was neutralized by crossing it with a fork.

Augurs and omens would be read from the stars and the moon; a shooting star witnessed on Christmas Eve would be interpreted as a sign of great, usually positive, change. A crow landing on your windowpane on a Thursday night would carry more ominous messages. Omens were also taken from clothes and daily activities. From this, a whole range of superstitions developed, such as how mending a pair of trousers while still wearing them would be similar to sewing poverty into your life. When sweeping the house, if you left the broom to someone else to finish the cleaning you started, it would be seen as a token of coming death. Omens related to scent and the appearance of light phenomena in the night would likewise announce activity from the other side and would commonly be interpreted as bad omens. Finding a horseshoe or a four-leaf clover would, on the other hand, announce luck. Vaettir and troll could speak through unusual phenomena in nature, but they could also speak through fire by showing forms and imagery in the embers and burning logs.

Visions were another way of predicting the future and judging a situation. People prone to visions were commonly considered born with this troll-gift which was considered necromantic at its root. You could gain this gift, for instance, by crawling like a snake under a table where a corpse was laid out and then crawling back out again. This would bestow the gift of visions, as would biting the muscle of an animal immediately after its slaughter, holding the bite with the mouth closed around the muscle until the animal gave up its life completely.[53]

Dreams were also considered an important avenue for communication between man and nature. Dreams could both be provoked as well as observed as omens in their own right. One method for provoking dreams was the use of dream-porridge. This porridge was made by three unmarried young girls who, during the preparation, had to remain absolutely quiet and avoid smiling.

---

53 Tillhagen. 1968: 19.

As the water for the porridge boiled, one of the girls would add a handful of flour and a generous amount of salt to the water and, after the porridge was ready, it was served in three equal portions. It was forbidden to add milk or butter to the porridge and it was also forbidden to drink anything. The three girls would eat it up in silence, and with the porridge consumed, they would go to bed where they would dream of their future spouse coming to offer them something to drink.

The choice of place and time seems to have been important for making predictions. It could be as simple as tossing a coin at a crossroad at nightfall on a Thursday or it could be as complex as the practice of year-walking.[54] This method of divination would provoke visions and augurs in great quantities and appears to mimic the wanderings of Odin amongst men as the year-walker had to undertake his task in complete silence and absence from contact with humans. Tillhagen writes of several modalities and one of them is as follows:

> If the year-walk was done each year for seven years, one would encounter a rider on a white horse and he should then without fear run towards the horse and secure its bridle. This would gain him the power to see what was hidden and he would also be able to see what was living beneath the earth, like the huldre-people. If he did this for more than two years he would, on his wandering in the ninth year, witness a gathering of dwarves that would do what they could to provoke laughter from the wanderer, but he should avoid laughing and instead focus on stealing one of the dwarves' hats. Wearing this hat would give him the ability to look into the future and predict it.[55]

THE TROLLISH FORCE OF THE WISE ONE

Hugin and Munin are related to qualities believed to be possessed by the wise one, and in particular Hugin. Hugr is a concept we might describe as a form of mental power, not unlike the idea Renaissance philosophers had about divine imagination as an active and creative quality. Hugr was considered "thoughts", but thoughts fueled by an emotional charge and possessing a capacity to radiate in a way that would cause effect in the world. Hugr was considered a quality of the

---

54 In Swedish "årsgång".
55 Tillhagen. 1962: 57.

soul-complex. Effects of hugr when they had wicked consequences could be called *finnehugr* or *trollhugr*. If the capacity for hugr was strong enough, it was possible to allow the hugr to take shape and fly out in a monstrous or eerie form. This was called *hugrham* and was responsible for sudden cruelty and accidents, and also for nightmares as well as the appearance of doppelgangers.

The use of hugr could be both voluntary and involuntary, triggered by willful thoughts or strong emotions. A wicked hugr coming your way would frequently give some form of premonition akin to a feeling of something evil coming. In the Old Norse literature this was referred to as *trollrida, myrkrida, tunrida, gandreid* and *kveldrida*. There was little difference between the witch riding-out in the night in a different shape than the riding of mara or *mararida* which lives on in the word nightmare.

Hugin and Munin would then represent this capacity of flying out in different *ham*/shapes (i.e. shapeshifting) as well as the creative powers of Memory and Imagination. In the Edda it is said this ability is possessed by *trollkjerringkvind* or a witch, and in later folk beliefs hugr was associated with storm and tornado-like winds.[56] Interesting to note is that hugr could be prominent in given body parts, especially fingers; hence, a wise one or a witch pointing a finger towards you could unleash wicked hugr. It is also interesting to see that a concept like this assumes that memory could be inhabited not only in the mind, but also in the body itself. This might partly explain why a magical object like the hand of glory was said to possess a variety of virtues, and might be related to an idea of hanging forcing the hugr to the extremities and in particular the hands where planets were assigned and futures could be read.

Another concept tied to hugr was *vard* and fylgja which, just like hugr, could also travel in a different *ham* or shape. Superstitions in the west of Norway speak about the importance of opening the door for strangers when they are leaving so one can be sure that the vard is also leaving with them. From this we have the word *vardøger*, which is the premonition of a certain person coming, or actually seeing the apparition of a person that is about to arrive. This could be due to the natural skills of the one seeing *varden* or it could be due to strong hugr possessed by the person about to visit. This idea is in turn related to the concept of the doppelganger. Varden was a type of vaettir and so through the vard or fylgja the soul could experience a deep connection with nature and nature spirits, and here we find the songs called *vardlokker*, songs that would summon the vaettir.

---

56 Lid. 1935: 8.

It appears to have been hugr and vard that were the qualities that made possible effective gandr and galdr, also called troll-songs, frequently seen connected with seidr and *gandreid*.[57]

Birkeli[58] describes in great detail the vard/vord and fylgja, and discovers an important distinction between them which will enable us to better understand the idea of the soul.[59] Birkeli comments that *vord* and hugr are, in general, seen as related to one another. In the same way as fylgja can ride out in a different *ham* or shape, so can *hugren*, represented by the vord or the person's will and desire, also ride out in what is called *hugrham* – and it is when this phenomenon occurs we see doppelgangers and *vardøger*. In an attempt to describe the differences and meeting point between *vorden* and fylgja, he defines *vorden* as "the little soul" and fylgja as "the greater soul"[60] in the sense that the *vord* is the part of the soul that is guarding and expressing the personality of the individual, its will and desire, and hence it is in this realm or level that gandr is done, whilst seidr tends to use the greater soul, associated with fylgja, the fetch that connects the person to nature and the vegetal and animal kingdoms.

Sending out the curse

In Norway, and especially in the north of Norway, the Old Norse word for a curse or any form of malefica is *ganne*, derived from gandr. In *Darradarljód* stanza 5 we find a variation of gandr being used, *göndull*, which gives to gandr a wolfish quality and attributes it to the *Valkyries*, the army of Freya who in the poem *Sorla Tátter* is given the very name of *Göndull*. In addition, Odin in *Ynglinga saga* is referred to as *Göndlir*, a master of gandr, just as Freya is described as "the owner of gandr". This means that gandr, like seidr, is attributed to Freya and Odin, but whilst seidr carries a number of bird motifs, gandr invokes the imagery and force of the wolf, giving it a distinct predatory and violent character.

---

57 See the *Laxdaela saga* and *Ynglinga saga* for further details.
58 1944: 204-207.
59 The concept of the soul will be discussed in detail in Chapter Seven.
60 It is interesting that Birkeli perceives in the Nordic perception of the soul a similar idea as we find in West Africa, Madagascar, Borneo and other places, as also in Haitian Vodou where the soul of a man is considered a composite of the physical body (corpse cadaver/*ham*), the spirit of the flesh (n'ame/*hugr*), the little soul/good angel (ti bon anj/*vord*), gwo bon anj (big soul/ good angel/*fylgja*) and zétoil (the star/destiny/Fate/*örlög*).

Heide,[61] in his dissertation, presents alternative translations of the word seidr as cord, spindle, distaff, spinning, a spinning cord, girth, girdle, snare, a knotted cord and similar ideas, which harmonizes with gandr translated into "spinning" and "twisting", as much as the word *göndull* would suggest the capacity to send something out in a spinning form or shape. This spinning shape is found in folk traditions, not only in Scandinavia, but all over Northern Europe, where a whirlwind or any vortex of wind or fire is considered a gandr, and the remedy is commonly to throw a knife into the whirlwind to hurt the sorcerer that sent it out. So, while in seidr the practitioner is performing acts of skin-leaping into animal forms, the gandr is enabling the practitioner to ride-out in the shape of a natural phenomenon connected to the powers of the wind. In Snorre's Edda, we find several accounts where wind is used as a poetic reference to the mind in the sense of being a composite of hugr and Memory, supported by breath and spirit (*önd* and *anda*), hence a whirlwind that was sent out like a gandr possessed consciousness and direction and was seen either as a thought-form sent by the sorcerer or as the *önd* (spirit/soul) of the sorcerer being projected into this very phenomenon.

Nils Lid[62] comments from an account in the Norwegian west coast that the gandr was "a small body composed of various segments of wood that by the help of "trolldo" (in the sense of words and actions done) would be sent away to afflict its target." The gandr was experienced either as being shot, or as a blue fire that entered the target like a sting. Of notoriety was the *gandflue*, directly translated as *gandfly*, which might be similar to or related to *tunflua*,[63] described by Olaus Magnus as a bluish projectile of lead conceived as something conscious and ensouled that acted like an arrow. The horsefly also held similar associations.

The gandr was commonly sent out by the trollman while in a trance state, and in this way it ties itself to the core of the practice known as seidr. Gandr was something largely ascribed to the Finns, meaning both the Sámis and the foreigners associated with *finnskogen* and *finnmark*, and came to possess a largely wicked reputation due to the popular idea that it was the north wind that brought gandr. The north was also the direction where the altars were placed, where the chair of the patriarch at the table was placed, and where the stone of seidr was placed; it was the direction most sacred and also most volatile, because everything powerful was also tied to destruction and

---

61 Gand, seid og åndevind. 2006. PhD disertation. University of Bergen.
62 1935: 34.
63 *Simulium truncatum*.

darkness. The Sámis ascribed this gift to Vuokko, which is the spirit of the Snow Owl, and depicted the *gandfly* like this (see following page) according to the ethnologically inclined priest Johan Randulf in 1723:

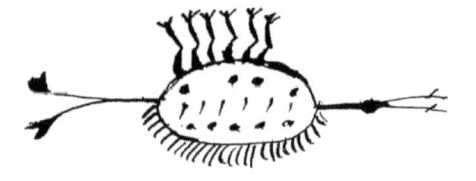

Lid also speaks of a perception of gandr from Österbotten, Sweden, where it was called *lappskott*, literally "shot by a Sámi" – a whirlwind announced the arrival of the fly, and if you looked closely you could see the cunning one in the shape of a bird, or a fly, in its center.

If we turn to *Historia Norwegiae*, we find gandr connected to *gandreid*: to ride out with sorcery/gandr. Here, the gandr was made possible through the use of *runebomma*,[64] a drum played by the noaids to enter trance and to connect with the consciousness they sought to send out. The riding-out happened through the way the drum summoned the fetch to bring the noaid out in some non-human form or shape.

If we add to this that the north Sámi word *sieidi* is translated to *seid* in Norwegian, but holds a slightly different meaning, it might expand our idea of what seidr is and connect it to sitting in places of power. *Sieidi* always refers to a given place that is considered powerful. It is always connected to stones, mountains or caves as a kind of crossroad or bridge where powers of air and land can interact with the living. Hence it is at these places that prayers and sacrifices were made, considering they were also vital intersections for connecting with the *radien*, or the world-ruler that was thought to be a destructive force constantly threatening to end the world.[65]

Communication, diagnostics and divination were done using the drum, called both *runebomme* and *trollbomme*, which was considered an entity in its own right, tied to the guardian spirits of the noaid and

---

64 See Appendix B for a detailed description of the symbols marked on the drum.
65 Kristiansen. 2005: 35.

the *radien*. Divination at the *sieidi* was done by placing a ring on the drum, and as the drum was beaten and galdr sung, the ring would move towards given figures on the drum and oracles would be taken from the ring's journey.

The designs on the drums would vary greatly, from symbolic and mythological landscapes to real time geography, but there were always some common features. Of these we find the presence of the Sun a frequent central symbol for a tripartite division in layers or circles. These three layers would represent, respectively, the realm of deities and light spirits, then the spirits active in our world, and lastly, the realm where animals, ancestors and the gods of the ancestors were depicted. Within these layers given narratives significant for the noaid could be found.

Amongst the important deities and spirits, we find the Lord of Thunder known by many names, but a reference to Thor is frequently found both in depiction and narrative. He was considered the ruler of the spirits of air, where we also find the Sun and the Moon. The Sun was considered a mother, benign and nurturing. During the Catholic synthesis, the Sun was called *Marianedni*, "Mother of Mary", represented by St. Anne. The Moon (*mánnu*), the younger brother of the Sun, was considered volatile and prone to destruction. One fairytale speaks about how the Moon took the shape of a *stallo*, a troll, that came down on Christmas Eve to murder children who were noisy and troublesome.

The powers of earth were tied into childbirth and seen as an extension of the Sun called *Máddaráhkká*. She had three daughters that served as midwives and weavers of Fate, and *radien* shaped into animals and men to lodge the souls as they were born into the world. Another earthen power was *Leaibolmmái*, the power of the hunt that was associated with the Alder tree, the most sacred tree, whose sap was used to trace the designs on the drum and draw magical markings and signs. The power of the hunt would frequently take the shape of a bear, its sacred animal, considered the ruler of the woods and an ancestor of the human race. Hence, bear could be appealed to as a great protector of humans, as long as humans were treating nature, especially the woods, with due respect.

The powers of water were associated with spring and summer, and were also connected to the rays of the Sun, and were considered a benign force empowered by the magical rays of the Sun, making all forms of water a magical fluid.

The dwellers of the underworld were known as *gufihtar* (vaettir), *ulddat* (*huldre*) and *hálddit* (vord/guardian/ruler), and were understood to possess similar qualities attributed to the subterranean dwellers in Nordic mythology at large. There were also the *saivo* people that would be considered a type of elf that were living in human-like communities, but were considered happier and more prosperous than humans. These people welcomed some humans when they died and, as such, they also held a portion of the realm of death. The *saivo* people were said to live inside mountains, in the same manner as trolls, and it was possible for cunning noaids to strike deals and even purchase saivo societies that would greatly increase wealth and fortune. The realm of death was found beneath the realm of the saivo people and was ruled by *Jábbmeáhkka*, a power that was considered female and sinister, and here we also find a sort of devil figure, *Ruto*, that was considered the deity of illness and plagues. It was not uncommon to sacrifice horses to him when a village was plagued by illness so Ruto could ride away on the horse.

It is important to recognize this worldview within which seidr and gandr were practiced and to also realize that seidr was tied to specific locations that gave access to powers. Hence, in practice, one would work with vaettir, huldre, vord, draugr and other chthonic and subterranean spirit allies, while the more powerful forces, like Sun, Moon, Thunder and Hunt would be appealed to so good fortune could manifest. However, there is little evidence indicating that magical work, like seidr and gandr, was done with the direct intervention of these greater forces.

In *Voluspá*, we find in stanza 22 a part that ties gandr directly to seidr which roughly speaks of how the knowledge of gandr makes up the art of seidr. Also, in *Fornalder saga*, we find in the second chapter that Thorstein is using a *krókstafr*, a crooked or cloven stave, to effectuate gandr.

In the north of Norway, a *gand* is still used not only to refer to the magic art, but also to a twig, or for branches and pieces of wood on which animals and humans accidentally hurt themselves. Nils Lid[66] concludes in his presentation of gandr that it was most likely used to signify an entire sorcerous art. If so, and if we invite in Heide's considerations concerning thread and spinning, we might conclude that gandr was a sorcerous art relying on the use of various woods and enchantments that used the winds and the drum and was made effective through the sorcerer's intimate connection with certain insects and animals.

There was also an alternative to gandr which was called *tyre*. It was described as a circular visceral object that possessed the power to release toads and snakes, and like gandr, it moved with the speed of wind and was considered a form of magical projectile. Contrary

---

66   1935: 38.

to gandr, tyre was something you could purchase and buy and send out yourself. Tyre means "wickedness flying" and appears to have been a spirit of less consciousness than what we find related to gandr. Tyre might have been perceived as a restricted active part of a given intelligence related to snakes and toads and was somewhat different from gandr which frequently used beings with wings, be it flies, mosquitoes or birds.

Clive Tolley and Maria Kvilhaug have both suggested that Odin's wolves Geri and Freki represent gandr and seidr, and as such stand for the intimate connection between the two arts. They are also connected to the mystery of wolves at a cosmological level as the wide-open jaws of Ginnungagap, and in this, stir origin through the aid of the Norns or Fates who were also deeply connected to wolves as well as snakes and dragons. The two wolves were also connected to the two ravens, Hugin and Munin, as the potency for effectuating gandr and seidr, which speaks of the importance of hugr and Memory for practicing trolldom.

Working harm

The cunning people were renowned for their ability to heal, but also in particular, to harm. Harmful trolldom was often referred to as *förgjordninger* or "annihilations", destructive workings in the sense that the target was drained of their vital forces, making them susceptible to illness and misfortune. These forms of workings were frequently tied to the graveyard and the use of graveyard dirt and human bones. A human bone sewn into the clothes of a person would, for instance, start a process of gradual and mysterious decay of the person's vital energy and luck. If we look at Tillhagen's[67] commentaries concerning the various harmful works, it appears that these forms of workings were aimed towards stealing a part of someone's soul, indicating that the soul was associated with vitality, power and courage.

A popular harmful working was to knock out people's eyes, and this could be done by forging a nail three Thursday nights in a row accompanied by certain enchantments that summoned evil Fate upon the target. On the third night, the nail would leave and harm the eye of the target. We also have examples of enchantment using images, like poking out the eye of the target in a drawing, photo or an image carved in a tree. Nails taken from coffins were also used for similar purposes, but with the greater intent of not only harming, but

---

67   1962: 65.

killing. It was common to carve the form of the target in a tree and nail the coffin nails in given points of the body to accomplish harm, illness or death.

One method for knocking out the eye of someone, in this case a thief, was collected by Bang and dates to 1770.[68] It goes like this:

> Gather Quicksilver, white chalk and human blood on a Sunday as Mass is being performed, blend it together until you have a dough and paint on the dough an eye. As it is there on the table you say (alternatively mark) the following words around it:
>
> Volacti, ada, Nola, Aprison
>
> Place then a needle (or a nail) in the center of the eye and read the following enchantment:
>
> Satan, Beelzebul, Balligel, Astriot, Babell, Zizilo, Erebi, Bumota, Rebos
>
> This nail shall stand as strong as the fearful Satan in Hell is standing solid, like the wife of Lot in Sodom, and like the unjust Judges in Hell are standing locked down, while they know what was right and spoke lies;
>
> And this shall happen in the name of Lucifer ✠ ha Stu jal Lucifer ✠ uc half Lucifer ✠ uci halfa Lucifer ✠ ucifhalfas Lucifer ✠ ucife halfast Lucifer ✠ ucifer bind it fast ✠
>
> Leave the nails in the eye for 9 hours, in this time leave your house, close the door and do not look back. Do this and the eye will be knocked out.

Trollskott/troll-shot[69] is the sudden onset of pain, often a nerve pain in the back or the legs, which could be caused both by the "other people" as much as by the cunning ones. One procedure speaks of how the handkerchief of the target is made into a rustic doll and affixed to a tree or hung in a tree at a crossroad. You would then make a bullet from scrapings of a church bell. If the target belonged to a different parish, you would need to get scrapings from the church bell of his or her parish as well. Graveyard dirt from the parish of the

---

68 Bang 2005: 648.
69 Also known as *finnskott*, *lappskott*, *elfshot* and *nordsending* (north sent).

target as well as your own would be mixed with some gunpowder and, instead of a bullet, a human bone was loaded in a rifle together with a silver bullet, preferably made from silver inherited in the family. Then, on a Thursday night with a waning moon, you would shoot the doll and, from the damage done to the doll, judge the harm done to the person. Variants of this working include carving the shape of the target in a tree and using a stolen host (stolen with this intent) affixed to the figure as its heart. was, however, slightly unpredictable, and it was said that the trollshot at times harmed people that were in the way of the shot before it managed to reach the target because the trollshot was using forms of wind and meteorological conditions to have effect. The whirlwind was especially considered caused by external occult agents and a knife thrown into the whirlwind would end its power.

More examples of enchantments against trollshot are as follows. The first one, from 1830, references the Norns and the second one, from 1882, focuses on the North as the wicked direction that also annihilates wickedness:[70]

> There are three beautiful maidens
> One for In-shot
> One for Fin-shot
> And one for all evil that flies
> In the name of God, the Father, his Son and the Holy Spirit x3
>
> Three woodsmen came from the North
> One mended the Finn-shot
> The other the shot of galdr
> And the third for all kinds of shot
> That in the world is found
> And now I will destroy you
> In the name of God, the Father, his Son and the Holy Spirit x3

Another interesting summoning or incantation is from 1882[71] which aims at generating restlessness in people who have caused offence:

> I summon you great Chieftain Lucifer that you with other
> Lords and dukes bring torment and plague upon this

---

70 Bang, 2005: 144, 145.
71 Bang 2005: 646.

human, that you will send this out to N.N., and making the effort, mighty Lord Gramatan so that also other goddesses and virgins, so that this human, which they have made offence against, this N.N. that he must be as unruly and restless as the waves at the ocean shore, may he be so turbulent and bitter of mind and thought, that it would seem to him that the heavens would fall upon him and the earth consume him, and this must go on for 5 or 6 days and that in the name of the Devil. Aasmedeus Norman ✠ Satan ✠✠✠ Belsebub ✠ Kobi ✠__ Buse ✠✠✠ Jeng ✠✠✠ Busel.

Another procedure involves closing off the possibility that the soul of a deceased person can go anywhere. This is called "the dead man's grip", where you summon the *Crue Christi Clavis est Paradisi*, the key to paradise, and then close the gates to the soul and lock him or her in "Hell and Grave". Apparently, variations of this formula could also be used to effectuate cures and healing, then the terms would be about locking every door to Heaven and Hell and grave until the ill person was healed.

In general, harmful workings do follow similar structures. An enchantment is done where a specific force or collective of forces is summoned to effectuate the will of the practitioner. Such workings may or may not involve the hair and nails of the target, and may or may not involve the use of figures, images and poppets. What seems reoccurring is that something physical is often done, commonly on a Thursday or during Mass, like forging a nail, carving something like an arrow, or making something like bread. The enchantment and the physical labor would then be accompanied or done in the spirit of a specific hugr or feeling that would be the energetic fuel for accomplishing the aim of the working.

To Enchant Lust

The cunning ones were also reputed to possess great skills in erotic and passionate workings and could set passions aflame as much as annihilate lust. We find a great number of spells, enchantments and workings that resort to items in natural harmony with love and lust, such as urine from animals in heat, or the use of the heart of animals said to be particularly lewd or faithful, depending on the desired outcome, as well as herbs and plants that were frequently used to bind and entice lust and passion. Of particular interest is how proximity to the target seemed crucial, and for a spell to work some form of physical contact seemed involved. Three spells from 1770 give the following procedures:

> Take three raisins, prunes or figs and place them in your left armpit, leave them there until they have been well soaked in your sweat and give them to the girl you want to love you and she will fall in love with you.

> Get a swallow and take its heart and fry it. You will then place the tongue of the swallow under your own tongue and when you see the girl you want to love you eat the heart. You will then, still with the tongue of the swallow under your tongue kiss the girl you want three times while you say to yourself, "you will love me as much as the swallow loves its young" in the name of the Father, the Son and the Holy Spirit.

> Take the tongue of a snake and carry it with you to church for three Sundays and carry it after that with you at all times. When you meet the girl you want to love you place the snake tongue under your own tongue and kiss the girl and you will certainly be given her approval.

Hugr was, in particular in the west of Norway, associated with the Norwegian word *elsk*, which is the same as love, often of an erotic nature, and used interchangeably to also refer to desires that were out of control. So one expression of wicked hugr was to infest someone with erotic desires. Many of the love spells we have testify to this element of the hugr besieging someone in intoxicating ways; the word "elskhugr", overcome by passionate love, was defined as a spiritual disease. Hodne comments that erotic trolldom was in several places in Norway called "rune" in reference to the secret element in a love potion that made it effective.[72] This use was probably from the arcane use of *manrunar*, or "summoning runes", that were the form of runes used in erotic trolldom spoken of in *Hávamál*.

Two spells, also from 1770,[73] that use blood, a natural element for invigorating lust and passion, go like this:

> Take your own blood and the blood of a mole and write on your hand her name and your name. Giver her then your

---

72 Hodne. 2008: 79.
73 Ibid. 364, 265.

hand and tell her the following words:
"May your love and my love be commingled like my blood is commingled with the mole. In nomini patris et filii et spiritus sancti. Amen"
Take your own blood and write hers and your own name on a piece of paper, touch this on her naked skin with the writing touching her body and read to yourself immediately the following words:
"I command you in the name of the highest savior, in the same manner as your name is commingled with my blood, so shall your love fuse with my love. In nomini patris et filii et spiritus sancti. Amen"

Yet another format is to enchant ale, as one procedure from 1735[74] advises:

Take a full cup of ale and share it with the girl you love, while you in secrecy whisper down into the ale the following: "Melchisedch qvi siiguet gros Religani." Between each work you must give breath from nose and mouth into the cup. Then she will love you.

Finding thieves and treasures

Another poplar service was to find thieves. Scrying in moonshine, various types of waters, or pouring lead into water to reveal the thief's identity was popular, as were workings to torment the thief to appear and confess. The use of liquids seems to have been the most widespread way of both finding and harming thieves. One variation from 1830[75] advises the following:

A Thursday night you will gather water in a bucket from a river running towards the north, in this water place a piece of bone taken from a thief, if you don't have this bone, add strong wine, and start naming the names of the suspects. When the right name is mentioned the face of the culprit will show itself in the water. If you want to mark him, you will then stab his left eye with a knife and the eye shall pop out.

---

74   Hodne. 2008: 81.
75   Bang. 1901: 685.

Variants of this formula are many and appear to have been one of the most favored ways of tracking down a thief and marking him so the stolen goods could be retrieved.

The workings aimed towards generating restlessness and dread within the thief so that he would come forward appear to have been largely done by resorting to the dead and draugr. The graveyard seems to have always been involved in works of stirring up feelings like paranoia, dread, fear, restlessness and insomnia with the purpose of forcing the thief to make visible what was stolen, as much as the same strategies were frequently used to find hidden treasure. This reveals a living belief in the connection between the dead and treasure that we find in everywhere in the world, perhaps most famously exemplified in Greek and Roman times, where Pluto was the owner of buried treasure and wealth was found in his realm, the sub-terrene realm that, in Scandinavia, was ascribed to the dwarves.

Another method was to take the footprint of the thief and burn it, or to take a human bone from the cemetery, tie it to a cord and leave it in a turbulent part of the river to cause extreme restlessness which would compel the thief to return with the stolen goods.

At large, the cunning one was considered able to command animals, both wild and domesticated, able to manipulate invisible forces and to cause supernatural phenomena like twisting people's perceptions in various ways, as well as to ride out in the shape of animals and monstrous beings associated with "the other side".

The cunning one gained his supranatural powers in various ways, as we have seen, but the dead seem almost always involved in one way or the other, from elaborate ceremonial procedures, to simple acts like purchasing a piece of human bone from the cemetery on a Thursday night between midnight and one o'clock. Bones, earth, fingernails, clothes and even moss and herbs that had been in contact with the realm of the dead were considered to possess the supranatural potency associated with the powers of the cunning ones. The second garland of power was the church: scrapings from the church bell, stolen hosts, holy water, etc.

THE SORCEROUS ARSENAL OF THE TROLLMAN

In addition to what has already been mentioned, we should also speak of the importance of two objects that were used for healing as much as for cursing, the troll-pouch and the troll-knife.

Trollpouches, trollhorns and troll bundles were common, which were horns or small bags containing objects possessing magical virtues from animals, minerals and plants in secret combinations that would, by their unity and enchantment, bring forth a particular virtue and function. These trollpouches could be made for protection and cure as much as they could be manufactured for harm and magical combat.

The troll-knife (*botarkniv*) was considered indispensable and was sanctified in various ways, most commonly with blood and honey on a Thursday night. It appears that the only directive was that the iron should go through the handle, i.e. the knife should be one entire piece. The knife was used for everything. It could be placed on an afflicted body alone or along with anointments of plants and waters, and would possess a neutral power that was given direction by the will and hugr of the cunning one. The knife could be used to carve runes and magical objects and was in itself a guarding talisman.

A fascinating part of the cunning arsenal was the troll box. Tillhagen describes one of these as being composed of nine types of wood that had been harvested on three Thursday nights by a person who was born between midnight and one o'clock. A person born on a Thursday night might also do the trick given the information we have. Nine symbols were carved into the box and it was secured with several types of locks. Nine types of wood and nine types of metals were a part of the contents in the box and it was largely used for healing. The person coming for healing would describe the symptoms, and was then asked to rest his left ring finger on the symbol corresponding with the symptoms as the box was opened and scrapings were taken from the objects and given to the patient. These scrapings were then thrown over the left shoulder as the illness was ordered to leave.

Two examples of works releasing binding and destruction, such as exorcisms, are found here:[76]

> Cut the nails on hands and feet and place it on a piece of butter and spread it on bread. Give this to a dog to eat and as you place it in his mouth say:
> "Take all my illness and my misfortune
> On this day, in this year
> And everything as long as the world persists
> In Satan's name"

> Thursday night between 11 and 12 go to the graveyard and cut a piece of peat or take a hand of earth and gather it under your right foot whispering:

---

76 Lorenzen 1872:21.

"I am abandoned and destroyed
I will never a home find
Until I have gathered earth below and above me
Now I have earth below and above me
Tomorrow the clock shall strike
On Sunday I shall rise boldly
In the name of God, his son and the holy spirit. Amen.
Word of God. Amen"

In the area of healing and curing we find several counter spells, as shown in the examples above, but we find also remedies that involve ointments, herbs, potions, enchantments and prayers. We find here an arcana of trolldom reminiscent of the ways of healing and blessing found throughout the Western world. For instance, Daggkåpa, *Achemilla vulgaris*, was considered a remedy against fear of darkness and melancholy. Three drops of its tincture would be administered on Thursday night in case of fear of the dark and on Friday night in case of melancholy. Another remedy to remove evil, described by Gårdbäck,[77] is to make bread from your own urine and rye that is shaped into six hag stone-like pieces the size of coins that, after being baked, would be strung together and hung up in a bush.

It was also possible to animate a given collection of items to generate what was called a troll-cat, and sometimes a troll-hare or a butter-cat, which was composed of thread, wool, hair, finger and toenails, parts of mouse and other *materia magica* and was given life by the Devil. The troll-cat could show itself as a wood cat or it could appear as it was made, like a dusty ball of wool. The troll-cat was used to steal milk from nearby farmers as the troll-cat would attach itself to the cow's udder and bring back milk to the owner. If on a morning it was discovered that one was milking blood from the cow, it was considered a sure sign of a troll-cat active at night, stealing milk. The techniques for making the troll-cat are largely tied to the heretic use of Ecclesiastical powers, and in this case, the use of Sunday for "doing the Devils business", perhaps aided by a belief that on Sunday God focused on what was going on in the church, so acts of diabolism could be done without attracting unnecessary attention from God. Two procedures go like this:[78]

If you want to make a troll-cat you need to sit with the distaff for seven Sundays in a row to spin, and on the seventh Sunday the cat will roll out on the floor from the distaff.

---

77 2015: 140.
78 Hodne 2011: 172, 173.

Prior to this you would cut your fingernails and toenails and also some hair and gather all things necessary on Sunday (probably during the time of Mass) and, with all things gathered, it should be wrapped up and taken to church in secrecy on a Sunday. During communion, the wine should not be swallowed, but you should collect it in a small flask and feed it to the bundle of necessary items. With all the things gathered, you would give up your soul to the evil one so he would give it life.

Forms of magical thievery of milk, cheese, butter and food were quite common everywhere, as was ascribing harm of cattle and plantation to the work of cunning troll-people or the consequence of the evil eye which was often called the "shit-eye". The shit-eye was considered empowered by envy, jealousy and hatred in general, and in other cases, it could also be activated due to an excess of personal power in the one possessing the shit-eye. Clearly, the large number of spells speaking about how to knock out the eye of thieves would suggest that the shit-eye was considered a serious matter and that knocking out a shit-eye was a legitimate solution to the problem.

Those possessing a shit-eye, just as those reputed to understand and use gandr, were feared for their curses. From the 6th century it was referred to as woe-prayer[79] which could be as simple as pointing a finger and uttering intent, be it death or misfortune, in determined anger while looking at the person. Hence, being cursed by a cunning man was not something anyone wanted to provoke. This fear naturally led to those possessing this fame to be treated like outcasts in society, yet it was important to also be respectful and avoid attracting negativity from them. In the 17th and 18th centuries, the cunning ones were resorted to for a variety of reasons, and it appears that they were always people who were not totally integrated into the society they were a part of, always existing on the outside and frequently appeased with money, food and favors for their services. They were like a trollish force or a vaettir that you ensured was content and happy, lest he or she wreak havoc upon you and your farm. In many accounts given by Flatin[80] and Hodne[81] of wicked as well as kind troll-people, this seems a constant theme in how their immediate society related to them.

Troll-letters were another popular method, similar to the Germanic and Pennsylvania Dutch *himmelsbriefe*,[82] and tie in with

---

79 In Norwegian: *våbønn*.
80 1991.
81 2008.
82 See Bilardi 2009: 307-313.

incantations (*besvergelser*) and talismans. They could be prayer-like letters with a summoning tone, smaller notes that carried a wish, barbarous and/or holy names, or they could be like this:

✠Alga ✠Algas ✠Algat ✠ana
✠Seketum ✠Essolatum ✠Dragor
✠Mecsit ✠Arnols ✠Artensie
✠Arthimei[83]

Other variations would be the use of barbarous words or sacred names recited in a way that would simulate the decrease of a given pain or condition, like this one for toothache:[84]

Kalamaris
Kalamari
Kalamar
Kalama
Kalam
Kala
Kal
Ka
K

Weather magic and marine magic was also popular and sailors could "buy wind" from cunning ones, who were in league with the denizens of the ocean, as much as they could buy luck in fishing. Offerings to marine spirits and knot magic appear to have been the most typical strategies used in this form of trolldom besides magic that would replicate what the cunning one wanted to happen to the sailors and the ship. One account speaks of how a bridal ship was sunk by the work of a cunning one who placed two eggshells in a bucket of water at a mound close to the ocean and started stirring the water. As she chanted and whispered until the eggshells fell to the bottom of the bucket, the waters became uneasy and the wedding boat fell to the bottom of the ocean killing the bridal couple.[85]

Finally, we have the many ways of stealing people's and animals' courage, stamina and life force; and also restoring it.

One for restoring life force is from 1800:[86]

---

83   Gårdbäck 2015: 229.
84   Bang. 2005: 458.
85   Hodne. 2008: 72.
86   Bang.1901: 153.

Our Lord was walking on a road where he met a brown horse.
"Why do you cry so painfully?"
"I must cry
"For bad people have taken the marrow from my bones
"And the blood from my limbs
"And the strength from my body."
"Wicked" said our Lord Jesus
"You shall have marrow in your bones
"And blood in your limbs
"And strength in your body."
In the name of God the Father, the Son and the Holy Spirit

A formula for stealing someone's force and courage also from 1800 is as follows:

Pax. Max[87]
Make it quick
Max, Max
Take this and on that
Which was on you placed
In the name of the Father, Son and the Holy Spirit x 3

The Trolldom-Philosophy of the North

We might conclude that trolldom, or the philosophy of trolldom, can be formulated into a few guidelines that constantly appear present in the Nordic Tradition whether we speak of acts of trolldom in the Eddas and sagas or in Nordic folklore. I have summed up these guidelines as follows:

- If it has a name it is. If it has a feeling it is, if it has a thought it is.
- Every Name is breath and Fate, that's why Names have Power.
- What "is" will at some point cease to be.
- What has a memory can be manipulated, what is remembered can be altered.
- Hugr and Memory is the power and wisdom of trolldom.

---

87 Ibid. 466.

If we look at the sorcerous technology of the North, we can say that it is rooted in a perception of sympathy between a thing and its effect, which, in a purely teleological manner, is born from the Aristotelian axiom that says the soul of a thing, or phenomena, shows itself in its action or use. If we add to this the notion that everything is ensouled and possesses a consciousness, typical features of what Charles Taylor called "the enchanted worldview", we arrive at an idea of the cunning one being exactly what the society around him or her perceived, someone who knew what was forbidden to know, namely, how to commune with and use the spirits of wood, stones, plants and beasts to affect the world.

This worldview was present everywhere and in every situation, and was translated into superstition and proverbs that would aid magical thinking and planning.

For instance, when one was in the proximity of where beer was fermenting, one should speak loudly to invoke the spirit of the jest in festive manners. When boiling blood sausage it was the opposite, you should speak low lest the sausage explode and rupture the skin it was held in. An example like this is interesting because it further testifies to a notion that nothing was ever "dead"; a sausage made from meat and bound in the skin of entrails could react to a feeling expressed in the form of loud talk. Another example is when making *lutfisk*.[88] Lid recounts how in Verdal, in central Norway, the preparations were accompanied by anger, and I mean real anger. The more angry and violent people got, the better the dish would be, like the feeling in the atmosphere would add a magical ingredient to the food and perfect the goal.

In the same way, telling someone beautiful that they were beautiful was considered a disgrace, as it was usually a comment born from envy and evil intent. We find this in numerous accounts everywhere in Scandinavia where praise for a newborn beauty was considered ill-mannered and salt was rapidly thrown to all corners of the crib, just as it was with gaining favorable words for one's cattle. The salt was thrown over the cow or ox as fast as possible to ward the beautiful from the wicked feelings of the ugly ones.

Speaking to crops and to animals, reciting poems and giving offerings to trees, stones, houses and plants were very common because everything was ensouled and held a consciousness. The more the practitioner generated a sympathetic energy, the more he or she would generate a bond that made the trolldom effective. When you built a house, you were using wood made from a particular tree

---

88 Dried cod tenderized by soaking in lye, which is rinsed off before cooking.

that held a unique spirit, and now as the tree was dead it regained a different kind of spirit in the angles and corners formed as the house was raised, as much as doors and windows would invite in other types of spirits. We might speak of Paracelsus' law of signatures, as much as Giordano Bruno's pantheism, to understand trolldom.

We also have other interesting factors in this regard, such as vernaculars that reveal some intensity of connection, like with bear and how bear is constantly referred to as "grandfather" amongst the Scandinavians, and also how berserkers were bear people directly linked to the father of men, Odin. Everything about the bear was sacred, and we might go so far as to state that the bear was the totem of the Northern Lands, the mirror of its people, its ancestor – the people of the bear as encoded in Skade, the deity of Scandinavia, who chose the polar bear, and by extension bears, as her companion. Skade herself is interesting in this regard as her name means both hurt, accident and wounded, which harmonizes with the Northern insistence of turning a bad fate into a good one.[89]

I am mentioning this here because the lady of a household might have held some of the virtues of Skade. The true name of the Lady of the House was Thora, but this name was forbidden to use. More common was *husbrei*, the one that fills the house. From the 17th century we have several accounts that speak about how the use of the name Thora would bring devastation to the house and the household, usually by being struck by lightning.[90] One account says that it is better to call her *Blia*, the smiling one who owns the house. Thora is a name not only mirroring Thor, the Æsir, but also thunder, revealing that the Lady of the House was considered someone in the ancestry of Thor, meaning that any woman taking charge of a household was representative of Frigg, Thor's sister.

We find this practice of naming something dangerous in kindly ways repeatedly, as though there is a knowledge that some benevolence is found in even the harshest and most wicked soul. We find, for instance, that *nøkken*, a marine and watery troll that usually wanted to consume life forms, could be appealed to either by gifts or sweet words – or by mentioning his benevolent names, which in the case of nøkken was Nennir. This would appeal to his more benevolent nature and give you freedom from his appetite. Hence, we find that everything had its "good name" and naturally the way to achieve the knowledge of the good name would be to actually understand

---

89 In runic terms we might say that we are all occupied with turning *naud* into *odal* through *fe*, *raid*, *laug* and *wunja*.

90 Lid 1935: 62.

and interact with the powers you were dealing with. *Kenningar*[91] was and is still important in Scandinavia, and most famous is perhaps Odin himself with more than one hundred kenningars, giving us access to particular strata of this magnanimous soul when we can call upon specific qualities of his rich personality. Yet the idea of everything having a "good" name and a "bad" name typifies the inherent neutral quality of all things, for it was very often the way a thing was called that gave it a given force a particular direction.

Trolldom was more often practiced with the aid of nature spirits than with the aid of Æsir. Æsir seem to have been used more as a summoning force, sealing the work through the practitioner's personal connection with a given Æsir, or through the place the trolldom was worked and the Æsir under which it was ruled. For instance, if work was done at a farmstead dedicated to Thor, it would be natural that the work, especially if it was an enchantment, would somehow call upon Thor as a witnessing force to the work done, or that the Æsir would be used in enchantments in the same way as Jesus and saints were used in magical parables to demonstrate the way and direction of the force utilized. The Æsir were commonly placated and fed at regular intervals throughout the year to maintain stability of a farm or a village, while trolldom was done by resorting to the spirits of house and land, as well as the dead.

---

91   Synonyms/nicknames, literally, "what I know you by".

Chapter Four

Magical Beings of the North

The nature spirits of the old inhabitants of the North might at one point have been nameless. Some of them over time were turned into demi gods and gods, while others were given names from the places in nature their dwelling were found, it was in mountains, in the air, in the fire, in waters or in earth. – I. Reichborn-Kjennerud[92]

When speaking of magical beings in the North we enter a field of intense complexity, because the Old Norse vision of the world was animist,[93] and what could be judged pantheist. Everything in the world was touched and made by Odin, an extension of primordial fire and ice that generated a world of extremes in the void where Fate gave meaning, purpose and deed. Every rock, flower and draft of wind possessed an indwelling spirit and was ensouled. Every creation Odin made or that man created gained a life of its own through its use. Hence, farming tools and swords gained names proper to their direction and use, for the blacksmith was considered the manifester of the creative potential of the world through the heat of the furnace and the coolness of the water.

We need to understand that for the Old Norsemen, the idea of a magical or supernatural being included more than singular or plural beings because it also counted geographical locations, stones and plants. Just because a spirit had not yet been named, didn't mean that it was void of soul. Naming was about recognition and pact, announcing a proximity to the human realm. Yet, many things remained unnamed and nameless in a world where everything was alive with its particular genius and spirit. Thus, the nameless would be named by its effect which defined what kind of spirit it was and what it was doing without further specification, like *uvaettir*, a vaettir of mischief and bad luck.

Many of these beings were tied to the house. The house or farmstead was considered a sanctuary and there were several rules

---

92 1928: 46.
93 See Reichborn-Kjenenrud, 1928, Birkeli, 1944.

concerning the cult of the house. Unfortunately, as Birkeli[94] laments, the material that describes the cult of the house is scarcer than we would like. Hence we need to resort to the oral tradition, old customs still kept, and a comparative attitude while seeking parallels in neighboring countries that will help us understand and replicate the idea of the house as center of the private cult that involves *disir*, vaettir, dwarves and ancestors as the key spiritual elements. For the ensouled human being, we find that the Norns, and by extension *hamingjer*, Valkyrie, and fylgja, stand out as vital. In the case of the ancestors and all things liminal, we find the huldre-people, elves, trolls, nøkken or nixie (a shapeshifting water spirit), and draugr or revenant.

In addition to this we have the magical beings of specific places, like rivers, under bridges, lakes and oceans. Space should be given to all of them, because by understanding the beings of a place, we will also better understand what kind of trolldom that place would generate, because trolldom is truly born from a fusion between the need of a practitioner and the forces available to accomplish the tasks in question, which can turn need into abundance and joy. The trolls will, at large, be left out of this chapter given that they will be prominently presented in the next chapter, and were given importance in the previous one on the origin of trolldom found in the Northern Tradition. Also, the importance of fylgja will be discussed in Chapter Eight when the concept of the soul is addressed in depth.

A World Woven by Fate

The Norns, or the Fates, held an important place in the Old Nordic worldview and in the *Voluspá*, stanza 19 and 20, we gain insight into the origin of these Fate makers:

Ask veit ek standa,	A standing Ash I know,
heitir Yggdrasill,	Yggdrasil it is called,
hár baðmr, ausinn	tall tree, watered
hvíta auri;	with foaming whiteness;
þaðan koma döggvar,	from whence all dew comes,
þærs í dala falla,	that covers the valley
stendr æ yfir grænn	ever green it stands
Urðarbrunni.	over the well of Urd.

---

94 1944.

Þaðan koma meyjar	From there
margs vitandi	wise maidens came
þrjár ór þeim sæ,	three have their home in the
er und þolli stendr;	hall beneath the tree;
Urð hétu eina,	Urd is one of them called,
aðra Verðandi,	Verdande the second,
skáru á skíði,	carving secret runes,
Skuld ina þriðju;	Skuld is the third;
þær lög lögðu,	law they made,
þær líf kuru	life they crowned
alda börnum,	for all men their
örlög seggja.	fate they sealed.

From this passage it is easy to conclude that the Norns are three, but as we see not only in the Edda, but also in the folk-beliefs in Scandinavia, "Norns" was a word used in reference to the part of the dead related to the *örlög* as a vital component of the ensouled being. The Norns were commonly viewed as a *fylgja*, fetch, and/or disir, protector spirit, given the fateful and protective role they played in the life of everyone. They could also defend the one they were protecting, which wouldn't be much different from a Valkyrie. Urd, a disir of death as Skuld, is also the name of a Valkyrie, hence, disir and Valkyries are woven into the mystery of Fate. This bridges them with the Vanir, expressed in the ability of foresight, clairvoyance and prophecy; *also*, Norns are found to come from elves and dwarves as well. Therefore, there is much indication that the Norns represent a particular function that was not ascribed to a given class of spirits, although as with almost everything else in the Northern Tradition, the Norns find their root in the Jotuns.

Urd, Verdande and Skuld were the arcane Fates, made famous in Shakespeare's *Macbeth* as the archetypal witch trio. These three were the original source of the many Norns that were found in great extension everywhere, tied to families and mankind at large. The Norns were spiritual forces related to destiny with an unlimited ability to bend and shape the content of a life and its end, and to acceptance of one's Fate, doing what was necessary to strengthen the relationship with your fylgja, or fetch. The Norns carved the law that man was supposed to adhere to in relation to a greater cosmic memory or law that was revealed in the concept of örlög, commonly translated as "destiny". Destiny was associated with a "law" that would be the particular compass for each person, indicating the best course of action to take in life to ensure a good memory was left as one passed on to the other side. Örlög[95] lies at the root of the word *örlög*, or *orlog*, the captain's logbook kept during travels at sea. It is tempting to suggest the imagery of every person in life sailing his or her own *naglfare* (the ship of death), where every act and thought is recorded during their travel and, at the end of their life, the contents of the book are compared to their life to see if they had lived in accordance with the law at the heart of their örlög. If so, it would explain the constant presence of death in the Old Nordic worldview and it would also reveal an idea of destiny similar to what we find in the Hindu idea of *dharma*, where every person is supposed to live according to a personal dharma or law that would play itself out harmoniously within the greater dharma or cosmic law. This suggests that destiny was not pre-destined as such, but that destiny spoke of a given way of acting upon the world that would ensure one left behind a good memory.

The Norns were absolute. Not even Æsir or Vanir could change what the Norns had predicted because they were analyzing actions done in relation to örlög, and from this, made precise predictions based on the rhythm of causes and consequence found in how a person executed their law in the world.

We see this from the names of the three proto-Norns. Urd, which means "to become", is also etymologically connected to the Anglican Wyrd, Fate. Verdande also possess a similar idea of becoming, but in the sense of what is temporarily in the present. Skuld refers to "what will happen" in relation to a consequence of the dictate at the root of the becoming and how this moves into the present, and then a prediction of how this will play itself out further is made. Skuld also contains the idea of "debt" which, in turn, appears in the path stretched out under the guidance of one's örlög.

The Norns were also present at the farmstead. In the past, every farm followed the design of Àsgard by having a *vordtree*, a ward-tree, planted at the farm, usually between the barn and the main house. In the *Hávamál*, stanza 137, Odin speaks of the importance of the "good vaettir" that live at the ward-tree and their significance in maintaining peace in the household, especially between the couple, as peace in the household was important for the continuation of the family. We also have remnants in several places in Norway and the Faroe islands[96] that show the importance of setting out porridge for the Norns at the ward-tree during childbirth.

---

95 *Orlog* also carry the meaning of war or battle, which is also interesting in the regard of fighting for one's manifest destiny.
96 Reichborn-Kjennerud. 1928: 53.

Likewise, white marks on the fingernails, called Norn-marks, were considered the presence of luck, a direct reference to how the Norns are said to mark Yggdrasil with white foam.

Their connection with healing and medicine is found in *Fjolsvinnsmál* where there is the mention of the nine maidens at Lyfjaberg who possessed the knowledge of all healing herbs. They were headed by the àsynje Eir, whose name means "calm", "protection" or "mercy".

It was these forces that were called upon when casting runes, and it was also these forces that worked through the volva. The volva is perhaps most commonly associated with the art of seidr, which will be discussed in detail in Chapter Eight, but prophecy was, as demonstrated in the *Voluspá*, the prime function of the volva. The volva was recognized by the *volvr*, or stang, that she held. This stang was always carried with the bark intact, given the belief that bad vaettir could, at times, live in the space between the bark and the wood. Therefore, keeping the bark intact would ensure that negative influences were sealed up. The stang was most likely cut from her vordtree, or patron tree, meaning that she would access her Norns and vaettir through her stang. Of interest also is that the grave of the volva Odin summons from the dead is located outside the Halls of Hel, revealing the liminal condition of the volva as much in life as in the afterlife, and marking how she was constantly dealing with the other side or what was outside the perimeters of where she was living.[97]

Hamingja, in the form of a female protector spirit, is the personification of luck assigned to persons and to families and has often been said to be the same as fylgja. But, hamingja, as we saw in the previous chapter, is also related to the part of the soul known as vord, a guardian that is more tied to the disir than to fylgja because it can be sent out as an extension of one's hugr and can also change shape. Hamingja literally means "to go out in one's own skin or fur", which plays on the idea that it was the guardian of one's hugr that went out and was activated in the form of "luck". Hamingja was the part of Fate that was "lucky", and it was possible to lend one's luck in case of need, such as in the story of when King Olaf II lent his hamingja to a friend.

Given how hamingja was rooted in an extension of someone's hugr, it is most likely that this was a vital part of the art of the volva and that it brought in the proximity of the Norns in benign ways. The volva also nurtured a deep relationship with Freya, and in this field the Valkyries enter in as important for the volva as much as

---

[97] Steinsland. 2005: 313.

they are for the Norns, with whom they are often associated. The Valkyries are warrior spirits in league with Freya and with a deep loyalty to Odin, as it is they who bring fallen warriors, called *einherjar*, to Valhalla – warriors that they choose to fall in battle.

Àsgardsreia, known as the Wild Hunt of Odin's army of the dead, most likely consisted of Valkyries as much as *einherjar*. Some of them were Jotun, like Skuld, but most of them seem to have been related to the *àsynje*, or female Æsir, like Bryhild. Their connection with the Norns lies in how they were given the role of choosing who would fall in battle, hence, this would imply insight into the örlög and the resulting Fate of the warriors.

Àsgardsreia could also be called *gandferd*; a similar "wild hunt" was ascribed to St. Lucy, most likely syncretized with Heid or a hulder, who on the 13th of December rode out in her sinister *lussiferd* with her legions of witches in the same manner as Àsgardsreia. This might be because the wild hunt of dead souls in olden days always happened at the big seasonal shifts, and particular in the midwinter as the chaos of darkness, death and dread announced the arrival of light. Hence it became associated with the Christmas-tide and is often called *Joleskreia*, "the Christmas ride".

As we see, life, death and Fate were overarching ideas that took shape through luck and misfortune. The veil between the worlds was never thick, one's vord and the involvement of the Norns through Valkyrie, vaettir or volva was always present, and the same forces and qualities were also mirrored in the farmstead and surrounding nature where it was possible to have more intimate contact with these larger forces.

A House of Spirits and the *Vaettir* of the Land

Disir is a name given to the Norns in *Grimnismál* and Valkyries in *Reginsmál* in the Poetic Edda, whilst in *Hálfs saga ok Hálfsrekka*, disir is described as a protective spirit with a clear war-like Valkyrie quality that secures luck and good fortune in a district. What all these associations of disir to Valkyrie or to Norn have in common is that they are considered the spirits of death and of dead ones. In *Hálfs saga ok Hálfsrekka*, Ulf comments that luck had run out because the disir seemed to have died, which would ultimately place them in a category of guardians of a land, a sort of extension of the land-vaettir and the ward-vaettir. Given all such references back and forth, it would appear that disir seem to have represented a specific function of certain female spirits, be they Valkyrie, àsynje or Norn, just like Æsir represented a specific function, no matter they be trolls, Jotun or Vanir. This function is similar to the function of the fylgja, or fetch, but this protective role was not limited to a given person, but to a family, a district or a region. In the cases where a disir is protecting a region, the disir will influence everything in that region, people just as much as the spirits of nature, with her protective presence.

In spite of obscure origins and much disagreement when it comes to defining disir, we know that they were significant, given the *Disablót* that was performed in February together with the *disating*, the parliament of disir, at Uppsala. This might suggest that dealings concerning Scandinavia at large were deliberated in the parliament of disir.

We also know that Freya was referred to as Vanadis, and that Skade, also known as Ondurdis, the patron-deity of Scandinavia, was a disir, yet also a Jotun. We also know that disir was connected to the family and to the home and played a role in pregnancy and childbirth. This would suggest that they were more associated with earth than death, as in the case of the Valkyries, and might have been more intimately related to the fylgja of families instead of a specific person. Given what we know, it appears that disir was a role given to female deities connected to earth and fertility and which had a specific role to play with Scandinavian people and its various families. If so, the disir would form their pact with Fjörgyn, the Earth, and ultimately be ruled by Frigg, the prime matriarch of the sanctity of the homestead, home, spindle and hearth-fire, who happens to be a disir herself. It's worth mentioning that disir is etymologically connected to the contemporary Norwegian word *dis*, meaning fog, vapor and cloud. Frigg being the one that weaved the clouds that hid Àsgard might give a hint of the protective function of the disir in terms of guarding a given place and people. Valkyries and any other female deity of a protective orientation related to preservation of family and its heritage counted as a disir, perhaps referring more to a function than a static social role. This at least appears to be the case of social organization in the Old Norse period. If we look at the most famous of all, the Æsir, they are composed of Vanir and trolls, but they are considered Æsir due to their role and function. If so, we find Frigg at the center of all things concerning the protection of the land, whilst Freya was the protector of the erotic, because it is through the erotic that a family continues. If we follow this suggestion, we see that the Valkyries were the protectors of the departed ones, ensuring that they can still support their family and land while disincarnated. If so, conclusions like those of Rudolf Simek in which disir are defined in reality as a general reference to the "Lady of the

House", "matriarch", or "Dame", might be fairly accurate, but it must include the expression that a disir is wise, protective and holds a connection to Norns and Earth through her age and position. If so, it would indicate the importance of Minne, or Memory, for the power a divinity would possess. The longer a memory is held and the richer a memory might be, the more influential its presence is in the afterlife, until the memory itself would generate manifestations, such as how the Jotun woman Skade is remembered as a disir, through her Fate-given function as the *protector* of Scandinavia, Skade's land with all its families and many, many vaettir.

Vaettir were, without any doubt, the most important beings in the Northern Tradition. In the saga of Thorstein Oxefot from the early 1300s, we find it written that no one should sail ashore to Iceland with a dragon's head on the front of their ship, and if they did sail with a dragon's head on the bow, they had to remove it when they saw land lest they scare the vaettir of the land.[98] Vaettir finds similarities in the concept of *genii loci*, the spirit of a place and was, like the word troll, used in reference to supernatural beings in general, but in particular to spirits that were somehow tied to a specific place, be it a mound, waterfall, house, land or grove. The vaettir of the homestead and house was particularly important. In Sweden, these vaettir were called *tomte*, which is the same word for "a piece of land". In Norway, they were often called *Gardvord*, which means "*protector* of the farm", and *Nisse*, which is derived from Nikolaus through the common name *Niels*. It was most important to keep this particular vaettir happy with offerings of food and ale, and during winter-solstice, a function which Christmas eventually appropriated, it was absolutely crucial to feed him ale, porridge, sour cream and butter lest misfortune fall upon the farm, leading to possible harm of the animals and people. The custom of placing out food to vaettir was widespread all over Scandinavia until the 18th century, and to this day many farmers place out yearly porridge, sour-cream, butter and ale to the vaettir that own the farm. In some instances, a bed of hay was also prepared in the storage house at midwinter where the vaettir could sleep.

Gardsvorden is commonly depicted as a short man, bearded, and dressed in traditional farmer clothing with a red cap. Several legends and customs indicate that he was connected to *vordtreet/ tuntreet*, or the *protector* tree of the farm. A custom found all over Norway says that fallen leaves should be gathered and placed at the foot of the tree lest you upset the Gardsvord, and there is another

---

98 Hodne.1995: 23.

custom of placing out food to him every Thursday night at his tree.[99] Some legends and folk tales state that he was the *ham*, the shape, of the first owner of the farm. If so, we find in observing the rules of the Gardsvord a strong link with the ancestry of the land. This might explain why vaettir and departed ones could at times fuse and mingle into the same being. It was also clear in this custom, as in dealing with all forms of vaettir, that humans were not the owners of the particular land or place, but were allowed to use it insofar as the contract was respected. This was further expressed in many customs, especially concerning the huldre-people which will be addressed later, including the importance of respecting the knowledge that humans could have the use of a piece of land for their animals during the day, but at night had to leave or find a shelter because the land was no longer up for rent after nightfall.

In the *Eyrbyggja saga*, it is suggested that the vaettir are ancestors, or at least some people who, upon passing to the other side, joined the realm of vaettir. In this saga we read how Thorolv treats a mountain as holy because he believed he would enter the mountain when he died, joining the protective vaettir of the land. Vaettir could be of a benign disposition, *hollavaettir*, or of hostile disposition, *meinvaettir* or *uvaettir*.

It was the vaettir that gave a particular place, plant, stone, waterfall, pond, mound and so forth its particular energy or vibration. Some places were meant for veneration, while others were avoided due to the hostility of the vaettir ruling it. Vaettir were also associated with illness, and it follows that cunning ones in their work of healing as much as cursing must have worked with vaettir in one way or another.

Also worthy of mention is that the word vaettir could be used as a reference to any non-human being manifested in nature, be it a *thurs*, troll, Æsir or elf. Also, it appears that all vaettir were somehow, at their root, related to death, revealing a simple dichotomy between that which is alive belonging under the Sun, and that which is dead belonging under the Moon. The preference for night is typical for all vaettir, with the exception of the elves. If they are woken from their slumber during the day, usually havoc and anger is the result.

Elves, or ***Alfar,*** are considered aerial spirits, but they are also a form of vaettir that has a strong association with the Vanir through Frey, called the "Lord of Elves", who lives in Alfheim, the home of the elves, with the Jotun couple Aegir and Ran, the owners of the Ocean.

---

99 Hodne.1995: 35.

The 6th Century Greek scholar Procopius of Caesarea says that elves were amongst the oldest of the nature spirits worshiped by the Norsemen. In the Edda, the elves are placed in a class of their own, on a similar dimension and level as the Æsir, equal with the Æsir, while also being considered a class of nature vaettir that was defined by foliage and the shape of water and wind. In Nordic folklore elves were considered "dead ones" that had merged with nature in various forms, but could take the form, *ham*, of fair humans, and like the huldre-people they could marry humans and have children with them. The *Lokasenna Loke* says that Aegir's hall at the bottom of the ocean is full of elves. *Alveblót* was done in late fall or early winter and the objective was to secure good health for the people on the farm and fertility for the crops. Elves could give illness, similar to that which the dead ones or draugr could give, like herpes or rashes of all sorts. The elves were also, like the dwarves, master smiths and were renowned for forging enchanted objects for the purposes of love and seduction or for victory in battle, like the Girdle of Freya or the Lance of Tyr.

We find reference to two types of elves: light-elves and black-elves. The light-elves live in Alfheim in the proximity of Midgard, whilst the black-elves live in Svartalfheim close to Urd's Well where the dwarves also live. Hence, the line between a dwarf and a black-elf is hard to define. Given that Frey is the King of Elves, it suggests that the light-elves were Vanir or at least vaettir of Vanir heritage and so, it might be suggested that an elf was like vaettir and troll was a vernacular used in reference to general nature spirits that were associated with powers found in the forest on a horizontal level and not underground as in the case of dwarves.

Dwarves are significant creatures, and since they were shaped from the maggots in Ymir's putrid flesh, they are both old and wise, possessing a particular cunning of enchanting objects through their mastery of the forge and metals. Always black from soot and considered cunning, crafty and moody, dwarves are never called "little people".[100] The corners of the world are supported by four dwarves, Austri in the East, Vestri in the West, Nordri in the North and Sudri in the South, giving an indication of their prominence in the structure of the cosmic fabric.

Dwarves are thought to dislike sunlight, as can be seen in the name *Dulinn*, "the one who can't stand the sunlight", and their home, Svartalfheim, is frequently imagined as a sub-terrestrial labyrinth that is not much different from the structure of anthills. Dwarves are loyal companions to the Æsir and have helped them with forging

---

100 Bø. 1987: 72

some of their most renown weapons, like Thor's hammer, Mjölnir, and Odin's spear, Gungnir, but also enchanted jewelry like Odin's ring, Draupnir, and Freya's bracelet, Brisingamen. However, the jewelry they made frequently came with a hint of trickery or potential misfortune, usually a consequence of the dwarf feeling forced or not sufficiently compensated for their work.

Dwarves, like elves and huldre, were erotic creatures, and were at times blamed for the abduction of women. In these accounts, the dwarves were always described as fair, but they tended to show off their mastery with the forge, and after a few days the abducted woman was allowed to leave the love nest with gifts of gold and silver. Their wisdom, and that they were present within the Earth as it was formed, might be an indicator that the land-vaettir were dwarves, or at least that they held a supporting function of the Earth itself from within their sub-terrestrial dwelling.

HULDRA AND THE HULDRE-PEOPLE

Huldre is the term given to the "hollow people", a species of spirits that lives inside mounds. They are similar to humans, but they have the tail of a horse or an ox and possess magical abilities. They are said to be hollow, and they are frequently said to have a cavity running along their spine that reveals this hollowness. The word huldre is from the old Norwegian *huldr* which means "something hidden", and over the years, the word holdr derived from it, which means "hollow". Most stories speak of encounters with huldra, a female force that sometimes seduces boys and men, and at other times kills them, and at other times drives them mad. A form of huldra is Mara, also known as *myrkaridur*, a dark rider, that is related to both the power of nightmare (in Norwegian *mareritt*, "the ride of mara"), as well as *vargulfr*, or werewolf and shapeshifting mysteries, as she is described both as a shapeshifter and a succubus.

The huldre-people lived in societies similar to the humans, but in a parallel invisible dimension, often in close proximity with humans. They were attracted by conflict and also drawn to beauty. If there were conflicts on a farmstead, they could, at times, appear to set things right either with kindness or with threats. With the advent of Christianity, the origin of the huldre-people was said to be the children that Adam begot with Lilith. One version says that Adam disliked the offspring and asked God to make their dwellings in mounds, close, yet away from him. Another version says that Eve tried to hide this offspring from God, and when God discovered that she tried to hide these children, He cursed them to live hidden forever.[101]

The hollow people of the mounds were originally thought to be a twin people to humankind, composed of the revenants and ghosts of people buried in mounds at the beginning of human life, and were, as such, considered to be a type of land-vaettir. With some frequency, the huldre-people married humans, but they were also responsible for changelings. Given the similarities between themselves and humans, they were reputed to exchange children born with some dysfunction with healthy human babies and to leave their own offspring in their stead. These huldre-children were noticed by their abnormal behavior, excess of crying and, after growing up, by creating havoc and disturbances in the household in all possible ways.

Mara is a form of huldra. In the *Ynglinga saga*, we learn that the seidr-woman Huld was riding King Vanlanda while he was sleeping. From this, we might say that the huldre-people were a part of the mystery of seidr, or that they were a form of witchcraft or trolldom where one could ride out in an erotic, yet often fearful, shape that was similar to the typical succubus accounts where pressure on the chest along with erotic dreams or orgasm happened. Mara could also give nightmares, and *myrkaridur* or *kveldrida*, inflicting nightmares, was an art the Jotun-women were reputed to master. People afflicted by Mara could exorcise her as in one piece of advice from 1786 states:[102]

> The person afflicted would take a knife, wrap it in cloth, pass it three times around the waist prior to going to bed and say the following prayer:
> "Muro! Muro! Muro!
> If you are inside
> You shall be thrown out!
> Here is scissor, here is lance
> Here Simon-Svipu is found inside!"

Simon-svipu was also known as *marisolv*, "what unties Mara", and was a broom-brush made from birch leaves that was placed under the bed along with a scissor and a knife.

Some people were reputed to see the huldre-people, like Peer Gynt in Henrik Ibsens' play with the same name. Peer is invited into the wild ride of an interested huldre. Such rides were reputedly something that would drive most people to insanity and delusion, most likely because after such an encounter the person would not

---

101 Hodne 1995: 22.
102 Bø 1987: 90.

be able to close out the "other world" completely and would have to walk in two worlds simultaneously. In the British Isles, this was understood as fairy-taken, so we might see in fairies a people closely tied to the huldre-people.

In Nordic folktales there is a strong erotic component related to marine creatures, like mermaids, and all sorts of mound-dwelling beings, especially huldra – a matter dealt with extensively by Mikael Häll who discusses all forms of erotic nature spirits that enter into relationships with humans.[103]

Draugr, Revenants and the Dead Ones

Draugr is the name of a revenant, an animated dead one, be it human, Jotun, dwarf or elf, and refers to the corpse itself, meaning "the corpse in the mound". In later years, a draugr was frequently viewed as the revenant of someone who died at sea, but we have both land-draugr as often as water-draugr. To some extent, draugr can be said to be the form of revenants that are generated by the lack of proper burial rites, or of someone who has not completed their task while alive. Draugr, for the most part, created misfortune and trouble; Àsgardsreia, led by Sigurd Fåvnesban or Odin, was largely composed of draugr.

With water-draugr and land-draugr, we find two meanings which seem more used than others, which are the association with apparitions and ghosts deeply connected to the graveyard and ghosts of those that died at sea, so much that in the North of Norway, algae is frequently called draugr-vomit. The class of spirits we know as dwarves (*dverge*) were intimately connected to death through their chthonic habitat in subterranean caves.

Dwarves, like Dáinn, whose name means "death", and Náinn, whose name means "corpse-like", would attest to this. Dwarves share the same theme of death with draugr and it might be that many dwarves were considered draugr just as the ghost of Olav Geirstadalv in *Ynglinga saga* was referred to as an elf. The classification of spirits was rarely as exact as we might like it to be. An elf, a troll, a vaettir, a draugr and a dwarf were all otherwoldy presences, and the distinction between them was not always as important for the common person as it would be for the cunning ones.

Draugr is also a word used in relation to rashes like herpes and psoriasis, *draugslag*, and also holds a strong connotation with

---

[103] 2013.

rheumatism, *daudklyp*. We also see the enormous use of bones, graveyard moss, cemetery dirt, scrapings of crosses, fingernails and hair of corpses and many other things possessing not only magical powers, but also curative properties. Other diseases, like the nail-shaped callous that can surface on feet under heavy pressure over time, were and are known as *likthorn* in Norwegian, meaning corpse-thorn.

Draugr also might have some relationship to *vorden*, the guardian spirit of the soul, due to the word "vord" in present day Swedish being a word that means a ghost or apparition. This connection between draugr and vord is quite evident in the Gardsvord, the ghost of the first man who cleaned the land to make a farm and who died there. Gardsvorden was both a vord and a draugr, but he showed himself as a man of rather short stature, as in our modern idea of a "dwarf". We are here touching upon the core of the cult of the house and the importance of the dead ones, a vital part of the Northern Observance that will be discussed in detail in the next chapter.

Nixen and Other Trolls and Vaettir

Forest-lakes, waterfalls and bridges were always places one should respect due to their association with vaettir of ill-intent often ruling over them. Fossegrimen, "the grim one under the waterfall", is one of these.

Fossegrimen is a curious figure in the Northern Tradition, and much indicates that this being is a vaettir form of Odin under the kenning Grim Fossegrimen, who like Nixen was poisonous, or dwelled in toxic waters. This connects to Odin through Odin being praised in *Ynglinga saga*, *Lodfafnismál* and *Sigerdrifamál* as the runemaster that also mastered medicine and healing, which might explain why the snake, the wise animal representative of the healing arts, was incorporated in Odin's iconography in the 7th century. Likewise, the cunning one that was a great healer in the *Fóstbraedra saga* was also called Grima, revealing a connection with Odin and the poisonous nature of Fossegrimen due to the need for healing should he touch you or drag you into his waters.

Nixen, or **Nøkken**, are beings that took shape in the 13th century through the personification of watery spirits of a volatile and hostile bent found in the woods, hence, *fossegrimen* is one type of nixen. Nixen was a shapeshifter and was reputed to play the fiddle extremely well; we see here motifs from continental devil-lore where the Devil with his fiddle was able to play people into insanity or ecstasy. Nixen can show himself in many forms: as a young man, as an old gray bearded man (again a reference to Odin, which plays on his grim yet wise form), or as a dwarf. In the motifs of the nixen as a master musician we also see a conflation with traditional European devil-motifs where one through ritual and pact could gain the gift of mesmerizing people with one's musical gift. Vigil at the cemetery, placing your hand in a hole in the church wall, vigil on the grave of a famed musician until summoning the Devil at the crossroad at midnight with gifts and promises of compact were all ways in which one could entice the nixen to teach you the fiddle. Most famous is perhaps the Hardanger fiddle, a fiddle with eight or nine strings instead of the usual four, that would work in such a way that resonance was caused to the back strings – this motion of the back strings that happened by resonance was said to be played by "the other one", i.e. the devil or the nixen. Those making this pact with nixen or the Devil were commonly said to be walking around with a "heavy shadow" as if in the concord made they had purchased a dark fetch.

The apparition of nixen was always a bad sign, announcing the death of someone, which ties this vaettir in with the Norns, as one who is able to announce the future and, in this case, when the Norns will cut the thread of life.

Mermen, Mermaids and Marine vaettirs

While the nixen and *fossegrimen* were vaettir of fresh waters, the sea offered its own vaettir in the shape of serpents, mermaids, and death-sailors. The sea-serpent is perhaps the one with strongest ties to Old Norse cosmology in the form of Jormundgandr or Midgardsormen and Nidhöggr, hence encountering the sea-serpent in olden days would probably summon the awe of being close to Jormundgandr, the child of Loke, which was coiling around the world. The sea-serpents were born on land, under rocks in the woods or in the mountains. As they grew up, they would develop a preference for human blood and after their first kill they tended to migrate to the sea or large lakes where they grew to enormous proportions. The Biblical Leviathan became synonymous with the sea-serpent in the 15th century and there have been instances where lambs and sheep have been thrown into the sea as indirect offerings to Jormundgandr, and directly to ask the forces of the water, including the sea-serpent, to give good weather and good wind. Sightings of sea-serpents have since the 13th century and up to present day been quite numerous, so numerous that Olaus Magnus in his *Magna Carta* from 1555 dedicated a generous amount of space to describing these beings.

Mermen and a smaller type of merman called *marmaele*, which simply means small merman, are written about in *Landnámabók* from the 9th century. These marmaele could bring luck with the fishing and they could also predict the future, which would perhaps be a natural trait for a being of water. Mermen were considered more like a troll and seeing them at sea was usually taken to signify that a storm was coming. Mermen appear to have been of a more somber type, while the mermaids, also called *margyger*, meaning sea-ladies, are described as having long, white hair, large wide eyes, a large mouth and wrinkled skin. When she appeared she also announced storms, but she also felt more easily threatened and could at times do damage to ships and try to sink them. In *Olavs saga* we find the story of King Olav in the 11th century who killed a mermaid at the mouth of a river ending in the ocean in Spain. This place was the site for the shrine of this mermaid, but Olav killed her because she was reputed to sink ships and to possess violent and horrible screams that she used in an attempt to make the sailors jump ship.

Ghost ships, like the Flying Dutchman, were called death-sailors and were considered a form of draugr most hostile and dangerous; just seeing one of these ghost-ships was considered ominous if not foreboding of disaster ahead. In addition to this there were also other vaettir found, like the waves which were spoken of as the daughters of Ran. It was frequently Ran and her daughters that were appealed to by seaside witches and sailors to get luck with fishing and good wind. This would naturally involve draugr and elves as well, as the Golden Halls of Ran and Aegir received those who died at sea, and are said to be populated with numerous elves.

A World Alive with Death

It appears that death and the dead were interwoven with all kinds of vaettir. In understanding how these forces were resorted to when trolldom, gandr and seidr were used it might be helpful to look at the powers found in the various places in nature to understand better the essence of these many vaettir. Let us first have a look at earth and land and see what mysteries we can unravel there.

The earth with its mounds, groves, dark woods, and graves was populated with death and beings from the other side in such richness that it is difficult to arrive at a conclusion as to where the dead end and the mysterious beings dwelling in the moldy nightside of the world begin. The idea of the afterlife was one of a transition of state and in some regards life was a preparation for a good death that was certainly not necessarily the end of existence as such. The dead ones would continue to give counsel to the living through dreams and omens, and to show themselves to the living as apparitions or revenants. These very lively societies in mounds and beneath the surface of the earth consisting of huldre, vaettir, elves and dead ones were at large referred to as earth-vaettir.[104]

The location where vaettir was believed to live was treated with reverence and there were rules for how to deal with such a place. Driving iron into the ground or leaving excrement or warm water (including urine) was thought to upset the earth-vaettir and could attract retribution in the form of illness or misfortune. In the same manner, when one was clearing land for construction it was important to avoid building directly over the dwelling of the vaettir as this would generate friction. It was necessary to find a harmonious field of co-existence with the spirits of nature and the vaettir. This agreement between realms would be symbolized by the farmstead's ward-tree as the representation of Yggdrasil, where the farm would mimic the concepts of Midgard and Åsgard and in a very real sense recreate sacred space on earth through observing the rules and establishing a benign harmony between the visible and invisible realms. The ward-tree would then be the connection with the vaettir of the land, the ancestors and the living or, as we read in *Egil's saga*, "the one that will live under the tree must also give it reverence". Earth herself, called Jord or Fjörgyn, was considered sacred and calling earth by her true names was considered something one should do with great care; nicknames aimed towards reminding her of her kindness and usefulness were used for her instead of her true name, in the same way as with every other vaettir. Jord is mentioned as the mother of Thor and the father of Frigg; Odin, in marrying Frigg, and by adopting Thor, would by this act affirm his pact with Jord. It also is tempting in this to suggest that the mysterious father/mother of Thor and Frigg was Nidhöggr, the dragon at the root of Yggdrasil, or at the center of the earth. In *Voluspá*, oath-breakers of various kinds are said to be sent to Nidhöggr as food; given how Thor represents social order and is associated with thunder which traditionally holds a serpentine motif, and how the secret name of Frigg as the Lady of the House is Thora, it would be most proper to see this serpent-thunder motif together with the children of Jord. Different kinds of earth, mold and moss were equally treated with awe as these elements were considered to possess particular virtues of Jord and would, by

---

104 Reichborn-Kjennerud. 1928: 9.

extension, also carry the influence of particular vaettir in a magical-thinking based on natural analogies and harmonies. Most of all Jord was considered the great healer, hence it was crucial to not "hurt" or "beat" Jord, lest healing was turned into affliction which would irritate the many vaettir who found places in the great kingdom of Jord as her *protectors* and wardens.

Trees and plants were considered the children of Jord and all of them were thought to be alive with a unique virtue, hence when a *skurdgud*, a carved image of a spirit or deity, was made from the wood of a tree, it was important to elect proper wood, representative of the energy or virtue one wanted to carve. In order to use a tree or plant, one had to sacrifice to the tree and ask its permission; these sacrifices were commonly ale and milk. Up to the present day we find in the Scandinavian countryside the custom of greeting trees, fields and vegetation as one ventures into their domain, to announce to the vaettir and to Jord that one is aware of one's place in creation and that one comes in respect. By extension, poisonous weeds were considered inhabited by wicked vaettir, while healing plants with benign ones. The more noble a plant or tree, the more elevated its indwelling spirit, like rye which was considered a manifestation of the Vanir Frey. Of trees it appears that folk-traditions venerated Aspen and Birch more than any other; it might be that these two trees were considered to stand in a particularly sacred relationship with Thor and Frigg as the children of Jord.

Certain animals were also considered more spiritually close to humans than others, like the toad which was frequently connected to the huldre-people and was treated as if a huldre was nearby in the shape of a toad. Flies, fleas, spiders and maggots in general were frequently seen as a sign that the Devil was around or that some nasty gandr was trying to anchor itself in the household. We also know that blót was done for cows, dogs, cows and horses that due to their involvement in human life were considered not only important but as close allies; it was important to keep these "ward-animals" content, because domesticated animals could also enter into the function of a ward for a person or a household.

Stones were also important; they were considered to be alive and were in some cases treated with the same awe as magical mountains and hills where the trolls, Jotun and *thurse*-people were living. The importance of the stone is perhaps most accessible to us through the importance of the border stones and the center stones in defining land, center and buildings in a farmstead. These stones were considered "earth-bound" in the same way as stones that were conceived of as growing through the surface of the earth – stones that were in direct communion with the spirit of Jord. These stones that marked center and border of the farmstead were subject to offerings. There are several folk-stories speaking about how people moving the border stones were attacked by the vaettir resting there[105] and suffered death – and in the afterlife were turned into the slave of the vaettir and given the eternal task of moving the stone they had dislocated back to its rightful place, over and over again. Up to the last century it was common to have a stone either at the threshold of the main house or close to the entrance of the main house; this stone was not only the seat of the *protector* of the house, but it was also a place where oaths and promises were made.[106]

The waters were just as alive as the earth and sheep were frequently sacrificed to the vaettir of lakes, waterfalls and rivers in cases where these places were on a farmstead or meaningful to a household. The bubbles from riverbanks were taken as a sign of the living, breathing vaettir dwelling at its bottom; in the same way that weeds and plants could be inhabited by good or bad vaettir, so it was with water in all its forms. Deceptive and dangerous rivers were seen as replicating the very nature of their vaettir, just as a calm and gentle waterfall expressed the nature of its particular guardian spirit. Lakes, rivers, and waterfalls were always given names proper to the vaettir living there. We have countless lakes and water sources which have names that bring attention to trolls in the sense that they are enchanted or dangerous; hence these places are called Jotunheimen, Trollebotn and other "trollish names". In the same way we find lakes and rivers named after benign elves or huldre-people, both to define quality as much as to assign ownership of that particular place in nature.

Fire was another element subject to veneration and from around the 14th century the fireplace held a strong association with Loke, especially seen in the custom of throwing milk teeth into the fire because this was Loke's part. This association between Loke and the tooth fairy is interesting, and combined with Loke being originally associated with air (through his name *Lopt*, meaning aerial) and locks makes this transition to a fairy living in the fire potentially indicative of how people saw the effects of Loke in the world – as a hot spirit that due to his aerial essence could with ease go through

---

105 This vaettir is known as *maerkestrollet*, the troll that marks.

106 It is curious to note that in West Africa these earth-bound stones are seen as manifestations of the orisa Esu and hold similar ideas, namely that these are places where one need to exercise truthfulness. Feeding such stones with palm oil and gin prior to making a pledge or to discuss matters is to this day done with frequency.

locked doors. In the Eddas we see how blót was done to the hearth and to the fire and sacrifices of ale, milk, malt, food, and cheese were frequently given to the fire-vaettir at the hearth of the house to ensure luck and prosperity in the household, and particularly aimed towards always having sufficient food, or as Odin says in *Hávamál*: "fire and Sun is the best for man."

Lastly the air was considered the playground for spirits and beings of all kinds; benign winds were moving around equally benign spirits and destructive and cold winds were bringing an increase of hostile spirits. It was also in this element that the *önd* or breath, the wind that gave life to the hugr, traveled in upon death, hence the air and the wind held this idea of being an animating substance. It was also through the air gandr was sent, and where birds and winged bugs, both harbingers of gandr, moved around. In illnesses like "alveblest", a skin disease said to be caused by the breath of hostile elves, we find an association with bad wind (as in acute lumbago which had many names) which in some districts was seen as being caused by the breath of a troll. The north-wind was considered the worst of all winds as this wind brought hostility of all sorts from illness to the mad wild hunt of Àsgardsreia, the army of dead riding through the air.

Clearly the Old Norsemen were living in a world made meaningful by signatures and correspondences that were seen as natural and logical given the enchanted worldview they held. A stone was never just a stone; a tree was never just a tree. A tree was connected to a vaettir and the vaettir was connected to dead men and women that were in turn connected to the living in an ever-dying cycle of perpetual renewal and transformation, singing the soft praises of the mysterious virtues of Jord.

Lastly it is necessary to mention two factors of importance in dealing with nature and its denizens. One is the interplay between silence and words and the other concerns the importance of colors.

Silence is a repeating theme in trolldom and seidr as much as in folk-magic at large. This demand for silence we find related to nearly every act where one is gathering objects. The journey towards the gathering of a given plant, object or stone is frequently said to be done in silence with the absolute prohibition against speaking with any person as one is undertaking such sacred sojourns. All forms of divination usually demand an absence of words, thereby allowing the silence to speak. In the same way words were of equal importance when used with precision, in particular concerning the true name of animals and vaettir, where one could use nicknames evoking their benevolence or, in the case of harmful gandr, names that would resonate with their capacity for harm. In the concept of galdr or troll-songs we also find the use of words to evoke harm and healing explicitly being said to be of importance as countless stories in *Egil's saga* demonstrate, like when he was writing in runes in blood on a drinking horn that was poisoned and was singing galdr to evaporate the poison. Names and naming were important as we see in the various troll formulas, where names and well-proven magical words, like "amen" and "In the name of N" were used along with Latin or Latin-like barbarous words to seal and effectuate a charm or a spell.

Of colors, black was the color of night and mystery and was relentlessly associated with trolldom, gandr and runes – but also healing. Enchanted animals were frequently black in color; black cats and black chickens and roosters were also used in trolldom, such as sacrificing a black chicken at the middle of a crossroad on a Thursday night for various ends[107] or boiling black cats alive on a Thursday night to generate either potions or healing bones. The color white belonged to the dead; draugr was, like ghosts and apparitions, described as white just as the hollow people living in mounds could show themselves in the guise of white mice. Blue was perhaps the color most used in active magic. The volva in *Eiríks saga rauda* for instance was dressed in blue, and in west Norway we find the custom of passing a blue cloth through the opening in a tree to infuse it with healing powers. Also, the huldre-people are frequently described as dressed in blue clothes, if not being slightly bluish themselves. We also see Hel, daughter of Loke and owner of Helheimen, being described as having half her face colored a dark blue. Red was also a color associated with trolldom; red silk threads were at times used to ward against Mara and held several associations similar to black – yet with an edge of something active going on as it is also a color of blood, fire and of poison. Red was also the color of passion, be it lust or sorrow, as we find with Freya crying tears of red gold when her husband Odr is away.

In this we see how nature could speak and how it was possible to communicate and interact with nature and its denizens. A red bird landing on an offer-stone on a Thursday night would be taken as a sign and interpreted as nature's own language as much as the silence of a graveyard wanderer, dressed in blue and black, searching for a particular human bone was in his silence and colors speaking with the revenants and ghosts in the realm of the dead and giving a statement of purpose.

---

107 Reichborn-Kjennerud, 1928: 107135.

Chapter Five

A Genealogy of Trolls

Then asked Gangleri: "What he (Odin) did before heaven and earth were made?" Hárr answered: "He was then with the Trolls of Ice (Frost-Giants)."[108] – *Gylfaginning*

The "gods" of the North are called Æsir, "shining ones", but we also find Vanir, a class of deity associated with wisdom and fertility which, in their description, remind us of fairies and elves. When the Æsir established their reign, they entered into a fight with the Vanir, leading to a truce where some of the Vanir were adopted into the ranks of the Æsir. The Æsir themselves were from two primordial origins, either of the Jotun-race or they were children of Jord, or Earth, herself. Jotun, like trolls, held an association with stones and mountains and were said to live inside mountains or in places guarded by mountains. The Vanir were deities tied to the forest and to the fields and it might be that the fusion of Jotun and Vanir in the fold of Æsir represented the merging of stone and greenwood, generating a world rich in virtue of difference. The Æsir took on this elevated role due to Odin, the first Æsir, who was also the one who created the world from the ur-matter of the body of the slain ancestor, Ymir. Yet, although he was the creative force of the world and of humans, he was never the origin of everything, for the world as we know it is the world as envisioned and made by Odin *and* his brothers. Hence the reason he is "father of all" and why perpetual entropy is built into the creation. Therefore, in order to understand the Northern Tradition, the main features of Odin, the son of trolls and his Æsir, will be presented. Also, *Gylfaginning* clearly states that Ymir was not considered a god as such, rather he was considered a slightly wicked ur-force and so his children were the frost-giants, or more properly, *thursar*, trolls made from ice and frost. Because of his heritage through his mother Bestla, it was amongst the thursar that Odin resided prior to the creation of the world.

Odin, the Allfather, the gallows god, the grim one, the god of the farm and of the battle, lies at the pinnacle of the Nordic worldview,

---

108 In the original text: Þá mælti Gangleri: "Hvat hafðist hann áðr at en himinn ok jörð væri ger?" Þá svarar Hárr: "Þá var hann með hrímþursum."

at least from the perspective of humans. It was Odin, who along with his brothers Vile and Vé, gave life to two pieces of driftwood and called them Ask and Embla, which became the first humans. Rydberg suggested in his oeuvre that the dwarves were also involved in the creation of humans, not only because *Gylfaginning* describes them as sort of proto-human, but because of their involvement in any kind of artistry and magic that binds beauty and form together into aliveness and enchantment.

According to chapter 9 of *Gylfaginning*, the three brothers Vile, Vé, and Odin were the creators of the first man and woman, just as they were also the creators of the world as we know it. The brothers were once walking along a beach and found two trees there. They took the wood and from it created the first human beings: Ask and Embla. One of the three gave them the breath of life, the second gave them movement and intelligence, and the third gave them shape, speech, hearing, and sight. Further, the three gods gave them clothing and names. Ask and Embla went on to become the progenitors of all humanity and were given a home within the walls of Midgard, the walls built from the wood made from Ymir's eyebrows for separation and protection in all directions. Stanza 17 of the *Voluspá* says:

Ǫnd þau né átto, óð þau né hǫfðo,
lá né læti né lito góða.
Ǫnd gaf Óðinn, óð gaf Hœnir,
lá gaf Lóðurr ok lito góða

Soul they had not, sense they had not,
Nor heat nor motion, nor a bright and healthy hue;
Ensouled breath gave Odin, spark and inspiration gave Hönir,
Blood and heat gave Lothur and a bright and healthy hue

Hönir, like Vidar, was referred to as "the silent one" that was delivered to the Vanir together with Mimir to ensure a truce. In the *Voluspá*, we see that Hönir gives Ód, or reason and intelligence, to the humans; while *önd*, the breath related to örlög or Fate, is given by Odin; and blood is given by Lothur.

Ód, the principle of reason and intelligence, is considered a deity in its own right; sometimes it is said to be an epitaph of Odin in the form of Odr and considered the husband of Freya. Ód, however, is not only a word describing reason and intelligence, but also signifies "inspiration" or "frenzy". Given that we find similar confusion with Ód and Odin, which is also something we find in relation to Odin and Hönir, perhaps the explanation here is that Hönir becomes what

A Genealogy of Trolls

he gives. Hence, in giving Ód, he is actually the same divinity, as attested by the fact that he was sent to live with the Vanir and Freya's husband, who was also known as Ód. The fact that Hönir is not capable of thinking without Mimir is also significant; the spirit of inspiration dislocated from Memory becomes silent and perhaps expresses itself in forms of frenzy and ecstasy. Odin is a complex deity, and understanding more of the nature of Odin might invite us to appreciate more of human nature. The name Odin means "fury", as in a fire-starting frenzy. His ancestry is one of trolls and giants, a legacy he tries to distance himself from yet from which he constantly seeks advice. He is the son of Borr and Bestla. Borr was the son of the giant Buri who Audhumla licked out from the ice. Bestla was the daughter of Bolthorn who taught the secrets of galdr to Odin, who in turn was the son of Trudgjelmir, the six-headed Jotun that was born from the decapitated toes of the primordial Jotun, Ymir.

Odin makes a blood-pact with Loke, a Jotun of great importance in the Nordic cosmology. He has a son, Thor, with the giantess Fjörgyn, also known as Jord. He also has Valé with Rindr,[109] another giantess and relative, if not daughter, of Fjörgyn. He marries Frigg, daughter of Fjörgyn, and is the lover of Freya, the Vanir, who is also counted as an Æsir together with her brother Frey. His most trusted allies are Mimir, a Jotun, and Hönir, who was most likely a Jotun also.

This means that the term Æsir is largely a genealogy speaking of divinities born from Fjörgyn/Earth and giants, but at the same time we find a Jotun like Loke also referred to as an Æsir, as much as the Vanir Freya is referred to as an Æsir, as much as Frigg who is solely said to come from Fjörgyn. Odin's occupation with Jord and Jotun might be seen as vital for creation itself given the prominence of stones and mountains that are seen as growing out from Jord, hence these dwellings of trolls and Jotun become the axis that connects the world with the spirit of Earth.

Odin fights in the front and he fights in the back, he is relentless with warding his domain against the Jotun-race, especially in Utgard, yet it is always there where deep wisdom is found, almost as if Utgard is what lies at the bottom of any well or deep spring, signifying the source of wisdom from which Odin is chronically thirsty to drink.

Odin is described as a one-eyed man in a deep blue cape and wide brimmed hat. He is flanked by two wolves, two ravens and a

---

109 Rindr as a Jotun is however slightly disputed and several researchers have suggested that she might be an elf, but given that she is the daughter of Billing, daybreak, and most likely Fjörgyn/Jord, we see here how Odin is constantly striving to strike pacts and alliances with Jord and her children.

horse. The ravens, Hugin and Munin, thought and memory, keep him constantly updated on what is going on in the world, clearly representing one of two avenues of *ham*riding as it speaks of his fylgja, just as his wolves, Freki and Geri, are the second. Their names refer to forms of greed and hunger, denoting both Odin's thirst for wisdom but also his domain over the arts of trolldom, such as gandr and seidr.

The war against the Vanir started with the murder of Heid, a word usually translated to mean "shining", or "hot". But, it might also be that the correct meaning is *heidr*, which means "uncultivated earth" and, when considering this in relation to the attack upon Heid that triggered the war with the Vanir, the idea that some conflict related to earth itself might be intuited due to the alliance Odin had with Fjörgyn or Earth in marrying her daughter, Frigg.

Looking at the Nordic genealogy we see that the deities we call Æsir are largely a fusion of Jotun with Fjörgyn. There are exceptions, like Heimdal, that in the *Rigstula* is credited with bringing increase to mankind and establishing social order, hence, we might conclude that the children of Ask and Embla were continued by the intervention of Heimdal, whose name means "the white one", which might simply be a reference to semen amongst many other things. Heimdal is the son of the nine sisters, commonly known as the daughters of Ran and Aegir. His paternal side is obscure, and given the mystery involved it might be Odin that is his father, which would invite its own logic between Heimdal and Odin as the fathers of mankind, or we might yet again see the rarely named Jord as his father, which would make him half-brother to Frigg.

This would then suggest that the "first gods of men" would be Fjörgyn, Ran, Aegir, Odin and Heimdal; along with Hönir, Lothur, Vile and Ve – 9 forces in all, which might point to yet another explanation of why the number 9 was always the most sacred and revered number in Scandinavian mythology and magic. With the truce between Æsir and Vanir, another divine strain entered Scandinavia through Njord, a Poseidon type, that most likely symbolizes the origin of the Vanir and their reconnection to the class of "the shining ones".

If we look at Nordic place names, we also see that the divinities Ullr and Tyr had rich domains, as had Frey and Freya. Yet Thor seems to have been the Æsir who was most placated after Odin. Also, from seeing how place names could change, it gives us the opportunity of cult and faith being practiced with a certain pragmatism: a "god" was good as long as he actually worked, and a god that didn't defend and ensure fertility could simply be discarded and replaced with another deity that proved more effective.

A Genealogy of Trolls

If we look at a text like the *Rigstula*, where Heimdal is going from farm to farm to generate the three stations of social classes (*jarl*, *karl* and *trell*), it suggests that men had a deep awareness of the proximity between Æsir and humans, hence the Allfather Odin was an Æsir that walked amongst men – after all, Midgard was considered a field where divinity and humans intermingled. If we look at the forms of cult practiced, Tacitus comments that there was no real difference between what the Nordic people did and what the Romans did, which hints at a possibility of turning to the Roman cults of the *lares* and nature spirits, as well as the more official religious expressions related to the veneration of planetary deities, for a reference in understanding the Northern Tradition.

The most vivid account of an official cult is related to the temple in Uppsala that apparently had a priesthood which was somewhat similar to the Roman *flamens*. If we consider both the accounts of official cult and the many folk-magic practices along with the particularly enchanted worldview of the Scandinavians in the Middle Ages, we will see a kind of religiosity appear that is quite different from what we are accustomed to in the Modern Age. It is fair to say that people had a deeper sense of ancestry with divinities, yet these ancestors were also considered lofty and mysterious, providing the possibility of appealing to divinities for the sake of protection and fertility, while maintaining a personal, yet respectful relationship with the divinities in the sense of families upholding veneration for them in this regard. Hence Odin as the father of all would necessarily not only be popular, but also intertwined in everything as the root cause of the human being. This is further perpetuated by Heimdal who would, from how he was perceived as a guardian of the rainbow-bridge that separated the visible world from the invisible, be conceived of as the guardian of the human race and civilization. This ancestral connection with the Æsir is clearly stated in *Ynglinga saga's* 5th chapter, where it appears that several of the Æsir settled in various parts of eastern and southern Sweden where they erected sanctuaries. Snorre writes the following:

> Odin took up his residence at the Mälaren Lake,[110] at the place now called Old Sigtun. There he erected a large temple, where there were sacrifices according to the customs of the Asaland people. He appropriated to himself the whole of that district, and called it Sigtun. To the temple priests he gave also domains. Njörd dwelt in Nóatún, Frey in Upsal, Heimdal in

---

[110] A place sacred to Gefjon, one of Frigg's servants associated with wisdom and fertility.

the Himinbergs, Thor in Thrudvang, Balder in Breidablik; to all of them he gave good estates.

Later we read that Njord's son Frey was made the King of the Swedes and was praised as a good, fair and generous king, just like his father. It was Frey that raised the temple at Uppsala and ensured that all the Æsir were given tribute, sacrifice and reverence.

If we look at the cult of Odin and the Æsir in Uppsala, at least from the account we have from Adam of Bremen, it indicates that the way of placating Odin was, to a large extent, to follow his example, and in this case, especially as the god of the hanged ones and in memory of the deed done in order to gain wisdom, to hang one's self upside down for nine days and nights on Yggdrasil.

In *Gesta Hammaburgensis ecclesiae pontificum*, Adam of Bremen provided a description of the temple in the 4th book. He writes that the temple at Uppsala was founded on a plain surrounded by mountains or mounds that, for him, generated the perception of a temple. At the side of the temple was a large tree, an evergreen of impressive and mysterious origin. At the tree was a well where sacrifices were made and wishes presented. Apparently, people were thrown alive into this well as a sacrifice, and if the person sank and died it would mean the wish was granted. The roof of the temple was adorned by a chain of gold that shone and flickered to show people their destination, and the abundance of gold everywhere was impressive. He says he found three wooden figureheads that were the center of worship: Thor, Odin and Frey; of these three, Thor held the central position. Thor is described as the ruler of air, thunder, lightning, wind, and rain; Adam also made a connection between Thor and Jupiter. Thor was considered the force that one appealed to for restoring order to potential threats like hunger, illness, and epidemics. Odin was described by Adam as a god of war, and naturally Adam associated Odin with Mars; Frey, depicted with a giant phallus, was said to be the one responsible for happiness, peace, and all kinds of pleasures, for the living as well as for the dead. Even if Adam did not comment on the Roman association, we see that Venus, Eros, Bacchus and Priapus are all facets of Frey, and that weddings were also under his domain.

Adam detailed the sacrificial practice at the temple, which he observed was celebrated at the spring equinox. Nine males of every living creature, including humans, were offered up for sacrifice, and the corpses were left hanging in the trees in the grove of the temple, particularly in the large evergreen. Adam commented on the bawdy songs that were sung and described a general repulsion for it all. Steinsland commented that the word Adam is using for temple is *triclinium*,[111] which is curious, because it would mean "banquet hall" more than a "sanctuary", and this sense of a temple which was an example of a social space showed how intertwined the religious and secular dimensions were, one sphere working within the other and vice versa. The most problematic matter with Adam of Bremen in terms of reliability is, of course, the fact that he never went to Scandinavia and that what he writes about is his rendering of the stories he collected from people who actually did go there. In this, we also find rumors and fantastical stories coming his way from all possible sources, credible or not, that were used to expand upon his vision of the "heathen north". Even so, if we look at the accounts given by Ibn Fadlan[112] along with Adam of Bremen, and along with what we later find in the writings of Snorre Sturlasson, we can agree with Rudolf Simek[113] and his critique of Adam as being not all that reliable, and that Adam took several freedoms in interpretation and invited in uncritical associations with for instance the temple of Solomon.

Orchard[114] states that "It is unclear to what extent Adam's description has a basis in historical fact rather than lurid fiction," yet that Adam's account contains "...a good deal of useful information." These are views also expressed by Steinsland.[115]

This perpetual disagreement is partly rooted in the varieties of perceptions people have when they study the Nordic ways, and in this is the chronic tendency to always understand the other in reference to ourselves. Our own time and culture will always present problems and potential for error in understanding a culture whose time, geography and worldview differs from our own. This is true for Westerners studying Oriental or Occidental cultures in the present day, as much as it is true for those standing within a given culture looking back in time with the belief that what has been a truth for one hundred years has always been true. It is important to be constantly mindful about these factors along with the dramatic difference between an enchanted and pre-modern worldview and the disenchanted modern worldview. With this in mind, it is also important to reconsider how the Æsir were actually understood and what roles they held in the "religious sensitivity" of pre-modern

---

111 2005: 298.
112 877-960.
113 2007.
114 1997.
115 2005.

Northmen. One example is from the *Sigerdrifamál*, stanzas 3 and 4, in an invocation that was not preoccupied with Thor, Odin, Frigg, Frey and Freya as being more important than other forces, but rather, suggests there are a composite of spiritual forces that are being met here that make the "runes", or magical secrets, possible. She makes this invocation prior to her speech about the runes:

Heill dagr!	I greet the Day!
Heilir dags synir!	I greet the Sons of Day!
Heil nótt ok nift!	I greet Night and Dawn!
Óreiðum augum	Turn towards us
lítið okkr þinig	with kind eyes
ok gefið sitjöndum sigr!	Give us, gathered here, victory!
Heilir æsir!	I greet the Æsir!
Heilar ásynjur!	I greet the àsynjer!
Heil sjá in fjölnýta fold!	I greet the ever good Jord/Earth!
Mál ok mannvit	Give us wisdom
gefið okkr mærum tveim	the gift of speech/prophecy/memory
ok læknishendr, meðan lifum.	and hands that heal in life.

Passages like this, which are rarely given much attention, coupled with the entire practice of trolldom with its spells and enchantments, present a very distinctive idea of "the gods" which differs from what we might be used to. Use of the term "the gods" might even be a misnomer in general, caused by a will to understand the alien with reference to the familiar, namely Christianity in the case of Adam of Bremen or Islam in the case Ibn Fadlan, or Teutonic Theosophy for the Germanic revivalists of the late 18th century.

If we look at the genealogy of the Æsir and Vanir, it appears that we could speak of another seed, something praeterhuman that was in touch with humankind before the age of men, and it seems that people could be incarnations of these forces, such as in the story in the *Ynglinga saga* of an Odin that settled at Lake Mälaren in Sweden. A physical location places the gods in a very different perspective, or at least it questions the entire transcendental quality we usually ascribe to gods and spirits. Not only this, although Odin created humankind, he had himself a legacy and ancestry going back to ice, fire and nothingness. Hence Odin, in spite of being the father of mankind, is not a first principle and not the creator of the gods, with the exception of those he fathered.

A Genealogy of Trolls

This means that the perception of people in medieval Scandinavia, when it came to Æsir, Vanir and cult, was in truth, not much different from what we find in Greek and Roman antiquity where gods and heroes, wood spirits and revenants shared in the same experience as humans. In other words, the distance between humans and "the other" was not so far and deep as is the tendency in the Modern Age. This, in turn, makes recent revivals of these customs and cults as faith or religion distinctively different from what they used to be due to adopting a theology alien from these people, a theology largely Lutheran and Calvinist. The most dramatic consequence of Lutheranism was that the saints and the dead ceased to have any importance. In severing the significance of the realm of dead which was so vibrant and vital for the Scandinavians of olden times, there were no longer intermediaries between gods and men. Thus distance took the place of saints, heroes and death, because, in truth, saints were little more than people considered to stand out, the Christian idea of the hero and the heroine, but instead of being people perpetuating social and philosophical ideals they became replaced with people who defended the new faith.

As we see from Nordic cosmology and genealogy, we find that "the Æsir" is a conglomerate in its own right. In terms of origin, there are basically three named sources of the Æsir which are three names for the same force: Fjörgyn, Jord and Erda, the latter two names for Earth. This mystical spiritual force is said to be both Frigg's father and Thor's mother – and which might also be the mother of Frey and Freya, which in turn generates all gods known to possess clairvoyance and prophetic abilities, be they Balder, Nep, Nanna and so forth, as great deities that appear to have some deep connection with either of the two celestial luminaries, Sun and Moon. Jord will be placed in better context as Loke is discussed towards the end of this chapter.

The Æsir all seem to possess a common quality, namely "to shine" in one way or another; hence we find a connection with fire, thunder and reflective surfaces that ties this shine into a nomenclature for wisdom, prophecy and clairvoyance, and in particular suggests that magically endowed beings are, in general, sort of meta-human. Here, a circuit of becoming is upheld through how Odin carved men from wood and how men in turn carved the images of the Æsir from wood to anoint those wooden images with the blood of sacrifice.

The greeting of Brynhild in the *Sigerdrifamál* calls the attention of Night, Dawn, Day, the sons of Day, Earth and then later "the shining ones", which would perhaps mean that the Æsir are a product of the spirit of Earth, Night, Dawn, Day, and that the sons of Day, just like

Aegir, Ran and Heimdal, are tied in to natural phenomena like fire (*lue*) and wind (*káre*) along with frost and snow which are all traced back to the Jotun, Fornjótr.

Fornjótr was a Jotun, also said to have been the King of Gotland in Sweden and Finland, perhaps emphasizing his outlandishness, and is an ancestor of Heimdal. His children were Aegi and Ran, the owners of the ocean, and *Logi*/fire and *Káre*/wind, the latter being the grandfather of "frost" and "snow", also considered Jotun. His name brings thoughts of some ancient origin, what was before what is now, and represents the origin of the wisdom that made wind, fire and water possible. Fornjot's family tree and family relations are as follows:

FORNJOT'S AND HEIMDAL'S FAMILY TREE

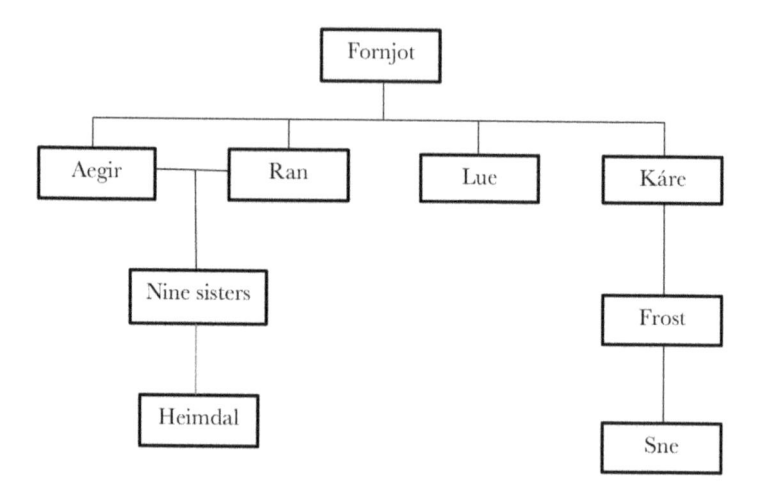

```
                    Fornjot
    ┌──────────┬──────────┬──────────┐
  Aegir──────Ran         Lue        Káre
              │                      │
         Nine sisters               Frost
              │                      │
           Heimdal                   Sne
```

Odin is, as established, also a Jotun, but his ancestry is different. He is deeply linked to the cosmic field of fire and ice that manifested earth, the farmstead and agriculture. His grandfather on his father's side was licked out from the ice by a cosmic cow, and on his mother's side we find Trudgjelmir, a six-headed Jotun born from the feet of Ymir, representing this fusion of fire and ice. Also, in the *Ynglinga saga*, there is a curious account of rivalry that mirrors intensely the world of men and the world of gods with equal measure, and we can of course speculate upon what Ottar Yngling meant when he said in the *Ynglingatal*, "The fair-haired son of Odin's race". If this is a reference to a heritage revealed in domestic cult or true succession of blood and memory is open for both interpretations. Odin's family tree and family relations looks like this:

A Genealogy of Trolls

ODIN'S FAMILY TREE

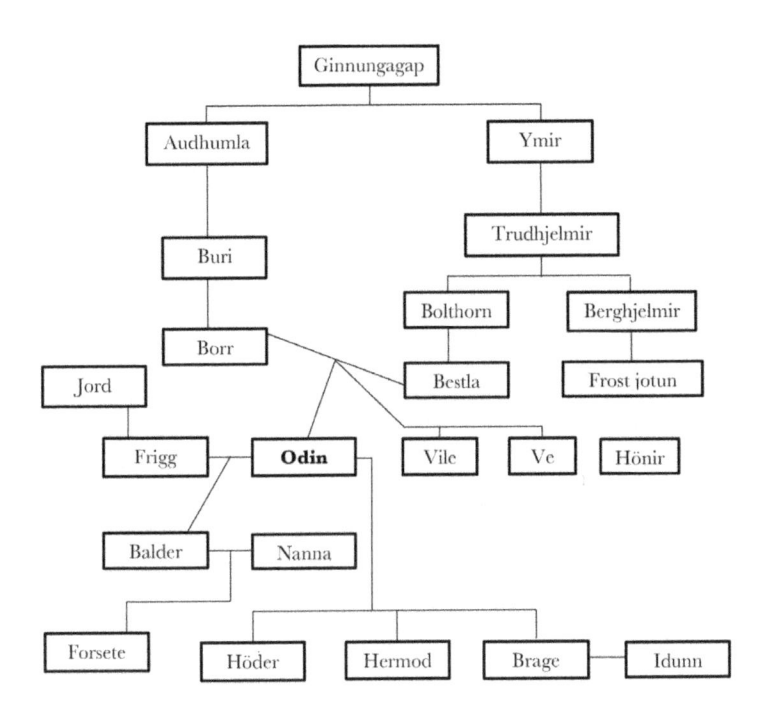

```
                        Ginnungagap
                    ┌────────┴────────┐
                Audhumla              Ymir
                   │                    │
                   │                Trudhjelmir
                 Buri              ┌─────┴─────┐
                   │           Bolthorn    Berghjelmir
                  Borr             │            │
         ┌─────────┤             Bestla    Frost jotun
       Jord        │
                   ├──────┬──────┬──────┐
                 Frigg  Odin   Vile  Ve   Hönir
                   │
              ┌────┤
           Balder─Nanna
              │
    ┌─────────┼─────────┬─────────┐
 Forsete   Höder    Hermod    Brage─Idunn
```

If we look closely at the Æsir, we see that they are largely of Jotun race and that there is a great fusion of pedigree involved. The Æsir loved to beget offspring with Jotun women, and always held them in high regard as well as equally in high contempt and awe and, as we have seen, there is an abundance of Æsir with Jotun-blood.

In going through some of the more popular and important *åsynje* and Æsir, it is possible to see how they represent principles and qualities with a double function, both cosmic and domestic. As principles, the Æsir were considered to have domain over larger areas and fields of activity. For example, in the instance of Thor, he would be the Æsir to which oaths and promises were made, which was frequently done at a given stone where the watchful vaettir would also observe the pledge and be able to execute penalties should the oath be broken. Likewise, we see in the past how Æsir names and animal names were given to children, a practice continued to this day, but with far less awareness of what it means to name a thing or someone. Names like Björn (bear), Gaup (lynx), and Ulf (wolf) speak of a connection with fylgja, or a power animal, which one wanted the child to inherit from nature. Names like Oddvar would connect the child to Odin, Thoralf to Thor and to the elves, Inga to Frey and Trym to the Jotun of same name, just to mention a few of the countless variants. In going through the more principal Æsir, it might be helpful to give some color associations to them which will denote cosmic and natural connections between the various Æsir born through color affinities.

Heimdal is the guardian of the world, of the Æsir and of Yggdrasil. He is clairvoyant and possesses prophetic abilities. His name can mean, "light of heavens", "shining home" or "cosmic brightness", hence, he is called "the white *ás*" – Snorre associates him with the idea of holiness. His home, Himinbjorg/Himmelberget, is located at the end of heaven. His horse is named Gulltopp and he is also known as Rig, from the Old Norse *rike*, or "kingdom". Rig is also an Irish term for chieftain/king as well as a word that etymologically derived Nordic words for "rich" (*rik*). He is also known as *Hallinskidi*, the forward leaning staff, which is a name referencing his connection to the ram as his sacred animal.

Heimdal is the son of the nine mothers and grandson of the giant Fornjot, with some interpreters suggesting Fornjot and Ymir are the same. Nevertheless, what we can see from this is that the origin of Heimdal goes back to a Jotun associated with some primordial potency, "the owner of what is ancient", which in turn is relegated to the mysteries of the Ocean, traditionally associated with secrecy, wealth, memory, death and ancestry. Heimdal, surging from the waters, born by the nine waves, rises as a beacon of light in the ocean's capacity of eating light, hence, Heimdal rises as a guardian of the mysteries, ever aware, ever alert; as he goes from water onto land he becomes the originator of social order, division and class (*Rigstula*). He might be viewed as the son of Odin, by adoption or blood, and considering his mother is the nine mothers, he might be seen as the one to continue the act of ordering the creative acts performed by Odin and his brothers when they ensouled Ask and Embla. Gro Steinsland[116] affirms the idea that Heimdal represents the axis mundi, hence, Heimdal is the marrow flowing through the core of Yggdrasil, the erotic light ebbing and flowing in harmony with the phases of the Moon and the seasons and stations of the Sun, the great harmonizer and natural guardian in his capacity of possessing arcane wisdom. He guards Bifrost, the rainbow bridge that connects the world of men and the world of the gods. Heimdal also represents the cycles and their changing. While his horn, Gjallarhorn, lies in quiet hiding in the roots of Yggdrasil near the Well of Mimir, the

---

116 2005: 221.

world moves on, but when he blows this horn the cycle will change, which is demonstrated in *Voluspá* when Heimdal blows Gjallarhorn, marking the end of the world as we know it and the rebirth of a new world. His colors are white and gold.

Frigg is the wife of Odin and is spoken of in the *Vaftrudnesmál* as equal to Odin in wisdom. Loke in the *Loketretta* indicates that she is equal to Odin in the amount of lovers she takes, of which Odin's brothers, Vile and Vé are counted. Linen and the distaff are sacred to her, and in this, we might see a strong connection to the volva and the art of gandr as well as seidr, for she was probably equal to Odin in those arts. When Balder died, the volva was the one that comforted her, signifying that Frigg was of special interest to her. Her name is etymologically related to the Old Norse *frjá*, which means "to love", and represents the steady fire of love in contrast to the ecstatic fire of erotic passion ruled over by Freya. Frigg, as well as Freya, were both protectors of midwives, with Frigg the protector of matrimony and the Lady of the House. Frigg's farm was called Fensalen and was believed to be rich in gold. Friday carries her name as well as Freya's in their common Venusian virtue. Her colors are red, gold and black.

Thor is commonly said to be the son of Odin, but again, it is difficult to state whether we speak of adoptive son or blood son. What we know is that he is the son of Jord and in this, the brother of Frigg. Thor is commonly considered the embodiment of strength, associated with thunder and goats. His home, Trudvang, is the home of the strong and his hall, called Bilskirne, is said to be as beautiful as Valhalla. It is said that every day, Thor wades through mighty rivers to get to the daily gathering at Yggdrasil. He is constantly depicted in battle with the Jotun and beings of Utgard, "the Outer farm", Nidhöggr, and other beings that are generally associated with the unruly and untamed, and it is in this capacity that we find the force that strikes limits and maintains the ebb and flow of perpetual order. Two things stand out in relation to Thor: one, that he seemed to have been the most venerated of the Æsir, most likely because of his capacity to warn of the wild and chaotic and to ensure bliss and fertility in the homestead; and two, that Thor and his famous temper caused the forging of a great number of weapons. The story goes like this: Loke decided one day to cut off the hair of Thor's wife, Siv. Thor, who was furious, demanded that he set right what he had done or suffer the consequences. In response, Loke went to the sons of Ivalde, the skillful dwarves, and had Gungnir forged, which became Odin's spear, the ship Skiblander that went to Frey, and for Siv a golden hair. In addition, they made the ring Draupnir that was given to Odin, the pig/boar Gyllenbust that went to Frey, and also

Mjölnir, the hammer that became the token of Thor. In the period of Christening in Scandinavia, the Hammer of Thor was used as a sign to demonstrate resistance against the cross. In this way, Thor represented the guardianship of the Old Ways and the patriarch of the warriors. While Odin represents the art of war, Thor represents warfare in action. His sons Mode and Magne continue their father's strength with both of them surviving Ragnarök and inheriting Thor's hammer, Mjölnir. Thor's colors are red and dark blue.

Balder is the son of Odin and Frigg. He is described as mild, kind, beautiful; he, like Heimdal, is a shining one, filled with light, just like the Sun. His wife is Nanna, daughter of the Moon, and they live at Breidablikk. Balder is immortal due to Frigg going around to all living beings and taking an oath from them that left Balder unharmed whenever they are involved, save for one plant, the mistletoe. It is eventually his blind brother Hod, etymologically linked to Heid, who, manipulated by Loke, suffers death by an arrow made from mistletoe. Balder will further be resurrected after the twilight of the Æsir, Ragnarök, and will be the instigator of the new world and the new races, continuing the legacy of Jord and Jotun as embodied in his parents Odin and Frigg. The perception of Balder has frequently been criticized as some sort of Christian propaganda given that his death and resurrection follow a central salvation theme in Christendom, but we should also take note that this theme, popularized in Christian mythology, is not a Christian idea. Death and resurrection are themes we find connected to Osiris as much as to Bacchus and thus represent a perennial and cosmic idea of regeneration. Hence Balder represents the accumulation of ancestral wisdom and the beginning of a new cycle. In this, we can say his colors are white, gold and red.

Forsete is the son of Balder and Nanna and was considered the wisest of all judges, and was the one called in to judge any dispute. He lives in a place called Glitne, "that which shines", again, a reference to gold and light connected to primordial wisdom. Forsete, being the child of the Sun and Moon, speaks of how the product of the two luminaries reveals itself in wisdom. Forsete is a master of solving disputes, a fair and wise king, similar to Solomon. His colors are said to be white, gold and dark blue.

Brage is another son of Odin, married with Idunn, and is the personification of eloquence and the patron of troubadours, testifying to the importance of poetry in Scandinavia, both as a virtue and also as a source for continuing ancestral memory, the secrets of galdr, and enchantments in general. His colors are said to be gold and red.

Ty or **Tyr** is one of the old deities, a precursor to Thor in many ways. He is said to be both a son of Odin, but also a son of the Jotun Hyme, which is the Jotun-friend Thor goes out with to catch Nidhöggr. Tyr is said to be the bravest and most wise one, and in this, represents a sort of warrior perfection, a combination of Odin's wisdom and Thor's bravery. It was Tyr who gave up his hand to Fenris in Ragnarök so the Æsir could chain him to the ground. He finally loses his life in a fight with the wolf Garm that marks the climax of Ragnarök and the defeat of the Æsir. The rune Tyr is one of the few runes that directly references an Æsir, and since the runes are cosmic building blocks in their own right, we might see within Tyr a perfect idea, an ideal representation of the art of war. His colors are white, red and blue.

If we add the Vanir, Frey, who was adopted into the Æsir family, we find another deity described as shining – through association with gold we see that the idea of light is most prominent amongst the Æsir. It is constantly about wisdom and bravery and to have that "shine" to you, a light Odin for some reason likes to hide and Thor is never said to have.

This means that, largely, the Æsir are beings born from Jotun and Jord/Earth, and that they appear very solar in various ways due to the element of light given to all of them, just Odin and Thor stand aside, with one hiding the light and the other being an activity which uses light in the form of lightning. So what appears here is a simple and traditional cosmology where the focus is largely on the source of light, the two luminaries in heaven, Sun and Moon, and how this light spreads wisdom over earth. Given the constant fight with forces considered chaotic and outside the hedge of the order generated by the Æsir, we find a worldview not much different from the transition of gods in antiquity in which the Olympian gods overthrew the Titanic gods ruled by Saturn.[117] If so, this means the reference to light held by the Æsir might be a memory of the light that ruled in the Golden Age of Saturn, before law and limits came to the earth. Hence, the Jotun race is similar to titans and the Jotun ancestry of Odin is equivalent to the legacy of Saturn. In this, when Tacitus described Odin as Mercurial, Odin would, for sure, take on this function and virtue as the Æsir of communication, eloquence and wisdom, just as much as with his ambiguity and position on the crossroad of night and day.

Vále is the son of Odin and the Jotun Rindr. Vále means a clearing, in the sense of cleaning and preparing a land prior to establishing the farmstead. Rindr means a mountain ridge. Vále, just twenty-four hours old, avenges the murder of Balder by killing Hod.

---

117 See Herodotus and his work *Histories*.

He is described as a master archer and is amongst the few Æsir that will survive Ragnarök together with his brother Vidar. His colors are white and blue.

Vidar is the son Odin and another Jotun woman, Grid, a name of uncertain etymology, who is described very much like a volva with her staff and magical instruments, and as an ally of Thor. Vidar is the strongest of all the Æsir and is also called "the silent one". Vidar is the one who, in Ragnarök, avenges his father by killing Fenrir, tearing off his jaws. His colors are red and blue.

Ullr is today a marginal Æsir, but his cult used to be very widespread and his reputation was probably as great as Skade. He was an Æsir who ruled skiing and hunting and was said to be a master archer. One of Odin's heiti, Ullin, suggests a strong relationship between Ullr and Odin. Saxo imparts that Ullr had, for a time, replaced Odin as Allfather, which would not only speak of the deep relationship between the two, but also of Ullr's significance. The shield was referred to as the Ship of Ullr which indicates that he was important for protection in combat. He was said to have mastered the art of seidr, being as proficient as Odin. It has been suggested that Ullr represented the promise of returning fertility in the guise of snow and winter, which would indicate, together with his craftiness in seidr, that he was originally a Vanir. Ullr means "something shining" which is perhaps a reference to the shine the snow gives off when hit by the Sun. His color is white.

Njord is a Vanir that lives in a place called Noatun, which means "harbor". His domain is the winds blowing over the sea. Njord is the father of Frey and Freya, with his not-named sister, yet much indicates that she is Nerthus, another name of Jord. Njord also married Skade as a consequence of the Æsir murdering her father Tjatse. But it was an unhappy union, as Skade didn't like to live at the ocean shore, and Njord didn't adapt to life in Trymheimen, the noisy trollish mountains where she was living. For a period, they lived nine nights in Trymheimen and nine nights at the ocean until the union dissolved due to a lack of true connection, denoting a qualitative difference between the mysteries of the sea and those of the mountains. His colors are white and dark blue.

Frey lives in Alfheim and is the King of Elves. Frey can mean both "lord" and "youthful one", and is etymologically connected to "seed"; words like *fridr*/peace and *frjandi*/friend were etymologically developed from his name. He is married to the Jotun woman Gerd, who is the daughter of Gyme, a relative of Skade's father, Tjatse, and Aurboda. Gyme means "wave" and Aurboda means "ominous", while Gerd means "an enclosure" in the sense of the farmstead, which

A Genealogy of Trolls

is represented in the rune Odel/Othal, the rune of one's inheritance in terms of the farmstead enclosed by the marking-stones. Frey is also tied to the rune Ing, seen as both a seed, as coitus and as virility. Snorre says that Frey is the best of all Æsir because he not only provides peace and heritage for people, but he is also the owner of rain and the rays of the Sun and, hence, secures the fertility of crops – an embodiment of the great provider of food. He is also the only Æsir in which Loke in the *Loketretta* apparently didn't have much negative to say about. Also, as we see in the *Ynglinga saga*, this royal line prided themselves over being the descendants of Frey. His cult was widespread all over Scandinavia since the 8th century, if not earlier, as we see both in place names and popular names, like Fröydis and Ingvar, which manifest a connection with Frey. In the temple at Uppsala, the carved image of Frey was an Æsir with a large phallus, and this form was replicated in metal figures, always ithyphallic and seated in a position of calm dominance. After the truce made in the war between the Vanir and the Æsir, Odin elevated Njord, Frey and Freya to "be gods" with him, a clear reference to how the Æsir-concept was one of class and not heritage as such – yet again we do see that Jord is moving around in the distance, just as in the name Njord, which can also mean, "from Jord". His colors are white and red.

Freya lives in a place called Folkvang, a place said to have a myriad of seats. The need for many seats is due to her being as much a war deity as she is a love deity due to half of the *einherjar*, those fallen in battle, belonging to her. Freya was also known by many names, like Mardöll, "the one who shines brightly", Gjevn, "the giving one", Syr, "the sow", and Vanadis, "protector of the Vanir". Her cart is pulled by cats. She can also ride her pig, Hildsvini, "bold swine", and fly out in the shape of a falcon. Wild cats in Norway are constantly linked to elves and, in some places, are considered the ward vaettir of a place showing themselves. Cats also bring a reference to the dress of the volva and the art of seidr. The association with the sow is not only a reference to her lustful sensuality, but it would also connect her to the huldre-people that are frequently said in Norse folk traditions as riding pigs in heat. She is nurturing, intimate, and has close relations with dwarves, making her a true Lady of the vaettir of nature. She is married to Odr, a name that means "frenzy" or "ecstasy" in both an erotic and "shamanic" sense. They had the daughters Hnoss and Gjersemi, both names meaning "precious", which hold references to night and day as Hnoss is said to be dark while her sister is light. Odr is often associated with Odin, but when we look at Odr's ancestry and descendants, we see yet again how Jord enters the equation. In the case of Freya, Jord becomes an important force through a pact in matrimony through Jord's mother, Nátt, the Night. Odr is the son of Nátt and the Jotun Naglfare, "he who sails the ship of dead men's nails". Nátt also begot a child with another Jotun, Ánarr, "ancestor", and this daughter was called Fjörgyn or Jord.

In the *Loketretta*, Loke called Freya lewd, saying that both Æsir and elves are amongst her lovers, and also emphasized how she is not only a wise woman, cunning in seidr, but also that she gives false and deceiving advice to the people she is helping. Freya is the one who taught seidr to Odin. In spite of her associations with night, crying golden tears in Odr's absence and ruling over half of those slain in battle, it is Freya as the personification of the erotic and lustful, Freya as the sow, that seems to have attached itself to her in greater degree. Her colors are red and gold.

Idunn is a Vanir, descendant of the lunar *àsyngja* Nep and Nanna, Balder's wife, yet she is counted amongst the Æsir and married to Odin's son Brage, who is the ruler of troubadours and poets. She is important for the Æsir as she has access to the golden apples of youth that the Æsir eat to stay young. In the Edda, we find a story that tells of how the Jotun Tjatse, instigated by Loke as always, abducts her and the golden apples and, as a consequence, the Æsir start to grow old fast. Loke borrows Freya's falcon-*ham* and manages to bring Idunn back to Àsgard. Loke in the *Loketretta* states that she is as voluptuous as Freya, which might be revealed in her name which means "to love again", and she is also associated with the waves of the ocean, hence, she might have been seen as someone ruling deeper loving emotions, not only the erotic which leads to pregnancy as in the case of Freya and Frigg. She, being married to the Æsir of poets, might reveal that her domain is more in the realm of courteous love and if the apples are borrowed from Christian mythology, Snorre might have wanted to emphasize her role as a temptress, or he could have had in mind the mythological garden of the Hesperidia, where Venusian evening nymphs are in possession of magical apples. Her colors are gold and red.

Loke is as intrinsic to the Northern Tradition as Odin, and is the Jotun-Æsir surrounded with the most ambiguity of them all, having as many diabolic references to his person and activities as Odin himself, as if he were the red fire to Odin's dark blue ice. Loke has been associated with fire and his name is derived from the Old Norse *loge* or *lue*. In truth, his name is a kenning of Loptr, which would mean the aerial one, so his association with fire would be more related to the bellows and to the air necessary to

A Genealogy of Trolls

make a fire burn. Loke is also genealogically important, being an ancestor of Thor and Jord as shown in the lineages of Loke below.[118]

THE FAMILY TREE OF LOKE, HEL AND THOR

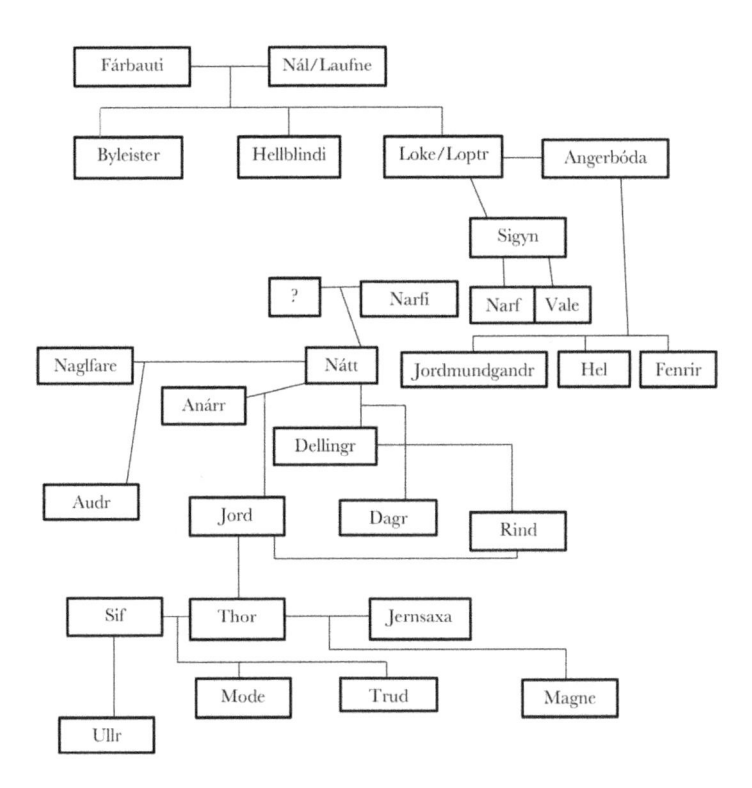

```
Fárbauti ─── Nál/Laufne
    │
    ├── Byleister
    ├── Hellblindi
    └── Loke/Loptr ─── Angerbóda
              │
              Sigyn
         ?    │    Narf  Vale
         │  Narfi
    Naglfare ── Nátt    Jordmundgandr  Hel  Fenrir
         │   Anárr
         │        Dellingr
    Audr   Jord    Dagr   Rind
         │
    Sif── Thor ── Jernsaxa
         │
       Mode   Trud   Magne
       Ullr
```

It is in his family tree we might get an idea of the complexity of Loke, both in terms of his origin, and what he became an ancestor for in his own right. In this, it is Jord who is particularly interesting, being in the same family as Loke together with principles like night, daybreak, ancestry and abundance, whilst Loke himself is the product of sharp objects, danger and violence.

Loke's ambiguity reveals itself in how he constantly brings great treasures to the Æsir, while at the same time he also orchestrates predicaments and difficult situations for them, and finally his

---

118 This flowchart expanded on what is found at https://bladehoner. wordpress.com/2017/11/29/hels-and-thors-family-relations.

children will, together with Nidhöggr, end the world of the Æsir, yet, he is there as one of the Æsir, Odin's blood-brother. The information we have about Loke is likewise quite sparse, and there is no mention of him being a subject for a cult or having places that were named after him.[119]

In Denmark, folk tradition refers to the flickering in the air during hot summer nights as signified by Loke, tending to his goats, just as the vaettir that was living in the hearth-fire was called Loke, and finally the folkloric mercurial figure in Scandinavian fairy tales, the Ash-Lad, overlaps greatly with Loke, the Jotun.[120] Heide suggests that the mythological Loke originated as a vaettir and was transformed into his mythological Jotun-form over time, a theory that would be in harmony with the original Old Nordic faith. He argues this while pointing out what Odin says about Loke in the *Lokasenna*, stanza 23: "eight winters below the ground, being a woman, milking cows [or being a milk cow and a woman], giving birth to children." This might be a reference to his primordial state as a vaettir of the hearth fire, as this vaettir was considered to bring abundance to the farm. This would also explain the disputed association between Loke and fire. In truth, Loke, as with so much Old Norse etymology, opens a host of possible associations, although Loke is most likely etymologically related to words that signify "to close" something.

Loke, or Lopt, is a Jotun; given Odin's root in the dark blue ice, it would make sense that Loke represents the red-hot fire giants that will contribute to the end of the world in Ragnarök, given how his children will be instrumental at the twilight of the Æsir. Loke is both fair and well-spoken and is the son of the Jotun couple Fárbaute, "he who hits hard", and Nál, "needle". His brothers are Byleiste, associated with strong winds and lightning, and Helsblinde, "he who is blinded by Hel", which is a heiti or kenning for Odin.

In one story, when he shape-shifted to a horse, he got pregnant with Sleipnir, an eight-legged horse he then gave to Odin. Like Odin, he had children with several women, the most important of them being the monstrous offspring he begot with the Jotun Angrboda, "she who brings distress", often suggested to be the same as or intimately related to Heid given that they both live in the Ironforest. These children were the wolf Fenrir, the dragon-serpent Jormundgandr and Hel, the hidden one who was given the responsibility of one of the halls in the afterlife. With his wife, Sigyn, "victorious one", he had the sons Narve and Vále. After Balder's murder, the Æsir went after Loke to punish him for instigating the deadly situation.

---

119 Bæksted, 2002: 88.
120 Heide, 2011.

He tried to escape by turning himself into a salmon, but Thor managed to get ahold of him and brought him to a cave. Here they also brought his children. They turned Vále into a wolf that tore Narve into pieces and used the entrails of Narve to chain Loke up inside the cave. At this point, Skade, the disir of Scandinavia, brings a venomous serpent and hangs it up over his face so the venom will drip over him. Sigyn is given permission to bring a vessel to capture the venom, but every time she empties the vessel the venom hits him with great pain, and Loke's agony creates earthquakes. Here he stays chained until Ragnarök. This Edda account is interesting in many regards. The more Æsir-like offspring of Loke are killed or transformed into monsters and the disir Skade herself entered the punitive situation, which would indicate that he managed to upset the vaettir of Scandinavia in its totality from having Balder killed. Finally, the wolf-motif is impossible to escape, seeing that Vále is turned into a wolf and that he also fathered a wolf, Fenrir. It was suggested in Chapter Two that Ginnungagap was envisioned as a wolf's jaw holding emptiness, and seeing that the world will end by the jaws of a wolf, Loke's importance for the world is revealed in its beginning and its end, a world brought into being in the spirit of a wolf that will also end by its bite. The wolf-theme will also add another layer to Odin's kinship with wolves as Loke is an integral necessity for the Allfather.

Ragnarök – The Twilight of the Æsir-Reign

With Balder's death and Loke's exile and captivity, the earthquakes caused by Loke's distress announce the beginning of the end. It is Jord herself that shakes as darkness spreads over the Æsir reign. A few will survive, but at large the Æsir and the Jotun will see their end at Ragnarök. Connected to Balder's death, the Æsir suffer much misfortune. Thor loses his hammer, Frey loses his sword, Sif, Thor's wife, loses her golden hair. Finbul-winter arrives, a winter that goes on for three years with no summer, freezing the earth to ice until fire and forest fires enter the scene and the Sun is eaten by a wolf. Steinsland suggests that the cataclysmic events and natural disasters are mirrors of the collapse of social order.[121] This is an interesting observation, especially if we see this in a relation to the *Loketretta* when Loke is listing all the shortcomings, vices and cruelty of the Æsir. If so, it is possible to see the *Loketretta* as Loke's last attempt of setting the Æsir

---

121 Steinsland, 2005: 122.

straight, calling attention to how they have entered corruption in the same way as the built-in entropy of the world cycle also reveals degradation and corruption, the world mirroring the social order and vice-versa as it moves towards its unavoidable destruction. Knowing that they are doomed, the Æsir go out to the battle as Heimdal sounds his horn and Loke sides with the destructive forces led by his children, Jormundgandr, Fenrir and Hel. Nidhöggr rises from the rotting roots of Yggdrasil on which he has been gnawing and chewing, testifying to the loss of cosmic center where chaos is the only option should renewal be possible. The *Voluspá* describes the shifting events surrounding Ragnarök as follows in stanzas 59-66:

59.
Sér hon upp koma
öðru sinni
jörð ór ægi
iðjagræna;
falla forsar,
flýgr örn yfir,
sá er á fjalli
fiska veiðir.

59.
Now do I see
the earth emerging
from the waters
ever-green;
waterfalls flowing
the Eagle flying over,
the one who catches
fish in the mountains.

60.
Finnask æsir
á Iðavelli
ok um moldþinur
máttkan dæma
ok minnask þar
á megindóma
ok á Fimbultýs
fornar rúnir.

60.
Æsir are coming together
at Idavollen
speaking of the mighty
serpent in Midgard
and the memory comes
of powerful tales
and Fimbul-Tyr's
distant runes.

61.
Þar munu eftir
undrsamligar
gullnar töflur
í grasi finnask,
þærs í árdaga
áttar höfðu.

61.
There shall yet again
the wonderful
golden board-game
be found in the grass,
the one they owned
in the olden days.

62.
Munu ósánir

62.
There fields with no seeds

akrar vaxa,
böls mun alls batna,
Baldr mun koma;
búa þeir Höðr ok Baldr
Hrofts sigtoftir,
vé valtíva.
Vituð ér enn – eða hvat?

shall flourish with grain,
all evil shall be mended,
Balder will come;
Hod and Balder shall dwell there
on the battlefield of Hropt,
the field of the elevated ones.
Do you know enough, or do you want more?

63.
Þá kná Hænir
hlautvið kjósa
ok burir byggja
bræðra tveggja
vindheim víðan.
Vituð ér enn – eða hvat?

63.
Will then Hönir
choose the Tree of Fate
and sons of them both
brothers shall dwell
in the wide home of the Wind.
Do you know enough, or do you want more?

64.
Sal sér hon standa
sólu fegra,
gulli þakðan
á Gimléi;
þar skulu dyggvar
dróttir byggja
ok um aldrdaga
yndis njóta.

64.
A hall she sees
more fair than the Sun itself,
covered in gold
on Gimle it stands;
there will families
free from deceit build
and live happy
all their days.

65.
Þá kemr inn ríki
at regindómi
öflugr ofan,
sá er öllu ræðr.

65.
Then will the ruler
come to his kingdom
powerful from above,
he who rules over all things.

66.
Þar kemr inn dimmi
dreki fljúgandi,
naðr fránn, neðan
frá Niðafjöllum;
berr sér í fjöðrum,
flýgr völl yfir,
Niðhöggr nái.
Nú mun hon sökkvask.

66.
And there comes the brooding
dragon flying,
shining, from below
Nitafjöll;
with corpses in the feathers,
flying over hills and mounds,
Nidhöggr.
Now she shall sink.

The *Vaftrudnesmál*, like the *Voluspá*, also speaks of how a new world is rising from the old, a world that emerges green from the waters and unfolds on its own. There is no mention of any Æsir or deities involved in the world that appears; it is like Jord herself is in charge and allows all things to move into place according to the natural law where a new Golden Age reveals itself, a world free from trolls and the Jotun-race, in so far as it is continued through the sons of Odin which carry on the seed of perpetual entropy as the great-grandchildren of trolls, ice and wolves.

Chapter Six

The Northern Observance

Since these creatures (dwarves, elves and the dead) also lived in the natural wild, it was easy for churchmen toiling for the greater glory of God to incorporate them with spirits, if only by virtue of the Augustinian principle according to which pagans worshiped demons. – C. Lecouteux[122]

When we speak of Nordic rituals and magic, we largely lean on the written accounts given to us by Olaus Magnus, Adam of Bremen, and Snorre Sturlasson along with archaeological discoveries in order to understand the public Æsir cult. This focus on the Æsir cult has come to overshadow the reality of the Elder faith, because when we add folklore, folk magic and what is handed down in oral traditions, we find that diversity was more the rule than uniformity. Also, leaning on the accounts of the mentioned historians, we are, in the case of Adam of Bremen and Olaus Magnus, speaking of an experience and understanding of the Northern Tradition limited both in time and location, and of course, naturally biased by the pre-judgments they held. Snorre stands as the most reliable of the oldest sources, but here we also have the problem introduced by poetry and the troubadour-tradition, which often gave versions of repeating themes that showed great variations in how given mysteries and lore could be perceived. As mentioned earlier, we also need to be observant of the fact that the public Æsir cult represented just one of many variants of faith in Scandinavia, in which a large part was practiced as a private cult, and which also involved diverse perceptions of the Æsir.

In order to understand the complexity of the Elder faith and its rituals and practices, it would be helpful to point out that Old Norse really didn't have any word that corresponded to the Latin idea of "religion". The word coming closest to religion is the Old Norse *siðr* or *sidr*, meaning custom, observance, habit, practice, the manner of how things are done. We find a difference between new sidr and old sidr in relation to Christianity introducing new customs,

---

122   2015: 61.

but curiously enough, we don't find sidr particularly rooted in *trú,* or belief, but more in how things are done.[123] It is also essential to keep in mind that prior to Snorre composing the Edda and the *Heimskringla,* the accounts of Nordic customs and beliefs that were preserved over time were written down solely by travelers, merchants and adventurers of non-Scandinavian descent and origin.

We should also take note of how the farmstead or homestead was, in its own right, a sanctuary, and any palace or temple was originally understood to be erected on the same principles as a household. Hence, the owner of a farm held a similar cosmic situation in relation to the world and his domain as would a chieftain or a king. The farmstead was replicating Àsgard in the way that all farms had a ward-tree close to the main house and often a well. The patriarch would then enter into the position of the "ruler" of his world in the same way that the Æsir were the rulers of their domains. Such perception invited in a proximity to all kinds of spiritual beings from this position of rulership in one's own realm.

Collective, public cults grew out from a commonality between the practices in given farmsteads that, over time, were taken as guidance for how the public cult should be done as each cult expanded from the intimate and private to encompassing and embracing larger and larger geographical locations, thus becoming more collective and representative for the public cult. This expanse from the private and personal to the collective, social and cosmic also invited in a flexibility, dynamism and richness of belief born from the customs and their execution in various places and situations. This would, in turn, invite in the possibility for a rich cosmogram where the public cult and the land itself would mirror one another both in similarities as well as differences. It appears, from place names, that the custom was to dedicate a given place to an Æsir that would then be the main protector of that place, often focused on appeasing natural forces like rain, wind, temperature and sunlight. If there were several farms in the same region, a yearly collective blót would be done to the ruling Æsir to maintain this protective influence, whilst the more regular observance would be the responsibility of the private vaettir-cult.

What we have then is that a given homestead could, in terms of a private cult, solely deal with the vaettir and ward-spirits of the farm, while the chieftain of the village would carry the responsibility of ensuring regular public offerings to some Æsir that were found to secure stability and ward off bad Fate. However, we know that it was not only the Æsir that received attention and offerings; of equal importance were *jotneblót, diseblót, alveblót* and a host of other customs

---

123 Steinsland, 2005: 268.

that consisted of offering and appealing to potentially disruptive forces and the many vaettir that inhabited nature. Since the private cult was restricted to what went on within the boundaries of the farmstead, it is natural to assume that the ways of dealing with the vaettir in one location would differ from how things were done in other places, mediated by the needs and the inclinations and nature of the vaettir of those different regions and places.

Seen within a continental perspective, Norse religious practices at the end of the first millennium CE mimic many of the key aspects of Iron Age rituals across Northern Europe, a regional variant of the pan-European paganism that was found in Britain, Germania and Italy, and was partly constructed from the ideological clash of Christianity with various deity cults consolidated in opposition to the Christian cult. As DuBois[124] states as his premise concerning pre-Christian Nordic cults, they were "…decentralized communities of belief, framing local relations with specific deities." Therefore, local variations were the norm, and what we find both universally consistent and of great importance were the seasons of the year, midwinter, midsummer, and the eclipses. Related to this are the archaeological findings from Fiskerton, Lincolnshire, presented by Mike Parker Pearson,[125] that consist of Viking tools and jewelry as well as Roman weapons and crafts all together in the same grave sites along with a great number of oak trees that, according to dating, were cut at times of eclipses. Findings like this show that eclipses, and by extension starlore, were important, yet the problem is the meager evidence we have access to which would help explain the role and importance of stellar phenomena. Yet, following the idea of Nordberg[126] and using Wittgenstein's concept of "family resemblance", we might understand a concept in one culture by looking at another, even if the concepts perceived as being related cannot be seen to have a mutual reference in the material culture *per se*. This idea of family resemblance, of how a mystery in one location and culture can be understood to reflect similitude with spiritual phenomena in other locations and cultures is better exemplified in the work of Claude Lecouteux. Claude Lecouteux[127] manages to present a rich tapestry of the Northern Tradition by analyzing family resemblances found in Germanic districts and Roman paganism, in which observations of how *lares familiars*, which are protector spirits of a household, would

---

124 1999: 60.
125 In *Old Norse Religion in Perspective*, 2006: 86.
126 In *More than Mythology*, 2012: 119 – 151.
127 2013 and 2015.

be similar to Nordic spirits of domestic importance. Lecouteux describes the Gardvord, various vaettir, elves and the spirits of the dead as "small domestic spirits...that roam through the houses at night."[128] Likewise, Johan Weier, also quoted by Lecouteux, writes that many lares and larva were called "little earthmen", which, yet again, holds a family resemblance with the vaettir of the farm. The similarities between the cult of lares, the cult of the ancestors, and the cult of the house in Scandinavia present significant family resemblances as will be demonstrated after having a look at the more public or collective rituals, which were known as blót.

Blót appears to have been a generic word loosely meaning "sacrifice" or "offering" in the sense of fortifying or bringing strength to something, and also "to spray" in the sense of using blood to anoint something, thereby giving it power by attracting the attention of gods and spirits to whom it was anointed. This means that you could in the vernacular speak of *blóta til Odin* in terms of giving a private sacrifice to a deity important for you personally or for the farmstead by offering the blood of an animal or pouring ale on the image or on the ground or on a stone in honor of the force placated. Blót was done at public places in given districts and sanctuaries were prepared and erected, called *hov*, and often the *ting* or court as well as the dwelling of the chieftain or king was in the proximity of the sanctuary. Any vandalism or desecration done to the sanctuary was punishable with confiscation of land and home and exile of the offender.

The public blót was ruled by the lunar cycles and the summer blót was celebrated around the 14th of April and was offered to the Allfather, Odin. So, we see from the date that some notion of Aries entering the sign of the Sun marked an important transition, both cosmic and material, and the exact time of celebrations were apparently adjusted to the moon phases. These spring/summer blóts were about embracing the summer and providing luck for kings and chieftains, victory in war and good wind for the ships.

In October there was the blót to Frey to mark the end of work and the arrival of winter. Slaughter was done and food was gathered in the food repository for the winter to come. Finally midwinter, known as *jól*, was also dedicated to Frey. At midwinter it was pigs that were given as offering, Frey's sacred animal. The exact time was again adjusted by the moon and was set somewhere between the end of December and the middle of January. The making of ale was central to *jól* – the Law of Gulating that was in effect until 1274 actually demanded that every farmstead should make ale for

---

128 Lecouteux, 2013: 120.

Christmas and have it blessed in the name of the Holy Virgin and Jesus Christ. Failure to brew beer for Christmas resulted in penalties paid to the bishop.

It would also appear from *Hymiskvida* that jól held a significant relationship to Amma, meaning "grandmother", being the mother of Jord. Amma is said to be a terrible and fearful creature, having nine hundred heads. Yet it is from her that Jord takes the horn of plenty and offers it to her son Thor. If so, the significance of jól would ultimately be about a time when abundance returns to mankind from the darkest nights, as Abundance, or Audr, is a child of Nátt or Night.

Also of importance was the disablót performed at least in Uppsala at the beginning of February and was dedicated to Vanadis, another name for Freya, and also to the "spirit of Scandinavia", Skade, who was also called Öndurdis, "dis who owns the Skis". Disir appear as an arcane class of spirits that, in temperament, are related to Valkyries, Norns and fylgja, but in effect they are female land spirits of a protective nature tied to childbirth and fertility, represented by rocks and stones. It is tempting to suggest that this shows a relationship between Freya, Skade and Heid relative to the protective quality of the disir, and is also why the disablót was given to the coldest month of the year. Perhaps, in terms of belief, February was ruled by cold forces like Skade and Heid, but Freya, with the fiery and fertile abundance of pleasure and the erotic, would, at all times, conquer the harshness of winter, especially considering how Freya's twin-brother, Frey, is ritually tied to the most important of the public blót where one secured good winds, good sun and great fertility for crops and beasts.

If we look at all these celebrations, be they private or public, they always held a communal focus and were, at large, a communion, not only with the people attending, but also with the spirits or gods fed as the focus for the celebration. Hence, the heathen practice of blót was similar to the Eucharist and the *houzle*, also known as the Red Meal, where bread and drink were offered to the dead and to the vaettir of Germanic practitioners of the Elder faith. If we cease associating breaking bread and sharing wine as predominantly Christian, and rather focus on the Roman roots found in the breaking of bread, offering food, drink, blood and wine to the lares (household spirits) as well as to the dead, it is a Roman practice that shows itself more than a Christian one. The technique we can call "communion" defines the generation of sacred space by summoning denizens from the other side, be they ancestors, sprites or gods, to dine with us and together partake in a Greater Banquette that literally makes the visible and invisible side of creation merge in a moment outside of time and space.

Meat and mead/ale were the two most important components of the blót; mead and ale, originally known as *alu*, was also a *rún*, or a secret magic word, which was just as important as blood and meat. In the *Hávamál*, stanza 137, Odin says the following about ale:

> When you drink the ale
> Seek the power of the Earth
> Because the Earth (Jord) will receive the ale

It should also be mentioned that ale and mead were drunk at special occasions, related to celebrations, and were considered to possess magic qualities, hence, the etymological relationship between *alu* and ale, and how, in the *Sigerdrifamál*, we find *ölruner* or ale-runes to possess great powers. It appears that the ale-runes and the magical properties of the ale were not much different from the *samudra manthan* spoken of in the Vishnu Purana, better known as the churning of the ocean of milk that produced *amrita*, the drink of immortality. This relationship was meaningfully explored by Dumezil and Rydberg in a comparative relationship, given the association of amrita and soma as intoxicating and provoking an altered state. Speaking of brewing, henbane and toadstool were frequently added to the brew for the sake of taste, as henbane in particular gives a pungent and rather regal bitterness to the ale in addition to its psychoactive effects. Toadstool (*Amanita muscaria*) was also added to the brew, at least in the case of making the berserker ale, and knowing that *bulmeurt* (mandragora) was held in awe, it might also have been an ingredient in a brew made for special occasions. Mead was less frequently made due to cost, given the amount of honey and fruits that were commonly used to make this special brew. Looking at the Edda, we see that when we find significant mentions of ale, Thor is not far away, such as when he decided to steal the brewing barrel of the Jotun, Hyme, or when he destroys the house of some kind farmers that gave him a bed for the night because they didn't have enough beer to quench his thirst. This might suggest that there is a connection between ale, alu and Thor in terms of some form of magic found in the alu/ale and expressed in the form of Thor. In the *Ynglinga saga*, 5th chapter, we find Thor described as a *godi* or priest of Odin, a chieftain of repute that made his *hov*/reign at Trudvang in Sweden. Given the amount of mjölnirs found in archaeological excavations in this region, we can yet again conclude that the hammer of Thor was used as a symbol of protection for the Elder faith, and in meeting with Christianity, became a counter-symbol to the Christian cross – a symbol of the old custom. Mjölnir is, according to Heide,[129] seen as an instrument for gandr, given how this magical object used the wind to fly out and attack, just like every other gandr. Hilda Davidson sees in Mjölnir a similarity in meaning as symbolizing Sun and lightning. This might lead to the suggestion of alu as a magic that was composed of drink, wind, Sun and lightning or to restate: some form of intoxication was used to enter an altered state or possession where the practitioners became firm and central, like the Sun, and could shoot out gandr, similar to lightning, on the path of the winds, and were, in this way, acting out the magic of Thor.

Positions in the official cult were communal as several people were in charge of given parts of the blót. The chieftain was responsible for getting the blót done, but he was apparently not a priest in the sense we would understand the role today. Some important roles were that of the Thul who was the troubadour, the one who ensured the memory of the particular observance and that this memory was passed on in a timely and timeless fashion with song, poetry and storytelling. The *Hávamál*, stanza 111, says that the Thul is placed at Urdabrunnir, the Well of Urd. Another position is *godir*, which is more known from Iceland; this appears to have been a position both political and responsible for preserving a place-bound ritual observance embracing a larger district, and would perhaps be similar to a fusion of a vicar and a mayor. Worthy of mention is also that this function was held as much by men as women, then called *gydja*.

Blót was done at what was called *horg* or *hov*, with *hov* referring to a noble court and *horg* meaning a pile of stones and rocks. Steinsland[130] highlights through various sagas that representations of the Æsir carved from wood were quite common, as were stones, both rustic and more refined, used to depict divinities and their attributes. The phallus of Frey was ever popular, and was represented in every erect tree and phallic shape found in nature, hence the tendency of carving symbols and divinities into the wood in a similar fashion as the totem poles known from North America.

In addition to the larger blót, we also find accounts of blót made for the elves which was quite different. It was administered by the Thora, the Lady of the House, and was usually done in autumn and was a private event. It was solely the family of the given farmstead that partook in the celebration that apparently included not only elves, but also the ancestors. In spite of not knowing much about the way Alveblót was done, it most likely consisted of the repeating

---

129   2006.
130   2005: 292.

themes of communion through food, blood and ale. In Kormak's saga we see that "reddening the mound" with the blood of a bull that is sacred to elves will bring instant healing and cure to a man that is seriously injured. Another private blót, one less restricted than the Alveblót, is described in the saga of Olav the Holy. It was called *völseblót* and involved the visit of a volva to the farmstead to present predictions and prophecy for the household. Again, it is the Lady of the House who is in charge of the blót; central to the ritual is what is called *völsi*, a mummified horse-penis – most likely representing Frey – that at the break of night was passed around to the people who were in the house with a given charm: *Þiggi mörnir þetta blæti*, meaning "May Mörnir receive this offering". Steinsland comments that *mörnir* is a kenning both for *völsi* as much as for a Jotun woman and suggests that Mörnir might be a kenning for the collective female powers of the Jotun. In relationship to the importance of trolls in Scandinavian culture, this would make a lot of sense, given this form of blót's intimate restriction to the homestead, while being an obligation for whatever guest might be there with or without intent. In order to fortify this suggestion, it would be good to point out that the phallic Frey married Gerd, daughter of the Jotun couple Aurboda and Gyme. Gerd was said to live far north, but whenever she lifted her arms, she lit up everything around her. Her connection with this peculiar shine ascribed to all Æsir might be why Snorre Sturlasson says in the *Skaldarskapermál* that Gerd is an àsynje, a female Æsir. Gerd and Frey had the son Fjolne together who was one of the legendary kings of Uppsala that were the decedents of Frey.

Another observance of very private character was the *vaettirblót*, or the way of dealing with vaettir, which might be said to be the practice or observance more common than any other. Vaettir can be said to be a word defining any chthonic spirit tied to a plant, tree, spring, well, house, angels of a house, and hinges of doors, crossroads and whatnot. Any place, location or geometric combination considered to possess power would also be considered to have a vaettir attached to it. This because we know that vaettir would secure movement and fertility of land, and if the vaettir of a particular place was driven away, then misfortune, illness and barrenness would usually be the consequence, as we know from the story of Egil Skallagrímsson who erected a *nidstang* when he was exiled from Iceland in order to drive the vaettir away from the land of the king of the Norsemen. Vaettir is, as we saw in Chapter Four, a large class of spirits that can be said to include *tomter* (pixies), *nisser* (brownies), *rådare* (rulers), elves, dwarves, and huldre-people.

In the previous chapter, Adam of Bremen's account of the sanctuary in Gamla Uppsala in Sweden was discussed. Given how it highlights what Adam considered heathen customs, in his description of public blót we find a curious place mentioned, also found in Sweden, known as the Trollchurch which invites an observance of a more secretive and private character. More specifically the Trollchurch is located at a place called Tiveden, now a national park. The Trollchurch was in use at least as early as 1604, and in the latter part of the 19th century. The legends around the Trollchurch say it was dangerous for Christians to go there because their presence would wake up the wrath of the trolls that inhabited the place. Also, local myth says that the place was worked by a secret brotherhood, and those stumbling upon their nocturnal rituals would either have to suffer death by being buried alive or accept being sworn into the brotherhood. The Trollchurch is, basically, a rock formation at the end of a long and narrow track through the woods. We find the ritual practice that took place there described in a poem collected by the folklorist Carshult. The poem is as follows:[131]

Kärken smyger på slingrande stig	The procession creeps on a meandering path
helst osedd till Trollebergen.	preferably unseen to the Troll mountains/hills.
Mässa skall hållas i dagarna tre,	A Mass shall be held for three days,
det varde början på helgen.	this will be the beginning of the weekend.
Kolten är sid, så den nåder vid marken,	The frock is long, so it reaches down to the ground,
håsorna äro i topparna vassa,	the socks are sharply pointed,
hättan dras ned, så hålen för ögonen passa.	the hood is pulled down so that the holes for the eyes fit.
Alla är lika förutom på längda,	Everybody looks alike except for the height,
prelatus han räknar på mängda.	the prelate counts their number.

---

[131] The poem with translation is found also in Wikipedia; changes have been made to the translation presented here.

Lösen den gives i lågmälder ton,	The password is given in a low voice,
prelatus han bjuder tre stötar i horn.	the prelate blows three times in a horn.
Elden den köllas av nio slags ved,	The fire is kindled with nine kinds of wood,
det är gammal sed.	that is old custom.
Offer till andarna skänkes,	A sacrifice is offered to the spirits,
med blodet sig allom bestänkes.	everyone is sprinkled with the blood.
Det bästa till andar föräras,	The best part is gifted to spirits,
det som blir över skall av männerna täras.	what remains is consumed by the men.
Uti midnattens timma	In the midnight hour
då sjärnor beglimma,	when stars glitter,
prelatus han tystnaden bjuder	the prelate asks for silence
och männerna alla det lyder.	and this is obeyed by all the men.
De falla till markone ner,	They fall down onto the ground,
prelatus han bistert mot rymderna ser.	the prelate looks grimly at the heavens.
Och svärjan och formlar i dälderna skallar	And incantations and summons echo in the dells
prelatus han kallar på andar.	the prelate is summoning spirits.
Allom de fick på sitt spörje ett svar,	Everyone received an answer to their question,
ingen av androm fick då höra varom det var.	no one heard from another man what the answer was.

From what the poem says we can get an idea of the central elements of what we might call *trollblót*, although Tiveden might mean the woods of Tyr, and hence, be dedicated to this arcane Æsir. We see that the ritual was three days duration and the walk out was most likely done on a Thursday night to embrace three days and nights of gathering. The members were all dressed like hangmen which might be a reference to Odin as the Æsir of the hanged ones, and hence make a parallel with Adam of Bremen's description of the ritual activities at Uppsala and the importance of Odin there. Nine different kinds of wood were gathered to make the fire, blood sacrifice was made and those gathered were asperged with the blood. Sacrifice of food was made to the spirits and communion in the form of food and drink was taken. At some point the stars take precedence and this is followed by enchantments and silence leading to acts of prophecy, fortune-telling and divination.

It is interesting to note that there is no mention here about any Æsir or Vanir, rather the term *anda*, or spirit, is used, which ties this ritual to the practice of seidr, where again the Æsir were not central, but the vaettir and trolls inhabiting nature as sources of specific powers are.

The anthropologist Emil Birkeli made in-depth studies about the belief in spirits, such as vaettir and trolls, and saw a deep connection with the importance of ancestor veneration and the cult of the homestead. In looking more closely at the veneration of the dead, it is also possible to understand this rich chthonic network and the cosmography of the underworld, realizing its intense importance for the Northern Tradition.

The cult of the ancestors was located at a mound on the farm, the burial ground of the first man to clean the field and prepare the farmstead. This mound would also come to attract all sorts of vaettir and become a hidden society in its own right. This custom lived on when graveyards were made and there was a demand for burying people there instead of the farm; the first one buried in a graveyard was taking on the role of the ruler. In effect, being buried in a mound would give access to, and in time, make one a part of the vaettir that were also living inside the mounds, especially elves. It was customary to make holes from the outside of the mound so gifts and offerings could be placed inside. The burial mound was treated as a sanctuary, and trees, grass and plants growing on it were left to grow; the vegetation that was naturally drawn to the mound would be empowered by the vaettir of the mound, and were therefore also considered extensions of the vaettir and under their protection and influence. The one resting in the mound was called *haugbu*, which means "he who lives in the mound", but mounds themselves were also called *tusse*-mound or troll-mound. In this it is possible to see that, at least in some places and epochs, the dead were thought to join forces with trolls upon death. The dead one that was living in the mound was treated as a part of the family. The family would go there with offerings of ale and food, seek advice, and inform the dead one about what was going on at the farmstead. In cases of distress and quarrels on the farm, it was not uncommon that the dead one in the mound showed itself as an apparition, in visions or in dreams, to sort out the situation that was bothering the family. There are also instances where the haugbu was said to have actually risen from the grave to execute punishment upon the family. The dead ones were perceived as living a life pretty much like the one they lived when they were alive, but on the other side they had access to greater wisdom and could better guide the living. Birkeli establishes in his research, in which he collected 68 tales speaking of the haugbu, that the haugbu was defined as troll in 12 of them; as draugr in the sense of a ghost in 14 tales; *tuss*, a variant of troll, 15 times; and as a part of the huldre-people in 4 of them. It is difficult to say with certainty if this would indicate a rather casual use of terms referring to vaettir as a group or if this was representative of the belief people held in relation to the transformation of the dead one that was to live in the mound. If so, it appears that transformation into a troll was a more widespread belief.

From 1267, the first prohibitions related to the Elder Faith consisted of the ban of waking up troll, draugr and haugbu, which in practice meant that there were penalties for those who were making offerings to the mound and those who practiced *utesitta*, sitting-out on the mound to connect with their ancestors. We also see here the first demonization of the old customs in denoting ancestors as troll and *draug* in a patronizing context.

It also appears that Thor and Odin were in a special relationship with the burial mound. From their exchange in the *Hárbardsljód*, life in the mound appears similar to the descriptions of the world of huldre-people, and it might be that in the earliest ideas of the afterlife the departed one was considered "hollowed out" and entered communion with the denizens of earth and roots. In stanzas 43-45 of the *Hàrbardsljód* we can read the following:

43. Þórr kvað: Hvar namtu þessi in hnœfiligu orð, er ek heyrða aldregi in hnœfiligri?	43. Thor sang: where did you learn such hurtful words, I never heard words mroe hurtful?
44. Hárbarðr kvað: Nam ek at mönnum þeim inum aldrœnum, er búa í heimishauga.	44. Hárbard sang: I was taught them amongst the old men that live in the mound at home.

45. Þórr kvað:
Þó gefr þú gott nafn dysjum,
er þú kallar þær heimishauga.

45. Thor sang:
Good name you give them
When you call them the
mound at home.

All the beings that lived underground were called *jardbu*, a term covering huldre, draugr, tusser and the haugbu. All of them lived in Heimrinn nedri, meaning the "home below", probably indicating the intimacy between the home above and the home below. There is, however, one big difference between the people of the mound on the farmstead and other vaettir. Vaettir which one sacrificed to outside the domain of the farm were usually sought out at dangerous or haunted places in nature and they were never offered food. The most common offerings were from nature, like leaves and stones and herbs that were gathered together where the vaettir was living, and at most, ale and milk were offered over these natural items. Another sacrifice was cloth. Tying cloth to the tree where particular vaettir were living as a sacrifice for the purpose of appeasing them, or to seek their counsel or protection, was also a common act that also served as a token of asking for permission to gather stones and plants in his field. A gathering of materia magica in such places would always consist of making an offering of what one collected as a way of giving back what one took which would also demonstrate cunning and intent in the gathering.

Revenants and ghosts were also dwellers in the mound, as well as denizens living on the other side and under the earth and therefore all matters concerning death and funerals were done with the utmost care. Funeral rites were subject to meticulous preparation and careful observation of omens. In Scandinavia, the art of taking omens from nature was subject to a very rich lore; in particular, when we speak of birth, matrimony and death, the omens were many. Death could be announced in many ways, but the most common sign was the presence of the tawny owl (*kattugle*) and her proximity to your house. If she entered your bedroom when sleeping, that was a definitive sign of death arriving. Similar attributes were held by the raven, crow, rooster, cuckoo and woodpecker. If the woodpecker knocked on your window and stayed there like he was looking after you, that was not a good omen, just as with crow and magpie. If the cuckoo was heard singing in the north, that was considered an announcement of someone dying, and the rooster singing in the middle of night brought a certain discomfort as it was outside the normal. Omens, like a cat curling herself into a ball in the crossroad, or a dog starting to howl towards some specific corner for no good reason, were also upsetting, especially if the dog was howling towards the north. Also, if the church bell rang in the night for no reason, an occurrence called *feigdarbell*, it meant someone in the parish would die that night. Also, we find the appearance of a blue light, referred to as needle light and known as *náljos*, or dragonfire, which also announced death. This light was most likely St. Elmo's Fire, which was believed to be departed ones returning in the shape of "lantern men" who came to bring relatives with them, and in particular, infants.

These omens announcing death were, for many, considered crucial for the preparation of death, because ensuring the transition to the other side was as smooth as possible was desired. This led to customs like holding a candle or a torch to light your way to the other side as you were dying, because unwelcome vaettir could interfere with the transition and sometimes take the place of the soul, and at other times steal the soul away. This phenomenon was often related to the presence of feathers of chickens and roosters.[132] If unusual things happened with the one dying and one suspected that the smooth transition was thwarted, a popular technique was to "beat the devil out" by beating the Bible all over the body of the dying one to make it uncomfortable for the curious presence to inhabit the corpse at the moment of the soul's transition. It was important to leave the doors and windows open so the soul could leave, and, at the moment of death, all the clocks in the house should be stopped.

After death it was important to throw the bedclothes and the thatch mattress (*likhalm*) on the fire, most likely to sever the connection with hair, saliva, blood and suchlike that, strictly speaking, still had an attachment to the departed one and could be used to manipulate them. To burn the thatch and bedclothes would help the departed one unchain from the earth and become aerial and free. You would also do this to prevent the departed one from becoming a revenant.

The body was washed and dressed, the nails cut and the mustache of men was always shaven off. This custom is old; in the Edda we find the story of the ship of death, Naglfare (traveler of nails/ ship of nails), that is made from the fingernails of the dead and which will be instrumental in Ragnarök at the end of the world as we know it. Making sure to cut the nails would therefore delay the construction of this ship. In the coffin the dead one was always given several things, items connected to their trade, jewelry, money, Bibles, a cross and almost always silver. The colors of death were always white, black and silver, save for the copper-coins resting on the eyelids as payment to enter Hel. The wake was very essential, because as long as the departed one was still above ground, nasty presences,

---

132 Hodne, 2011: 84.

spirits and beings were a constant threat. The wake was a social and religious gathering; prayers were present the entire time, but also play, song, dance and drink was a part of the wake. On the last night, they gathered either in the homestead of the departed one or at the graveyard with the farewell ale or tomb-ale. On the day of the burial the coffin was placed in the living room (for farmers the coffin was usually placed in the barn for the wake) and carried to the graveyard. The corpse was carried with the feet first out of the door and it was important to carry the coffin three times around the table prior to taking it out, making sure that chairs and furniture were kicked over in the process. In some instances, when a death had been particular ominous, some would cut a hole in the back of the house for the coffin to be brought through, after which this hole was immediately closed up. If the transition of the departed one had been troublesome, it was usual that a different route than the natural one was chosen, or that one avoided straight lines, to literally shake off hostile and unwanted presences. The coffin was then presented to the graveyard, speeches were given, and the last goodbye said. If the farewell-ale hadn't already been done, prior to placing the coffin in the earth, the tomb-ale was presented on the coffin lid and drinks were offered both to the departed ones, vaettir, subterrestrial spirits and all those present as they sent the dead one away with the last drink.

The graveyard itself had areas that were better than others. The south part was always considered the best place and north the worst, which was made even worse due to criminals and suicides being buried in the northern part of the graveyard. The head of the dead one should face towards the east so they could follow the natural course of the Sun from sunrise to sunset. This perhaps holds a deeper meaning of placing the departed one in such way so that they could witness the natural order amongst the living, and from this, realize his or her own place in this new cosmology of which they were a part. The burial done, people were quick to leave the graveyard and continued the celebration for the departed one with ale and food. Seven days later, there was a new round with ale and food, and it was at this juncture that inheritance was sorted out, for it was seven days after the burial that one could be sure the departed one had passed on as intended and hadn't turned into a draugr or a revenant.

We find several proverbs or axioms concerning death, dying and the afterlife. One of them is that "suicide insulted Fate",[133] a belief that must be old as we see in the Edda a tendency to accept whatever Fate is given to man. In truth, if we look at the *Hávamál*, it appears that Fate was often understood as bad, and as something

---

133 Lorie, 1993: 246.

you had to overcome by doing whatever was necessary, and in this way turn a *de facto* bad Fate into a good one. Suicide would, by this perspective, insult the Norns, the triple spirits of Fate that were in charge of birth and death, and ultimately the one choosing this way to the afterlife would be marked by weakness and cowardice, which were seen as vices in the old observation.

Concerning revenants and ghosts, the belief was that they, at times, chose to stay earthbound due to love and commitment, besides having unfinished business they needed someone to resolve for them. It also appears that the dead ones always had an ear to the other side of the ground and were listening in to what the living were saying about them, hence the prohibition of "never speak bad about the dead lest they come back to torment you". This belief is connected to the old practice of burying the dead ones at the homestead, sometimes under the kitchen, other times at the south of the main house, always so close to the world of the living that they could partake in the life of the farm, watchful from the other side. Hence the dead were never really dead, but kept on being aware while on the other side, a place conceived of as being underground and inside mounds. The dead could, therefore, be used in a variety of ways as the four modalities below demonstrate:[134]

> In order to conjure a dead person from his grave you will take some earth from the grave and place it in a piece of cloth and attach to it a long thread. You will then dig down in the earth until you find the chest of the dead man and here you will make a hole and tie a knot to the chest of the corpse. Hauling up the knot very slowly will make the corpse rise. Do it several times, rising and lowering the corpse repeatedly. This strategy is used if one wants to awaken a dead ancestor, no matter how long he or she has been in the grave. You will then take some chalk and write the baptismal and common name of the person over the doors of the house. You will then put a penknife over the name and together with this the following formula written in chalk:
>
> Comotote Prili Sali.
>
> Within two hours the dead one will come and enter one of the doors. No one should speak to the dead one, but let

---

[134] These formulas are found in their entirety in T. Johnson, (2013), *The Graveyard Wanderers*, S.E.E: UK.

the dead speak. When you want the dead to go back you go outside and erase the formulae and remove the knife. Go inside again and throw seeds (probably linen seeds or *papaver*/opium seeds) and quicksilver over the dead one and he will leave.

Another experiment is about asking the dead ones for assistance in which you will go to a grave and pull up a plant with its root. As you do this you will say:

When I take you, you who lie in this grave do not deny me this root
That I take for abundant blessings; rather give me your power and blessings
Rest soundly in your grave, I wish you no ill
Work peacefully in God's name

Bring the root home with you and guard it inside the house.

Another experiment is one where one borrows human bones; this was a widespread practice as human bones could be used for several purposes, ranging from healing and cursing to effectuating charms and spells. This one is about how to harvest a human bone to generate a spirit of protection for the house. You will go to the graveyard and dig up a bone and as you take it you will ask to borrow it for however long you decide. As you take the bone you must say the following:

I exorcise you, you spirit of the bone
By the Virgin Mary's birth and the paths of all the Apostles
And I wake you up to become a guardian of everything I own
So no thief, whoever it might be
Will be able to steal any of my food
But instead will be standing still in one place
Until I order my guardian to release him

As long as you have the bone locked down safely in a box, the spirit of the bone will be watching and guarding your house.

Finally, there were also instances where the dead ones were used to murder someone; one of the formulas is like the above one. You will go to the cemetery and borrow a bone. As you take the bone you must say: "Oh you, my brother or sister in the Christian faith, lend me this bone." You will then state your intent and for how long you intend to keep the bone until you return it. This bone will then be placed under the pillow of the one you want to sleep forever, and as you place the bone, there you will say: "You (name of the person) will sleep and you will never wake up." When the deed is accomplished the bone must be taken back to the grave.

In the past, the dead ones were, with great frequency, seen by the living. Seeing apparitions or revenants was always considered a bad omen. There were several understandings concerning why this would happen, the predominant ones being that the departed one was restless, still had things to do, or messages and demands yet to tell the family. In other instances, they are people who were wicked and difficult in life that returned from the grave because they wanted to continue to torment people. In the *Laxdaela saga*, we find one instance of someone wicked in life who continued to be wicked in death, such as in the case of Hrapp, described as "difficult and wicked". Hrapp wanted to be buried standing under the door to the hearth fire so he could keep watch over everything that went on in his house. The revenant of Hrapp, however, started murdering both the people in the house as well as the neighbors, and it ended with the people simply abandoning the farm. Abandoning the farmstead was a last resort. Before doing something that drastic, there were other things that could have been done to make the revenant find peace. Amongst the arsenal at one's disposal, it was possible to salt the grave, burn the corpse, or drive a stake through its heart to nail it to the ground, hindering it from getting up. You could also decapitate the dead one and then place the head at the feet or use a cloth to blindfold the head. It was also possible to burn the corpse and spread the ashes on the ocean or in a place far away, just as it was also possible to relocate the corpse and bury it somewhere far away from the farm.

Concern for the dead ones is also found in *Egil's saga* where we see that the night before he died he was *hamram*,[135] and very difficult to deal with, and where he had been quarreling with his son. He died sitting in bed, and as he died, his son came from behind to close his eyes to avoid being "seen by a dead man", something believed to bring great misfortune. Then they made a hole in the wall and carried the body out from the house through the hole and buried him far away from the farmstead to avoid the revenant finding its way back. There is no account of Egil returning to his family after his death, so apparently the method was successful. Similar concerns were observed in Scandinavia until the early 20th century where the corpses of difficult people were not carried out through the door,

---

135 We might translate *hamram* into being "in a bad shape", or "not being quite yourself".

but through a window or a hole in the wall. Likewise, to carry the corpse along a "crooked walk" was also advised in some cases in order to hinder the revenant from finding its way back to the house.

Finally, the many accounts of the Mass of the dead would illustrate how thin the veil was between the world of the living and the dead, as in one account by Gregory of Tours:

> In the city of Autun there is a church dedicated to St. Stephen, and a graveyard in which it was reputed that voices were frequently heard singing psalms at night. And so it happened that once two clerics decided that they would in the stillness of night visit these sacred places as preparation for the morning Mass. When they got close to the church of St. Stephen they all of a sudden heard curious songs and harmonies. Filled with joy to hear the music they entered the church and found a corner where they immersed themselves in prayers for a good while. When they stood up they saw that the church was full of strangers singing. What stood out as most curious was that there was no light of any kind shining, yet it was all bright. Then they noticed that the light came from the people themselves. Filled with bewilderment they stood there until one of the strangers came over to them and said: "You are making great wrong in disturbing our secret prayers, leave now, or die". One of them didn't need to be told a second time and ran away, but the other stood fast in anger and stayed until the Mass was done. He died a short time after.[136]

Two other rites of passage were subject to a similar care and observance as were death and funerals, those being pregnancy and birth, and matrimony.

Birth and pregnancy were always surrounded with ambiguity as while it was joyous to see one's family being continued, it was also dangerous and much could go wrong during the period of gestation and with the birth itself. It is not without reason that deities and spirits associated with midwifery and birth were often lunar with a darkside, like Hekate and the Egyptian frog goddess, Heqt. In folklore everywhere in the world we find several references to vampyric entities attracted to conception and childbirth; amongst the more famous is Lilith. Naturally, as in the case of funerals, pregnancy and birth omens were taken seriously and there were many rules to

---

[136] This account is from Gregory of Tours (538 – 594), found in Hodne, 2011: 96.

secure the arrival of the new person into the world and the family. Both Frigg and Freya were considered to preside over conception and birth; Frigg was said to possess an herb she gave at birth to ease pain. This herb, or "grass" as it is called in the Edda, was either opium or one of the *soleanums*, most likely Belladonna, which has a longer history in Scandinavia than *Papaver somniferum*.

Amongst the central and important elements following birth was the acceptance of the child into the family. The newborn was placed on the lap of the patriarch of the family who sat at the high seat of the table. Here the child was cleaned and after the 1st century, water was poured over the child as they were named in mimic of baptism. Naming the child was a serious act, as the omens around the birth, the temperament of the child and the atmosphere of the homestead in the moment of birth would have an affect on the child's name. The name could be related to an ancestor, to an animal, or related to a vaettir, elf or Æsir in such way that the name would demonstrate a continuation of a strong relationship with the other side in one or several forms. In this, we can find names like Thoralf, which is a name pointing towards both a connection with Thor and the elves or Thor and Frey – a name that evokes double royalty and would remind the child of its aspirations and connections. In the same way being named after dead ancestors would enliven the memory of the departed one in a new form in the child. Naming was closely related to the influence of the Norns, as the name would reveal a part of the child's destiny and prowess in the world.

When pregnant there were some activities that were better avoided, such as walking through the woods at night, lying down directly on the earth or staying home alone after dark. The pregnant mother was frequently a target for elves and the hollow people after dark. It was equally important to avoid looking at ugly and displeasing things and it was also vital to avoid negative sentiments and fear, as all the mother's impressions potentially affected the gestating child. Likewise, it was good to avoid ominous animals like snakes, bears, wolves, crows and owls, as encounters with any of these animals would transmit certain traits to the child.[137] This could result in the child becoming extremely furry under the effect of a bear, or in being born with problems with the eyes should the mother suffer encounters with snakes in the wood.

Easing pain through delivery was not only subject to herbal decoctions, but one also resorted to magical intervention. In the *Sigerdrifamál*, Brynhild speaks to Sigurd about certain runes that should be marked in the palm of the hand that, along with prayers

---

137 Hodne. 2011: 137, 138

to the disir, would lead to a healing grip which would reduce pain. Moving through time to around 1700 we find that Frigg has been substituted with the Virgin Mary in prayers to ease delivery-pain, yet the old custom of "reading runes into ale" is maintained as the operative factor in making the prayer effective. One of these prayers says that you should read the prayer into ale, water from a stream or saltwater and then give it to the women in labor to drink. The prayer is as follows:[138]

> When Jesus the Christ came to the world the midwives eased
> the pain of the virgin Mary, the Holy one, with these words:
> Torment and pain be still
> Don't hurt you more than me
> You shall give birth
> To the savior of the world
> It is with this gospel I greet you
> The pain of all women in labor
> Shall reach the heart of Jesus and the Virgin Mary
> Jesus with his kind Mother
> Tell your Mother present
> To loosen this woman
> From the contractions and pains of this birth
> In the name of Jesus
> In the name of Our Father x 3

The bear was thought to be an animal very interested in unborn children, and so it was possible to use the paw of a bear rubbed over the belly to ease labor-pains. It was also possible to use Thor's thunderstone, i.e. a stone axe, that was passed over the belly. Also, something called a "vaettir-kidney", a magical item found at the ocean shore which was the seeds of the Sea-bean (*Entada gigalobium*), could be passed over the belly or turned into a decoction and drunk.

The birth itself was full of omens. To be born with a caul was seen as a sign of luck, a sign that hamingja was still attached to the newborn. These children were often considered to possess special skills, like clairvoyance or some magical capacity. Often they were also thought to be immune to danger, such as animal attacks, bullets and knife wounds. The caul could be kept as a lucky charm or it could be offered to the fire spirit guarding the house. Likewise, children born on Thursday nights were considered "lucky", albeit this would also denote a child with a strong connection to "the other side". Birthmarks also spoke of the life to come, as a birthmark close

---

138 Hodne. 2011: 137, 138

to the heart or visible in the upper part of the head was commonly regarded as announcing early death for the infant. To be born at the time of an important blót or on a special day, like Christmas Eve or Sunday morning, was considered a good omen. It was also possible to infuse the infant with certain characteristics by, for instance, placing weapons in the cradle to allow the infant to grow courage, strength and hunting skills. Until the 17th century, the custom of planting a patron tree for the newborn was widespread. The tree would be either of the same type as the ward-tree of the farm or, if omens during pregnancy indicated otherwise, a tree proper to guard the child was planted. The tree would then not only give the child access to the vaettir and other invisible forces, but would also be used both to diagnose illness and effectuate cures should that be necessary. The tree was considered an extension and a guardian of the child, for what happened to the tree also happened to the child and vice versa.

Matrimony was of great significance – it was not only about love and the couple that married, it was something of great social consequence, as it would unite families and rearrange parts of the social structure. And so, matrimony was not only about a pact and an oath, but it also touched upon possessions and heritage. Steinsland[139] comments that matrimony was not a matter without complication, as it would, in many instances, concern the future of the farmstead. Hence, matrimony's entire process was a collective process involving both heart and reason. Prior to matrimony, the groom and his family would make a formal visit to the family of the bride to discuss the terms of the marriage regarding possessions, inheritance and also to agree on the *heimanfylgja*, or cost for purchasing the bride, as well as what gifts would be given to her. With the agreement done, a feast was made to set the date for the matrimony. The marriage feast was celebrated for at least three days; anything less would be seen as petty and shameful, as the abundance of the marriage feast would be reflected in the couple's abundance and happiness. Hence, it was important that the celebration was joyous and that there was an absence of quarrels and trickery of any wicked kind.

Up to the 16th century, remnants of the old customs could be found. The àsynje Vár, Spring, one of Frigg's handmaidens, was the one who accepted the oath itself from the couple, whilst Frigg and Freya were called upon to guard the couple. Sometimes, Mjölnir was placed in the lap of the bride, which not only speaks of the importance of Thor himself, but also how he was tied to loyalty, strength and the capacity to produce heirs. It might also indicate that Frigg was considered the patron of the bride and Thor of the

---

[139] 2005.

groom as the Lady and Lord of the Farmstead, emphasized in the true name of the Lady of the House as Thora.

We find much magic tied to finding a proper partner and to discovering who one should marry. A popular method was to look into a well on St. John's Eve after an entire day of fasting to see the reflection of one's future husband or wife. Another common form of divination was to walk backwards around one of the houses on the farmstead three times. One would then meet one's future spouse either as a reflection from the future, or the man in question would be drawn to the house as one made the turns. Doing this could also lead to omens of death; meeting a person carrying a shuffle would announce the presence of death. Likewise, on Christmas Eve or another important day, two lights could be lit on a shelf and you would then sit down on a chair with your back to the lights while holding a mirror. You would then ask the mirror to show you the one you would marry. You could also use prayers, commonly prayers involving the three magi who came bearing gifts at the birth of Jesus. Yet another custom was to make the thread of Fate, as in a formula from 1887 where spinning threads into a ball on the last three Friday nights before Christmas would lead to one's future husband arriving at the farmstead at the Christmastide and being drawn to the thread in such way that he would take hold of it. Dream divination was also popular; you would then consume given foods, like porridge, milk, cheese or anchovies prior to going to bed, and then as you fell asleep you would in dream see your husband-to-be.

Easter is a Christian observance, but it is interesting to view Easter as an example of how the heathen ideas and beliefs lived on in this observance, making Easter a beautiful heresy. Easter is the most significant period in the Christian mythology in which the Eucharist is renewed and continues to function. It is when Jesus died and made salvation possible, and in this interim of Jesus' absence, we find its heathen reflection in how this was a tide when celestial and magical powers were up for grabs. From the little we know about the beliefs the new Christian Scandinavians held about Easter, we find King Olav at around 1040 forbidding human burials during Easter. This would, in the imagination of the people, tie Easter dramatically to the realm of the dead. We can only speculate how the heathen people, in a culture where dealing with the dead was an almost casual, yet sacred, activity, interpreted a prohibition like this. That this was a tide of prominence for the dead would be implied as there were given restrictions upon their realm due to the presence of a different and mysterious death-cycle. In all cultures where Roman Catholicism colored folk-customs, we find that the Easter tide was the time when the Devil and his legions were allowed to roam around in Jesus' absence. In Iberian and Balkan folk traditions, we find lore saying that the Devil took the celestial power possessed by Jesus and ruled the Earth for the three days of Jesus' absence. That a similar idea existed in Scandinavia is not only suggested from the host of penance one is advised to perform during Easter and the placing of various forms of warding objects at threshold and gates, but also in the arrival of the Easter witch in the 17th century. Here we find the belief that from Maundy Thursday to daybreak on Saturday witches were gathering in their mountains, celebrating communion with the Devil. Brooms were often laid across the threshold in case a witch would come to the farm. She would then take the broom and leave the people and animals alone. With Sunday's sunrise, this tide, signified by torment and danger, was over as the Sun signaled the resurrection of Christ for the Christians and the end of the Sabbath for those of more heathen inclinations. Easter, being a tide adjusted according to the Moon, would also make sense for those following the Elder faith, and remind them of *jól* and how the interplay between Sun and Moon marked significant times during the celebrations and blót during the year. Also, Easter fell on dates already tied to the annual blót to Odin in the middle of April, so there was already an anchor in the old customs, giving rise to Easter as a time where the Wild Hunt was active in the form of *myrkaridur*, the dark ride. Likewise, St. John's Eve was easy to fit into a culture that already venerated the summer solstice as an important yearly event where the fires where lit, wishes made and magic gathered in the form of prayers, visions and plants, as everything was thought to possess maximum magical potency on this night. What stands out, looking at these sacred periods during the year, is that these were times when divinations were done, magic spells worked and omens taken. It was viewed as a magical crossroads where some spiritual afflatus was pouring out into the world and these virtues could be harvested or worked with to a greater effect than usual.

The Northern Observance was ruled by the Sun and the Moon in a play of absence and presence. The celestial drama between the two luminaries affected the Earth, and stations throughout the year were thought to possess an overflow of virtues that could be used for whatever ends. This could range from mundane matters, like sealing a deal, proposals, and rituals of the home, to magical acts and larger offerings and rituals. Weddings, for example, were often done in May, the month of Vár, the *àsyngja* that guarded the marriage oath, or at midsummer where the healing forces of Sun and fire would nurture the union and invite in a positive virtue to work in the marriage.

Chapter Seven

The Stars and Wells of Yggdrasil

Askr Yggdrasils
drýgir erfiði
meira enn menn viti:
hiörtr bitr ofan,
en á hlið fúnar,
skerðer Níðhöggr neðan.

The ash Yggdrasil
suffers deeply and darkly
more than men can know:
deer bites at it above,
in its side it is rotting,
with gnawing Nidhögg beneath.
— *Grimnismál* 35

In Snorre's *Landnámabók* we can read how Aevarr walks up to a mountain until he finds a place he names Mobergsbrekkur. Here he places a stick into the ground and states that this is where his son will build his farmstead. Lecouteux[140] recapitulates the central elements of how to lay claim of the land, noting how fire is carried around the borders of the land which announces the act of taking possession to the vaettir and nocturnal spirits dwelling there. This act would be like walking the land with the Sun in your hands, marking the land by virtue of Thor. The circumference of the land could also be marked by shooting flaming arrows into the corners, and placing marking-stones wherever the arrows fell. Taking possession of a piece of land would usually take two or three days, as it was vital to appease the vaettir of the land and to place the land under the protection of an Æsir, or, with the advent of Christianity, a saint. The central staff and the border markers were considered sacred, as vaettir would attach themselves to both the center pole and to the border markers. In doing this, the one taking possession of the land would re-enact how Odin made Àsgard, a sanctuary in the world of darkness, where the border markers would signify where Midgard met Utgard. The pole would be replaced with a ward-tree and the house would be built close by, mirroring the sacred landscape of Àsgard.

Yggdrasil was placed at the center of the world, the crown reaching upwards and the roots downwards in such way that Yggdrasil became the axis mundi, the meeting place of all realms in the world created by Odin, with the farmstead at the center of the world. By understanding the qualities of Yggdrasil, we can also better

---

140 2015.

understand the unspoken and natural worldview of the Scandinavians, and we can better understand the gloom and entropy permeating everything. Yggdrasil is rotting and it is fed upon. Yggdrasil literally means "the horse of Ygg", which is not only a metaphor for all the activity happening in the tree, but is also a reference to the gallows, as Ygg is a kenning of Odin, meaning "the terrible and ugly one". Yggdrasil is also known as Mimamidr, Mimir's tree and Læradr, which can mean both protector as well as destroyer.

Læradr is the name given to the tree that grows on the roof of Valhalla, where the goat Heidrun produces the mead for Valhalla and the stag Eikthyrnir feeds on its leaves. From the dew on Eikthyrnir's horns is shaped drops that fall to the well Hvergelmir, the source of all rivers. We know that the fixed stars in Gemini had some meaning for Snorre, and it might be that Eikthyrnir, the red deer, corresponds to the fixed star Aldebaran. Aldebaran, having as its herb the milky thistle, is said to bring riches and honor as the eye of the red bull. This would give to the goat Heidrun Capella, the goat star, which is also reputed to bestow honor and riches, with wormwood being one of its plants. This would together give a reference to the sap and dew of Yggdrasil and the bitter essence of the tree itself – yet honor is what the tree bestowed on deities and men. Another suggestion is that Heidrun and Eikthyrnir was the twin stars Castor and Pollux, the eyes of Skade's father that Odin threw up in the heavens, and since Snorre never tells us which of those options is correct, it is left to careful discernment to decide which suggestion makes more sense. Andrén[141] also comments on another variant of the world tree found in the *Volsunga*, saga 2, namely the big oak called *barnstokker* or "trunks of children". Odin had buried a sword in this tree, a sword only Sigurd Volsung would be able to pull out. This would naturally remind us of the Arthurian sword in the stone, as the tree itself would carry the memory of how the first humans, Ask and Embla, were made from logs of wood.

The roots of Yggdrasil are connected to Jotunheimen and Hel and take their nutrition from three wells. The well connected to Jotunheimen is Mimir's well, the root connected to Àsgard is Urd's well; both are relegated to the Norns and are also the place where the Æsir meet and pass judgment and counsel. The well connected to Hel is Hvergelmir, the source of all rivers which is constantly fed by the dew from Eikthyrnir. Coiling around the wells and roots we find the dragon Nidhöggr chewing on Yggdrasil's roots.

In the crown of Yggdrasil, we find four stags or deer, eating its leaves, all of them children of Eikthyrnir, the red deer that is found on

---

141 2014:32.

the roof of Valhalla. At the top of the tree we find the eagle Raesvelg, eater of corpses, who is responsible for natural catastrophes. On the beak of Raesvelg, we find the hawk Vedrfölnir who is "made pale by wind and weather". We should also mention that at the foot of Yggdrasil is found six large snakes and many lesser ones, all of them dwelling in Hvergelmir. The mercurial squirrel Ratatosk runs up and down the tree exchanging insults from the dragon to the eagle and vice versa. Already in this imagery we see how the end of all things is encoded in the world. Through restless communication, from top to bottom, the world of Yggdrasil is gradually collapsing, all made pale by wind and weather until the earth swallows everything in the turbulent waters generated by Raesvelg's winds.

Yggdrasil as the world tree, the axis mundi, will also describe a specific condition for the world and the powers necessary for its manifestation, continuation, destruction, and rebirth. Also, the axis mundi is always a symbol for the spiritual North, the Hyperborean land that represents the spiritual center, and hence, the Saturnine navel of the Golden Age, the true Sol Invictus, which by traditional analogy is the Hyperborean Apollo. In Scandinavia this was represented by the white nights of the summer solstice in Cancer and the solar star Sirius.[142] This invites an Apollonian or solar symbolism[143] in the choice of Yggdrasil being made of an ash, which Ficino says is Apollonian and emphasizes its ability to expel poisons.[144] This is interesting given how Nidhöggr is in *Grimnismál* associated with malice and poison, hence the ash would be the ideal ward-tree of the world to deal with expelling the poison embedded in creation.

Yggdrasil is the center that ties the underworld and the celestial world into a common dimension – a meeting ground where "gods walk amongst men" in an entropic cycle that will lead to destruction and resurrection, because everything that lives must also die. This "cycle of woe" is also found in the role of the three Norns that spin, make, and cut the thread of Fate for every living being; it is the arrival of these three Norns at Àsgard that announces the beginning of the end of Odin and his reign. This process is mirrored in the spiritual and material North where the spiritual ideal, upon manifestation, instigates a cycle of gradual decay which ensures that the world slowly twists itself away from its axis and succumbs to fire and water, to be regenerated in a different form. Realizing the Apollonian

---

142 Sirius culminates at 14° Cancer.
143 For more extensive discourse on this see Andrén 2014 and Guénon 2001.
144 Ficino, 1989, *On Life* 3, 13-14.

theme in the Nordic worldview, we can see an Orphic theme playing itself out in the mystery of Yggdrasil and Odin's role in creation and the importance of the Fates.

When Odin hung himself in Yggdrasil for nine days and nine nights,[145] Apollonian Odin becomes a lunar mystery. Prior to his hanging, he gave up one of his eyes to Mimir, which might indicate that he sacrificed his Apollonian consciousness so he could drink from the well of night and wisdom. This would indicate that his journey towards the wisdom hidden in the lunar North is what crowned him with ravens, wolves and serpents: all animals of Saturn, the Lord of the Golden Age. This would speak of how he triumphantly gained kingship of the Hyperborean North through his self-sacrifice on Yggdrasil in an attempt to turn the current and restore stability to the cosmic center. This was to no avail – not even the Hyperborean Lord could avoid the dictate of Fate. Knowledge was not sufficient to reverse the turning of the axis of the world.

The hanging upside down on Yggdrasil might be a mirror of how Shemyaza, the leader of the *Grigori*, the watcher angels, fell as punishment for bringing knowledge to humans. Shemyaza was hung upside down in the constellation of Orion, a constellation important for the mystery of Odin as the constellation was often known as simply Odin and not Orion from the 14th century.[146] Odin, in attempting this reversal, did as Guénon explains in *Man and his Becoming*, where he observes that the upside-down position of the tree is, according to Vedanta: "an analogy, here as everywhere else that must be applied in an inverse sense. Like the Hanged Man card in the Tarot, what is true for the inner spiritual reality is inverse to the external material one. The roots are above because they stand for "the Principle" and the branches spread out below to represent the deploying of manifestation."[147]

This means that Yggdrasil was an axis mundi composed of Mimir's influences, the Fates and Nidhöggr represented by the three wells. Mimir was considered to possess the wisdom of origin; even when Mimir was decapitated during the war with the Vanir, Odin kept Mimir's head as oracle. Mimir means "memory", but in the sense of remembering the past and bringing it into the present. It is "wisdom remembered" and not just any kind of wisdom, but fundamental wisdom concerning origin and beginnings. The decapitation of Mimir might be seen as the particular moment in the

---

145 3 x 3, which would be a symbol of the work of Fate in the three dimensions or levels of existence.
146 Mitchell, 2011.
147 Guénon, 1925/2001.

world where the axis loses its consciousness and becomes dislocated from its origin, starting its process of twisting away from its center which leads to the inedible collapse of the world.

The Norns

Of the Nordic Fates, called Norns, three are named. They are said to be Jotun women who do not necessarily come from the sea as many other Fates are said to do. These three, according to the *Gylfaginning*, come from a subterrestrial hall at the side of Urdabrunnir. These three are Urd, Verdande and Skuld. Urdabrunnir is the sacred well that links the Norns with the dragon Nidhöggr. This connection is not spoken of, but placement in such proximity would indicate the dragon as the source for the powers of the Norns. The central item used by the Norns are the distaff or spindle, mirroring the wheel of life, the thread passing through the distaff being life itself. What Fate dictated was unavoidable, and it was always associated with necessity and the end of a life span. If we bring our attention to the Orphic Ananke, mother of the Greek Moirai which correspond to the Norns, we might find an interesting reference. Ananke is associated with necessity, lots and parts and is depicted holding a spindle. Additionally, she is one of the *protogenos*, the deities that emerged uncreated from the cosmic matter, much like the offspring of Ymir emerged while he was sleeping. Ananke was naturally bound with another serpentine protogenis, Khronos or Time. Together they crushed the cosmic egg and the world and cosmos as we know it began, hence, necessity and time makes up our allotted part, or Fate. This would suggest that Nidhöggr is not only representative of the clarity of vision the Norns possess, but also embodies the concept of Time. The two luminaries of heaven, Sun and Moon, represent the contrast of the turning of the world and mark significant tides on earth. In summer, the Sun is celebrated because she is in her fullness and during winter she is reminded to return. The solar motif is contrasted with a lunar motif, tied in with ice, giants and the three wells on which the axis mundi feeds. This polarity is represented by the two solstices symbolized by the dragon Nidhöggr and the eagle Raesvelg, who both speak of the common titanic foundation of the world created by the Æsir, where Night will eventually consume the Sun and everything on earth.

In the *Vaftrudnesmál* and the *Voluspá* the three chief Norns are of Jotun heritage, as we see in the *Voluspá* where the arrival of three giantesses from Jotunheimen in Àsgard announces the beginning of the end. They are given names and attributes: Urd is assigned the position of handing out the "law" in the sense of what would rule a given destiny; Verdande gives life to everything; and Skuld is given the rulership of Fate itself. Several researchers have suggested that the three Norns also mirror vital components of the Nordic soul-complex, namely fylgja, hamingja and the vord, which will be discussed at the end of this chapter.

The names of the Norns are all tied in with Fate in an ominous way, as Urd shares etymological roots with the English "wyrd", Verdande is not only linked to the vord, but also *what is*, while Skuld represents necessity and also debt, most likely in the sense that death is the debt generated by life. An interesting observation in this regard is that Norn is frequently used in reference to a witch in Iceland.

In stanza 49 of the *Vaftrudnesmál*, the three Norns are acknowledged as Jotun but they are also called hamingjer in the sense of being the disir of fortune, and here it is Frigg that possesses this knowledge. If we add to this what we find in the *Fáfnismál*, where Sigurd speaks with the dying Fafnir in the shape of a dragon, Fafnir expands on the Norns as being more than three and describes them as a class of deities that are not necessarily from *jotnírs:*

Sigurðr kvað:	Sigurd sang:
Segðu mér, Fáfnir,	Tell me Fafnir
alls þik fróðan kveða	given the esteem you are given
ok vel margt vita,	that wise you are,
hverjar ro þær norns,	where are the Norns,
er nauðgönglar ro	that help in Need
ok kjósa mæðr frá mögum.	and come to women when they give birth.
Fáfnir kvað:	Fafnir sang:
Sundrbornar mjök	From heritages many
segi ek norns vera,	I believe the Norns are,
eigu-t þær ætt saman;	nor are they from the same family;
sumar eru áskunngar,	some are from Æsir,
sumar alfkunngar,	some are from elves,
sumar dætr Dvalins.	some are the daughters of Dvalin.

This would suggest that the three named Norns might be the original forces which, in turn, gave this power to Æsir, dwarves and elves who were taught the arts of giving, measuring and ending

Fate. Dvalin is given here as one originator of Norns, and this might be due to him being the one who taught Odin how to carve runes. Hence, the runes themselves must be a secret that is ultimately guarded by the Norns, which explains why it is only through nine nights of symbolic death and inversion that Odin is given insight into this secret.

The fact that they are referred to as disir would give them a liaison with ghosts, but also tutelary spirits which would serve as protectors for clans and families. Disablót was commonly celebrated in winter, never earlier than the beginning of autumn, which suggests a connection with the darkest night at winter solstice. This, in turn suggests that disir were intimately connected with the cult of the house and the homestead, and were particularly tended to at winter solstice to fortify the protective spirits of the land and house.

The fact that they are also understood as disir and hamingjer would suggest a connection with Freya, while their entire symbolism related to the distaff and the thread would suggest Frigg as being at the heart of their mystery. They are associated both with luck or hamingja, but also with Fate as something depressing and unavoidable. Lastly, it is reasonable to suggest that Nidhöggr is also involved in this mystery. He lies there at the root of everything and gnaws on the roots that stretch to all three wells, amongst them Urd's well and Mimir's well, spreading his poison through the tree – the same rotting tree into which the Norn's carve man's destiny. In this regard it is a tempting reminder of the temple of Apollo in Delphi, which was a cult of oracles and serpents.

The serpentine motif that binds the protogenetoi together is interesting as we do find it in Nordic cosmology as well. For instance, Trudgjelmir is said to have six heads, and whenever we find a reference to some titanic force having so many heads in any other mythology, we always speak of snakes and dragons. Between the roots and wells of Yggdrasil, we find the dragon Nidhöggr who is said to have its dwelling in the halls of Sindri, a place made from pure gold deep inside Nidafjöll, "the black mountain" in the underworld. Nidafjöll is most likely to the North, because Nidhöggr, "the one that strikes with poisonous hatred", is said to be sucking on the corpses of the dead. It might be that the corpses which Raesvelg are consuming from his position in the crown of Yggdrasil end up at the roots of the tree in Hvergelmir and Hel.

Raesvelg, eater of corpses, the Jotun that looks like an eagle and is responsible for chaotic weather, was placed in the far north where he most likely is in the company of Nidhöggr, since both are denizens of the spiritual North. Nidhöggr is also a name given to the constellation Draco which, in turn, leads to Yggdrasil as it is related to Polaris. Known as the eye of Odin, Polaris is the guiding star that moves the celestial axis, turned into the primordial tree ever-circled by the poisonous dragon that eventually will bring an end to the cycle as we know it. This would be in harmony with the lore of Draco in several parts of the world, where this constellation is associated with betrayal, treachery, poison and the force that is constantly threatening to overturn the status quo.

The Stars of the Dragon

We don't know much about Nordic starlore besides that it was significant. Like with so many things practical, such as seidr and trolldom which are not really described in any great detail, so it is with starlore and the importance of the celestial bodies. We only know that the Moon, Sun and several stars and constellations held prominence. There also seems to be a connection between Yggdrasil, the world tree represented by Polaris, and the starry reflections of the animals having a function and role in relation to the tree, like the deer, squirrel, eagle and serpent-dragon. The connection between constellations and these animals make sense if we approach Yggdrasil as the axis mundi, the pole or center of a temporary condition that follows a cyclical movement towards destruction and resurrection, and mirror this against similar themes through recognition of family relations and similarity.

From the few hints given to us in the Edda and what has been transmitted orally in the form of folklore and proverbs it should be possible to present a plausible blueprint of Nordic starlore. In the references we have, the twin-stars in Gemini, the fixed stars Aldebaran and Capella, the constellations Orion, the Lyre, Ursa Major and Minor, Cassiopeia, Perseus and Polaris are mentioned either directly or in vague code.

There is not much written about the nature, effects and reason a star was important in Snorre's writings or in the sagas, except for laconic mentions here and there that stars, seasons and lunar phases were taken into account and held significance. But we are left with little details, as with most things Scandinavian, that rarely go into much philosophical reasoning of why a certain ritual course is followed. Hence, yet again, we need to resort to the traditional themes and measure them against what we find standing out as central in the Nordic cosmogony so we can arrive at a plausible and solid epistemology of the importance of the stars and their connection with the material world for heathen Scandinavians.

The Stars and Wells of Yggdrasil 175

In the Northern hemisphere we find two constellation families, and it is natural that amongst them we find the stars and constellations significant for the Norsemen. These are the ten constellations in the Ursa Major family in which seven of them are animals. These are: Boötes (the Herdsman), Camelopardalis (the Giraffe), Canes Venatici (the Hunting Dogs), Coma Berenices (Berenice's Hair), Corona Borealis (Northern Crown), Draco (Dragon), Leo Minor (the Smaller Lion), Lynx, Ursa Major (the Great Bear) and Ursa Minor (the Little Bear). We also find all the constellations in the Perseus family except Cetus (the Whale). These are Andromeda (the Chained Maiden), Auriga (the Charioteer), Cassiopeia (the Queen), Cepheus (the King), Lacerta (the Lizard), Pegasus (the Winged Horse), Perseus and Triangulum (the Triangle).

The constellations:

Yggdrasil is also called Mimameidr, Mimir's tree, and Mimir is also the brother of Sigurd Fávnesbane's foster father, Reginn, who has the ability to shape-shift into a dragon, which might suggest that Mimir holds an ancestral, or at least spiritual, connection with Nidhöggr.

One of the three wells that feed the roots of Yggdrasil is Mimir's well which stretches through Jotunheimen and the realm of the frost giants. It was at this well Odin gave up one of his eyes so he could partake of the boundless wisdom that was owned and guarded by Mimir. The eye he gave up might be Polaris, as this star is also called Odin's eye. His other eye is perhaps Betelgeuse in the constellation of Orion, a star that is almost exactly on the same degree of the ecliptic as the pole star.

The seven stars known as the Pleiades in the constellation of Taurus lie between Orion and the big bear. This constellation is associated with Odin and his wagon, as Ursa Minor is commonly associated with Thor, but at its tip we find Polaris, the eye of Odin. Both of them are in the north known as "the seven stars", although in the majority of cases Polaris is involved in the mystery of the seven stars, and so it is the bear constellation that takes precedence.

From this, there are many plausible theories which present themselves; of these to simply see Polaris as representative of Yggdrasil as the axis mundi gives us Thor in the shape of Ursa Minor, and Odin in the form of Ursa Major, spinning around the axis with Nidhöggr in the shape of the constellation of Draco outside the two bear constellations. From this, we might see the Northern stars give us Orion as the home of Odin and Frigg, Hercules as the home of Thor and so forth, but an assignment like this will not invite in the many animals and other mysteries that are related to Yggdrasil and so we look to another theory, more elaborate, rooted in directions of the winds being both symbols as well as true directions.

Yggdrasil represents its own stellar mystery; it is the constellation Cygnus that was viewed as Yggdrasil. Cygnus was, in Antiquity, known as Orpheus in his elevated form and rightly we find the Lyre at Cygnus' side, the harp given to him by Apollo, which is charming for a culture that placed poetry in such high regard as did the Nordic culture. Also, when we look at the shape of Cygnus, it can be viewed as a cross, a crossroad or a tree. The the star in its head, Daneb Algedi, is aligned with Polaris, being a natural candidate to represent Yggdrasil as much as Polaris, yet more specifically the crown of Yggdrasil given this is the resting place of Raesvelg.

In the Greek legend of Cygnus or Orpheus the constellation is sacred to Zeus, and in the constellation is encoded the story of Zeus' seduction of Leda, the Queen of Sparta. After the seduction she, however, also slept with her husband, King Tyndareus, and from this she laid two eggs. From these, amongst several versions, was born Castor and Pollox who were placed under the protection of Aquilo, the North Wind. In the north, Cygnus was always understood as a cross, hence its most used name to this day is Northern Cross. It has frequently been associated with the Cross of Calvary, a most apt symbol for Odin's ordeal and initiation in Yggdrasil. Also, for the Norsemen the Northern Cross was at times viewed as an owl or a tree falling into the Milky Way, which is associated with Helvegen, the road to Hel, in the sense of the realm beneath Yggdrasil where we find the dragon, the Norns and the three wells. Yet, the Milky Way is also attributed to Bifrost. Robson says about Cygnus that Cygnus' nature is contemplative and dreamy, that it is cultured and adaptable, yet its affections are unsteady and reckless. She attributes it to the 20th Tarot trump, judgment, which remarkably fits the entropic idea of cruel Fate associated with the rotting Yggdrasil. In the head of the Northern Cross we find the tail of Capricorn, the fixed star Deneb Algedi, a star that is reputed to cause climate change, and especially storms and tornadoes at sea,[148] the very same nature we find ascribed to Raesvelg, the eagle in the crown of Yggdrasil.

Sitting between the eyes of the eagle we find a hawk or falcon called Vedrfölnir, "the one who is withered or bleached by wind and weather". It might be that the story which speaks in depth about this stellar mystery is the one about Tjatse, the father of Skade, the protective *dis* of Scandinavia and skiing who is considered to be an àsynje due to her marriage with the oceanic Vanir Njord, as told in the 8th century poem *Haustlong*. It is also later retold in the Edda, where Odin, Loke and Hönir make a meal from oxen they had sacrificed but are unable to make the meat tender due to the enchantments of the giant Tjatse whom the three Æsir finally invite to eat with them. Tjatse, however, takes all the best parts of the oxen. This enrages Loke, who then starts beating the giant, which leads to Tjatse, who is in the *ham/*shape of an eagle, flying away with Loke and demanding that Loke bring Idunn to him in exchange for being let safely down onto the ground. Loke agrees, and through trickery, he manages to bring Idunn and her apples of youth and immortality to Tjatse. But without Idunn and her apples, the Æsir start to get old fast and it is imperative to get her back, hence Loke borrows the falcon-*ham* of Freya and flies to Trymheimen, where Tjatse lives, transforms Idunn into a walnut and abducts her. Tjatse however immediately realizes what is happening and flies after Loke in the shape of an eagle. As

---

148 Noonan, 1990: 36.

Loke arrives at Åsgard the Æsir manages to burn the feathers of the eagle, and as Tjatse falls to ground, Thor kills him. Skade however comes to Odin and demands retribution, whereas Odin throws the eyes of Tjatse into the heavens where they turn into the twin stars Castor and Pollux in the constellation Gemini which rises brightly over Orion in the month of April.

Tjatse himself is associated with the oak, sacred to Jupiter. According to the *Gylfaginning*, Tjatse has a relationship with Yggdrasil and Valhalla through Eikthyrnir, "thorny oak", the deer which stands upon Valhalla together with the goat Heidrun. This oak-deer is understood to be the same as the deer that are protecting Yggdrasil, or the father of the four deer that protects the world tree. The Icelandic scholar Finnur Magnusson[149] is of the opinion that the four deer are the four winds, and so he sees in Dáinn, "the dead one", and Dvalin, "the unconscious one", the calm winds, while Duneyrr, "thunder in the ear", and Durathrór, "thriving slumber", represent strong winds. He arrived at this conclusion due to how the deer are eating/moving the branches and leaves on the tree in a similar manner as winds moves branches and leaves. Dáinn and Dvalin are dwarves, and dwarves are seen as the forces that support the four major directions, given that we have dwarves named North (Norðri), South (Suðri), East (Austri) and West (Vestri). If so, we have the four compass points in the dwarves as protectors of and dwellers in the tree, which brings us a natural connection with the Norns who would also be from the heritage of dwarves, more specifically Dvalin.

This would suggest that Dáinn, who with Nabbi made Hildsvinet, the fighting boar on which Freya rides, might be represented by the constellation the Lyre and the fixed star Vega, a star that holds connotations with things poisonous, the end of cycles and the destruction of old structures in favor of the new, hence it is proper for Dainn's name.

Dvalin, "the sleeper", would then be identified with the constellation Cepheus, who stands with one foot on Polaris, the North Star. He was also one of the four dwarves that made the necklace Brisingamen for Freya and taught Odin how to carve runes, hence we find in Dáinn and Dvalin a common reference to Freya and the red deer. Aldemarin is the most famous star here; it is not one of the fixed stars, but a star associated with the memory of royal deeds as much as the gallows, hangings and crucifixions, which is beguiling, given the deep connection Dvalin holds with Odin and his understanding of the runes.

---

149 1824.

This would ascribe Duneyrr, "drooping ears", to the constellation Aquila and the star Altair, related to reptiles and mischief; Durathrór, "sluggish beast", would then have Perseus as its home. Algol, the head of Medusa, is ultimately represented by Nidhöggr. Here we have the two destructive winds being associated with stars of destruction, while Dáinn and Dvalin are not identified with, but are in the proximity of Polaris and Vega, two stars that would represent the current state of affairs and the poisonous destruction that will enable Vega to take the crown of Polaris, represented by the cosmic drama between Odin and Loke. The squirrel Ratatosk, "gnaw tooth", might be assigned to Cassiopeia, another constellation given rank and recognition, as it is there resting over Deneb Algedi in the head of Yggdrasil and constantly revolving around Polaris.

If we now return to Orion, the constellation of Odin and Frigg, we find that the belt of Orion is invariably called Friggerocken or Mariarocken, "Frigg's distaff" or "Mary's distaff". Frigg was said to spin the clouds that veiled Àsgard and rested over Midgard. This would suggest that the constellation, even though referred to as Odin, is, in truth, the constellation of Frigg. Here we find one of Odin's two eyes in the shape of the star Betelgeuse; the other is Polaris, because it is Ursa Major that is commonly understood to be the wagon of Odin, while Ursa Minor is the wagon of Thor. Ursa Minor is surrounded by the constellation Draco, which would naturally be Nidhöggr who is conceived of as coiling around Polaris on three sides. This is in harmony with the three wells, especially when we consider that the Greeks also saw Polaris as the tree of Hesperidia and Draco as the snake that was coiled around the tree to protect the apples – and yes, this legend was most likely the inspiration for the myth of the tree of knowledge in the biblical Garden of Eden. Furthermore, we should keep in mind that starlore everywhere in the world connects Polaris to judgment in one form or another and Romani-lore sees in Polaris the arrival of the grandfather of Cain on Earth which, in the Nordic context, would be Odin in the *ham* or shape of a bear.

This would then invite us to consider a dual mystery here, where Ursa Minor and Ursa Major together with Draco and Orion represent the mystery of origin, and the constellations and stars surrounding Cygnus are concerned with the temporality of the world created by Odin and represented by Yggdrasil, the Northern Cross, the pole star which is doomed to leave its position for the next star that will be the "new north".

Yggdrasil and the Behenii

The fixed stars were, prior to Ptolemaic precision of stellar bodies, the most significant luminaries in the heavens, and continued to be of great importance even after Ptolemy (100-173 CE) and his mathematical calculations of star and planet positions. With Ptolemy, the fixed stars took on a new prominence, as celestial markers of the ecliptic and of the poles of the equator. Ptolemy also, in his *Tetrabiblos*, gave dual planetary associations to each of the fixed stars in an attempt to explain how the fixed stars would be similar yet different to known planetary vibrations. This means that the fixed stars do mark the 360 degrees of the zodiac, with bright stars in each of the zodiac signs that bring the year around. We find that none of the classical fixed stars are found in Pisces and Aries, both because the area of sky shared by these constellations marked equinoxes, the beginning of the astrological year, and because they were not really defined as separate constellations until the Babylonian reform of astrology. Amongst several theories explaining this, we find that prior to the Babylonian revival, Aries was a part of Taurus and Pisces was a part of Andromeda, but we can also see in Pisces and Aries the oroboros, the alpha and the omega, the astrological starting point announcing the cycle. In this, it should be mentioned that the four royal stars, Aldebaran in Taurus, Antares in Scorpio, Formalhaut in Pisces Australis and Regulus in Leo, were the earliest markers for the cardinal points.

Nigel Pennick in his *Runic Astrology*[150] gives a presentation of the meaning of the behenii, or fixed stars, in relation to runes and the Nordic Tradition; it would be interesting to present here an expanded version of his initial presentation. In Pennick's view, Frigg, Odin, Tyr, Thor and Loke stand out with great dominance, and he makes further correspondences by creating associations where Heimdal works through Regulus, Heidrun through Capella, Frey and Freya through Alcyone, and the Pleiades in the shape of the boar and by extension the Valkyries. This would harmonize greatly with the importance of these Æsir in Scandinavia, and it would also suggest that, for Pennick, the fixed stars represent the Æsir rulership. It is only natural that the apocalyptic theme of Ragnarök is the canvas for understanding how the influence of Æsir and stars as elements are played out within the greater apocalyptic theme we find in the *Voluspá*, as the drama of the behenii plays itself out between the two celestial wolfs' jaws. This invites into this cosmic drama the idea of

---

150 1995: Chapter 7.

The Stars and Wells of Yggdrasil

the wolves being integral to Ragnarök in tandem with Nidhöggr, a sentiment that would be in tune with how Polaris mediates the stars of Nidhöggr and the behenii in the heavens, unavoidably turning into perpetual change and renewal. Here, I will present a suggestive simple diagram applying virtues, deities and runes in accordance with the vibration of the behenii.

The Northern constellations, marking the behenii:

Polaris is the eye of Odin, the ideal Yggdrasil; lodestone, periwinkle, cypress, iron nails, the runes Fé and Algiz are sacred to this star. It is located at the tail of the bear at 27° Virgo.

In extension of Polaris and its symbolic representation of Frigg's distaff, the belt of Orion, representing the three Norns – our *wyrd* that Frigg is spinning around the pole star – should be noted as having a traditional meaningful relationship to the Hyperborean North and the importance of Fate encircling Polaris in such way that Orion can be seen as the full form of Polaris as he shows himself in our age.

The **Pleiades**, in particular the fixed star **Alcyone**, gives us the boar's throng, mimicking the wedge-shaped formation of attack which was called *svinfylking*, boar riders, the army of Frey and Freya. Alcyone brings destruction, ruin, blindness and ties in with the Valkyries as Freya's army, proper for a star that is said to summon the dead. The runes Ken and Ing together with fennel and quicksilver belong to this star located at 29° Taurus.

Capella is the star of Heidrun, the she-goat of Odin which makes special ale, and is located at 21° Gemini. Capella gives honor and exalts men and possesses curative properties. Wormwood, mint and mandrake are amongst its virtues and Gebo and Wunja are its proper runes.

Arcturus is a star that possess great healing qualities, is related to jasper and the evergreen, and is located at 24° Libra. It provides justice and good repute, and it follows that Tyr and Thor are proper powers assigned to its influence along with the runes Tyr and Sol.

Antares, located at 9° Sagittarius at the heart of Scorpio, gives both good memory, but also violence and corruption are part of its virtues. Saffron is related to its benevolence and all herbs bitter and juicy to its sting. The runes Thurs and Perth are proper here as are Fenris, Jormundgandr and also Odin's ravens Hugin and Munin.

Aldebaran, found at 9° Gemini, is the star of Eikthyrnir and the stags feeding the tree. It is a star of strategy and it brings increase of wealth and honor. Its plant is hellebore, and its runes are Fé, Ur and Eihwaz.

Betelgeuse, found at 28° Gemini, is in many ways similar to Aldebaran, the other eye of Odin in Orion, as it also gives honor, but there is also something primal and dark in this star and so aconite and wolfbane stand out as a plant allies to this star of Odin along with the runes Hagal and Laug.

Deneb Algedi is the star of Raesvelg, the Jotun eagle in the crown of Yggdrasil, and is located at 23° Aquarius. The star gives grief, malevolence, loss, storms and natural disasters. Marjoram and mandrake are amongst its virtues and Jera, Naud and Eihwaz are its runes.

Sirius, the greater Dog Star, is located at 14° Cancer and was in the North known as *Lokebrenna*, Loke's fire. It is a star of tremendous solar qualities, considered to be the source of the Sun, and gives fame and guardianship. Its herbs are mugwort and pennyroyal and in this can give luck. Its runes are Ansu, Sol and Dag, its Æsir Jord, Frigg, Frey and Balder.

Procyon, located at 25° Cancer, is also called the torch-bearer as well as being the lesser Dog Star. It is related to craftiness, lust, success or failure, disagreements and divorce. Its virtues can be found in pennyroyal, heliotrope and horehound; its runes are Naud, Raid and Eihwaz, and its deities are Sleipnir, Fenris, Frigg and Odin.

Sirius and Procyon mark the midsummer and are attributed to Loke by virtue of their shared "heat". Whilst Snorre depicts Loke as a troublemaker and author of mischief, a less judgmental interpretation might suggest that Loke is ultimately the force that makes the fire of the Sun possible and represents the union of its benevolence and malevolence reflected in these two stars.

Regulus, found at 29° Leo, makes men temperate and removes melancholy. It is proper to assign this star to Heimdal, the bright and white one. Liquorice, St. John's Wort and lily of the valley are sympatic herbs. The star gives success and fame in projects and runes like Bjørk, Man and Odel would be natural candidates for attracting this benevolence

Alphecca, located at 12° Scorpio, is a star that gives poetry and brilliance, but can also ensure chastity. Rosemary is amongst its virtues and Frigg, Vár and Idunn would be powers in resonance along with the runes Wunja, Jera and Laug.

Algorab, located at 13° Libra, is a star that brings destruction and malice. It causes wicked dreams and provokes wickedness in men, hence henbane, mugwort and black pepper are amongst its virtues along with the runes Perth and Thurs, with a strong presence both of Thor, Tyr and the frost giants.

Vega, located at 15° Capricorn, is the star of Loke. It gives idealism and direction; it also makes people fearless. Plants juicy and stingy, slightly toxic and plants that increase the fire in the body would be seen to possess Vega's virtue. Its runes would be Ken and Tyr.

Algol, located at 26° Taurus, is the star of Nidhöggr. Holly, hellebore and the Christmas rose along with mandrake would speak of the virtues of this star which finds itself in the runes Is, Naud, Eihwaz, Perth and Laug.

Spica, located at 23° Libra, is the star of Frigg and Odin, Frey and Freya. It is a star of union, harmony, love, the erotic and sensual. Sage, honeysuckle, jasmine and rose are all of its virtues and Ken, Wunja and Tyr are amongst its runes.

There is naturally much more that can be said about these matters, especially concerning the deeper mysteries of Orion itself and its other stars, such as Rigel and Bellatrix which invite in Mimir in the shape of Rigel and Freya in the heart of Bellatrix, but at this point the correspondences and musings presented should suffice to give a stellar dimension to the Northern mysteries, as a turn towards the ontology of man in light of Yggdrasil will conclude this chapter.

The Ontology of Yggdrasil

Yggdrasil can, with great ease, be taken to represent the constitution of man. At first glance the eagle in the crown would be associated with the intellect and the importance of the eyes as windows for sense experiences. Nidhöggr at the root represents the drives and impulses at the base of man. Then we have the Norns that carve the Fate of every man and living thing into this tree which is already rotting and will die, reminding everyone that the mark we make in the world is fated to wane. This would make man a cosmic actor in the great drama of existence. In considering the ontology of Yggdrasil, we need to address the concept of the soul and discard the idea of the soul as a singularity. The idea of the soul associated with breath as a singular representation of self entered the Scandinavian consciousness with the spread of Christianity. In many ways, Herman Hesse in his book *Steppenwolf* gives a fine description of the concept of the soul as it was experienced in heathen Scandinavia:

> even animals are not undivided in spirit. With them too, the well-knit beauty of the body hides a being of manifold states and strivings...You will have to multiply many times your two-fold being and complicate your complexities still further. Instead of narrowing your world and simplifying your soul, you will have to absorb more and more of the world and at last take all of it up in your painfully expanded soul.[151]

The term coming closest to the idea of a soul was hugr. Hugr was said to rest in the heart but also possessed intellectual capacity, and was able to express itself in emotions.

Hugr is an Old Norse word meaning: "mind-spirit, thought". In generic use, hugr is the psyche. It is the mental life of the individual. Hugr is a representation of the words we now call "thought, wishes/desires, personality" but is commonly used to refer to the entire soul in general. It was believed that every person had a hugr, and what the hugr did and could do was complex. The hugr could be detached from the body, be in different places at the same time, could come in the shape of an animal or another person (often it's thought the hugr was similar to the doppelganger, in that it would look like the person to whom it belonged). "Hugr-stolen" was a term sometimes used to

---

151 1963: 72, 73.

refer to someone with mental abnormalities or physical disorder. To "hugr" somebody meant to manipulate them using your own hugr.

There was also such a thing as "hugr-turning" in which a person could do a rite to either turn hugrs towards them or away from them, making them friends or enemies. Related to the "shape" aspect of the hugr, it was thought that a person's hugr could be strong enough to eventually take a shape. Most commonly the shape would be that of the person it represents, but it could also be in the shape of an animal. Because of the physical-thought that was associated with hugr, it was thought that if the hugr suffered damage outside of the body, the person would suffer physical damage as well. This is because it was believed that while the hugr could be separated, its ultimate home was within the body. The concept of elsk, or being passionate about someone, was considered a faculty of hugr, and was intimately linked with the spirit of envy, which was considered a reflex of passion tied into the concept of *hugrsa*, meaning "desirous", usually in relation to a goal.

The body was called *hamr*, literally the skin or fur in the sense of one's physical appearance. Hugr could also describe a person's personality and temperament. The hamr on the other hand could do what was called hamferd, which is simply astral travel and the shapeshifting abilities of those cunning in the arts of seidr and gandr. For instance, in *Ynglinga saga*, when Odin is allowing his hugr to run out when he is sleeping, this is referred to as *hamleypa*, the form that runs or leaps.

Connected to the hamr we had the part called hamingja, which would be the part of the soul complex connected to the disir, and thus this connection would establish the amount of luck and good fortune a person would have in their life. Hugr can be understood to represent the soul as reflected in personality as much as describing the essence of a person. Also, the hugr could be stolen, which would lead to a person decaying, losing power, stamina and courage. Likewise hugr could increase and decrease, much like a flock of birds, and so the person with a strong hugr would be conceived of as someone possessing a larger gathering of soul birds than someone weak and unimpressionable. The allegory with birds is found in the icon of Odin and his two ravens, Hugin and Munin, representing the connection between hugr and memory and how someone strong in memory would also be understood to possess a strong hugr.

The hugr had its shadow, called fylgja, which was its guardian and associated with the fetch, which in turn was frequently understood as man's connection to the realm of beasts. Thus it was the presence of fylgja that made it possible to shape-shift and allowed the hugr to ride out while the body was asleep. The fylgja of men would frequently show itself in the shape of bears, wolves and other animals. In this way, the fylgja would represent the character of a person and would also be the gateway to the oneiric realm. How connected hugr and fylgja are to dreams is clear in how words like *manna hugrir* and *manna fylgjur* were both used as references to riding-out in dreams.[152] This means that for the heathen Norsemen dream and reality was not a meaningful distinction; these were realms equally real, only differing in the presence and absence of the hamr. Hence, we find in the sagas several examples of how people, who were dreaming true, *draumspakr*, were sought after for counsel and advice. To gain this gift, folklore says to sleep in foreign places and to count the wood logs in the roof until trance occurs and one enters the world of dream; sleeping on a grave would also give one this ability. Fylgja can in this way be said to be the guardian of man's hugr, something that would be more or less powerful in relation to the magnitude of one's hugr.

We have yet another concept connected to the hugr/hamr complex, namely the vord, the guardian. Given how the vord is frequently spoken of in relation to the harm that it causes, it appears to be a protective force that connected the person to the land and by extension to the world of vaettir. Vord means protector, guardian, and it could also be stolen. A person lacking their vord would be like a person without their shadow; they would be incapable of making decisions and behave in senseless ways, lacking direction in life. In the *Hávamál*, stanza 155, we learn how the volva can summon back a lost vord, so it "returns to its own hugr and hamr". Both Reichborn-Kjennerud and Birkeli point out that frequently physical illness is related to something being wrong with one's vord. Considering that physical illness was equally frequently ascribed to the work of vaettir and elves, this suggests that vord was the part of the soul complex which connected man to this realm.

As the extension of hugr we find concepts such as örlög which is understood as the original cosmic law, which is beyond social law, and is manifested in *önd* or breath, indicative of our "spirited" state as human beings, hence breath was not associated with being given soul, but being given Fate. This concept is related to Wyrd or Fate in the sense that in the greater örlög we all have a unique wyrd to fulfill. As an aid in fulfilling our wyrd we have fylgja, which is our guardian spirit that enables the possibility for changing hamr.

This gives us a unique soul complex where hamr is the physical appearance, the clothing of the hugr. The hugr is guarded by the

---

152 Reichborn-Kjennerud, 1927: 33.

fylgja, just as the hamr is guarded by the vord which gives man access to the realm of vaettir and beasts and also enables us to move around in the oneiric realm and to change shape. When we are born and take our first breath, we are being given our örlög, or Fate, and depending on our constitution, which is directly related to the reputation of our heritage, the strength or weakness of our hamingja is established.

Chapter Eight

The Way of Seidr

> ...the task of the sejd-woman was to unravel and understand the causes for crop failures and illness as well as gaining insight into the Fate of given persons. You would in this regard assume that the ward-spirit (vorden/varð) was related partly to the vaettir of the farmstead, those that were ruling over man's contentment and progress and partly to the fylgja of given persons. – D. Strömbäck[153]

Seidr/Seiðr is etymologically disputed, however the sense of seidr being related to thread, circumference, a bond, or something that approaches, are amongst the more established definitions of the word itself. This leads to Heide[154] seeing in the idea of seidr something that spins, a spirit thread, a circular movement mimicking the distaff that induces trance. Seidr can be used both to describe how Jormundgandr embraces the circumference of Earth, and how a shoal of fishes gathers in a forward motion. Seidr is also commonly interpreted as the shamanism of Scandinavia, a term that might escape the spirit technology inherit in seidr and its purpose on a particular level, yet insofar as shamanism concerns itself with a trance state that invites in the possibility of undertaking journeys or "soul-flights", the term might be adequate in a general and broad sense. From the accounts in the Edda, seidr was considered a form of trolldom, a trolldom unsuitable for men to practice given the element of ergi, or "perversity" involved in the art. In the *Ynglinga saga*, stanza 7, the following account is given about seidr:

> Odin could transform his shape (hamr). His body would lie as if dead, or asleep, even though he would be a bird or beast, fish or snake and be off in a twinkling to distant lands upon his own or other people's business. But he could also do other things: with words alone he could quench fire, still the ocean in tempest, and turn the wind to any quarter he pleased...Odin understood also the art in which the

---

153   2000: 124. First published in 1935.
154   2006.

greatest power is lodged, and which he himself practiced; which is *seidr*; by means of this he could know the fate of men and foresee what has not yet happened, he could bring to men death or misfortune or ill health, he could take sanity and strength from men and give it to others; but with this form of *trolldom* comes so many unmanly matters that men could not perform it without shame, that's why they thought *gydjene* [priestesses] this art.

From this account in the Edda it seems that seidr was twofold. On one hand, it was concerned with prophecy and the mystery of fate which would connect seidr to Frigg and the Norns, and on the other hand it could bring misfortune upon people and change their luck and fate, which would clearly define seidr as the art of the Norns given how manipulating Fate was a part of the art. Skin-leaping was an integral part of seidr, but not necessarily lycanthropy.[155]

The skin-leaping related to seidr would be one where the hugr went out while the body was still. As we see, this trance state allows Odin to take on various shapes and fly wherever he desired, unrestrained by mundane geography. It would seem plausible that this is a presentation of seidr as part of a larger generic tradition referred to as trolldom, emphasizing the importance of trance and the ability of establishing magical bonds with other beings in nature. It also seems that seidr was the trolldom from the Vanir, while the trolldom known as gandr held more of a Jotun connotation. Gandr and seidr shared in common the necessity of altered states and the use of galdr and song, i.e. what we would call enchantments that would effectuate a state of otherness and establish the bonds that made it possible to travel out in various forms.

Practitioners of *seid* were known by many different names such as *seið-maðr* and *seið-kona* in particular, but also words like *seið-skratti*, *seið-stafr*, *seið-berendr*, *seið-hjallr*, *seið-læti* are used. The oldest accounts we have date to the 10th century: *Lausavisa* of Vitgeir, and *Seidmadr* and *Sigurdardrápa* by Kormakr Ogmundarson. Both accounts were used both by Snorre in his Eddaic poems and by Saxo Grammaticus in his *Gesta Danorum*. In the Poetic Edda we find three direct references to seidr: *Voluspá* stanza 22, *Lokasenna* stanza 24 and *Hyndluljoth* stanza 33. In addition, we find in *Balder's draumars* stanza 4 and *Helgakvida Hundingsbana* stanza 37 seidr mentioned in relation to this being the practice of the volva.

The account in *Hyndluljoth* stands out, as here we learn that the first *seid* practitioner, called *seiðberendr*, came from Svarthöfdi and was

---

155 See Appendix B about the mystery of the *vargulf*, the Nordic werewolf.

a Jotun. It might be that in the blackness of Svarthöfdi we find a reference to Heid, the three-times burnt, because Heid is significant in the practice of seidr. Both in the *Ynglinga saga* 4.7 and in stanza 22 of the *Voluspá*, we see that seidr was introduced to the world by the volva Heidr, an art already in the Edda associated with *illrar brúðar*, or wicked maidens. In the *Ynglinga saga* we also see that Freya is the one who is teaching the art of seidr to the Æsir and in particular to Odin. This has led some to conclude that Freya and Heid are the same person.[156] This is however quite doubtful, yet it is in this relationship seidr is often considered the trolldom of the Vanir. An important detail here is that while Heid is directly referred to as a practicing volva, there is no account specifically describing Freya practicing seidr, although naturally in her capacity as a teacher of this art she would also be an apt practitioner. It would perhaps be more logical that Freya was a student of Heid and was taught these arts from this mysterious Jotun woman lodged in the origin of creation, the first volva. This would also explain why this art was so important for Odin; in mastering this art he would have access to yet another level of knowledge that would enhance his foresight and cosmic understanding of the world and its mysteries.

Also in the *Ynglinga saga*, Snorre writes about another volva from Finland called Huld who, through seidr, ensures the fall of two kings. Finally, in *Eiríks saga rauda*, we find an account of how a volva is arriving at a farm and takes her place on a high seat and gives prophecies of the fate of the farm. Similar accounts focusing on the prophetic dimension is found in *Hrólfs saga kraka* and *Örvar-Odds saga*, which will be discussed in detail shortly, but now we need to look more closely at Heidr.

Dag Strömbäck is the one who pioneered the study of seidr in his dissertation presented at the University of Lund, Sweden in 1935, and later published in various editions. Strömbäck anchors his dissertation in what is written about seidr in the *Voluspá*, stanza 22, and is particularly fascinated by how seidr is described with the words hugr and *leikinn* or *hugrleikinn*. *Leikinn* means "playful" or "playful performance", but can also mean "taken" as in being possessed, whilst hugr is a word of some deeper complexity. We find the word hugr in the names of one of Odin's ravens, Hugin, meaning "thought". Hugin flies with Munin, "Memory", and thus we can in the icon of Odin see there is something that ties memory to thought. When we look at the context in which the word hugr is used, it is evident that we are speaking of something more than the intellectual faculty, especially in a word like hugr-taken which

---

156 Simek, 2007: 123.

refers to a deep desire caused by the memory of the object of desire taking shape in one's mind. The importance of hugr as the very act of recalling a specific memory sustained by an emotional charge is an element found in several Black Books. Also in the *Voluspá* it is the memory, the hugr, which is used to access a prediction for the future.

According to stanza 22, seidr is ascribed to a Jotun woman known as Heid or Heidr, often considered the same as Gullveig; the similarity in the meaning of their names might attest to Gullveig and Heid being the same. Gullveig means "golden road" or "golden liquid"; Heid means "shining one" or "bright one". Three attempts were made to murder her by fire, but she could not die. In the figure of Heid we find a mysterious figure; she lives in the Ironwood, a place every Æsir dreads to venture, and is viewed as a wise prophetess, not unlike the pythonesses at Apollo's temple in Delphi. The stanzas in question, 21 and 22, are as follows:

21.
Þat man hon folkvíg
fyrst í heimi,
er Gullveigu
geirum studdu
ok í höll Hárs
hana brenndu,
þrisvar brenndu,
þrisvar borna,
oft, ósjaldan,
þó hon enn lifir.

21.
The first murder I remember
the first on Earth,
when Gullveig
was pierced by spears
and set on fire
in the Hall of Odin,
three times burnt,
three times born,
frequently murdered,
yet she still lives.

22.
Heiði hana hétu
hvars til húsa kom,
völu velspáa,
vitti hon ganda;
seið hon, hvars hon kunni,
seið hon *hugr* leikinn,
æ var hon angan
illrar brúðar.

22.
Heid was her name
the one who sought people out in their homes,
volva wise in foresight,
gandr she guarded and knew;[157]
seidr she did, whenever she could,
seidr she did, with playful hugr,[158]
supreme she was amongst
the wicked women.

---

157 Alternatively: *vaettir* she woke up with *gandr*.
158 A reference to a form of ecstatic trance, maybe sexual in nature.

Vexior[159] suggests in analyzing the genealogy of Heid that she is the daughter of Berghjelmir. Given that Trudgjelmir, his father, was the only one of the frost giants to escape Odin's slaughter of them, and the near obsession Odin and the Æsir had with ending Heidr's life (while wanting to gain access to her art), this suggestion becomes very plausible. Also, in annihilating Heid and possessing her art in full, Odin would be the sole owner of all the available trolldom in the world. There is also this element of her "shining", just like the Æsir are described as being shining. This would suggest that in truth, she should have been considered an Æsir, but what was experienced as her "wickedness" made her unsuited to become part of the Æsir fold. Hence, it was perhaps less threatening to invite in Freya who possessed the same knowledge and eroticism but was considered less "wicked". Nevertheless, the prototype of the volva was Heid and the supreme mystery of seidr was related to how it was possible to manipulate Fate through an intense connection with the Norns. Naturally for Odin, access to these mysteries would give him a chance to avoid Ragnarök, but alas, what the Fates have written will come to pass; only what is yet unwritten can be manipulated and it is in this field that misfortune along the thread of Fate can be inflicted. The volva, being a manifestation of Heidr, would also explain the ambiguous role she held in society; prophetic seidr was lawful, whilst malefic seidr was not. The volva was an accepted actor in the public seidr or custom, yet not all of what she did was considered lawful. This is further emphasized in how the volva Odin resurrects to give the prophecy called *Voluspá* is summoned from her grave outside Hel, so even on the other side the volva was a figure existing at the hedges of the wild and the orderly. In this, the volva would reflect the idea of the "witch" better than anything else in the Northern Tradition. With the word "witch" I have in mind someone who brings solace and perspective from this place on the outside of everything – the solace of peace or death, the solace of an end of suffering. The witch is a Fate-maker, someone who understands how to ride nature into trance and how to build bonds with vaettir and nature spirits, someone who is one with their fetch due to having their roots in the wells of Mimir and Urd in such way that they can predict the future as much by looking backwards as by interpreting the consequences of the present.

Freya enters this mystery by virtue of being a volva herself, yet in practicing the art, it is Heid she manifests, so to speak. If we want to generate a closer proximity, we might understand Freya as a benign form of Heid due to a single comment in the *Ynglinga saga* where

---

159 2010: 52.

Snorre writes that Freya was the last surviving one of the Æsir to maintain the old customs. In this, we might see the omega to Heidr's alpha, the head and the tail of Jormundgandr.

In *Eiríks saga rauda*, we can read about the typical form in which the volva showed herself when she was going to perform prophetic seidr.

> She was wearing a black mantle with a strap, which was adorned with precious stones right down to the hem. About her neck she wore a string of glass beads and on her head a hood of black lambskin lined with white catskin. She bore a staff with a knob at the top, adorned with brass set with stones on the top. About her she had a linked charm belt with a large purse. In it she kept the charms which she needed for her predictions. She wore calfskin boots lined with fur with long, sturdy laces and large pewter knobs on the ends. On her hands she wore gloves of catskin, white and lined with fur.

It seems that most rituals of seidr were performed after dark according to what we can read in *Örvar-Odds saga* and in *Eiríks saga rauda*. In these sagas we see the importance of singing the *vardlokkur*, songs to protect and to enchant, like in the ritual referred to in the *Volsatattr*. Here we can read about how the volva and other women of the community come together to praise a cult object called völsi. The völsi was packed in pure cloth together with onion and herbs and sent from woman to woman who sang songs to praise its size and fertilizing abilities. The völsi was the mummified member of a horse, a representation of Frey. When the praising of the völsi was completed, a young virgin, not menstruating, was lifted over the threshold of the main entrance of the house so she could look into the future.[160] It is worth pointing out that we can, in this practice, see similarities with witchcraft of a more traditional orientation in how a specific animal is treated, in this case the horse, which connects the practitioners to spirit travel and also to an Æsir, in this case Frey, whilst the songs and enchantments are done to appease and bring protection from the vaettir of the land. In addition, the act of being lifted over the threshold, the communion with night, and the enchantments in general would stand out as interesting.

---

[160] The hagiography of Olaf the Holy tells about his participation in this ritual ending with the king throwing the *völsi* to the dogs, leading to the entire household converting themselves to Christendom.

The Way of *Seidr*

The divinatory seidr was of a different caliber than the malefic seidr. While the divinatory seidr was solely focused on prophecy and soothsaying, largely referred to as *at spá*, the malefic seidr would enable the practitioner to twist and thwart the laws of nature. The predictable would be unpredictable in this act of hollowing or turning the worlds. What the two expressions had in common was the importance of guiding spirits. Seidr could not be performed unless the practitioner had a deep and intimate relationship with the spirits of the land and the dead.

The secrets of the runes Odin received by descending to the halls of Hel in the nine days and nights he hung in the tree were both necromantic and divinatory in nature. This suggests itself if we realize that it was by hanging in the tree that he descended to Hel. The gift of prophecy and sorcery were given by descent to Hel. This tells us further that the land was crucial, and it follows that the most common method for seidr was what was called "sitting-out". By entering the woods or mountains at night and making contact with the spirits of the land (landvaettir[161]), it was possible to access the potency which informs this powerful and dangerous art. Sitting-out was simply about sitting still in a silent place of sacred nature by night and calling for inspiration and vision. This practice was considered so effective that it was forbidden by law as late as the 15th century. The significance of landvaettir is crucial to note because it is these beings that maintain stability, fertility and happiness in the land. If they leave, the place in question becomes subject to hostile influences and barrenness and melancholy enters in their place. This is precisely the effect of erecting the so called *nidstangr* (staff of disgrace), a staff carved with runes and enchantments where the head of a rotting animal is placed on top, facing the place one seeks to hex. The decaying gaze of the animated head will cause the landvaettir to leave the place and, in the absence of fruitful and stabilizing forces, gloom and barrenness invades the location.

We find many instances where both witches and gods are told to sing over wounds to heal them, or to sing over runes that have been carved. One of the most fearsome forms of galdr is the variety known as *níd*. Originally this word spoke of ridicule and harm, and was often very vulgar in its imagery. Today it has come to be used much more for ridicule, and has lost its magical reference. Some of the famous people connected to this art were called Kveld-Ulfr

---

[161] The term *vaettir* denotes as we have seen a large class of nature spirits, similar to the Roman *lares*. The word is perhaps etymologically related to the Anglo-Saxon "with" which refers to creature, being, spirit, demons, etc.

(evening wolf) and another one was said to be "half troll". Egil Skallagrímsson is himself the most famous due to his conflict with King Eirík and Queen Gunnhild. In his saga it is worth noting the significance of the stang, as the *volva* was literally the "stang-carrier". This story from *Egil's saga* might indicate a use of the stang and from this how different forms of wood might be used for different ends, while subject to the same method, chanting and carving:

> Egil went up onto the island. He took a hazel pole in his hand and went to the edge of a rock facing inland. Then he took a horse's head and put it on the end of the pole. Afterwards he made an invocation, saying "Here I set up this scorn pole and turn its scorn upon King Eirík and Queen Gunnhild" – then he turned the horse's head to face land – "and I turn its scorn upon the nature spirits [landvaettir] that inhabit this land, sending them astray so that none of them shall find its resting-place by chance or design until they have driven King Eirík and Queen Gunnhild from this land!" Then he drove the pole into a cleft in the rock and left it to stand there. He turned the head towards the land and carved the whole invocation in runes on the pole.

The most famous act of divinatory seidr is found in *Voluspá*, the poetic rendering of the end of Æsir and the coming of a new golden age. Here the practitioner is referred to as "volva". Prior to Christianity, and certainly in some centuries to follow, she was treated with utmost respect. This is because the position of the volva in the Nordic religious life was one of religious interpreter. Usually she was an old woman, old as defined by loss of menstruation, where she left her position as woman and mother and became something else. In this context, she became a prophetic channel, a spokeswoman between men and gods. Volva often carried a *volr*, literally, a stang, symbolic both of Yggdrasil and the dual acts she was capable of by being able to both bring fertility to a land or household or to take it away. So great was her position and status that even Odin himself goes to her to learn of the fate of the world and the gods. These divinations were usually lengthy processes that included songs and enchantment, galdr and silence. A shape of hamr often occurred, all done in concert with the spirits aiding the practitioner. She would then lie as dead, while her hamr left the body together with the attending spirit host.

The reference to the use of cat fur is interesting, as it clearly connects the art with Freya. Freya is said to arrive at the burial of Balder in a chariot pulled by cats, probably denoting the presence of Heid in the form of Freya. Further, the association of cats with sexuality and freedom, as in the cult of Cybele, is worth mentioning as is the reputed double-sight of cats. The ability of seeing the past and present, the visible and invisible world simultaneously is a quite proper motif. This does suggest that seidr was an art intimately tied to sexuality, but not necessarily fertility, which was the case in the public cults.

The researcher Clunies Ross[162] has pointed out regarding the typical practitioner of seidr that she seems to show a traditional segmentation of the divine feminine into its white, red and black phases or faces. She relates the similarities between Gullveig in the *Voluspá* and Freya in the *Ynglinga saga* and then lastly remarks on the fierce goddess/volva Heidr. Heid is said to be a black goddess who is three-times burnt but resurrects again. She lives in the forest of iron where only the black elves dare to venture. This insight Ross presents points towards the triple form of the divine feminine as in Hekate Triformis and will reveal a traditional color scale counting black, red and white/gold.

Freya represents the red phase associated with menstruation, Gullveig the white phase associated with abundance, generosity and youth, while the black phase represents the days of the blackened moon, when the blood is no longer rejuvenating the womb. Heid might be seen as the gateway to the enigma of malefic seidr. In *Örvar-Odds saga*, the *seidberendir's* name is Heidr. There is also mention of an old woman in *Eiríks saga* with awesome powers called "the angel of death" who is most likely Heid under one of her many aliases. Heid is depicted as a being both human and divine, but with a malefic and wicked disposition that accords her powers prominence in the outskirts of the world. But if this underlies for us that seidr was an art deeply related to the female cycle and essence, why would this wisdom interest Odin?

ODIN, THE MASTER OF SEIDR

Seidr was considered a female art and both in *Lokasenna* and *Ynglinga saga* we can read that Odin's interest in seidr was described as unmanly. Seidr was said to be ergi, meaning something perverse. We read in *Lokasenna* stanza 24:

---

162 2010.

En þik síða kóðu Sámseyu í,	But you once practiced seidr on Sámsey,
ok draptu á vétt sem völur;	and you beat on the drum like a volva;
vitka líki fórtu verþjóð yfir,	in the likeness of a cunning one you walked amongst men,
ok hugða ek þat args aðal	and that I thought the hallmark of a pervert [ergi]

Here Loke gives several interesting associations concerning what seidr is about, which is beating the drum to change his hamr and walk around in this other form. Already Odin has his horse Sleipnir, who with his eight legs demonstrates the ability Odin has to ride between worlds, in both the quarters and mid-quarters, up and down. As always, everything with Odin is black. It is about the night, the natural domain of the womb, the un-manifested possibility of becoming. I believe this is exactly the realm of reason for seidr. It is the realm of invisible powers, unruly and turbulent, that is entered with the desire to shape one's own destiny.

Odin is compared to a volva which, like the noaids, uses a drum (*vétt*). Odin is referred to be both *argr* (negative connotation) and *vitki* (positive connotation), two words that in Sámi refer to practitioners of trolldom, by virtue of its connection to the large class of nature spirits close to humans, both benefic and malefic. The importance of the drum is found both in African cults as well as what is today largely referred to as "shamanism" in which the drum provides a pathway of sounds, a ladder of descent for the spirits and a way of ascent for the practitioner. We might say that the drum is the sound of the crossroad of the worlds. It should also be noted that the use of sex and orgasm was not uncommon in the practices of the noaids – a practice very similar to the descriptions of seidr.

In *Lokasenna* Odin is called out for his "unmanly" magic in reference to the practice of seidr, where Loke attributes *argr* and *vitki* to something perverse or shameful. This passage is interesting because this is the only time Odin is mentioned as indulging in perverse or unmanly activities. Worthy of note is also that this account in the *Lokasenna* is the only time *seidr* is linked with ergi, so clearly it is related to the modus operandi used by Odin in the performance of seidr.

Also, it is worth pointing out that there are only three accounts of seidr in the Edda that refer to seidr as being baneful and wicked; the other twenty accounts found in the sagas present the idea of seidr as a radical and respected art. Socially, there was not a conflict between being a man and practicing seidr, although it was unusual, so it must have been something about the methods Odin used that caused Loke's upset. It could merely have been Odin's behavior in the trance of seidr that made him behave unmanly, or improperly for the Allfather, or it can also simply be that Loke, irritated by Odin constantly taking an interest in men and walking amongst them, is calling Odin out as a pretender of sorts, calling his actions a disgrace.

Odin and his relationship with the art of seidr has been the subject of much speculation; one idea leaning towards queer theory has been presented by Britt Solli.[163] Her thoughts are interesting also in how she takes note of the importance of the transgressive element and connects this to Odin's gluttonous disposition when it comes to wisdom. On one hand it might be reasonable to assume a form of spiritual gluttony being present as revealed in the names of his wolves, Geri and Freki, names which refer to greed and gluttony, but which also are seen as metaphors for gandr and seidr, i.e. Odin having mastered the two principle arts of trolldom. At the same time we have the fact that Odin was originally associated with the night and the ice. He was a nocturnal deity said to bring storms and winds, a domain predominantly female. He is also accompanied by the ravens, Hugin (thought) and Munin (memory). Birds are yet again a female symbol and also a symbol for prophetic abilities, so it is also possible to read into this that Odin searched for some sort of completion or totality which he couldn't have without entering into the domain of women.

Ergi refers to something perverse or wicked and even if we cannot be absolutely sure of what was really contained in the term and what acts caused a person to become ergi, passive homosexuality has been frequently suggested. Passive homosexuality was condemned by law given the idea that taking the passive role in male/male coitus was to forfeit your natural place in the sex act.

That homosexuality caused the ergi of Odin is a popular theory, but also dressing up in women's clothing could have been the ergi Odin was accused of by Loke, which suggests that by dressing up like a woman he would also take on the submissive position in sexual intercourse. But it can also be that allowing possession and being taken in ecstasy were considered "unmanly", and that it was simply the ecstatic/hysteric ways of the art which caused Loke to patronize Odin, who had behaved in unmanly ways by practicing an art that was a part of the women's mysteries.

Seidr was an art that belonged to women. It was Freya, the Vanir, who brought this wisdom to the Æsir – in particular to Odin, who became a master of it. Names given to the practitioner, such as

---

163 2002.

Seidberendr, are suggested by for instance Solli to refer to "the art of the cunt", thus speaking clearly of a female connotation. Actually, it was considered quite complicated for a male to indulge in these arts as the accusation of ergi easily could arise. This term is frequently translated as homosexuality; strictly speaking it isn't homosexuality, but more to take the submissive part in a sexual relationship. In fact, laws were quite hard when it came to accusations of ergi, so hard that the offended one had the right to murder the offender as his reputation as a virile male was damaged. By being subject to this particular form of accusation, one could lose respect, work, wife and income.

It is a quite fascinating imagery that surfaces from this. On one hand Odin is a transgressor of limits by getting involved in a form of magic that is not only subject to a somewhat bad reputation, but he is also venturing into the field of women. This highly mercurial tendency is interesting to note conjoined with the fact that he goes to the volva for divination. This indicates that he in the end demonstrates obedience towards the traditional channels for wisdom and spiritual sustenance. This mercurial orientation is further revealed in how his poles are colored by his wife Frigg, a stable mother figure, and his lover and teacher Freya, the untamed desire, with sexuality itself being shared by both Frigg and Freya if we believe Loke's words in *Lokasenna*. He is, as such, an excellent representative for nocturnal Mercury, yet crowned by Saturn, Moon, and Jupiter, constantly longing for union with Venus.

The astrologer William Lilly commented in his magnum opus, *Christian Astrology*, that "Mercury is good with good and bad with bad," which by extension says that Mercury is female or male according to the planet he is conjoining. When Odin is hanging in Yggdrasil "to sacrifice himself to himself" he is simply becoming the fullness of what he in essence is – a paradox. Odin is definitively moving into a territory of tension when he is being taught the arts of seidr and night flight, how to connect with the spirits of the land and to use them for prophecy and malefica.

Heide[164] makes the following conclusion about the matter of seidr and ergi:

> All in all, despite the fact that seiðr-practitioners were almost systematically viewed as foreign and potentially holders of a strong disruptive force, these men and women were apparently not targeted by systematic public ire. The social situation of several of the most notable of

---

164 2006.

those seiðr-practitioners could even be quite high up. The only element that could maybe set them apart from other Norsemen is the repeated accusation of ergi against them. As we have seen, with the exception of Óðinn, no seiðr practitioner is ever described as being or suffering from ergi. This point I think, should prove once and for all that practitioners of seiðr were definitely not seen as obscene or perverted individuals whose seiðr-magic would make them misfits in the world they evolved in.

Both healing and cursing, performed by using seidr, are associated with Freya and Odin; many Edda poems speak of this, which might hint towards the use of the erotic in effectuating certain forms of seidr. For instance in *Fjolsvinnsmál* 49 Freya says whilst awaiting Odin's arrival:

Long I waited
on Lyfjaberg,[165]
day on day I waited for you;
now it has happened,
that I anticipated,
my lover, you have come to my halls.

"To my halls" can indicate that the object of desire actually died and came to the halls of death where he became Freya's lover, or it could simply mean coming under her spell, as it can suggest rituals of erotic nature. This confirms the ambiguity and complexity of Odin as a god of contradiction and tension. If we look more closely at the way he was inducted into the secrets of runes, namely by hanging in Yggdrasil for nine nights, we should take note that Yggdrasil is also a reference to the horse. In other words, for nine nights Odin was traveling along the world tree from root to top and this night ride gained him great wisdom. The secrets of the world opened up and he at last found peace with himself.

Solli[166] has suggested that this ritual of initiation was of a sexual nature, supported by Adam of Bremen's commentaries of the blót at Uppsala where the songs and enchantments sung were so rude and repulsive that he would not even repeat them in his historical annals. This can suggest that there was a sexual character to the initiation focusing on asphyxia and its sexual connotation as a stepping stone towards trance and insight. That a god of tension and transgression

---

165 *Lyfja* means trolldom/seidr, so it means the mountain of trolldom.
166 2002.

seeks the extreme for further transgression does seem to fit the picture quite well. Not only this, but it also hints subtly at a methodology for a male practitioner to symbolically "give himself to himself" – at least this is the silent message presented in the course of initiation. There has not been much academic research on this, but it is tempting to remember Maria de Naglowska and her activities in France in the 1930s. She performed Golden Masses in her ecclesiastical faction called *Fleche d'Or*, which centered on ceremonial hanging with the purpose of entering the realm of death in a state of awareness – at least from the perspective of Julius Evola. What is interesting in this detour from our subject is exactly how sexual stimulation culminating in orgasm led to asphyxia during the mass and thus was believed to open the gates of death, with the journeyman as a conscientious wanderer in the underworld. There is of course not much research to back up this theory, but considering the hanged men in the trees at the Odin blót at Uppsala as told by Adam of Bremen, one plausible explanation is that these men were had failed their initiation and thus were served as offerings.

Seidr and its Mystery

Interestingly, the apprentice in the arts of seidr was sometimes referred to as "the apprentice of the moon", as the keys to the art were thought to be hidden in the art of poetry and the abundance of soul. The Moon as the author of muses, song and poetry is naturally a powerful force for whomever wants to make use of galdr and seidr properly, as the incantations were highly poetic in style and recitation. It was a feature of unique persons said to possess a double soul. These people were, as Hultkrantz[167] notes, considered the Moon's Apprentice – yet again a female concept enters the stage.

The Moon, Gullveig, is the fullness itself in its phase of giving; the pale whiteness of her dark face is as Heid, because Gullveig (drink of gold), is the Jotun-wife of Loke, himself a Jotun, but brother by blood and troth with Odin, and the harbinger of sorrow is known as Angrboda.[168] Seeing the deep relationship these three forms have

---

167 In *Current Anthropology*, Vol 24 (1983), pp 459.

168 Angrboda is a highly complex figure, both in function and by ancestry. Most likely she was a Vanir raised by Jotun. Her triple manifestation as Angrboda-Gullveig-Heid focusing on the heart as the seat of resurrection is likewise a mystery of traditional depth that unfortunately falls outside our scope as such discussion would occupy too much space. She is the mother of Fenris, the wolf, Jormundgandr, and Hel, the

to Ragnarök as described in *Voluspá* it becomes quite evident what immense powers were hidden within the seidr. As the story goes, of Loke's children, three of them would bring on the end of the world. These were the serpent Jormundgandr, the wolf Fenrir, and Hel, the mistress of the underworld. The roles they play are evident in *Voluspá* where Loke and his children are instrumental in restoring the golden age. It is only natural in a greater cosmic scheme that Loke appears more and more malevolent and misunderstood as the world is facing its annihilation. We might see in Loke a similar role as we find in Judas Iskariotes, the one who takes the blame of the world on his shoulders to set in motion the undoing and rebirth of the world and in so doing fulfills his Fate.

It is also here in the form of Loke that the distinctions between good seidr and bad seidr enter, where we find the friction between Jotun and gods, often presented by the two realms of Utgard and Midgard. Loke attempts to bridge this gap through his oath with Odin, but still the oppositions fight themselves out in order to strive towards oneness. In the Edda we find one story that tells of how Thor went to Utgard together with Loke. A fight between Thor and the creatures of doom occurs while Loke fights his own Utgard-reflection. The land at the outside seems a form of mirror image of the orderly world where one's oppositions are confronted and brought into harmony with one's destiny. Utgard was a place of secrecy, darkness and trolldom, literally "the farm outside", speaking of the reputation trolldom had in society. By extension, those who were involved in malevolent seidr were somehow connected to this chaotic farm on the outside, inhabited by giants and trolls, the dark shades of all that is good and familiar in Midgard.

Silence was one important factor of the art and the other was enchantments, the galdr, and carving runes. Runes of hexing or healing could be carved and sung to facilitate visions or night flights, or to effectuate blessings or curses. Odin says of the power of the runes in *Hávamál*:

> The runes you must find and the meaningful letter,
> A very great letter
> A very powerful letter
> Which the mighty sage stained
> And the powerful gods made
> And the runemaster of the Æsir[169] carved out

---

owner of the realm of Death. We should just point out the importance of Death, the wolf and the snake in the arts of seidr.

169 Which was Dvalin.

Galdr followed certain rules as well. Sturlasson in his handbook for poets speaks about certain meters used for galdr, what he calls *ljódahattr* and *galdralag*. Stanzas 144-166 in *Hávamál* systematically demonstrate the type of meter used to make ones galdr effective.[170] The meters most commonly used to indicate effectiveness were consonant rhymes in a jambeau/troche interaction that would sound like verbal punches.

The act of uttering words of bane was considered most powerful. It was almost as though a word spoken in hate or love assumed the form of its intent upon its uttering. The verb used in these instances was *gala*, so galdr could refer to a song or chant in the sense of charm or spell. Interestingly, this word is also used to describe an insane person. We can assume that it referred to a special state of mind during the utterance of the word. This state of mind is often ascribed to poets and troubadours, those who function as the "memory" of the culture, the *skáldskapr* or the troubadours.

Bestiality and madness were occasionally associated with trolldom and those sorcerers who displayed these features were considered outlaws and were occasionally chased away from society or "sent to the halls of Ran".

Acts of malefic sorcery were largely ascribed to seidr. In Norway, during its Christianization, unsanctioned and unlawful practitioners of this art were, in the Law of Gulating, from 1250 subjected to exile and confiscation of property. Not only this, a few cases tell of how practitioners of seidr were abducted and tied to a rock in the ocean to wait for the tide to drown them. This was done in order to send them to the halls of Ran, and not to Valhalla, in the afterlife. Since Ran was thought to capture her victims, spending one's afterlife in her golden halls was considered a form of imprisonment, less glorious than the constant feast of food, drink and laughter in Valhalla. In terms of punitive sanctions of seidr it should also be mentioned that the sagas and the Eddas frequently in conflict in terms of the social status of the practitioners of seidr. This goes back to the idea of lawful and unlawful forms of seidr; it was particularly the act of "waking up trolls" that was considered problematic, not the prophetic element *per se*. The status of Hallstein in *Laxdaela saga*, who is both a chieftain and a practitioner of seidr, suggests that it was about how one used seidr, not about the practice itself.

It is said in *Ynglinga saga* that Odin was a master of this art. Whether awake or asleep, Odin's hugr was carrying out deeds for him. In *Lokasenna* Odin's knowledge of seidr and shapeshifting were originally an art marked by tension and taboo. The female emphasis

---

170 The important stanzas in *Hávámal* will be discussed in Part II, Runatál.

is further described in both sagas and the Edda in which we find accounts of *myrkaridur* and *kveldrida,* meaning "those who ride at night" connected to seidr. These nocturnal rides were usually said to be either the dead, or hags and witches flying around in the night, using different bodies to mask themselves. They could ride pigs or horses and were at times said to ride men in erotic nightmares, assuming the name mara and inducing night-mare, an important reference to the mare, the female horse. This being said, the word mara itself is double-sexed and can refer to both males and females.

It is here in this altered state the importance of fylgja enters. We have already commented several times that sorcerous acts could not be performed without the aid of the spirits of nature – and by the same measure it could not happen without fylgja. *Fylgjur* were considered the guardian spirits of men, connected to a specific person and/or families. The fylgja was a repository for advice and revelations of omen and, when showing itself, it was usually in the form of some animal or a woman. One can say that the fylgja was a man's mirror in the spiritual dimensions, but more importantly, this spiritual double was considered "the female follower".[171] This again emphasizes seidr being a female form of trolldom, which in the hands of males brings out tension on a spiritual, sexual and social level. What is interesting is that the fylgja was always considered female, and it is perhaps here we find the connection between seidr and how this domain could open up for men who chose to venture to the borders of organized society.

While Sleipnir, Odin's horse, has eight legs and is the compass itself of the world tree, the night-flying witches take the shape of a mare, the very symbol of ergi, which is unmanly in itself, but reflects the true nature of the fylgja and affirms seidr being the art of effectuating a mild or radical change of perception or location for various ends. This might even suggest that Odin could ride his horse, Sleipnir, "the slippery one", just as the wise women could ride or take the shape of mares to ride the night. Thus we can conclude that the riddle is quite simple. By moving out to the outskirts of society, the laws of society dim and the rules are to a certain degree annihilated by the practitioner. In the particular case of Odin, he is not only a man amidst men, but he is also a god who can take the shape of a horse. His mercurial orientation turns him into the perfect amalgam for contradiction and he can as such freely venture into whatever domain, divine or mundane. Since he is operating outside the social order, he naturally has no need for orienting himself to the laws pertaining to an orderly society.

---

171 Lecouteux, 2003: 45.

The Practice of Seidr

What we can say about the practice of seidr in terms of technology is that it was commonly performed by a woman who was termed volva. Volva or *Volve* derives from *volver*, carrying a staff, giving importance to how she was holding Yggdrasil in her hands; planting the staff in the ground would be similar to erecting holy ground, allowing the world tree to stretch its roots to the ground and enter into contact with Nidhöggr and the Norns. Seidr was best practiced at night and the songs and enchantments were crucial. The vardlokkur would inform the warding vaettir of what was happening and the purpose of the seidr. The songs and enchantments would instigate a trance state in the volva in which would be prophetic due to her access to the wisdom of the Norns and the communion and bond she had struck with the vaettir. In *Laxdaela saga* the vardlokkur is described as "fierce lore sung in the form of enchantments", which would mean that stories, or simply memory, were used to remind the vaettir and whatever spiritual forces were around about the lore they were a part of, the lore surging from Nidhöggr and the Norns. Both in *Laxdaela saga* and *Hrólfs saga kraka* the vardlokkur is also described as galdr when the purpose is healing. Galdr appears not to have been used to stimulate prophetic trance but was more a part of practical magic done through the art of seidr. Archaeologist Neil Price summarizes seidr as follows:[172]

> There were seiðr rituals for divination and clairvoyance; for seeking out the hidden, both in the secrets of the mind and in physical locations; for healing the sick; for bringing good luck; for controlling the weather; for calling game animals and fish. Importantly, it could also be used for the opposite of these things – to curse an individual or an enterprise; to blight the land and make it barren; to induce illness; to tell false futures and thus to set their recipients on a road to disaster; to injure, maim and kill, in domestic disputes and especially in battle.

This condensation is good, because it reflects the wide variety found in the twenty-two accounts in the Edda and in the sagas. We find that six of them are explicitly about prophecy and five are about cursing and hexing, while the remaining ones are for protection, healing and manipulations of various kinds, especially for weather and for love.

---

172 2013: 64.

An example of using seidr for the sake of love is described in *Heimskringla* where Snorre writes about Harald Hárfagre and his relationship with Snefrid, daughter of the noaid Suási. Snorre states that the Sámi noaid had used seidr to spellbind the king so he would abandon his kingdom and stay with Snefrid in constant lust and devotion. King Harald begot four children with Snefrid before he snapped out of the enchantment. An account like this shows similarities with Homer's account in the *Odyssey* when Homer meets Circe, also described as a prophetess or seeress as well as a poisoner and herbalist. The history of Circe would be well known to the educated and well-traveled Snorre, and it might be that he conceived of Circe as a meaningful representation of the volva for him, because in truth a comparative study between iconic witches like Circe and the volva would have been an interesting undertaking.

In several sagas, like *Eiríks saga rauda*, *Laxdaela*, *Hrólfs saga kraka* and others we find that seidr was performed on a *seidhiallr*, or a seidseat, which was elevated – given that *Laxdaela* mentions that people broke their neck after falling from the seat, we might be speaking of a significant elevation. Grimm in his *Germanic Mythology* has pointed out similarities with the elevated seat of the pythoness in Apollo's temple in Delphi, yet we also find seidr being performed at tables and on mounds in nature, called more precisely *utesitta* or sitting-out.

The use of galdr[173] or vardlokkur seems common, given that seidr is worked in states of trance and ecstasy. Additionally, in the account in *Eiríks saga Raude* we find that an assistant is singing the vardlokkur which is clearly used for the purpose of "attracting spirits". Of importance is to note that vard is another word for fylgja; it can also refer to any guardian spirit known as vaettir in Norway and *rådare* in Sweden. We find ward-tree, *gårdssvard*, the guardian of the farm, and many other similar connections making the vard not too different from the genii loci of Antiquity. In the same manner as seidr attracted vaettir and fylgja, so utesitta was said to wake up trolls, and then again, troll was not only a reference to the Jotun, but often a term used to describe any mysterious being. Utesitta could be done in nearly every place of power, and one of those was crossroads[174] where this form of utesitta was defined as *nigromanticus*, thus there

---

173 Which is also a poetic meter similar to *ljodhattr*, but with a seventh iambus added.

174 For more information see the work of Arnasons Tjódsogur (1899) that speaks of practices dating back to the 17th century found at: https://archive.org/stream/mythologyofallra21gray/mythologyofallra21gray_djvu.txt

was an element here of waking up the dead ones. This is only natural seeing how the heathen concept of the dead and nature-spirit was one where they were living on the other side or in mounds and how the dead could merge with these beings from the other side upon death. Considering that meddling with vaettir or one's ancestors were both considered necromancy, it makes sense that those possessing a Christian temperament would jumble it all together in an unlawful activity pointing towards the subterranean realm.

If we return for a moment to vardlokkur we find that Strömbäck points out that the word *verdir* or *vórdr* is both related to *genii tutelares* as well as to the soul. The necromantic element might be more complex than it appears, this because sometime after the 16th century seidr became an art ascribed to Freya and the Vanir. Through one of Freya's epitaphs, Vanadis, we find a connection to the Valkyries of Odin, considered disir, as were the Norns, which in turn makes them similar to fylgjur, but fylgjur of the world at large.

The connection between Freya and seidr is suggested in *Hervarar saga*. When speaking of disir and the disablót that was performed at Odin's temple in Uppsala, we see that is was Alfhildr, the daughter of King Alf in Alfheim who performed the sacrifice. Knowing that Alfheim was the homestead of Frey, it is likely that Alfhildr is another name for Freya serving as the guardian of the mysteries and the mother of seidr as preservator of this art amongst the Æsir.

The fact that seidr is often related to concepts such as *kveldrida*, myrkrida, túnrida and other forms of riding- or going-out in the shape of something else at night, transformed in the powers of night and sleep, is tied in with the concept of soul in Scandinavia. The soul was not considered singular, but a composition of several parts. The fylgja or vord is the faculty of the soul that is instrumental in enabling the shifting of the *ham* or flying out to other places, seen clearly in the accounts where Odin is changing ham/shape. A word like hamr can mean shape, but also body, and can also be a reference to pelt, fur or coat and covering. We might say that hamr is the visible part of the soul, the presence of spirit a man has, but when we look at words like *hamstolinn*,[175] literally that the hamr has been stolen or taken, we find a term used to refer to someone unfortunate, someone that attracts misfortune. If we see the relationship between fylgja as the guardian of the *ham*, hamingja, we might conclude that the idea of the ensouled human being was someone in whom the fylgja was strong because the hugr was equally strong, which makes the fylgja uncannily similar to the genius and daimon of Socrates and Plato.

---

175 Still in use in the countryside of central Norway in the state of Trøndelag in particular.

The Way of *Seidr*

Hugr on the other hand is probably the concept most similar to the Christian concept of the soul, as something particular, unique and singular, both the essence and upholder of life, deeply associated with what maintains the breath. Strömbäck[176] remarks that hugr in the Edda is equated with *vind*/breath and in some instances "trollwind", or a "wind of witchcraft" in an allegory of how the hugr of a *fjólkynning*, *seidrmadr* or *galdraman* was like a whirlwind. Hugr also is related to thought and mind in the form of will and desire as much as it is tied to memory. In this manner it is the hugr which, aided by fylgja, goes out in the hamr, changed or not, and in the hamferd can visit other locations or take over animals and both sense through them and also control them. This reveals an idea of the soul as something resting in the mind which when fueled by memory, will/desire would then be the faculty making seidr possible.

Concerning the ecstatic element of seidr it is interesting to look at the practice amongst the Sámi noaids as this form of "shamanism" they performed might be similar to seidr. This would also give substance to seidr being an art derived ultimately from Heidr, someone from the outskirts who was not allowed to become part of the Æsir group. This might suggest an origin amongst Nordic "outsiders", like noaids and all things "Finnish", which counted actual Finns, the Sámis and other nomadic groups. The ecstatic shamanism of the noaid was from around 1710 referred to as the Mass of Trolls or Mass of the Devil by clergy in the north of Norway. Pollan[177] gives a few examples of how this Mass of Trolls was conducted. In one account she describes how an old noaid inducts a new noaid into the mysteries. The people of the camp should gather and dress up in their finest clothes. The noaid will be dressed simply and with all clothes inside out. He will have his drum and also a gathering of tools like several types of horns, carefully selected stones, an axe and several items made from brass and iron, like knives, chains and scissors. He starts banging the drum and singing, what is called "to rune" in the account. At some point he will take the chain and the axe and kneel in front of the fire and at this point what he sings is repeated by the people gathered. At the fire is a cauldron with a mixture of cod liver oil, lye and parts of fish that he needs to drink for the purpose of singing better and so that his throat does not get worn out. After drinking the decoction and singing for some time he enters trance and starts knocking himself in the head with the axe. He removes his clothes and sits down in the burning coals, screaming and singing while the people throw coals all around him. He finishes

---

176 2000: 175.
177 2002: 35-40.

the decoction in the cauldron and then jumps towards the opening of the tent and here he falls down unconscious at the pole which marks the entrance to the "other side". At this point a woman will take his place and sing while he is gone, or is "diving down to the land below" as the noaid called it. While the noaid is gone the woman taking his place needs to follow him and bring him back, both by going out herself in some form of trance but also by constantly singing. When he returns from the other side, he starts immediately singing again in honor of the woman who brought him back. These songs are described as extremely sexual and lewd in content, while the song itself is described as distorted and ugly screaming, leading to the noaid giving himself to the woman so she can quench her sexual lust with him in whatever way she wants. This being done the noaid will share the knowledge and counsel he was given on the other side.

Another account is simpler, and it is here translated in its entirety:[178]

> When a Sami gets seriously ill, they believe that the soul has left his body and is resting in Jabmeaimo (the realm of death). The noaid is summoned together with all the neighbors so the healing ritual can be made (*noaidi-kionka*). Those gathered will then sing (*joik*) as an act of prayer to Jabmeakka (the goddess of the realm of death), asking she accept an offer so the sick one can leave her realm and return to the body. The noaid is *runing* about the same time as he is drinking distilled liquor and is very agitated. He kneels down with greet speed, takes fire in his hands, cuts his hands with a knife and bangs his drum. When he has done this for some time he falls down as if dead and remains senseless for about three quarters of an hour. During this time he is travelling to Jabmeaimo with his guiding spirit to bargain with Jabmeakka to give her an offering. In return she will release the sick one. And even if the rule in Jabmeaimo is that the soul is exchanged against an offer of such and such size, it also happens that the noaid, by speed and cunning, manages to snatch the soul out from her realm with him without any other dead ones noticing.
>
> All the time while the noaid lies down breathless, it is absolutely necessary that a woman is singing with great vigor without stopping, to remind him about his mission

---

178 Ibid. 83, 84.

in Jabmeaimo, but also to bring him back to life. For this essential singing she receives payment from the noaid.

When his guide (*passevare guolli*) has led the noaid unharmed from Jabmeaimo and back to his body, he will start to breath again and tell about what happened on his journey and what offer must be given to Jabmeakka before she'll give back the soul he bargained for.

Etymologically it might be that seidr derives both from *sid*, meaning thread, both the thread that was spun as well as the threads and knots making up the fisherman's net, or possibly *reid*, to ride, which in the context of seidr would mean to ride-out. These might all maintain parts of the mysterious origin and nature of seidr, as this art was taught to Odin by the Vanir Freya; the Vanir were most likely an elven race from the ocean, hence the reference to thread, as in the fisherman's net, might speak of an origin and even the way of riding-out. The occurrence of a thread as a means for finding one's way back to oneself is common, be it Ariadne in the dungeon of the minotaur or following the silver thread during bodiless travel, or the concept of ley-lines which are said to be energetic lines passing like threads across the globe. We should also note the frequent occurrence of threads and knots in folk magic and witchcraft in general, and how in the coastal regions of Scandinavia and the British isles we find the recurring idea that hanging up the fisherman's net close to the entrance door will ward against revenants, vampires and hostile spirits as they are always compelled to count the knots before venturing in.

What we can conclude from the few accounts we have about seidr is that there is clearly an element of ecstasy involved just as there also seems to be a flying-out from the body. Yet, this is not a given. Sometimes seidr appears simple, as in the carving of some runes with the proper enchantments, hence the accounts we have most likely describe the arsenal of tools at the disposal of the volva. The practice of the art would be connected to possessing a power – something about the hugr of a person makes seidr effective. Perhaps the very essence of seidr as a power possessed by the practitioner can be better understood in binding gandr and galdr to seidr.

Binding Seidr to Gandr and Galdr

The concept of galdr, commonly translated into a form of sorcerous enchantment, was integral to seidr. One form might be found in *Eiríks saga Raude*, but galdr would refer to a form of enchantment or song that would wake up powers.

When speaking about seidr, the idea of gandr should be taken into account. The term is still in use in the north of Norway and signifies a hex, curse or enchantment, commonly ascribed to the Finns in the sense of the noaids that live in the northern county of Norway called Finn-mark. In *Grimnismál* we find Odin being known under the name or heiti of Göndlir, gandmaker or gand possessor related to *gandreid*, which is in turn similar to *myrkrida*, *oskorsrea* and other outlandish bands of spirits that ride out in the wind. Hence, we see from the Reformation and onwards the reference to gandr being equated with demonic spirits. Gandr appears to define the active effect of something, and is often associated with wind, be it in the forms of wind itself, aerial spirits, or being "like the wind".

Heide is in his dissertation about seidr[179] goes through in methodological fashion every single occurrence of gandr in the Nordic sources and demonstrates that gandr can refer to the storm that makes a tree bend, the wolfishness of the wolf, and the ability of Jormundgandr to stir the ocean, hence seidr and gandr relied on a power possessed by the practitioner. Laura Strong in her article about gender and the supranormal in Scandinavia discuss at length Finnish terms like *väki* and *luonto* which were all descriptive words signifying an effect caused by something inherent in the practitioner or a given environment. These terms might be valuable to look at as gandr is relentlessly seen as something stemming from the "Finns".

The term väki on the other hand refers to any gathering or grouping of supernatural beings, or as she describes it; "Väki was the essence of an object or animated being, but *not* the power evoked by a magic ritual or incantation."[180]

Väki was a power that could be harvested; one account speaks of how a healer, in order to extract the väki of a rock, had to find one with natural cross-like fissures or markings and offer three silver coins in the fissure as enchantments were sung or recited. With an old knife, parts of the stone were then removed and placed in a bag, ensuring the sun would never shine upon this mineral again. Water väki had similar ways of harvesting its powers as had all things in

---

179 2006.
180 In Raudvere et. al. (eds), *More than Mythology*, 2002: 157

nature, hence väki might be similar to the concept of virtue and might be in terms of meaning identical with gandr, in which strength or weakness was dependent on the quality of the person's luonto, which might be equivalent to hugr.

Luonto is a word signifying "to create or make" and is used in reference to a person's ability to influence his or her surroundings. All people were believed to possess luonto, which could be either soft/weak or hard/strong and would also correspond to the strength of a person's hugr – the thickness of a person's "gathering of birds".

Noting that galdr was used for the purpose of cursing and hexing it might be that utesitta was more a part of this form of galdr, which would explain why seidr involving waking up trolls were shunned and subject to penalties as in this practice bonds with harmful vaettir were generated and used. Prophetic seidr was connected to the Norns and offered possibilities for rectifying a situation and bringing back good things.

What we are then left with is a far less uniform and static concept of seidr, gandr and galdr than what is commonly believed. Seidr is about generating bonds with nature and specific places through the use of trance and ecstasy aided by drum, enchantment and song.

As we've seen, seidr could be a "shamanic" trance in which going-out was aided by drum and galdr, as in the case of the noaids, the use of ecstasy with the aim of connecting to some disir, vaettir, vord or similar for the sake of prophecy, performing gandr or making magic, or to ride-out in a different shape for a variety of purposes. It could be a formal ceremony as in the case of the volva sitting herself on a seid-seat or it could be an informal sitting-out. The elements seem to be about possessing luonto and knowing how to attract proper powers and spirits that will enable the goal for the seidr.

Given the etymological relationship with spinning and thread, and that any work involving cords and knots known from the folk magic of the world in general was also a part of the seidr, I would also suggest that utesitta was used for the sake of connecting with vaettir or for the sake of the seidr itself. The rosary used by Catholics is one example of cord and knot magic accompanied by enchantments and prayers being used as a tool for focus and ascent. This is magic rooted in connection with spirits of the land, like geni loci and geni tutelary, which will then bring in a traditional element to the practice of seidr reminiscent of the Roman practice dedicated to working with lares, but also using ecstasy and trance as tools for communion.

From this we see that contemporary ideas involving summoning Æsir and Vanir in the seidr were really not a part of original seidr. As such they are a more modern development which might have been used from the 15th century onwards where we see especially Frigg, Freya, Frey, Thor, Tyr and Odin figuring excessively as aids for spellwork, trolldom and gandr. Yet I believe these forces were summoned more as witnesses to the work done with the spirits of the land, and as a way of connecting with practitioners and calling their attention to following in their footsteps and continuing the "custom" taught by Heid to Freya and then to Odin. Hence if any Æsir or Vanir should be addressed in this practice it would be those six (and perhaps Loke), yet we must be mindful that seidr works by calling the attention of vaettir, troll and disir, which in the last instance means that seidr is to work intimately with the Norns that guards the wisdom of Fate hidden in amongst the roots and in the wells of Yggdrasil.

It follows that the practice of seidr rests upon establishing a bond, a connection with Norns and vaettir simultaneously, which will then utilize both hugr and fylgja to make seidr functional from a gift or power resting within the practitioner itself. This would further indicate that seidr, being the art of Heidr, is a power better held by an amoral individual, strong in hugr and with a fierce connection with the spirits of Fate. From this essential definition a variety of tools can be used, be it the elevated seat in a house, or the sitting-out, preferably on a mound or grave where songs and chants are used to fortify the bonds. Offerings of ale and bread were most likely a part of generating these bonds as well as the typical vaettir offerings, which where objects from nature gathered into mounds at places of power to awaken the attention of the spirits with which one sought to commune. Establishing these bonds would invite in the possibility of direct work with these spirits, as it would open communion with the other side either in a trance state or in possession.

Chapter Nine

The Black Books of the North

The only real way of obtaining a Black Book is to be given it by the Devil himself in person, and it is only given by pledging your soul. In return you are given the magical power that makes the Black Book effective. – V. Espeland[181]

The Black Books in Scandinavia were considered *scienta occulta*, a hidden natural science, and were commonly possessed by priests, noblemen and other learned people. It is also possible to see a shift in the contents of the Black Books around the year 1670. Prior to 1670, the Black Books were more collections of what was known as "wise women's advice and remedies" and consisted of a great number of collections which speak of the use of herbs and enchantments for getting rid of illness and spiritually inflicted misfortune. After 1670, there was a distinct increase in the production of Black Books and the content takes a more diabolic turn. Here we find the arrival of "the Black Book priests" in Scandinavia, affirming the deep connection the black arts held with the clergy. The reason for this will be addressed shortly, but first it will be meaningful to look at the contents and structure of the Black Books.

The oldest Black Book discovered so far is the *Vinjeboka* which dates to 1480, a manuscript found hidden close to the altar in a church in Vinje, Norway.[182] The manuscript is quite typical in terms of what the contents of a Black Book would be. The language used, how the manuscript contained eleven hymns to the Virgin Mary, and how the book relied on the owner having a good understanding of Vulgate, would indicate that it was a book in possession and used by the priest of the church. Besides the hymns and prayers to Mary, the book is dominated by formulas for healing ailments amongst men and horses, formulas for stopping blood, spells to become more eloquent, to find thieves, for justice, and enchantments for making an enemy's sword dull and weak.

---

181 In Bang, 2005: 10.
182 Published in 1993 by Mary Rustad under the title *Vinjeboka*. Solum forlag: Norway.

The Danish folklorist Ferdinand Ohrt defined four main types of formulas found in the Black Books. These were summoning procedures that had a demanding ceremonial method using will and direct command towards a given effect. This could be simply:

> In the name of Saint Bartholomew
> I am binding your hands and legs
> I bind your blood and liver
> I bind your tongue
> And demand the fire of Jesus' burning heart
> to burn your body
> In Belzebub's name!

Another one, this from 1880[183] to cure irritations of the eye, especially those that would give a sensation of having sand on the retina, is as follows:

> Take the black on the blue
> Take the blue on the white
> Take the white on to an earthbound stone
> In the name of Thor, Odin and Frigga

You will read this over a spoon of water three times and pour it onto the eye.

Another format was the epic one, where mythological themes are used to tell a story that will quicken a given resonance and virtue leading to the desired result, like this one which is about cutting the evil eye and envy from 1750:[184]

> Jesus went across the wide bridge,
> here he met the annoying Envy.
> "Where are you going," Jesus said
> "I am going to the farm of that man," he said,
> "and obstruct all of what he has."
> "No!" said Jesus.
> "I will myself turn you around to
> "whoever sent you
> "and until the End of the World
> "in the Mountain Blue[185]
> "you shall stand

---

183 2005: 21.
184 Ibid, 104.
185 Mountain Blue is a common reference to the dwelling of trolls.

"until doomsday morning.
In the name of the Father, the son and the Holy Spirit x 3

Ritual formulas were about ritual actions that were done with or without words, such as this one to maintain an erection or at least remaining rigid for twenty-four hours from 1770:[186]

In silence take holy earth from the cemetery just before sunrise. Blend it well with quicksilver, also in silence and place it under your left arm, also in silence and you should be safe for the reminder of that day.

Lastly we have the secret formulas that would contain barbarous words, Kabbalistic words and words and signs from secret alphabets, like a "troll-letter" against toothache from 1780:[187]

You will write the following words on a piece of paper:
Àgerin-Nagerin ✠   2
Wagerin-Jagerin ✠   2
Spagerin-Sepia ✠   2   1

The paper is then cut into three pieces and at night one of them is wrapped around the tooth and then in the morning it is given to the hearth fire; this is done for three nights and the toothache should be gone.

This formula is interesting in how it is affirms the connections between teeth and fire and how teeth, especially the milk teeth, belong to the fire vaettir protecting the home through the hearth fire.

The *Vinjeboka* contains examples of all four modalities, yet it stands out as quite unique given how the majority of the Black Books were written between 1670 and 1887. It is in these years that other names for the Black Books enter, names such as "Cyprians" in Norway and Sweden which most likely seeped in from Denmark through Germany along with the Faustian legends that took hold of the population from the 17th century together in the early days of clerical fixation on witchcraft and Satan. The Black Books were frequently owned by the clergy, and with freemasonry established in Sweden in 1735, their ownership spread to also included aristocrats which meant a greater preservation of magical books at large, including the Black Books. It is important to note that the Black Books were manuscripts owned and preserved by the clergy, as Eytzinger

---

186 Bang. 2005: 186.
187 Ibid, 445.

writes: "The priest had access to many types of information. He was indeed a person on the threshold, between what was accepted and what was not, between the cultivated and the wild."[188] We find the vernacular "Black Book priest" used in Scandinavia from the 17th century for priests and clergy who were reputed to know more than just "Our Lord's Prayer". The prototype for the Black Book priest was the priest and poet Petter Dass (1647-1707). Dass himself contributed to the myths formed around him; it appears that he saw himself as a fusion of Simon Magus and the Exorcising Christ in how he presented himself as a priest who had, through the use of the Black Book, managed to dominate the Devil and all his minions in order to learn the dark arts for the purpose of exorcising the Devil from all holy works. One legend tells us that he was given the Black Book when he studied at the University of Wittenberg, and it was there where his first trick occurred. According to legend, the last of the priests ordained each year would be the one to receive the Black Book and be taken by the Devil. Dass however managed to distract the Devil and the Devil only managed to take his shadow. Returning to Norway, he actually used this legend to create a myth around him as the one who had dominated Satan, and he made no secret of how he used the Black Arts against the Devil himself given his extraordinary exorcising gifts. In this, Dass represented quite a problem, and it is truly odd that he was not persecuted for heresy in his use of exorcisms. This was because Lutheran reformators like Calvin and Zwingli considered exorcisms, and even benedictions, as enchantments, and thus they had no place in Lutheranism.[189] Luther himself was less hard on this given that Jesus himself was performing exorcisms, yet Dass was clearly making use of much Catholic material, and Catholicism was, in his time, banned from Scandinavia and considered heretic. Yet, Luther was open to a limited use of exorcism, like in baptism where unclean spirits were exorcised to give room to the Holy Spirit. In this image of Dass we clearly see how the iconic St. Cyprian is moving around in the shadow of the holy almost as an archetype of the Black Book priest.

In Finland, the Black Books were usually called "black bibles" and this is actually significant, because the diabolic Black Books grew out from the main magical grammar, the Bible. In the late 17th century, it was not uncommon to refer to the Black Book as a "Sixth Book of Moses", given how Moses was considered the archetypal magician that accepted the true God – still he entered Christian and magical mystical thought as a magus, not much different from St.

---

188 2013: 29.
189 Bang, 2005: 10.

Cyprian that became the Faustian and heretic reflex of Moses, the magus turned to the true faith that still served Satan. In regards to the clerical connotation of the Black Book, Stephen Flowers writes about the legendary Bishop Gottskalk Niklasson the Cruel who was Bishop of Hólar, Iceland from 1497 to 1520.[190] He was, according to the myths around him, in possession of at least two magical books, one called *Raudskinnir*, "red leather", and another called *Gráskinnir*, "gray leather". Upon the death of the Bishop, a scholar named Galdra Loptur tried to raise the Bishop from the dead to gain access to his knowledge but was not successful in his pursuit, rather, he got tormented by the ghost and legend says he went mad. *Raudskinnir* was said to be written in golden letters, whilst *Gráskinnir* was said to be a book of galdr or troll songs. I would also guess the good Bishop was in possession of a book we could easily call *Svartskinnir*, "black leather", given that bibles were often bound in black leather, or it could be that, in this case, his Latin bible was bound in gray leather. I am suggesting this because, at this time, there was actually a powerful book bound in red and written with letters of gold used by the Church, namely the Book of Exorcism. Clearly, the Holy Bible was the magical book of Catholicism, containing words and formulas in barbarous Latin that affected healing through unction, exorcisms and turning wine and bread into blood and flesh. The Black Books fused the magical use of the Bible together with the handbooks of wise ones, and contained formulas for healing that were often summoning in character, along with the traditions of Cyprians and Faustbooks from Germany, developing into the rich and varied selection of Scandinavian Black Books we have today. When going through the collection of nearly 150 manuscripts found at the University of Oslo, the contents of these Black Books ranges from small collections containing formulas for toothache or rheumatism, to several formulas for taking care of horses and cattle, to quite elaborate operations, all exorcising in nature, all ceremonial in form and diabolic in essence.

Amongst the more fascinating Black Books in the collection of the University of Oslo we find one tome, written on parchment, from 1850 carrying the title: *Cyprian's Art Book*, written at the academy of Wittenberg in the year 1345 and later found at the castle of Copenhagen in 1665 in a marble chest.[191]

This Black Book stands out as quite representative as it is both holy and diabolic, and shows inspiration both from continental

---

190 Galdrabók, 1989: 27-29.
191 This mss is listed as NM: 106: I in the trolldoms-archives at the University of Oslo.

grimoires, German Faustbooks and Nordic healing manuals. Besides the lengthy and wordy summoning of Cyprian that follows the format of the Catholic exorcism, amongst its content we find the selected formulas translated below:

1.2.6. So that Wolf and Bear do not harm cattle and sheep:
"Virgin Mary walking to her dwelling
"woke up her blessed Son, close now
"for the tooth of wolf and the tooth of bear
"and for raven and for troll-women
"and for all creatures fragile
"that they may not break
"and this in the name
"of God the Father, the Son and the Holy Spirit.
"Amen."
This prayer shall be read in the Easter-malt and salt
That has been resting in the chimney since Christmas Eve
You will charge the malt and salt with this prayer first time as you lay it out at spring.

1.9.4.4 How to cast bullets that takes blood:
Take a viper before the Mass of the Cross
and cut off its head and in the head place a pea.
Plant it in the ground, so the pea will grow.
When it is mature you will gather and guard it to make bullets.
You will cut them into small pieces and mix them with the lead.
These bullets will never miss their target, but
will hit what you want, except shooting for gain,
that is for you forbidden (with these bullets).

1.8.2.2 Sword letter:
Write the letter as described and carry it on you.
When you are in a fight and it will make you hard
for the enemies' sword and bullets, although
only for 12 hours counting from when the fight starts.

Sole, Mando, Ocsilutas, Saba,
Spesis, Sera, habat, Tabenta,
Doza, Sanas, Qvadua, Dimas,
Pulmorumsamma, Sei...es-esapas,
Crema, Alfuis, Debæmus, Seara
Sierasla volo, Seuruto – Babi,

Colubos, ie Nominematris,
Silius Spiritus amen.

When you carry this letter nothing evil will
manage to afflict harm upon you.

1.12.1. To be invisible:
Take the ear of a black male cat
and boil it in sweet milk and anoint your
face with this milk together with the blood of a bat,
or drink, or eat, the ear and you will
be invisible for nine hours.

4.3. 3 To Summon Evil Spirits to make a thief bring back what he stole:
"I summon you devils that for all times possess power and
"dominion
"to bind on earth what is bound in Heaven ✠ and Hell ✠
"I command you to go out and bind
"the man who has stolen from N.N. and I summon
"you devils by Heaven and Earth, do not allow this man who
"has stolen from N.N. to find peace or calm in heart or in mind
"until he brings back what he has stolen from N.N.
"In will and in dreaming thoughts,
"awake or walking or riding,
"he shall never find rest or joy
"on earth unless he brings back
"what he has stolen from N.N.

"I swear this to you evil spirits,
"by God the Father and the Holy Spirit,
"by the majesty of God and his Power, with the Son,
"the Moon and the stars.
"You shall never find rest
"neither in Hell nor on the rich earth
"until you bring this man who stole so and so from N.N.
"Abraham, Isaac, Jacob and the wise Solomon that
"once cast you out shall find you again.
"Oh! Holy Cross buried in the mountain of Calvary
"which Helena the Queen found first and in this
"venerated you, you holy ✠
"Lay down the thief in front of Him.
"Day and night on the road

"where our Lord Jesus went to his guiltless death and torture.
"Lead this thief from the east by our Lord Jesus ✠
"Lead this thief from the south by our Lord Jesus ✠
"Lead this thief from the west by our Lord Jesus ✠
"Lead this thief from the north by our Lord Jesus ✠

"I summon and command you by Angels
"and Patriarchs and prophets
"and Malbelle and all his rites,
"virgins and goddesses,
"by the mighty power of the Highest Majesty
"I demand that you lay this thief
"before me.
"I command you, Sun, Moon and Stars
"that you shall not shine over this man,
"but consume his waters and bring upon him
"plague and torture done by the most evil
"of the devils that resides in Hell.
"Asmodeum ✠ Bellial ✠
"Cordi ✠ Belelsebub ✠
"Norman ✠ Cweurg ✠
"Richel ✠ Diefael ✠
"Jachel ✠ Bufo ✠"

The Black Books of Scandinavia were, for the most part, composed in a time characterized by two forces, the Reformation and the increased attention given to witchcraft as a consequence of the Lutheran Inquisition, especially as it took place in the district of Trent and spread out like wildfire on the continent. What actually happened at the council of Trent in 1545 is that the Inquisition set out to try to re-convert the Lutherans by treating them as heretics and actively using torture. The St. Bartholomew's Day Massacre where the Huguenots fled France was rooted in a Catholic persecution of Protestants. In the wake of the Counter-Reformation, the focus was turned to witches which was largely a Protestant interest. The consequences in Scandinavia, and in particular Norway, were that Lutheranism and Catholicism existed in a mutual field despite how Lutheranism appeared both suddenly and unwanted.[192] In practice, the transition from Catholicism to Lutheranism was slow as the Church of Luther didn't change the clergy, but instead gave the Catholic priests new theological directives, which amongst the more significant was that the priests could now marry. This gave the clergy

---

192 Amundsen, 2010.

access to marriage as a tool for gaining political and social influence, given how the new theology was handed down to Catholic priests who, with some resistance, mostly acknowledged Lutheranism as the new form of Christendom. Thus, we find that theology could be understood and presented very differently from parish to parish. What we see is a larger number of Black Books composed between the arrival of Protestantism in 1537 until the ban on Catholicism was abolished in 1842.

Looking over the 263 witch trials in Norway, we find that the majority of the "witches" spoke of how they used prayers and how they prepared herbal remedies for cures. Rarely do we find those accused of witchcraft involved in pact-making with the Devil. This was more an accusation born from unrightfully – and effectively – using prayers in heretical ways, as much of what came up in the witch trials is found in the many Black Books we have access to today.

Stokker[193] comments that it was most likely the clergy themselves who imported much of the more diabolic material in the Black Books due to the Church Ordinance of 1627 making a university degree a prerequisite for Lutheran ordination. It was common to study at a Danish and German university, and Luther's University in Wittenberg was naturally a popular choice. Hence the more Faustian elements found in Black Books from 1730 to 1850 most likely came from the "Black Book priests" and are a testament to how heretic Catholicism, healing arts and folk magic were combined and understood as the black arts. In Lutheranism, healing was a complicated issue given how Lutheranism saw the use of prayers and herbs for effectuating healing in God's name or a saint's name as an attempt to influence God, thereby thwarting divine providence and making it a heresy. Hence, if such formulas worked it was because the Devil made them work, because surely God would never listen to the demands of mortal sinful men. The field between Lutheran theology and how Christendom was understood in practice would be pretty much understood as Stokker comments:[194]

> Apparently the almue found no conflict between their folk beliefs and the pious Christian faith that they observed with equal devotion. Rather than resisting official church doctrine, the almue simply supplemented it with traditional beliefs and practices that addressed the practical needs of their daily lives. In the wake of the sixteenth-century Reformation, the almue similarly supplemented the official

---

193 2007: 82.
194 Ibid, 89.

faith with customs – including pilgrimages to St. Olav's spring and lovekirker and Catholic healing prayers – that featured the direct appeal to the deity that Catholicism had encouraged but Lutheranism denied.

It is natural that it is in this field we find the nerve that made the Black Books possible as a continuation of herbariums and healing lore fused with diabolism, summoning rituals and natural and ceremonial magic of various forms. The importance of the clergy in relation to the Black Books has been demonstrated in the figure of Petter Dass. One of the earliest witch prosecutions in Norway is also interesting as here we see how the Catholic-Lutheran priests, now married, enter the realm of political and clerical intrigue.

In Norway one of the first and most important victims of the witch prosecutions was the wife of a priest in the city of Bergen, Anne Pedersdotter, who was burned in 1590. This case is curious in how it ties the practice of trolldom in with the clergy, and opens the way for the intensity of the witch persecutions in the west and north of Norway that took place from 1620 onwards.[195] Anne was the first person accused of the practice of trolldom which led to the demise of her husband's uncle, the bishop Gjeble Pedersson, thereby opening this position for her husband. Already at this time the political powers, represented by the mayor and the clergy, were in opposition. Anne Pedersdotter was absolved from the accusations; however, because of those allegations, she never forgave the people around her. So upon the death of her husband, the rumors again started to spread, and this time she became agitated with anger and with curses, leading to the reopening of the case against her. This time, due to all the cursing and wickedness she was thought to be spreading around her, she was convicted for active use of trolldom, which included the murder of six people who died from sudden and agonizing illness. In the verdict she was also accused of having killed a pear-tree, which perhaps was seen as a form of malefica aimed towards driving away the ward-vaettir of the land; it is interesting to note that this heathen belief was subject to penalties in a Christian court. Also, by this time the sabbatic meetings of witches in "troll-mountains" were vivid in the imaginations of the people, and so the accusations against her included that she had been seen flying to the witch mountain outside Bergen, Lyderhorn. Some had even witnessed, whilst hiding in the bushes, her participation in demonic gatherings of lewd and orgiastic rituals.

This account from the early days of the persecution of witches commences with the increase in Black Books, by far most of them

---

195 Hagen, 2015.

owned by the clergy and several of them found hidden away in churches. It testifies to the attitude of the people that a dual observation was practiced by many priests and it was in this dual observation that it was possible to secure this rich legacy of folk magic in Scandinavia.

Part II

RÚNATAL

Chapter Ten

Origin of the Runes

Due attention to the runes was given for the first time in writing by Olaus Magnus, who, in his 1554 work about the Nordic people, published a runic *futhark*, or alphabet. This *gotthicum alphabetum* was published five years earlier in the work *Introduction to the Chaldean Language* by Theseus Ambrosius (1469-1540), an Italian friend of Olaus Magnus. In this futhark, we see that there are 19 runes, revealing that the runes replicated by Magnus were the runes used for calendar markings from late medieval times. In addition to the runes from the younger futhark we find three extra runes: *àrlaug*, *tvímadr* and *belgthorn*.

On this and the following page we find the 1554 futhark of Olaus Magnus (Fig B:1), the runic calendars (Fig. B:2), the traditional Younger futhark (Fig. B:3) and then the Elder futhark (Fig. B:4).

Fig. B.1

230 TROLLRÚN

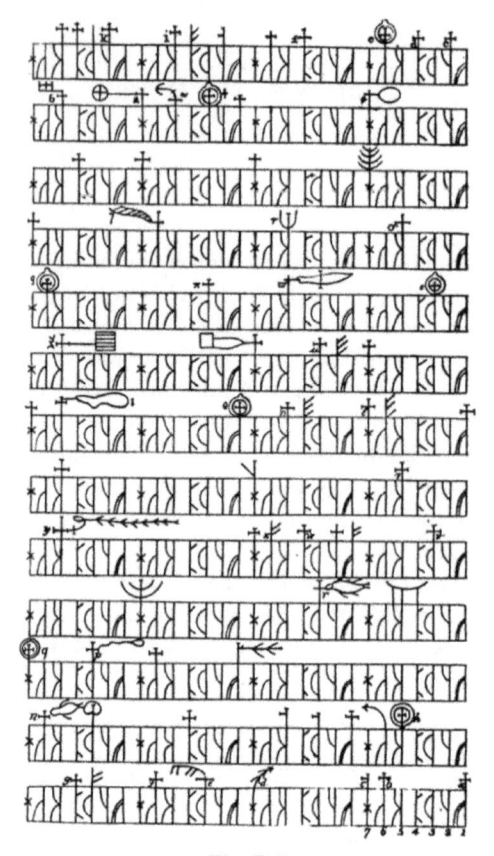

Fig. B.2

Fig. B.3

Fig. B.4

The nineteen runes presented by Magnus testify to developments of the runes within a medieval indigenous tradition, a fusion of a Latinized adapted typography combined with what was at the time known as a *helstungna* or Swedish runic futhark. At the same time that Olaus Magnus published his treatise about the Nordic people, the first Lutheran Archbishop in Sweden, Laurentius Petri (1499-1573), and his brother Olaus, were occupied with studying the runes. In their findings they describe each rune in some detail, discuss their pronunciation and also talk about the tree calendar runes. Unfortunately, this work was never published, but was thankfully discovered by Johannes Bureus (1568-1652), who, after a six-year study of their work, published his own rune tablet and runic interpretations in 1599. This work caught the attention of the Danish physician Ole Worm (1588-1654) who held the view that the Catholic Church had deliberately tried to undermine the magic of the runes. He published a significant work about the mystical idea of the runes in 1626, which was badly timed, as heresy was widespread and heretics and their books easily ended up on the flames of a separated, confused and bigoted Church. With Magnus Celsius' attempt at runic interpretations in 1674, we find the last written work about runes until they resurface again 200 years later with the works of Norwegian anthropologist Sophus Bugge (1833-1907), who established runology as an academic science through his discourse of the Elder futhark.

A clearly defined and undisputed theory of the origin of the runes has yet to be made. The Elder futhark appears to have found the form we know today in the 1st century in the southern parts of Scandinavia. This suggests that the runes predate this time period in some form. Theories proposing Etruscan, Greek and Latin influences on the origin of runes[196] are all still in vogue and suggest more of an enigma. Due to the Roman Empire slowly cracking and shattering, Etruscans, Greek and Latin speakers were all influential in the age of change, trade and migration, all in harmony with the wide geographical distribution of runic inscriptions. Therefore, looking for a specific origin of the runes might be futile. Instead of searching for lost pieces of the puzzle of origin, perhaps we should, rather, be simply content with defining the time and place that runes were developed in southern Scandinavia in the 1st century, and study runes from a different angle, namely, their use and meaning.

---

[196] See the studies by Derolez 1998, Moltke 1985, Simek 2007, Düvel 2011, to mention a few, to see how disparate and ambiguous runology is.

With Düwel[197] we can affirm what we know with certainty about the origin of the runes is as follows:
The runes were not solely a Germanic creation; they were subject to outside influences.
Some Mediterranean alphabets influenced the runes.
We are tied to archaeological dating of runic inscriptions, both in terms of locality and time, in making our suggestions.

The Latin theory was proposed by the Danish runologist Ludvig Wimmer in the 1870s, and suggested that the Latin alphabet was at least the inspiration and model for the emergence of the runes. Given the wide circulation of the Latin alphabet in the 1st century and the similarities between letters like f, r, b and m, this is a noteworthy theory that possibly explains a part of the origin of the runes.

The Greek theory, proposed by the Norwegian runologist Sophus Bugge in the early 1900s, suggested that it was the Greek alphabet that inspired the first emergence of runes. As with the Latin theory, the Goths living around the Black Sea and those living in the southern parts of Scandinavia were understood to be key spreaders of runes. This theory sets the development of runes to around the 3rd century, but since the 1st century appears far more likely as the century of runic development, the Greek origin theory has become weaker over time.

The Etruscan theory was proposed by the Norwegian historian Carl Mastrander in the 1990s and suggested a connection with the Etruscan alphabet through the Germanic part of the Pyrenees and the Alps, a theory that finds agreement with the considerations of Tacitus in Germania who spoke of the tribe of Cimbru that tried to enter Danish territory from the Danube and through the Alps in the 1st century.

I would say there is merit to all of these theories and if, in our contemplation, we add the indigenous and pragmatic uses of the runes, as we see in the example of the construction of runic calendars,[198] we are left with very little we can say with absolute certainty save for what has been stated so far in this chapter.

In addition to these three main theories of origin, it is important to return to the legacies of Bureus and Worm which were forgotten for nearly 300 years. The work of Bureus and Worm was developed at a time best represented by the impact of Christian Rosencreutz upon the continent with the tracts *Fama Fraternitatis* in 1614 and the *Chymical Wedding of Christian Rosencreutz* in 1616. This influence

---

197 In *Runes, Magic and Religion* 2004.

198 For an in-depth study of runic calendars I recommend the monograph written by Carla Cucina from 2011.

added a dimension of wonder and marvel to the imaginations of the Scandinavian intellectuals and spiritualists who aimed towards unveiling, understanding and integrating the great traditional themes that were found at all the corners of creation. A presentation of Bureus' *"runosophie"* will be given in the last chapter.

The more esoteric side of the runes that was concerned with magic saw a great resurgence in Germany and in Scandinavia through the Teutonic theosophical theories of Sigurd Agrell (1881-1936). Agrell developed the theory that the runic cipher was revealed in esoteric truth by placing the Fé rune last, giving an Uthark. Personally, I find the theory a bit of a stretch, but at the same time it demonstrates the flexibility of the runes and also a modality of "picking up the runes" to own personalized secrets from within the cosmic fabric. In 1952, the studies of the Dane Anders Bæksted (1906-1968) systematically dismantled and discarded any magical use of the runes, and in particular, Agrell's theory. Agrell suffered a severe blow from this which shook not only his theory, but runic studies in general.

Bæksted's conclusions are, however, too radical because of how he dismisses historical accounts of divinatory uses of runes. The Edda tells us of many instances where rune carving was unmistakably a magical activity, and we must not forget that when Odin "took up the runes", he became cunning of secrets aimed toward manipulating the world. Clearly, a magical content is found in the runes. Not only this, but as any linguist should recognize and know, the letters and numbers of a language find play between each other in relationship to their meaning and states and objects, as, for instance, is quite evident in the Greek alphabet.[199] Bæksted was one of those academic minds that fiercely opposed any irrational element in his paradigm of traditional materialism, a true child of conservative modernism, discarding the significance of the enchanted worldview that certainly influenced the understanding of the runes in the Middle Ages and the Renaissance.

If we turn towards archaeology, we have one finding and its associated theory that is currently in discussion which appears more inclusive than many other theories. This archaeological finding is known as the Negau A helmet,[200] and suggests a use of runes related to a group of people or a type of practitioner by the name of erilaʀ.[201] In the 1st century, we know there was a group of people known as the Heruli who opposed the Danes, who are suggested to have been

---

199 Pennick, 2015.
200 Found in present day Slovenia in 1812.
201 In *Runes, Magic and Religion* edited by McKinnel et al. 2004: 13.

a "cultic band of warriors". If the Heruli were a social cluster with both a military and a religious or magical elite, it would suggest uses for the runes both as language and for magic. Not only this, but this archaeological find would affirm the Etruscan theory, at least in part, and also the Latin theory. This finding, combined with what we know about the inhabitants in the southern part of Scandinavia (defined at this time as the Danish islands, the northern and Eastern parts of present-day Germany and the southern parts of Norway and Sweden and Estonia), indicates that the runes might have been developed by a sophisticated tribal nation with a connection to the Goths. It might even be that the Heruli and Cimbru were actually variants of the same Gothic family bound by blood, ancestry or kinship in some form or combination.

Pliny the Elder, in speaking about the Heruli, states that they originally came from Thule (Scandinavia, usually understood as Iceland or Norway) and migrated to the lands around Danube and the Black Sea side-by-side with the Goths, suggesting an intimate bond between these two tribal nations. The reputation of the Heruli was one of avarice and violence, and, in general, it was believed that they offered up their military services to the highest bidder. Hence, they were hired as special troops in the Roman Army. According to the historian Procopius, they also had a reputation for sacking and plundering, especially around the district known today as Ukraine. The modern historian Roland Steinacher (2010) proposes that the Herulians experienced a definitive blow by the Lombards around the year 500 which led to a wide geographical spread of the Heruli as far away as Egypt, whilst the greatest concentration went back to Thule, in particular the Danish islands, the Gothic districts in Norway and Sweden, and the Balkans. Given the affectionate bond between Scandinavia and the Balkans since before the Viking Age and up to our current age, it indicates that this theory of origin might be the most plausible one, as it would simply explain the many theories of origin, the wide geographical spread of runes, and also produce an origin for the Odinic *ulfhednar* and berserker that later was known as *männerbunde* in Germania.[202]

The Heruli were, like the Goths, a sophisticated nation, focused on grooming a military elite that was supported by a well-organized culture. Given the connection they held with the Roman army as a phalanx or troop in their own right, some resonance might have been found between themselves and the Mithraic cult, something suggestive of the solar design carried on the shields of the *Heruli senioris*. If a common solar factor is found to connect the two, we are

---

202 See Kershaw, 2000.

easily led to the recent research of Swedish archaeologist Anders Andrén,[203] who proposes that the same culture that developed the runes were a solar military cult, as discussed in the chapter on Nordic cosmology. These theories are interesting in their own right, and they may help to shed more light on why Odin was always presented as the Æsir who first gained insight into the use and mysteries of the runes, or it might suggest the presence of a sorcerous magical elite that used the runes both as language of communication as well as a system of magic.

The number of runic inscriptions we have using the Elder futhark ranges to around 200 findings in addition to some 160 bracteate designs. When the Younger futhark rose in use between 700 and 800 CE, the spread of runic inscriptions took on vast proportions both in numbers and in area, probably due to the commencement of the Viking Age. In Sweden alone, we find as many as 3600 runic inscriptions carved in stone, the majority of them dating to the 11th century when survival of runic inscriptions is much more numerous, partly explained by the use of the more durable material of stone instead of the wood which had been more common for inscriptions using the Elder futhark.

The cutback from 24 runes in the Elder futhark to 16 in the Younger went through a process of reduction as testified by the occurrence of what is known as long branch runes and short twig runes which used runes from both futharks, sometimes called Danish runes. This transition led some to see the runes spoken of in the *Hávamál*, the Younger futhark, as the magical runes Odin gained knowledge of in the nine nights he hung in the tree; however, this remains speculation. It is equally easy to see a magical meaning in the Elder futhark with its 24 runes parted into three *aettir* of 8 runes each, and to see each aettir speaking about the three levels of forces that constitute the human journey: the first aettir speaks of the cosmic principles at play in the world, the second aettir speaks of the human journey as tied closely to the Norns, and the third aettir addresses social and global forces. Such interpretation also justifies the focus on the number 3 recurring in the Edda, suggestive of the common oracular use of the runes where one picks 3 runes 3 times to obtain an oracle, a 3 x 3 with 9 in total, the number holding the most magical potency in the Scandinavian tradition.

Why the number 9 was regarded with such reverence is still partly veiled in mystery and open for interpretation, but if we follow the triple modality given to us by the Elder futhark, we can then see that it is rooted in the Norns. Urd (past), Verdande (present) and

---

203 2014.

Skuld (future) have their say about the three levels of human activity as related to the human journey itself, but are also related to the forces ruling the person and the outcome of their actions. If you look at this theory in light of the Old Norse and Icelandic rune-poems we have, a sensibility for a theme like this reveals itself as will be made clear when the runes are discussed rune by rune in Chapter Thirteen.

Tacitus' *Germania* from the 1st century CE presents us with the oldest account of the runes and how they were used. In the 10th chapter of *Germania* he writes that a branch was cut into pieces and each piece marked. These pieces were then thrown over a cloth and interpreted, followed by prayers and taking omens from surrounding nature. This process was possibly repeated three times. This short account in full reads as follows[204]:

> To the use of lots and auguries, they are addicted beyond all other nations. Their method of divining by lots is exceedingly simple. From a tree which bears fruit they cut a twig and divide it into two small pieces. These they distinguish by so many several marks, and throw them at random and without order upon a white garment. Then the Priest of the community, if for the public the lots are consulted, or the father of a family about a private concern, after he has solemnly invoked the Gods, with eyes raised up to heaven, takes up every piece thrice, and having done thus forms a judgment according to the marks before made. If the chances have proved forbidding, they are no more consulted upon the same affair during the same day: even when they are inviting, yet, for confirmation, the faith of auguries too is tried. Yea, here also is the known practice of divining events from the voices and flight of birds. But to this nation it is peculiar, to learn presages and admonitions divine from horses also. These are nourished by the State in the same sacred woods and groves, all milk-white and employed in no earthly labour. These yoked in the holy chariot, are accompanied by the Priest and the King, or the Chief of the Community, who both carefully observed his actions and neighing. Nor in any sort of augury is more faith and assurance reposed, not by the populace only, but even by the nobles, even by the Priests. These account themselves the ministers of the Gods, and

---

204 https://www.romansonline.com/Src_Frame.asp?DocID=Ger_Bk01_10

the horses privy to his will. They have likewise another method of divination, whence to learn the issue of great and mighty wars. From the nation with whom they are at war they contrive, it avails not how, to gain a captive: him they engage in combat with one selected from amongst themselves, each armed after the manner of his country, and according as the victory falls to this or to the other, gather a presage of the whole.

In the late 5th century, we find an account from the Bishop of Poitiers who, in a letter to a friend, describes the runes as a written language used in the same way as Greek, Latin, Hebrew or Persian, testifying to the runes used as a common writing system. 300 years later, we find the Abbot of Fulda, Hrabanus Maurus, stating in a small tract that the runes were used to give account for the poetry, magic and predictions made by the Northmen, suggesting their use both as a written language for communication as well as having a magical function.[205]

From this, we conclude that the runes should be viewed as a magical language, much like Hebrew, Latin, Persian and Greek hold clear magical implications due to their communicative virtue and the various sounds they were replicating.

---

205 Enoksen, 1998.

Chapter Eleven

Magical Runes and Runic Magic

The word "runes" is instantly associated with the Nordic letters, the futhark, or alphabet, but this is a limited idea of what a rune is. A rune refers to a secret, an enchantment, a whisper, something mysterious, something magical which is not really limited to the letters in the futhark but spans much wider than that. A Runebook is, in many folk songs, used as a kenning for a Black Book, as a magical prayer would at times be called "a runic prayer" in reference to its secret and magical potency.[206]

Two recipes reproduced by Lorenzen[207] are fascinating enough to replicate here in terms of the use of the word runes in relation to magic.

S1

To gain insight into secrets and hidden dealings, turn yellow cheese (a jarlsberg type of cheese) into powder and carry this under your left armpit whilst Mass is read. Then place this between her breasts and you will use the following runes:

or these (i.e., runes): Elam, Eloy, Galoy

When she sleeps, and upon questioning her, she will answer in a loud voice all she had done and all that she knows.

S2/S3

So that you will not suffer any form of accident anywhere, write the following runes with your own blood on a Thursday morning between 11 and 12 o'clock and tie to your chest the secret and when this is carried no accident will harm you and your enemy will flee from you:

---

206 Reichborn-Kjennerud, 1927: 10.
207 1872: 49, 50.

In the Edda, there is a particular part of the *Hávamál* called *Rúnatal* which speaks of the varieties of Northern magic, and in the *Sigerdrifamál* there are thirteen stanzas in which runic magic is spoken of. *Rúnatal* will be detailed in Chapter Thirteen, so in this chapter the focus will be on the stanzas in the *Sigerdrifamál*.

As always, Nordic texts are short, to the point and laconic, hence, we are presented with the core of functionality with little written detail about the process. In stanzas 6-19 in the *Sigerdrifamál*, we find the following considerations given by the volva Sigerdriva, better known as one of Odin's Valkyries, Brynhild, the "victorious one", who is passing secrets taught to her by Odin on to Sigurd Fávnesbane. The key stanzas read as follows:

6.
Sigrúnar skaltu kunna,
ef þú vilt sigr hafa,
ok rísta á hjalti hjörs,
sumar á véttrimum,
sumar á valböstum,
ok nefna tysvar Tý.

6.
Winning-runes learn,
if thou longest to win,
and the runes on thy sword-hilt write;
some on the furrow, and some on the flat,
and twice shalt thou call on Tyr.

7.
Ölrúnar skaltu kunna,
ef þú vill annars kvæn
véli-t þik í tryggð, ef þú trúir;
á horni skal þær rísta
ok á handar baki
ok merkja á nagli Nauð.

7.
Ale-runes learn, that with lies the wife
of another betray not thy trust;
on the horn thou shalt write, and the backs of thy hands,
and Need shalt mark on thy nails.
Thou shalt bless the draught, and danger escape,
and cast a leek in the cup;
for so I know thou never shalt see
thy mead with evil mixed.

Magical Runes and Runic Magic

8.
Full skal signa
ok við fári sjá
ok verpa lauki í lög;
þá ek þat veit,
at þér verðr aldri
meinblandinn mjöðr.

8.
Birth-runes learn, if help thou wilt lend,
the babe from the mother to bring;
on thy palms shalt write them, and round thy joints,
and ask the fates to aid.

9.
Bjargrúnar skaltu kunna,
ef þú bjarga vilt
ok leysa kind frá konum;
á lófum þær skal rísta
ok of liðu spenna
ok biðja þá dísir duga.

9.
Sea-runes learn, if well thou wouldst shelter
the sail-steeds out on the sea;
on the stem shalt thou write, and the steering blade,
and burn them into the oars;
though high be the breakers, and black the waves,
thou shalt safe the harbor seek.

10.
Brimrúnar skaltu rísta,
ef þú vilt borgit hafa
á sundi seglmörum;
á stafni skal rísta
ok á stjórnarblaði
ok leggja eld í ár,
er-a svá brattr breki
né svá bláar unnir,
þó kemstu heill af hafi.

10.
Runes that save learn,
if a healer wouldst be,
and cure for wounds wouldst work;
on the bark shalt thou write, and on the leg of the birch
when its boughs to the eastward bend.

11.
Limrúnar skaltu kunna,
af þú vilt læknir vera,
ok kunna sár at sjá;
á berki skal þær rísta
ok á baðmi viðar,
þeim er lúta austr limar.

11.
Speech-runes learn, that none may seek
to answer harm with hate;
well he winds and weaves them all,
and sets them side by side,
at the judgment-place, when justice there
the folk shall fairly win.

12.
Málrúnar skaltu kunna,
ef þú vilt, at manngi þér
heiftum gjaldi harm:
þær of vindr,
þær of vefr,
þær of setr allar saman
á því þingi,
er þjóðir skulu
í fulla dóma fara.

13.
*Hug*rúnar skaltu kunna,
ef þú vilt hverjum vera
geðsvinnari guma;
þær of réð,
þær of reist,
þær of hugði Hroftr
af þeim legi,
er lekit hafði
ór hausi Heiðdraupnis
ok ór horni Hoddrofnis.

14.
Á bjargi stóð
með Brimis eggjar,
hafði sér á höfði hjalm;
þá mælti Mímis höfuð
fróðligt it fyrsta orð
ok sagði sanna stafi.

15.
Á skildi kvað ristnar,
þeim er stendr fyr
skínandi goði,
á eyra Árvakrs
ok á Alsvinns hófi,
á því hvéli, er snýsk
undir reið Hrungnis,
á Sleipnis tönnum
ok á sleða fjötrum.

12.
Thought-runes learn, if all shall think
thou art keenest minded of men.

13.
Hropt arranged them, and them he wrote,
and them in thought he made,
out of the draught that down had dropped
from the head of Heithdraupnir,
and the horn of Hoddrofnir.

14.
On the mountain he stood with Brimir's sword,
on his head the helm he bore;
then first the head of Mimir spoke forth,
and words of truth it told.

15.
He bade write on the shield before the shining goddess,
on Arvak's ear, and on Alsvith's hoof,
on the wheel of the cart of Hrungnir's killer,
on Sleipnir's teeth, and the straps of the sledge.

16.
Á bjarnar hrammi
ok á Braga tungu,
á ulfs klóum
ok á arnar nefi,
á blóðgum vængjum
ok á brúar sporði,
á lausnar lófa
ok á líknar spori.

17.
Á gleri ok á gulli
ok á gumna heillum,
í víni ok í virtri
ok vilisessi,
á Gugnis oddi
ok á Grana brjósti,
á nornar nagli
ok á nefi uglu.

18.
Allar váru af skafnar,
þær er váru á ristnar,
ok hverfðar við inn helga mjöð
ok sendar á víða vega;
þær ro með ásum,
þær ro með alfum,
sumar með vísum vönum
sumar hafa mennskir menn.

19.
Þat eru bókrúnar,
þat eru bjargrúnar
ok allar ölrúnar
ok mætar meginrúnar,
hveim er þær kná óvilltar
ok óspilltar
sér at heillum hafa;
njóttu, ef þú namst,
unz rjúfask regin.

16.
On the paws of the bear, and on
Bragi's tongue,
on the wolf's claws bared,
and the eagle's beak,
on bloody wings, and bridge's end,
on freeing hands and helping
footprints.

17.
On glass and on gold, and on goodly
charms,
in wine and in beer, and on well-loved
seats,
on Gungnir's point, and on Grani's
breast,
on the nails of Norns, and the night-
owl's beak.

18.
Shaved off were the runes that of old
were written,
and mixed with the holy mead,
and sent on ways so wide;
so the gods had them, so the elves got
them,
and some for the Wanes so wise,
and some for mortal men.

19.
Healing-runes are there, mountain
runes there are
and all the runes of ale,
and the magic runes of might;
who knows them rightly and reads
them true,
has them himself to help;
ever they aid,
till the gods are gone.

Sigerdrifamál speaks of runic magic with a focus on two particular runes, Tyr and Naud. He informs us that several runes exist that can be used for magic, and he gives us the following list of magical runes:

Sigrúnar, victory runes
Ölrúnar, ale-runes used both for protection and for good luck
Biargrúnar, runes that save or rescue, particularly related to childbirth
Brimrúnar, sea runes for protection at sea
Limrúnar, limb runes for healing wounds and damage of the body
Málrunar, speech runes for oratory qualities, poetry and convincing verbal arguments
Hugrúnar, thought runes aimed towards gaining wisdom

In addition, we have *meginrúnar*, runes that strengthen, and *bótrúnar*, runes that heal (and which might also be used for casting erotic spells), giving us 9 runic secrets in total. In stanza 18, we also find one method of how these runes were used and activated. The five stanzas prior to this speak both directly and in code about the materia magica considered when working runic charms, whilst the preferred material for rune carving is clearly listed in the stanzas.

Basically, the method is to sanctify ale, and then carve the desired runes on an object as vaettir, Æsir, elves or Vanir are summoned to witness the act and bring about its effect.

The sanctification of the ale is most likely tied to the mysteries of Mimir. The various wells of wisdom represented by the ale are encoded in the magic word *alu*, which has been translated into many things, frequently as a word that signifies magical protection, or a seal, or an oath of some form, perhaps like "amen" in the way that it seals an intent. Next, the runes are marked and then scraped off into the ale and drunk.

There is no information about what kind of material was used, nor a concordance, nor is a list of signatures and their use given, but, considering the importance of greenwood and trees, it is logical to assume that the runes were marked either with saliva or blood, some form of natural ink, be it from rowan, berries or colorful juices of specific trees, and then scraped off with a knife and ingested.

In terms of *sigrúnar*, we find as late as the 12th century swords inscribed with a double Tyr rune at the shaft in accordance with the instructions in the *Sigerdrifamál*. We also find the Naud rune used in similar ways, as a finding from the 11th century from Rogaland, Norway shows it as part of a SATOR square.

Therefore, we can conclude that the mere carving of runes, in particular Tyr and Naud, carried magical virtue in its own right and would then perhaps be seen as the beginning and end of a runic sequence encoded in the runic spell itself, spelling out a given direction that is then sealed with the power of need.

Any of these runes could be carved onto something physical: for example, *limrúnar* could be carved on the nails, *brimrúnar* on the ship and *biargrúnar* on the bed where a birth was taking place as they could all be carved, scraped off and ingested in a glass of sanctified ale.

This would reveal to us a direct and pragmatic use of runes ranging from a simple Tyr rune to a complex runic formula. The more complex runic formulae would be either in the shape of *lönnrunes* (secret runes), or in the form of a poetic enchantment commonly written in the poetic meter known as *ljóðaháttr*.

The rune Tyr symbolizes the Æsir Tyr, who represents courage, honor and justice and would, in this way, suggest that a certain approach or temperament is necessary for the magic of the runes to play out. Tyr himself is relentlessly tied to wolves, and the maintenance of order and self-sacrifice. First, he sacrificed his hand to Fenris, and later, he sacrificed his life to Garm in Ragnarök. He also stands in a peculiar relationship with Thor in their shared hunt for the vessel that was big enough to brew ale for all Æsir. Also, in terms of genealogy, we find a discrepancy in the *Hymiskvida*, in which Tyr is said to be the son of the Jotun Hymir, while in the younger Edda he is said to be the son of Odin. A similar inconsistency is found when it comes to Thor, who is the son of Odin, but it is said Thor is the son of Fjörgyn who is also known as Jord, which makes Thor Odin's foster son and brother-in-law as Thor is the brother of Odin's wife, Frigg. If we consider that Thor is the Æsir mentioned most in the engravings which we have at our disposal, and figures more prominently in any text referring to the magical use of runes and Nordic magic in general, then together with Tyr, we must conclude that there is a fundamental mystery encoded in what Tyr and Thor represent in terms of Nordic magic.

The mere carving of the rune Tyr should be accompanied by the memory of Tyr himself, his qualities roughly found in his uprightness and courage, qualities necessary to deal with potentially ill and hard Fate given in the rune Naud. In this way, we can see the type of attitude necessary to placate the Norns and turn a bad Fate into a good one.

Magically speaking, this would indicate that any runic work should start with a summoning and identification of Tyr and/or Thor, leading straight to a call for the Norns to enter the magical sphere of action and bend things in conformity with how the rune-worker approaches the secrets. This is further emphasized in the consistent use of Thursday, primarily sacred to Thor, but also to Tyr, who in totality owns Tuesday, the day of Mars. This might suggest that both Tuesday and Thursday were seen as martial days, but in an active and passive relationship where powers might be gathered on Tuesdays and then put into motion on Thursdays.

On the practical side of Sigerdriva's magic, we need to realize that she is simply sharing the principles and protocol of given mysteries, but in accordance with dogmatic formulae we need to accept the possibility that a person having "picked up the runes" will also know the use of the runes, hence every situation is unique, and a unique set of secrets is needed for the formulae to act upon the world. So, in pursuing victory, a double Tyr carved on a Tuesday or Thursday upon your sword, accompanied by offerings of ale to Tyr and Thor, would be sufficient. But, if we are speaking of childbirth, we find that matters are perhaps more complex, and engraving Tyr, Naud, and Birch on the bed whilst offering ale to Tyr, Thor, the Norns, and Frigg, might be sufficient. This invites in the development of runic charms or the use of "secret runes" that are carved, scraped and drunk along with being engraved permanently on the bed.

In this, we can also see a formula for working with the runes related to Mimir. A cup of ale is presented, preferably in the presence of a well or a spring which represents wisdom. Here, the rune one seeks to know is carved or marked on wood particularly elected for its resonance with this rune. Mimir is then summoned, as are Hugin and Munin (the ravens of Odin), along with the three Norns, followed by the carving of the rune as its name is sung or whispered and the rune-worker connects with the rune Tyr as its axis and Naud as its cradle. The rune is then scraped off into the ale, a portion given to the earth and the rest drunk. This suggests working *hugrúnar* in the way Odin did, which is why we would leave him out of the ceremony and instead do things as he did. In doing as the Allfather did, we will tend to call upon his attention by effecting magic that follows his example.

Beneath such simple actions of rune magic we find a cosmic complexity residing in the marking of secrets and desires with carvings and engravings, whilst being witnessed by forces aligned with those same secrets that are imprinted on the material world, in a sacred sequence of will made manifest.

Bringing into the equation the materia magica of the North, we are presented with several items understood to possess power in and of themselves. In folk magic, we find saliva, semen, menstrual blood and the placenta used as nearly universal "power-houses" for whatever type of enchantment or "runic work", and naturally in high frequency where matters of the erotic are concerned.

Eggs were another important power-element used in both folk medicine and magic as something that would attract energies, be they good or bad. Passing an egg over an inflamed eye would cause the egg to suck up the illness, and in the same way, eggs of different birds could be used to pass over certain places to imbue the egg with the desired virtue. In this way, the egg could be used in all forms of magic, for healing and for cursing and also as a container for a specific magical virtue.

Hair and nails were thought to be direct links with a given person and hence, possessing the hair or nails of a person was sufficient to cause harm and healing on that person.

Naturally, we find several plants believed to be endowed with unique powers, the troll-plants, and we find in a number of trolldom recipes the significance of using "nine types of wood" when a working is done. It should also be mentioned that it is surprising to see how many of these troll-plants are ascribed to Thor, which would indicate his importance as a patron for trolldom. Amongst the most used troll-plants both for healing and magic are the following:

Alrune (*Mandragora officinarum*), the mandrake, was the subject for much lore and magical use, but also possessed great protective qualities, and it was believed to enhance one's magical capacity if one carried a mandrake on one's body.

Alvenever (*Peltigera aphthosa*) is a moss that should be gathered on the northern side of the tree and was used to "wash away" illness caused by elves and trolls.

Apple was a significant tree, sacred to Frigg, Freya and Idunn, and carried the virtues of love and the erotic.

Barley was an important plant, sacred to Frey and the vaettir that serve him. Barley was also known as Byggvir. Barley was considered to embody the essence of Jord herself which might explain why ale was considered so important and holy. **Oats** were the other important grain, considered of a protective nature and of course important for the sake of food such as porridge and various types of bread. **Rye** on the other hand was the corn of trolls and was an ambiguous plant.

Birch/Aspen were trees of great reverence, considered the first trees, and hence there is reason to believe that the first human couple, Ask and Embla, were carved from these two trees. The sap and bark of Birch was used for a variety of matters and the bark of Birch was a popular substitute for parchment, frequently used to carve and write on. This tree was always associated with Frigg, as Aspen had longstanding associations with Thor and Tyr. Birch also held remedies against the mischievous huldre-people, and would keep away Mara.

Eik/Oak was another sacred tree, well known for being important in all cultures where it is found, and is especially sacred to Thor. Odin holds a strong connotation to Oak, although Holly is more "his tree".

Eineren/Juniper was thought to be one of the most powerful ward trees and it was considered particularly dangerous to offend this tree. Leaves and berries were used for a great number of situations, both as an exorcising agent and as cures for everything from hysteria and complications related to birth, to the plague.

Flismegras (*Linnea borealis*) was connected to elves and especially the afflictions caused by elves, in particular skin rashes like herpes.

Furu/Pine is another important and powerful tree; it is at the roots of the pine we find the huldre-people living. The tar produced from its roots and the resin from its marrow were both used as universal remedies; however, its extraction was considered dangerous as it would always involve the vaettir of the tree, and so, either of these substances were considered a vaettir medicine at large.

Geitved/Buckthorn (*Rhamnus cathartica*) is another herb with diabolic connotations and folklore. It was given its name "goat in the wood" because of a story in which the Devil was riding a goat and rammed into a tree with such force that the goat got stuck between the wood and the bark with its pelt hanging out. Hence, Buckthorn is truly a "devil-tree". We find a similar reference related to Tyr's Birch (*Betula sp.*) whose name, Björk, refers to it having been subjected to a similar driving mishap on the part of the Devil.

Hegg/Bird Cherry was also one of the nine woods, a popular remedy, and considered a favorite amongst the many vaettir. Having a lot of this bush on your land would naturally attract benevolent and powerful vaettir.

Hyll/Elderberry (*Sambucus*) was a tree considered a protector of the peace at the farmstead and was in particular interested in preserving harmony and attraction between married couples: hence, a tree important for Frigg, Freya, and Vár.

Karve/Caraway was popular as a spice, but it was also believed to be a powerful exorcising agent.

Korsknapp/Peppermint (*Glechoma hederacea*) was a potent protector and expeller of wicked vaettir.

Lauk/Leek was one of the most sacred vegetables, and with Lauk or onion, we do speak of all forms of onion, but in particular of the leek. It would ward against evil eye and wicked vaettir and was in and of itself a source of physical healing.

Linden was another important tree, associated with snakes, but also with *vargulfr*; it was believed that Linden and its pact with the full moon possessed the mysteries that caused the werewolf curse.

Linen/Linseed belongs to Freya and Frigg and is amongst the oldest and most reputed enchanted plants said to possess strong protective potencies. Linen, linseed and leek together form a powerful ward against wicked vaettir.

Marihand/Hugvendel/Marsh orchid (*Dactylorhiza*) is a well-known aphrodisiac used in erotic works, and also to treat cows with lactation problems.

Maure/Lady's bedstraw (*Galium verum*) was believed to offer protection to infants.

Misteltein/Mistletoe holds similar qualities as the Rowan in so far as it guarded against wicked vaettir and trolls.

Nykleblom/Primrose (*Primual veris*) was a popular ward against curses.

Older/Alder tree was also sacred and was almost always one of the nine woods used to perform magic.

Rogn/Rowan is also one of the nine woods and gained prestige by being the savior of Thor. In Finland it is called Rauni, "red one", and considered the wife of Thor. A person plagued by huldre-people and revenants could go to the Rowan and carve his name into the tree, which would loosen him from the attention of the denizens from the other side.

Selsnepe/Water hemlock (*Cicuta virosane*) was another plant associated with thunder and Thor, and often was one of the nine woods. It is imperative that the root is dug out in the night to preserve its magical virtues.

Søtrot/Sweetroot/Gentian (*Gentiana purpurea*) was used as a remedy against plague and similar afflictions. In spite of its rather bitter taste, it was important to call it "sweet root" as this would evoke the benign aspect of its vaettir protector.

Tjøregras/Silene (*Viscaria viscosa*) was another protective plant.

Tobacco was considered a universal expellant for driving away harmful trolls.

Torhjelm/Helmet or **Thor/Trolls hat** (*Aconitum septentrionale*) is a powerful toxin and is a frequent participant in the nine types of wood necessary to perform magic.

Trollbær/Trollberries/baenberries (*Actaea spicata*) was revered for its fast and dramatic poisoning that led to coma and death, naturally possessing the virtues of the most vile and harmful vaettir.

Trollgras/Trollweed (*Paris quadrifolia*) was used to combat diseases caused by trolls and in particular swellings of the throat.

Trollhegg (*Rhamus frangula*) was frequently used as a component in troll pouches, given its protective qualities and that it possessed troll virtues in and of itself.

Tysbast (*Daphne Mezerum*) was, for some, considered a representation of Tyr and was therefore commonly used in runic magic and troll-pouches. However, it is not derived from Tyr, but from the Germanic Tyfel/Diefvel/Teufel, or Devil, revealing this as a diabolic herb that is ever-present in the world of trolldom.

Vendelrot (*Valeriana officinalis*) was considered a root detested by huldre-people and dwarves, hence, it was a powerful ward against them.

Villrot/Henbane (*Hyoscyamus niger*) was a common participant amongst the nine woods and was considered a plant with amazing magical abilities and a ward against ill-intended elves.

There are two other modalities that should also be taken into consideration; one of them is in the findings of Magnus Olsen, given in his curious little tract *Om Troldruner*, "On Troll-runes", from 1917; the second is divination.

What Magnus Olsen discovered is that, in some instances of cursing, a different meter was used, namely *dróttkvaett*, which was the poetic meter selected when composing verses in praise of noble men. He found that this meter was also used as a "cursing meter" that had an edge of satire to it. Used in this way, it would provoke harm on the person who was turned into the target of the poem. He discovered that some of these curse-poems followed a stringent use of 72 runes. This is true for several curse-poems he examined, as it is also true for the verses in the original Icelandic text that details how Egil raised the curse-pole, as discussed earlier in this book. Unfortunately, it is not possible to arrive at a concise explanation of why 72 was considered numerically significant. Clearly, 7 + 2 adds up to the sacred 9, and of course the most meaningful of all is that 72 divided by the number of aettir, 3, gives us 24. It might be that the use of 72 runes would involve each of the three Norns to work through each of the runic letters in the Elder futhark. If this were the case, it would support the theory that the secret of the runes was mediated by a cunning elite of sorcerers, as in the example of the Heruli or ErilaR.

If we consider that the word "rune" is used both as a noun and as a verb in Scandinavia, it should be recognized as imperative to take into account that in speaking of runes, we are not restricting ourselves to merely the futhark, but also looking at how each of the letters represents a sorcerous secret in and of itself, and that the runes represent intelligent spiritual building blocks woven into the fabric of creation. To work with a rune is to work with the spiritual intelligence of an elemental on a deeply personal level born from wisdom and sacrifice.

Speaking about divination, it appears that divination by runes was similar to the casting of lots. Hence, it would appear that a simple call to the Norns was made and then the runes were thrown onto the ground or picked up from a horn or pouch. Today, there are several divinatory innovations found using the format of "spreads" born from associations with tarot and astrology, however, I personally find what Pennick calls "the grid of nine" a better method. Here, you summon the Norns and pick three runes for each of the Norns, generating three runes that describe the past pattern, three runes that describe the current pattern, and three runes that describe the natural progress and outcome of what took place in the past and what is currently going on in the present.

Chapter Twelve

Runic Cryptology

Runic cryptology, how to veil a message and develop it to become even more secret, is perhaps better exemplified by the runic staves found in Icelandic magic and Scandinavian Black Books from 1780 and onwards. In these are a great number of symbols and shapes, taken from the classical grimoires and also constructed using secret alphabets and runic formulae, which in some cases rest on the simple premise of runic cryptology addressed in this chapter.

We have several instances of the use of secret or cryptic runes, either as anagrams or coded abbreviations, in the form of single stave runes and bind runes. We find several examples of this where a single rune in a sequence stands in for an entire word. We also find letters re-arranged in simple ways, such as DINO, or written backwards like NIDO, to encrypt a name like ODIN.

The most common and most useful of the secret runes are the use of "twig runes", also known as *hahal* runes, or "hook runes". The twig runes can be written using the single stave from top to bottom or bottom to top where the left side of the stave signifies the aettir and the right side the position of the rune in the aettir used. Let us give a few examples here and first look at hook runes:[208]

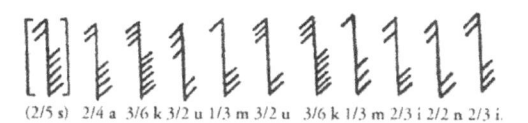

(2/5 s) 2/4 a 3/6 k 3/2 u 1/3 m 3/2 u 3/6 k 1/3 m 2/3 i 2/2 n 2/3 i.

These traditional hook runes can then be bound together in a way that might have inspired Icelandic magic's combination of bind runes, signs and symbols, like this:

2/5 s 2/3 i + bi   3/2 u 2/3 i + a   3/2 u 2/4 a + ri

---

208 The illustrations in this chapter are reproduced from McKinnel et. al's *Runes, Magic and Religion* 2004: 28-30.

Here, the diagonal lines are connected with the two ends pointing up and the two ends pointing down. Starting from the top left going clockwise will give us two runes. These runic crosses can be written in sequence or used as anagrams or as abbreviations.

A third form is as follows:

3/3 2/3 2/5 2/4 3/5 3/5 3/2 2/2 2/4 3/5
þ i s a r   r u n a r
Ill. 7: Twig runes from Maeshowe; they read: **þisar runar** (from Düwel: RK 2001, 186).

These twig runes can in turn be used as bind runes, where each branch is used to form a cross of 4 or 8 arms composed of a single rune on each arm, referring to aettir and placement in the aettir.

The rune letters corresponding to this are as follows:

	1. rune	2. rune	3. rune	4. rune	5. rune	6. rune	7. rune	8. rune
I. ætt	ᚠ f	ᚢ u	ᚦ þ	ᚨ a	ᚱ r	ᚲ k	ᚷ g	ᚹ w
II. ætt	ᚺ h	ᚾ n	ᛁ i	ᛃ j	ᛈ p	ᛇ ë	ᛉ R	ᛊ s
III. ætt	ᛏ t	ᛒ b	ᛖ e	ᛗ m	ᛚ l	ŋ ng	ᛞ d	ᛟ o

Finally, it is also possible to get more creative with this form of runic cryptography in the following manner:

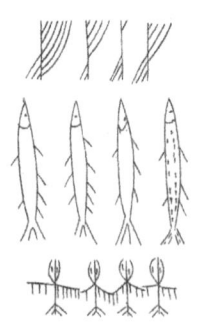

The shape of these runes suggests a basic concept of the field where the runic sequence is supposed to work. In this case, it is related to fish, Ran, Aegir and oceanic mysteries, and perhaps wealth, food and richness.

Twig runes pertain to the basics of runic bindings, and, in their construction, we are truly utilizing the secret levels of the runes to give shape to a more intricate symbol that in turn will carry a more complex effect into the world.

Chapter Thirteen

The Secret of the Runes

The section in *Hávamál* known as *Rúnatal* is the text which most directly speaks of the nature and secret of the runes in the Edda. *Rúnatal* is written in the poetic meter known as *ljóðaháttr*, associated with magic and wisdom expressed in poetry. The Old Norse is also replicated here to show how this magical meter was used and what it looks like, because this will give an idea of how an enchantment was composed and what poetic laws guided its composition.

In *Rúnatal*, we find a complete listing of the magical arsenal available to Odin, as we also find hints speaking of how mystery was penetrated and how secrets were taken. *Sigerdrifamál*, as well as *Hávamál*, uses the word "runes", and in hearing this word we may understand that the word rune not only refers to the symbols, but also to the secret of the rune itself and the whisper which was the way of communicating a secret. And so, it follows that any attempt to relate single runes to secrets spoken might limit what is mentioned here. When Odin speaks about how he took the runes, certainly we can see how each of the runes represent parts in a fundamental creative matrix, but I would also say that each of these secrets speak of combinations of runes and of particular types of magic and sorcery. Hence, a commentary, verse by verse, might instill a greater clarity of the secrets Odin learned as he hung for nine days from the World Tree. I have also given the stanzas in the original Old Norse language as I have made several changes to existing translations, so it is good to have a reference to understand the choices of the translation.

138
vindga meiði á
nætr allar níu
geiri undaðr
ok gefinn Óðin
sjálfr sjálfum mér
á þeim meiði
er manngi veit
hvers hann af rótum renn

I know that I hung
upon a windy tree
for nine whole nights,
wounded with a spear
and given to Odin,
myself to myself
on that tree
no one knows
to where the roots stretch

In the beginning of *Rúnatal*, Odin speaks of the conditions necessary for receiving secrets and understanding runes. He is sacrificing, or in truth he "gives" himself to himself, in ways that suggest restraint of movement and a 180° inversion of the body due to Odin staring downwards from the tree in the next verse. What we see in this verse is that Odin does this to connect to the roots of the World Tree. These mysterious roots are most likely 3 in number and related to three wells, each directly related to the three Norns. These are Urdabrunnir, Hvergelmir and Mimisbrunnr. Urdabrunnir is guarded or tended by three Jotun maidens, who are said to be hideous to look at. These Norn maidens go by the names of Urd (Past), Verdande (Present), and Skuld (Future). Hvergelmir is a root/well that is said to stretch all the way to Nifelheimen, and to be where Nidhöggr lies gnawing at the roots of Yggdrasil which moves Ragnarök ahead, guarded over by Hel. Mimisbrunnr is said to be located towards the direction of the frost giants, but is clearly the root/well that holds and secures the particular wisdom that existed before time and the ages started to move the world, and also might be a reference to the water or sweat gathered from when Ymir melted out from the ice.

The technique spoken of here, this turning upside down and being immobile, is remarkably similar to what Austin O. Spare wrote of in his book titled *The Book of Pleasure* in 1919, that is bringing your body into an uncomfortable posture, similar to Atu 12, the Hanged Man in the Tarocchi, and controlling your breath to access deeper psychological, spiritual and magical levels of being. The excerpt from *The Book of Pleasure* is so profound that it is only just to give the section in full, as follows:

The Death Posture

Ideas of Self in conflict cannot be slain, by resistance they are a reality – no Death or cunning has overcome them but is their reinforcement of energy. The dead are born again and again lie in the womb of conscience. By allowing maturity is to predicate decay when by non-resistance is retrogression to early simplicity and the passage to the original and unity without idea. From that idea is the formula of non-resistance germinating "Does not matter – please yourself."

The conception of "I am not" must of necessity follow the conception of "I am," because of its grammar, as surely in this world of sorrow night follows day. The recognition of pain as such, implies the idea of pleasure, and so with all ideas. By this duality, let him remember to laugh at all times, recognize all things, resist nothing; then there is no conflict, incompatibility or compulsion as such.

Transgressing Conception by a Lucid Symbolism.

Man implies Woman, I transcend these by the Hermaphrodite, this again implies a Eunuch; all these conditions I transcend by a "Neither" principle, yet although a "Neither" is vague, the fact of conceiving it proves its palpability, and again implies a different "Neither."

But the "Neither-Neither" principle of those two, is the state where the mind has passed beyond conception, it cannot be balanced, since it implies only itself. The "I" principle has reached the "Does not matter − need not be" state, and is not related to form. Save and beyond it, there is no other, therefore it alone is complete and eternal. Indestructible, it has power to destroy − therefore it alone is true freedom and existence. Through it comes immunity from all sorrow, therefore the spirit is ecstasy. Renouncing everything by the means shown, take shelter in it. Surely it is the abode of Kia? This having once been (even Symbolically) reached, is our unconditional release from duality and time − believe this to be true. The belief free from all ideas but pleasure, the Karma through law (displeasure) speedily exhausts itself. In that moment beyond time, a new law can become incarnate, without the payment of sorrow, every wish gratified, he8 having become the gratifier by his law. The new law shall be the arcana of the mystic unbalanced "Does not mattter − need not be," there is no necessitation, "please yourself" is its creed.

In that day there can be deliberation. Without subjection, what you wish to believe can be true. "He" is pleased by this imitation, the truth revealed to me by all systems of government but is himself ungoverned; Kia, the supreme bliss. This the glorious Science of pleasing one's self by a new agreement, the art of Self-love by recognition, the Psychology of ecstasy by non-resistance.

The Ritual and Doctrine

Lying on your back lazily, the body expressing the condition of yawning, suspiring while conceiving by smiling, that is the idea of the posture. Forgetting time with those things which were essential – reflecting their meaninglessness, the moment is beyond time and its virtue has happened.

Standing on tip-toe, with the arms rigid, bound behind by the hands, clasped and straining the utmost, the neck stretched – breathing deeply and spasmodically, till giddy and sensation comes in gusts, gives exhaustion and capacity for the former.

Gazing at your reflection till it is blurred and you know not the gazer, close your eyes (this usually happens involuntarily) and visualize. The light (always an X in curious evolutions) that is seen should be held on to, never letting go, till the effort is forgotten, this gives a feeling of immensity (which sees a small form), whose limit you cannot reach. This should be practised before experiencing the foregoing. The emotion that is felt is the knowledge which tells you why.

The death posture is its inevitability accelerated, through it we escape our unending delay by attachment, the Ego is swept up as a leaf in a fierce gale – in the fleetness of the indeterminable, that which is always about to happen becomes its truth. Things that are self-evident are no longer obscure, as by his own will he pleases, know this as the negation of all faith by living it, the end of the duality of the consciousness. Of belief, a positive death state, all else as sleep, a negative state. It is the dead body of all we believe, and shall awake a dead corpse. The Ego in subjection to law, seeks inertion in sleep and death. Know the death posture and its reality in annihilation of law – the ascension from duality. In that day of tearless lamentation the universe shall be reduced to ashes . . . but he escapes the judgment! And what of "I," most unfortunate man! In that freedom there is no necessitation, what dare I say more? Rather would I commit much sin than compromise myself. There are many preliminary exercises, as innumerable as sins, futile of themselves but designative of the ultimate means. The death posture in the reduction of all conception (sin) to the "Neither-Neither" till the desire is contentment by pleasing yourself. By this and by no other are the inertia of belief; the restoration of the new sexuality and the ever original self-love in freedom are attained. The primordial vacuity (or belief) is not by the exercise of focussing the mind on a negation of all conceivable things, the identity of unity and duality, chaos and uniformity, etc., etc., but by doing it now, not eventually. Perceive, and feel without the necessity of an opposite, but by its relative. Perceive light without shadow by its own color as contrast, through evoking the emotion of laughter at the time of ecstasy in union, and by practice till that emotion is untiring and subtle. The law or reaction is defeated by inclusion. Were he to enjoy an hundred pleasures at a time, however much his ecstasy, he does not lose, but great increase takes place. Let him practise it daily, accordingly, till he arrives at the center of desire. He has imitated the great purpose. Like this, all emotions should find equipoise at the time of emanation, till they become one. Thus by hindering belief and semen from conception, they become simple and cosmic. By its illumination there is nothing that cannot be explained. Certainly I find satisfaction in ecstasy. I have now told you a secret of great import, it was known to me in childhood. Even by sedulously striving for a vacuity of belief, one is cosmic enough to dwell in the innermost of others and enjoy them. Among men few know what they really believe or desire, let him begin, who would know, by locating his belief till he sees his will. Existing as dual, they are identical in desire, by their duality there is no control, for will and belief are ever at variance, and each would shape the other to its ends, in the issue neither wins as the joy is a covert of sorrow. Let him unite them.

139.	139.
Við hleifi mik sældu	Bread was not given to me
né við hornigi	nor any horn of drink
nýsta ek niðr	I gazed intensely down below,
nam ek upp rúnar	I took up the runes,
œpandi nam	screaming I took them,
fell ek aptr þaðan	and I fell back from there.

This verse directly speaks about the trance state necessary for penetrating the realm of runes. Inversion is clearly stated as the premise, and if this is about hanging upside down in a tree of power or an inversion of any other form, such as the death posture, the aim may be towards the same result, namely the exhaustion involved when the body is brought to a threshold where only spirit can enter. Hence, in this process a return to body awareness is marked by a scream, most likely screaming the names of the secrets, suggesting a rhythm from silence through whispers to screams as a specific modality of gaining access to secrets. This replicates the idea of creation, mirrored by Ymir, Odin's great-great grandfather, who melted from the ice slowly and was at some point murdered by Odin and his brothers Vile and Ve, and turned into the world as we know it.

140.	140.
Fimbulljóð níu	Nine enchanted songs/spells I
nam ek af inum frægja syni	was given
Bölþórs Bestlu föður	from the mysterious son
ok ek drykk of gat	of Bolthorn, the father of
ins dýra mjaðar	Bestla,
ausinn Óðreri	and I got to drink
	of the precious mead,
	poured from Odrörer

In this section we find a reference to the "well-like barrel" used to store ale and mead, in this case Odrörer, translated to "what ecstasy is made of". Odr is itself an ambiguous presence. It is a word meaning "frenzy" and "ecstasy", but it can also refer to spear and arrow heads, as well as being a reference to the ecstatic quality of Odin himself, highlighting the ecstatic element related to intoxication. Odrörer, Son, and Bodn were barrels/wells that were used to store the particular mead related to troubadours, poetry and enchantments. We also know that henbane *(Hyoscyamus niger)* and toadstool *(Amanita muscaria)* would be used together with juniper when brewing ale. Henbane with its bitter taste and euphoric effect would serve well as a plant that stimulated ecstasy, tearing down the veil between the visible and invisible worlds. Further, Odin speaks here about how he obtained nine secrets, a number that in the enchanted Scandinavian world could very well have been used not as a specifically exact number, but a plurality of magical wisdom no matter the amount. We also see here that the one teaching Odin these songs and spells was a son of Bolthorn, Odin's grandfather. We know that Bestla, Odin's mother, had a brother with whom Odin was very close, his uncle Mimir, who was sent to the Vanir in an attempt to create truce and concord. However, they decapitated him and sent his head back, which was reanimated at one of the three wells at the roots of Yggdrasil. In this verse, we might see a relationship between Mimir's Well and Ordrörer which speaks to a particular ecstatic component of Odin's magic that is born from some sort of intoxication. Hence, we can deduce from this verse that there is little Norse magic done without the presence of mead or ale and herbs of power, whether they be subtle and spiritual, or proper intoxicants and entheogenics.

Clearly Odin sees himself as the guardian of the wisdom that existed before the world was created from Ymir's slaughtered body. He guards Mimisbrunnr, the well of wisdom, and is himself born from these primordial Jotun forces that existed before our world was begun. Odin, together with his brothers, held the capacity of the material world's author, known as the Allfather, Father of All. Together with a select grouping of other spiritual beings, he created a gathering and named them Æsir, which we can understand to mean as something elevated, something that lives on a hill, or a dweller on a mound. Clearly, the word Æsir holds the idea of something or someone elevated.

141.	141.
Þá nam ek frævask	I stepped up, to the front
ok fróðr vera	and became fertile
ok vaxa ok vel hafask	grew fruitful and well-
orð mér af orði	disposed
orðs leitaði	to grow and to flourish;
verk mér af verki	speech fetched my speech for
verks leitaði	speech,
	action fetched my action for action.

This verse appears to highlight the ecstatic and Bacchic frenzy already mentioned. Again, the deity Odr appears to take on important proportions in spite of his obscurity. However, we should take note of the fact that the Greek and Roman gods were not unknown to people like Snorre; nor was the Nordic tradition unknown to historians and explorers like Tacitus and Herodotus who quickly found stellar and planetary references in Nordic ways, in particular with the Æsir. This stanza might also suggest erotic elements with phrases like "being well disposed" and "growing fruitful".

142.
Rúnar munt þú finna
ok ráðna stafi
mjök stóra stafi
mjök stinna stafi
er fáði fimbulþulr
ok gørðu ginnregin
ok reist Hroptr rögna

142.
You can find runes
and interpret the staves,
very mighty staves,
very strong staves,
which a mighty sage/sorcerer colored
and mighty powers made,
and Ragna-Ropt carved.

Again, Odin is addressing a deep secret, namely the necessity of returning to the state of mind from before time as we know it became manifest, a sort of timelessness. In this, he imparts, through partially veiled ways, that when we speak of runes or staves we are accessing primordial energies, and that we are not speaking about the runes sacred to given spirits, but that runes are mysteries in their own right. *Ragna-ropt* is one of the heiti of Odin.

143.
Óðinn með ásum
en fyr álfum Dáinn
ok Dvalinn dvergum fyrir
Álsviðr jötnum fyrir
ek reist sjálfr sumar

143.
Odin among the Æsir,
Dain for the elves
and Dvalin for the dwarves,
Alsvidr for the Jotuns
also, I myself carved some.

In this stanza, Odin goes deeper into what was spoken of in the previous verse. Here we find the powers we need to access as gatekeepers for the mysteries, which might be seen as constituting the corners of the timeless world we need to access to gain the wisdom of runes and staves. Dainn is the first name given here after Odin, and is in the Eddas said to be both an elf and a dwarf and associated with the constellation of the deer, or what we commonly know as Orion. His name is found on King Högni's sword Dáinsleif ("Dáinn's legacy"). It is laid with a curse which says it must always kill a man when it is drawn, which might connect this elf king to the mysteries of the hunter at large. Dvalin is a dwarf, said to be the most cunning of them all. He made the necklace Brisingamen for Freya and the sword Tyrfing; both of these items having a deadly twist to them, just as in the case of the sword associated with Dainn. Lastly, we have the Jotun Alsvidr, meaning "most learned", perhaps an epitaph of Mimir or a distinct Jotun in his own right. What all of these have in common is their relationship with a primordial condition and in this, the constellation of Orion which holds Dainn or "the deer". In this we might see Odin as Orion himself placed in the well of wisdom we know as space, the origin of liquid waters. This would suggest that these are the powers we need to incorporate in order to perform a traditional runic working aiming towards picking up the runes. This modality is at times associated with utesitta, the sitting-out in a location in nature that holds power. Here offerings to elves and dwarves are given, and the wisdom of Jotun called upon as we sit under the constellation of Odin/Orion in stillness and whispers.

144.	144.
Veiztu hvé rísta skal?	Do you know how to carve them?
Veiztu hvé ráða skal?	Do you know how to interpret them?
Veiztu hvé fá skal?	Do you know how to color them?
Veiztu hvé freista skal?	Do you know how to tempt them?
Veiztu hvé biðja skal?	Do you know how to summon them?
Veiztu hvé blóta skal?	Do you know how to sacrifice to them?
Veiztu hvé senda skal?	
Veiztu hvé sóa skal?	Do you know how to send them out?
	Do you know how to ward them off?

In this stanza Odin is laying out the *modus operandi* of actual work with runes and staves. The act of coloring them is vital. This would be done with some form of anointing using ale, honey, blood, juice of rowan, oak-bladder or a variety of other coloring agents that held some meaningful relationship with a particular virtue. The same goes for summoning, sending and warding off these powers. There is a consistent lack of step-by-step formulae in the Eddas. This is most likely due to the importance Odin gave to the act of "sacrificing oneself to oneself" and the importance of entering into these mysteries of one's own accord. Hence, these mysteries are protected by the self-sacrifice required to seek them out.

145.	145.
Betra er óbeðit	It is better not to invite
en sé ofblótit	than over-sacrifice,
ey sér til gildis gjöf	gift demands gift in return,
betra er ósent	it is better left and not given
en sé ofsóit	than over-immolated.
svá Þundr um reist	This Tund carved
fyr þjóða rök	before time and ages
þar hann upp um reis	when he rose up
er hann aptr of kom	and when he came back.

In this verse, Odin speaks about some form of balance between taking and giving, and a ritual precision seems involved here. His considerations are reminiscent of ideas we find in "Kongo sorcery" where there is a consistent idea that food for a spirit should not be excessive, lest the spirit gets lazy and greedy, nor too meager, lest the spirit does not have sufficient fuel for action. We also find consideration of proper food for given spirits, which would mediate virtues with precision in the form of "food" and "drink" that would aim towards "feeding" a given direction or force. The most interesting thought here might be that gifts demand gifts in return, hence, it appears that Odin speaks here about a contract/pact/agreement as a bond better worked with runes. Thus we might avoid approaching these mysteries as friends bearing gifts, but rather by treating this as an agreement that is paid for, be it with food, ale, blood or an eye. These considerations are written by Odin assuming the form and name Tund, of uncertain etymology, but most likely a reference to the Tundra, which is earth penetrated by ice and cold to such extent that a primordial stillness is embedded in it. Alternatively, it might refer to the field, *tun*, around the farmhouse that is assigned its own retinue of guardians.

In the stanzas that follow, Odin speaks of various forms of runic magic, but he does not give any formulae as such; he has already given the way to gain these secrets, and now he is listing the various secrets that are possible to retrieve, or at least those secrets he gained access to and in what realms of activity the magic can accomplish change:

146.
Ljóð ek þau kann
er kannat þjóðans kona
ok mannskis mögr
hjálp heitir eitt
en þat þér hjálpa mun
við sökum ok sorgum
ok sútum görvöllum

147.
Þat kann ek annat
er þurfu ýta synir
þeir er vilja læknar lifa

148.
Þat kann ek it þriðja
ef mér verðr þörf mikil
hapts við mína heiptmögu
eggjar ek deyfi
minna andskota
bítat þeim vápn né velir

149.
Þat kann ek it fjórða
ef mér fyrðar bera
bönd at bóglimum
svá ek gel
at ek ganga má
sprettr mér af fótum fjöturr
en af höndum hapt

150.
Þat kann ek it fimmta
ef ek sé af fári skotinn
flein í fólki vaða
flýgra hann svá stinnt
at ek stöðvigak
ef ek hann sjónum of sék

146.
I know the songs
that no king's wife knows,
nor man or maid:
the first is called "Help",
and it will help you
with disputes and grievances
and all sorrows.

147.
I know a second
which the sons of men need,
those who want to live as
physicians.

148.
I know the third:
if great need befalls me
for a fetter for my enemy,
I can blunt the weapons
of my enemies,
that no weapons nor cunning
will have effect

149.
I know the fourth:
if men put
fetters on my limbs,
I sing a trollsong so that
I can go:
fetter springs from my feet
and bond from my hands.

150.
I know the fifth:
if I see the spearhead/arrow of
the enemy
arriving in haste,
I can make it halt
No matter how strong its flight
As long as I can reach it with
my sight.

151.
Þat kann ek it sétta
ef mik særir þegn
á rótum rams viðar
ok þann hal
er mik heipta kveðr
þann eta mein heldr en mik

152.
Þat kann ek it sjaunda
ef ek sé hávan loga
sal um sessmögum
brennrat svá breitt
at ek honum bjargigak
þann kann ek galdr at gala

153.
Þat kann ek it átta
er öllum er
nytsamligt at nema
hvars hatr vex
með hildings sonum
þat má ek bœta brátt

154.
Þat kann ek it níunda
ef mik nauðr um stendr
at bjarga fari mínu á floti
vind ek kyrri
vági á
ok svæfik allan sæ

155.
Þat kann ek it tíunda
ef ek sé túnriðir
leika lopti á
ek svá vinnk
at þeir villir fara
sinna heimhama
sinna heimhuga

151.
I know the sixth:
if a warrior wounds me
with the fresh root of a strong tree
and calls forth hatreds from me,
then the harms eat the man and not me.

152.
I know the seventh:
if I see a high hall
and fire around the sleeping ones,
no matter how bright it burns
I will save the hall,
when I scream this trollsong.

153.
I know the eighth,
which is useful to know
if hatred grows
among the sons of kings,
I can quickly cure it.

154.
I know the ninth:
if I need
to save my ship afloat
I can calm the wind
on the wave
and lull the whole sea to sleep.

155.
I know the tenth:
if I see witches
playing in the air,
I can so arrange it
that they go astray
from their proper shapes
and proper thoughts.

156.
Þat kann ek it ellipta
ef ek skal til orrostu
leiða langvini
undir randir ek gel
en þeir með ríki fara
heilir hildar til
heilir hildi frá
koma þeir heilir hvaðan

157.
Þat kann ek it tólpta
ef ek sé á tré uppi
váfa virgilná
svá ek ríst
ok í rúnum fák
at sá gengr gumi
ok mælir við mik

158.
Þat kann ek it þrettánda
ef ek skal þegn ungan
verpa vatni á
munat hann falla
þótt hann í fólk komi
hnígra sá halr fyr hjörum

159.
Þat kann ek it fjórtánda
ef ek skal fyrða liði
telja tíva fyrir
ása ok álfa
ek kann allra skil
fár kann ósnotr svá

156.
I know the eleventh:
if I must lead old friends
to battle,
I sing under the shields,
and they go victoriously:
safe to the battle,
safe from the battle,
safe they will return home.

157.
I know the twelfth:
if I see up in a tree
a hanged corpse swinging,
I carve
and color the runes
that the man moves
and speaks with me.

158.
I know the thirteenth:
when the warrior is young
I pour with water and
enchantments
So he cannot fall,
though he may come to war
the man does not fall before
swords.

159.
I know the fourteenth:
if I must amongst men
name any spiritual being,
I know the details of all
the Æsir and the Elves
the unwise man knows that
not at all.

160.
Þat kann ek it fimmtánda
er gól Þjóðreyrir
dvergr fyr Dellings durum
afl gól hann ásum
en álfum frama
hyggju Hroptatý

160.
I know the fifteenth,
which Thjothreyrir sang,
the dwarf, before the doors of
Dellingr [father of Dag/Day]:
He sang the might of the Æsir,
the courage of the elves,
the understanding of
Hroptatyr [a heiti of Odin].

161.
Þat kann ek it sextánda
ef ek vil ins svinna mans
hafa geð alt ok gaman
hugi ek hverfi
hvítarmri konu
ok sný ek hennar öllum sefa

161.
I know the sixteenth:
if I wish to have all the heart
and pleasure
of a wise maiden,
I turn the feelings
of the white-armed woman,
and I change the whole of her mind.

162.
Þat kann ek it sjautjánda
at mik mun seint firrask
it manunga man
ljóða þessa
mun þú Loddfáfnir
lengi vanr vera
þó sé þér góð ef þú getr
nýt ef þú nemr
þörf ef þú þiggr

162.
I know the seventeenth,
that the youthful maid
will never avoid me;
Loddfafnir, you knew
these charms
now forgotten,
though it be good for you if
you get them,
useful if you take them,
needful if you receive them.

Loddfafnir appears as a student of Odin, and in this stanza, it might be that Odin is addressing "the failed student". Odin is perhaps speaking of the responsible use of these secrets, given that he is here speaking of Loddfafnir in the same stanza where he speaks of troll-songs which can cause the erotic to stir in young women – but a type of woman not referred to as wise as in the previous stanza. This might refer to some component of character and wisdom being necessary to actually make cunning use of these secrets.

The Secret of the Runes

163.
Þat kann ek it átjánda
er ek æva kennik
mey né manns konu
alt er betra
er einn um kann
þat fylgir ljóða lokum
nema þeiri einni
er mik armi verr
eða mín systir sé

163.
I know the eighteenth,
which I never teach
to maid or man's wife,
everything is better
when one person understands it,
it belongs at the ending of spells
to none but she alone
who is wrapped in my arms
or is my sister.

This mystical verse appears somehow connected to mysteries more dominant in alchemy, and in particular the alchemy of Nicolas Flamel where he insisted that the creation of the Philosopher's Stone is only possible in its truth and excellence bound with the mystical marriage, which, in his case, was as much spiritual and as it was material. Odin might be speaking of the importance of Frigg as the power that allows magic to happen in her capacity as the owner of the house, the axis of the *tun*/field representing the world itself that radiates from the hearth-fire of the home guarded by Frigg. This theory might explain, to some degree, Odin's interest in seidr, a magical tradition ascribed to part of women's mysteries. The reference to the woman or his sister wrapped in his arms might allude to both Freya and Frigg as symbols of what is necessary to bring an enchantment full circle and into effect.

164.
Nú era Háva mál
kveðin Háva höllu í
allþörf ýta sonum
óþörf jötna sonum
heill sá er kvað
heill sá er kann
njóti sá er nam
heilir þeirs hlýddu

164.
Now the sayings of Har are spoken
in Har's hall,
very needful to the sons of men,
harmful to the sons of giants.
Hail to him who spoke!
Hail to him who understands!
Let him benefit who took them!
Blessings on those who listened!

The runes of the Elder futhark consist of 24 letters parted into 3 aettir, families, of 8 runes each. Each rune represents particular secrets in and of itself and the sequence is not random.

1st aettir/family:
ᚠᚢᚦᚨᚱᚲᚷᚹ

2nd aettir/family:
ᚺᚾᛁᛃᛇᛈᛉᛋ

3rd aettir/family:
ᛏᛒᛖᛗᛚᛜᛟᛞ

There are two ways of seeing the Elder futhark which are complimentary to one another. One is to see the 24 runes as scales on Nidhöggr where the cyclical entropy of the world is made visible from Fé, the first rune, which gives the spark in the abyss of possibility until the new day rises in a renewed world where the same sequence repeats itself. The other perspective is to see the first aettir as dealing with matters of the world, the second aettir as dealing with matters related to the human journey, and the third aettir speaking of the rhythm within the social fabric. Personally, I find both of these approaches useful and meaningful, and it would aid not only in the use of the runes as mnemonic tools but also in making the runes your own, as the wisdom taken will be firmly lodged in the tradition of Thule itself. Here, I present the runes in a flow of 24, giving focus to the cosmic and sorcerous dimensions to each rune, which will, in turn, prove useful for divination and practical work with the runes.

ᚠ

Fé is commonly associated with wealth, represented by cattle and livestock. Fé, placed as the first rune, can be seen as having a particular relationship with Othal, representing enclosure, inheritance, gathering, gain through the span of life, and a gathering of wealth that is yours to pass on. In this way, Fé highlights the accessibility of wealth, riches and the possibility of gaining life as an offering. In this way, we can see Fate, represented by the three Norns, taking form in this rune through its offering of possibility for gaining wealth and all that represents.

Regarding Fé as the energy of beginnings, it is common to see the cosmic cow Audhumla licking the ice that unleashes the Jotun race. In this, we can see Fé representing movement, be it the melting ice or be it the motion of an arm or leg freeing itself from bondage so it can act upon the world.

The Old Norse rune-poem says the following about the core of Fé:

ᚠ Fé væeldr frænda róge;
føðesk ulfr í skóge.

ᚠ Fé
Wealth is a source of discord among kinsmen;
the wolf lives in the forest.

This poem highlights that with wealth and the possibility of gain, envy, discord and enmity enter the world as a natural reflex. Here, we find within Fé the mention of the wolf, the animal that, in the *Völuspá*, announces the end of the world, Ragnarök, and the end of the Æsir, by eating the Sun. This would imply that in Fé, wealth and gain is the underlying force of enmity between the Æsir, and hence, it is greed, envy, jealousy and gluttony that ends the world and breaks the Othal, the gathering of wealth, into nothingness. The Icelandic rune-poem gives us two more stanzas about the nature of this rune:

ᚠ Fé er frænda róg
ok flæðar viti
ok grafseiðs gata
aurum fylkir.

Fé – Wealth
Source of discord among kinsmen
and fire of the sea
and path of the serpent.

This poem highlights how Fé is the beginning of the end, suggesting a cyclic worldview at play where everything that has a beginning also needs to find its end, and through that, renewal. This is mirrored in the story of Jormundgandr or Nidhöggr, the dragon that will rise up from the ocean in fire and strike its path across creation to bring the end of the world and begin a reality of renewal. Also, we see how wealth is not only associated with money, but also with friends. Considering this, a word like "foe" might be etymologically related to Fé, a reminder of gathering friends as a part of accumulating wealth, yet it also comes with the warning that wealth also attracts foes.

Materia magica associated with this rune is: nettle (*Urtica dioica*), Elder tree (*Sambucus nigra*), salt, ice, fire, meteorite, and fur and horns of livestock, as well as any evergreen tree and plant, anything of wolf and snake, and anything used as monetary currency. We can also add to this certain trees like the coconut palm that depend on saltwater to give fruit. The idea behind Fé is about beginnings and endings and it is in following this idea and concept that we apply this rune for magical use.

ᚢ

The rune **Ur** is commonly associated with the aurochs in a direct reference to Audhumla, the cosmic bovine that in licking the cosmic ice released life from its motionless stand, and in this Ur represents movement. To give a proper etymological explanation and translation of Audhumla is problematic as *aud* can refer to both wealth and void – yet also fate – and I am tempted to go with the latter meaning being predominant. As Ymir is drinking Audhumla's milk, she is licking out from the ice Odin's first ancestor, Buri; in this rune creation is properly begun, which is why runologist Sigurd Agrell insisted on the secret of the runes being encoded in the *uthark* and not the futhark, placing Ur as the beginning of all things. I find this theory interesting, but all movement needs a spark to get it going and this spark is represented by Fé that moves Ur and hence we find the beginning of creation staring with Ur, but caused by Fé.

As mentioned, Ur might be linked to Fate more than anything else, because with Audhumla feeding Ymir and releasing Buri she is also setting down the premise for the Fate of all living beings, be they mortal or immortal: hence we can see in Ur the Norn Urd, the Norn who is connected to the past in the sense of everything done is already making up the past. The three Norns represent the past (Urd), future (Skuld) and present (Verdande), but Fate itself is most likely represented by Urd herself in being the warden of acts done. Her sister Skuld, who is connected to the future, is also connected to consequences as we can see in her name, *skuld* giving meaning to words like guilt, blame and debt in modern Norwegian, while Verdande most likely refers to what is going on presently. There might be a connection here with veritas or truth, although it is difficult to say if the etymological succession can be verified. Considering the valor of truth, honor and uprightness in Scandinavian cultures, it will at least have a meaningful understanding in terms of truth and uprightness motivating the present in reflex of past and future in order to provide a good and worthy bane, where one in dignity carries the guilt and blame (or its absence) caused by one's own action. If we accept an interpretation like this, we will also see that we are all the tailors of our own Fate.

If we have a look at the rune-poems, first the Nordic and then the Icelandic, we see that both verses carry some form of gloom I related to drizzle, be it of bad iron or from the clouds in form of drizzling rain. The verses are presented below, the Nordic first and the Icelandic after:

ᚢ Úr er af illu jarne;
opt løypr ræinn á hjarne

ᚢ Ur
Dross comes from bad iron;
the reindeer often races over the frozen snow.

ᚢ Úr er skýja grátr
ok skára þverrir
ok hirðis hatr.
umbre vísi

Úr – Shower
Lamentation of the clouds
and ruin of the hay-harvest
and abomination of the shepherd.

Both verses speak of a certain hardship attached to life and in overcoming life we need strength, stamina and perseverance, hence the reference to bad iron and its dross will also refer to spineless and weak people who succumb to Fate rather than forging their Fate.

Materia magica associated with this rune are moss and the silver birch, but given its association with the Fates, yarrow would also be under the rulership of this rune, horns of bovines, milk, honey, and hops (*humle* in Norwegian), the herb used for making beer. Obsidian and fulgurite as well as the resin from pine trees, fern and hay suitable for feeding livestock would also hold a relationship with Ur.

ᚦ

The rune **Thurs** is commonly attributed to Thor but is more properly the rune of the Jotun-race or giants. It is also the first rune which is a combination of two others, namely Is (ice) and Ken (a kindling fire), and would as such refer directly to the powers that were freed from the ice due to the work of fire. As we know, the first form released or shaped from the ice was Buri, the grandfather of Odin. And so, this rune is primarily speaking of the arrival of the giant race and secondly about the friction caused by giants. Hence the need for protection was also generated, in the form of Thor's hammer Mjölnir, for example, and any thorny sharp objects, be they thorns of plants or sharp weaponry.

Thor enters here as both the son of Odin and the brother of Frigg. Frigg having a different ancestry than Odin, namely Fjörgyn, often associated with Erda or Earth, suggests the possibility of Thor actually being the stepson of Odin, more so than Odin's blood son. This origin of Thor might explain his antagonism towards the giant race and his constant travels to Utgard with the aim of killing Jotun, just as it also accounts for his chronic distrust and friction with Odin's blood-brother Loke, also of Jotun pedigree.

Fjörgyn is in the Edda referred to as both male and female and is as such described as the father of Frigg and the mother of Thor, these deities being born from earth itself. Earth was created by the mutilation of Ymir and thus we see a specific genealogy, different from the Æsir that originated from Buri, or more directly from his son Borr and the children he had with the Jotunwoman Bestla, great granddaughter of the six-headed frost giant Trudgjelmir. It was this couple that begot Odin, Vile, Ve and Hönir; Odin in turn created the first human forms, Ask and Embla, from driftwood.

If we look at the Old Norse rune-poem it says the following about this rune:

Þ Þurs vældr kvinna kvillu;
kátr værðr fár af illu.

Thurs
Giant causes anguish to women;
misfortune makes few men cheerful.

Clearly it is about the arrival of the giants to the world and in this Thor appears as a controlling force, a protector of Midgard, a protector against misfortune. We should also take notice of how this rune is associated with anguish for women, and it is nearly impossible to escape the Enochian legend elaborating on the biblical comment from Genesis 6:4:

There were giants in the earth in those days; and also after that, when the sons of God came in unto the daughters of men, and they bare children to them, the same became mighty men which were of old, men of renown.

This is interesting in the light of the Icelandic rune-poem that refers to the giants being Saturnus, as well as bringing in the need for *vardrunar* or protective runes, and again we see the reference to how this force represents something hostile towards women.

Þ Þurs er kvenna kvöl
ok kletta búi
ok varðrúnar verr.
Saturnus þengill.

Thurs – Giant
Torture of women
and cliff-dweller
and husband of a giantess.

We know that the Enochian legend invariably states that these giants or *nephilim* took by force or seduced by charm women and had offspring with them, and later in Genesis we can read how, as a consequence, evil spread across the earth and led to the deluge.

I will not enter too deeply into this beyond pointing out the quality and representations of giants in biblical mythology and that the Icelandic association between giants and Saturn most likely reference both the popular imagery of Saturn eating his children in an attempt to avoid Jupiter, the ruler of the world, along with being himself the king of Titans.

This means that this rune would ultimately be the rune of the giants, the Jotunrace at large and in particular what appears from the melting ice. It represents suffering, agony and chaos – particularly for women – and thus it is in calling upon the need of protection represented by Thor that this enters as a martial balancing force, the fire to the dominant ice.

This rune is also associated with one of the weekdays, Thursday, which repeatedly in the Nordic tradition of sorcery is the auspicious day for doing any form of magic. It is also the only day where we meet taboos for what cannot be done, taboos largely about avoiding handling any form of round objects, for instance, or spinning or riding a wagon. It is also overwhelming in the Black Books to see how Thursday is used as the magically favorable day for nearly any magical operation, which suggests what tremendous forces we can access through this rune.

This will give us a key to what materia magica would be under the rulership of Thurs, namely all things Saturnine, such as lead, poisons, bramble (*rubus fruticosa*), blackberry, blackthorn (*prunus spinosa*), mandrake (*mandragora spp.*), flint, obsidian, and onyx. We would add to this the various magical staves of protection, and those for sleep, like vardthorn or *vardunar*, and sleepthorn. The association with sleepthorn, magical diagrams and signs with the aim of enhancing sleep might be a reference to the hamingja, and the changing of shape happening when one falls into a deep sleep and allows the fylgja to ride out in a different hue/form/ham.

ᚨ

The rune **As** is commonly associated with the Ash tree (*fraxinus excelsior*), or Yggdrasil. But we can also see the Yew tree here, simply due to these two trees apparently serving as general jargon when speaking of trees related to the axis mundi. The Ash tree represents the giver of life; the Yew represents the giver of death. As for the latter, we can see how the Yew is the lord of death, both due to its frequent occurrence as a tree planted in cemeteries and also because it appears to be naturally attracted to graveyards. Yggdrasil on the other hand is represented by the Ash tree, the tree that was found in the center of Midgard, the dwelling of the Æsir. We also find Yggdrasil being a reference to Sleipnir, the eight-legged horse of Odin, son of Loke. Another association is with Mimameith, the Tree of Mimir, but this might not be an Ash at all, but rather the Linden tree, associated with the metamorphosis of the form encoded in the phrase *hugr ok hamr*, from "thought/will to shift of form".

The rune is the first of the series of Odin runes we encounter in the *uthark*; the Norse rune-poem says of this rune the following:

ᚨ Óss er flæstra færða
fǫr; en skalpr er sværða

ᚨ As
Estuary is the way of most journeys;
but a scabbard is for swords.

As usual we find a breath of gloom in this rune associated with centeredness and the arrival of the Æsir in constructing Midgard – but with Midgard also comes Valhalla, the realm of death given to brave warriors who would naturally be under the rulership of the Yew and not the Ash. Yet the rune-poem mentions the estuary being the end of most journeys which speaks of how when we find fertile land we find rest, but also the estuary is metaphorically where new life begins in the meeting of fresh and salt water, where fertile mud gives the medium for perpetuating new life. As the second line states, when we find a good place, that is when we lay our weapons to rest and prepare to enjoy life.

The Icelandic rune-poem is even more poignant in ascribing this rune to Odin, using here one of his heiti (praise names), Gautr, which means someone who pours metals. We also find the dual reference to both Valhalla and Asgard, the very dwellings of the Æsir. The poem reads as follows:

ᚼ Óss er algingautr
ok ásgarðs jöfurr,
ok valhallar vísi.
Jupiter oddviti.

Óss – God
Aged Gautr
and prince of Ásgardr
and lord of Vallhalla.

"Jupiter oddviti" is a curious phrase here and has been left out of the translation; *oddviti* means someone who is crafty with sharp weapons, in particular arrowheads and lance heads. This connection to Jupiter might refer to Odin as Allfather and his cunning with sharp weapons, an extension of the mention of his heiti, Gautr, and thus highlights Odin as a craftsman, blacksmith, and a forger of weapons. This in turn might bring us to Zalmoxis (due to his ambiguously simultaneous chthonic and celestial being, and association with spear heads) and Volund (Wayland) serving as worthy references explaining the nature of Odin as Allfather.

This rune is thus one of stability, supremacy, victory and clarity of vision. It announces life as much as it brings the "good death". It is an Odin rune, but it is about Odin as the creator of a still center, and as a forger of weapons. Materia magica under the rulership of this rune would be sulfur, iron, steel, silver, quicksilver, ash, yew, anything turning liquid by fire, Star of Bethlehem, Rose of Jericho, spinach and horses.

ᚱ

Raid refers particularly to the wheel on a wagon, composed of a circle and with its spokes hinged on a center/axle that makes it roll forward. Ash, oak and hickory are examples of the types of hard wood used for making wheels. In this simple representation we find

Raid representing travel, movement and relocation, both for the joy in as much as the need for travel.

Two other perennial symbols can also be associated with this rune, one being the Sun, and the other Fortuna and her Wheel; Raid is to a certain extent related to the concept of Luck and in this, the spinning wheel commanded by the Norns. This makes this rune represent a force that touches everything that has a movement in whatever direction.

The Norse rune-poem says the following of this rune:

R Ræið kveða rossom væsta;
Reginn sló sværðet bæzta.

R Reidh
Riding is said the worst thing for horses;
Reginn forged the finest sword.

We find here the mention of the dwarf Regin, foster father of Sigurd, renowned for slaying the dragon. Regin's brother was Fafnir, who was affected by greed for gold and dominion caused by the Andvaris' ring, and was turned into the dragon slain by Sigurd. Fafnir's fame was renewed by Tolkien's *Lord of the Rings* trilogy which serves as backdrop for the metamorphosis of Smeagol into Gollum, yet the entire drama surrounding the ring became the main plot in this work. Odin's ring Draupnir should also be mentioned as it was also forged by dwarves and was reputed to give both riches and unhappiness to its owner.

The fact that this rune is related to dwarves is significant due to dwarves being related to riches and wisdom, but there is also a certain murkiness related to the dwarves, who guard secret treasures and live in hidden-away places, preferably underground. In this last, they are perhaps particularly related to the genii loci of given places that in Sweden are known as *rådare*, which in English would be "rulers".

In the story of Sigurd we also find the idea of a quest, another powerful perennial theme presented in any account involving a knight rescuing a princess from chaotic and destructive forces. The Icelandic rune-poem says the following:

R Reið er sitjandi sæla
ok snúðig ferð
ok jórs erfiði.
iter ræsir.

The Secret of the Runes

Reid – Riding
Joy of the horsemen
and speedy journey
and toil of the steed.

We see that both verses highlight that what is the joy of one is the sorrow of another, and thus emphasize this polar contrast existing in the world and how the world will always be a realm of knights/jarls and thrells/servants.

And so Raid is far more than just about the travel – it is the journey at large, whether we are speaking of the journey of the Sun, the journey of the yearly cycles, or the quest of a knight, or about guarding a precious center or the Fate given to each one of us by the Norns spinning and cutting the threads of life.

It is a rune we often use as the first rune worked to accomplish anything, as it is a force that pushes and moves what we seek to accomplish.

Materia magica belonging to Raid would be any kind of wood used for the making of wheels, and in particular oak, ash and hickory. Given the association with dwarves, gold and coal would naturally find resonance here. Dandelion, mugwort, yarrow, and lily of the valley would also be natural candidates for this rune as well as any edible weed growing along the wayside.

ᚲ

The rune **Ken/Kaun** represents fire in a great variety of expressions, including the fire of fever announcing illness and the acid heat that generates ulcers. The rune is also speaking of the female genitalia and might be seen as a euphemism of the witch fire itself burning strong in every woman and outwardly represented by the hearth fire, and also the forge of the blacksmith.

The rune is also associated with the torch, and in this with the pine, which is a sparkling wood that burns with joy and ease.

In the rune-poems below we see that both speak of infant illnesses such as chickenpox and measles. The first is the Norse and the latter the Icelandic.

ᚲ Kaun er barna bǫlvan;
bǫl gørver nán fǫlvan.

ᚲ Kaun
Ulcer is fatal to children;
death makes a corpse pale.

ᚲ Kaun er barna böl
ok bardaga [för]
ok holdfúa hús.
flagella konungr.

Kaun – Ulcer
Disease fatal to children
and painful spot
and abode of mortification.

This rune highlights the workings of fire pure and simple and how it works for good as well as for bad. In this the rune is suggested the idea of containment being central, as it speaks of the central fire being a place that attracts forces and people and leads to a gathering around.

Its associations with children and hearth fire emphasizes how this rune is represented more than anything by the vagina, and in this the potential for new life, for comfort, for the fire of passion, for mystery; and also for any form of illness related to heat and fire and any kind of fever, be it playing itself out in life or being the fire that kindles the ecstasy happening in the practice of seidr and galdr.

As such any wood that burns with ease, and "red" plants, would be sacred to this rune, such as mulberry, bilberry, cranberry and rowan. Cowslip (*Primula veris*) and *Tribulis terrestri* would also be under her domain, as would fruits associated with the vagina such as the fig, the apple, the mango and melon. Metals and stones would be bloodstone, rose quartz, carnelian, copper and rust.

X

The rune **Gebo** represents two hands crossed, two sticks crossed or one hand giving and the other receiving. The cross shape is equal armed and is commonly considered a union harmonious in nature, representing the gift of union, friendship, pact and oath. Yet in this it might also signify sacrifice, as when Tyr sacrificed his hand in the mouth of Fenrir announcing the Ragnarök.

The rune would also suggest natural locations where powers meet and submerge into something else, namely a place where we can unite with forces, as in the practice of utesitta (sitting-out) which effectively consists of locating a spot in nature where powers are already present and appealing to them. The purpose would be subject to the gift of some spiritual power or prophecy, but this means that you would also need to come bearing gifts to that location. This being done, the gift received might be a good gift or a troublesome one...

Also, we should keep in mind that a gift is not always given without conditions and so the idea of a gift would in some instances for the Scandinavians call upon questioning the reasons behind the gift, expecting that some sort of demand or request would be forthcoming. And so it can signify a helping hand, either to take something or to give something. Also connected are Elm (*Ulmus Glabra*) and Aspen (*Populus tremula*), the latter generally considered giving in the sense of comfort and remedies, while the Elm represents the negative side of Gebo in the way it is prone to catch fungi that destroys it – a deadly gift so to speak. Hence we find fungi belonging to this rune as we also find metals like gold and silver, diamond, ruby.

A rune-poem for Gebo that would remind us of the ambiguous nature of a gift could be like this one:

> A gift given with wish of being returned
> Soon enough becomes a ransom holding
> Your joy hostage in a withering concord

ᚹ

Nigel Pennick suggests the rune **Wunja** represents the wind vane and speaks of joy and lust in the way it naturally measures where the wind is coming from; as such it demonstrates an agility, turning in relation to what is going on. It is a good metaphor to understand the Nordic concept of joy as a capacity to take advantage of whatever form of wind, be it good or bad. Pennick further sees this rune as the union between Odin and Frigg which would suggest joy coming as a consequence of a harmonious union in Gebo, and represents marriage and similar unions that exalt lust and joy in one's life.

A proper rune-poem for this rune could be as follows:

> A life journeyed well
> Will always call upon the winds of joy
> Contentment rests in the joyful smile

The association between joy, winds, and lust suggests fullness of life resulting in agility in life, preferably in togetherness and perpetual renewal.

In this way, Wunja coming as the last rune in the first family of runes would suggest that joy will be the reward of a journey well traveled.

Flax (*Linum spp.*) would be a good candidate for an herb related to this rune due to its global association with luck and good fortune. Any light and invigorating metal or mineral like lapis lazuli, sapphire, jade and tin, and any sappy greenwood like cypress and cedar would naturally hold some of these virtues.

ᚼ

Hagal is one of the major Odin runes. In representing hail itself it also carries the memory of Odin's ancestry. The Norse rune-poem says the following about this rune:

> ᚼ Hagall er kaldastr korna;
> Kristr skóp hæimenn forna.

> ᚼ Hagall
> Hail is the coldest of grain;
> Christ created the world of old.

Of note is the association between grain and hail which bears a similar concept to what is necessary for bringing forth new life. The Icelandic rune-poem follows in the same vein, saying the following:

> ᚼ Hagall er kaldakorn
> ok krapadrífa
> ok snáka sótt.
> grando hildingr.

> Hagall – Hail
> Cold grain
> and shower of sleet
> and sickness of serpents.

Here is emphasized the merciless weather conditions related to snow falling in the form of ice and turning into sleet, which makes both seeing and walking difficult. For coldblooded beings like snakes it is everything but benevolent, yet this threat upon their life also brings out their survival instincts.

Pennick states that this rune is also related to örlög or a man's fate, symbolized by the rune also representing a hedge and a gate as much as a fence. If so, we find in this rune the Norns being active; they might be attributed to the three pillars the rune is composed of. Örlög is itself an interesting concept. On one hand it is used to signify a man's Fate or Wyrd, often linked to Urd and her well, the well of Fate; on the other hand it also means the breaking of an oath and the commencement of war or dispute, usually at sea. Furthermore the word is also related to the ship log, hence we see that örlög commonly describes an ill Fate. If we accept that this is an Odin rune we will therefore need to look at Odin and his Fate to understand its deeper nuances.

The idea of ill Fate might rest in the fact that Odin left his own, and in creating humans he also generated an isolated farm for the Æsir. It might be these choices that led to his demise as foretold by the volva in *Voluspá* – or it can simply be that anything that begins will end in a cyclical fashion. As a seed is born true to its inherent nature it will ultimately find its end and death. As such this rune can be said to signify the beginning of the human journey, the gestation of possibility, a good beginning given over to the possibility of accepting an ill Fate, signified by the surrender to darkness and the hunt for wisdom and knowledge.

A good summary is given by Krasskova:[209]

> Wyrd encompasses the sum total of one's individual actions and choices, as well as whatever destiny may have been predetermined by the Nornir for that individual. In many ways, wyrd may be likened to Fate, but it is far more interactive. Essentially, wyrd is causality and consequence. It is the sum total of every action a person has ever taken interacting with that of their ancestors and their communities at large, as well as whatever destiny may have been predetermined by the Nornir for that individual. Wyrd is a web of choices that constantly shifts and changes – one's own choices, the choices of others, the choices of one's community, and even the choices of one's ancestors impacting each person's current evolution and awareness.

---

209 http://www.northernpaganism.org/shrines/norns/writing/understanding-wyrd.html

If so, anything that brings dramatic changes in the cycle of life, like poison, will naturally be ascribed to this rune, as would certain marine plants and organisms as well as what cold ocean water might bring.

Yew, bryony, mandrake, onyx, opal, iron nails, seeds and corn, and in particular seeds and bulbs that are resistant to cold weather would naturally be a part of the materia magica of Hagal.

ᚼ

Naud, a word meaning need, distress, and net (a fisherman's net), is encoded in the popular Norse proverb "distress and need teaches naked women to weave", which is also the deeper layer in the old Norse rune-poem:

ᚼ Nauðr gerer næppa koste;
nøktan kælr í froste.

ᚼ Naudhr
Constraint gives scant choice;
a naked man is chilled by the frost.

The Icelandic rune-poem emphasizes how this rune is contained in work and toil as rooted in oppression:

ᚼ Nauð er Þýjar þrá
ok þungr kostr
ok vássamlig verk.
opera niflungr.

Naud – Constraint
Grief of the bond-maid
and state of oppression
and toilsome work.

It is traditionally a rune related to both the Norns and to Odin. The rune itself represents the two sticks needed to make the "need fire", which is made by using a stick of hard wood rubbed into a softer wood to generate fire by friction. In this way this rune represents the creative power of need and necessity that results in the development of new skills.

The rune is also interesting in the way that its cross shape is not representing two straight roads, but the road in-between laid out upon the upright axis which is symbolic of searching for solutions outside the norm and also defying the obvious route of one's life, leading to a slowing-down where we actually sit down and do what is necessary.

This is a rune of demand, direction, stern intent and desperate will bent by patience, where passions are tamed by the time necessary to generate what is needed.

If we look at Naud in relation to the rune Hagal's other written variant (a variant adopted by List in his Armanen runes), we see a sequence related to the Norns. This form is given here which is then followed by Naud and then Is/Isa:

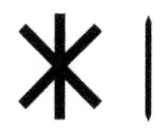

So in Hagal the cruel Fate of man is laid out, in Naud choices are made, and in Is one's Fate is done and directed.

This means that Naud will always be represented by two elements, something hardy and something volatile, whether a hard wood and a soft wood, or a soft plant and a thorny plant, and of course anything that can be used to bring fire, like flint, pine, and in particular the rowan tree given its association with fire and redness, witchery and need, solace and resistance. Rowan and holly would for instance be a good fusion of these powers, as would rowan and oak, flint and granite, or soap stone and hematite.

Odin is naturally connected to this rune, but we can also see Loke, the fiery one, found here, and it might be that Naud is also speaking of what happens when fire gestates offspring as Loke is the progenitor of Sleipnir (Odin's horse); the children he had with the giantess Angrboda, like Fenrir and Hel/Is, are also found in the rune following Naud, namely Is.

But we also see this rune active in acts of desire, as when Freya desired the necklace Brisingamen so much that she entertained sex with the four dwarves that had made it, due to her need moving her desire. The suggestion of *brising*, meaning fire, amber, or the draft needed to generate fire, is also interesting here in terms of the symbolic dimensions in this story, where Freya actually has coitus with primordial powers associated with the four corners of the world to gain this amber, fire or the draft that makes fire possible. Hence amber might be seen as the mineral and resin most aligned to this rune. The rune is also related to Valborg and Valborgsmesse (1st of May).

I

Verdande, the Norn of the present, that which is in this moment, is encoded in the rune **Is/Isa**. It is directly related to ice, of being frozen and standing still, a lack of motion, and is in turn a reference to the idea of the Nordic Hell, a place cold, dark and still.

The Norse rune-poem says this rune represents a bridge, specifically Bifrost, the bridge that connects Utgard and Àsgard, but also the bridge leading to the realm of Ice, the abode of Hel, Loke's daughter. In this way this rune represents the inevitable end of the human journey as much as it represents the very act of finding a temporary center and being still, whether it be in life, contemplation or in death.

As the Norse rune-poem says:

| Ís kǫllum brú bræiða;
blindan þarf at læiða.

| Isa
Ice we call the broad bridge;
the blind man must be led.

The Icelandic rune-poem highlights glaciers and the ice covering waters and the danger that comes with these. A hole in the ice is covered in great haste; a man falling through the ice is finding his ice-cold doom and becomes one with the realm of Hel, as the poem goes:

| Íss er árbörkr
ok unnar þak
ok feigra manna fár.
glacies jöfurr.

Iss – Ice
Bark of rivers
and roof of the wave
and destruction of the doomed.

In the sequence of Hagal, Naud and Is, we can see how Is represents the succession of multiple choices given by Fate, how choices made lead to Naud and how this, once acted upon, gives us the returning present, the path emerging from Fate and necessity which we must walk.

In this we find a certain persistence in this rune, a call to go on no matter what. Is means endurance and stamina that leads us directly to an inheritance in the shape of tides turning and legacies encoded in Àr/Jera. This is the rune that follows Is; it speaks of natural cycles and new beginnings, hence Is also represents the midwinter, the coldest and darkest tide of the year, a time for hibernation and contemplation, a time to feed upon what we have reaped up to this point, by Fate and need. In this way Is speaks loudly about the harsh weather conditions in Scandinavia and the promise of doom and difficulty that winter can bring, just as it also brings isolation and stillness due to ice and snow covering the earth and turning everything into the domain of Hel for some time.

Materia magica belonging to this rune would naturally be fossils, ice itself, snow crystals and whatever freezes easily as well as anything white, and the bark of trees (due to bark in the past having been used as a food supply under extremely harsh weather conditions). Somehow we can see the presence of Heimdal in this rune, the white one who guards the bridge Bifrost, and so opal would be a stone in resonance with this rune, as would bones in general.

Àr/Jera: Àr means literally "year" and refers to the cycle of the year, but in particular the late spring announcing summer. It is the bounty gained after the suffering of Is which offers the chance for renewal and new beginnings. The rune can be seen as two ploughs, hinting towards the importance of ploughing the ground and making the earth ready to receive seeds. As such it is related to the concept of fertility represented by Frey and Freya as mentioned in the Norse rune-poem, here under the name of Frode, meaning "youthful one" in reference to the virility of youngsters. As the poem goes:

> ᚼ Ár er gumna góðe;
> get ek at ǫrr var Fróðe.

> ᚼ Ar
> Plenty is a boon to men;
> I say that Frodi was generous.

We find this idea further encoded in how Àr is composed of two Ken runes turned towards one another, suggesting the union of ovum and sperm necessary for growth and beginnings as being the prerequisite for having a bountiful harvest. The Icelandic rune-poem highlights how this rune is related to summer itself and in particular midsummer, and in this represents a very different form of fire than what we find in a rune like Naud, which is also a fire rune. The fire of Àr is the easygoing jovial fire of contentment and lustful mingling, the heat of desire and the joy of merging.

ᚼ Ár er gumna góði
ok gott sumar
algróinn akr.
annus allvaldr.

Ár – Plenty
Boon to men
and good summer
and thriving crops.

Given that Àr is related to Frey/Freya, this rune is also sacred to the disir. We know that Freya was referred to as *vanadisr* and that disir was a class of female spirits/entities connected to fertility and childbirth. Both fylgja and Valkyries were referred to as disir. *Disablót*, sacrifices to the disir, were commonly performed on the vernal equinox – and I would suspect midsummer – given that the purpose was to enhance fertility of crops.

Plants like rosemary, marigold, rye, wheat and dandelion would be sacred to this rune, but we can also see plants like plantain and banana and sugarcane, being a greenwood, in resonance with the tremendous fertility and sweetness encoded in Àr. The milky sap of plants and semen would also be a part of the mystery of this rune as would the fertile soil itself. Gold and brass would be natural metals sacred to the idea of bounty as would stones like lapis lazuli and emerald.

The last four runes in the second aettir will be dealt with here in the same lesson, this because three of these runes were actively used for magical purposes and healing in variants of themselves, as we shall see. If we focus on all four of these runes, we will see that the Nazi occultists of the Third Reich based large parts of their idea of power and domain on exactly these four runes.

ᛇ

First let us have a look at **Yr/Eihwaz**, commonly considered the rune representing the ash tree or Yggdrasil proper, being composed of two Laugar runes, both meaning waters – the waters of wisdom and "leek". The leek is a generalized word referring to any form of onion, reputed to be ardent, which holds water and serves as an important part of the nutrition for the Norsemen, and is even made part of pacts, marriage agreements and is an object of bestowing blessings and more. So, in this rune we might see Yggdrasil as much as we do the leek. This rune being the tree where Odin hung himself to gain wisdom would then represent any "bleeding" tree and in particular trees of red sap, likes Dragon's Blood.

As we see in the Norse rune-poem, we find that Yr represents a fire that is controlled and silent, reproducing the properties of the ash wood as replicated here:

Ýr er vetrgrønstr viða;
vænt er, er brennr, at sviða

Yew is the greenest of trees in winter;
it is wont to crackle when it burns.

The Icelandic rune-poem is mentioning the Ynglinga, the shapeshifting family of Odinists reputed to know the mysteries of how to change *ham* to Bear and Wolf, and is even hinting towards the importance of the gateway made by the yew generating an arch related to Fårbauti. Fårbauti is the father of Loke and his name simply means the striking lightning that results in wildfire, which then would be the true essence of Loke.

Ýr er bendr bogi
ok brotgjarnt járn
ok fifu fárbauti.
arcus ynglingr.

Yr – Yew
Bent bow
and brittle iron
and giant of the arrow.
The arch of the Ynglingr.

This reference is quite interesting and when we look at the medieval magical rune called *wolfsangel* (see below) we do see how this rune is clearly modeled on Yr:

ᚠ

Wolfsangel represents the pothook in the kitchen on which the cooking cauldron was hung. Pennick see it as a wolf hook, a weapon designed to combat wolves. It was used by the Waffen SS division – yet originally was a symbol used by Germanic peasants in the 15th century as the sign of their revolt against the oppressors. Naturally this "magical rune" would be apt in binding and controlling dangerous forces. Its sound is like "SZ" mimicking the sound escaping from food or water boiling in a cauldron.

ᛈ

The rune **Pert/Pertho** has invariably been seen as the cauldron hung upon Yr, the pothook – but it is also seen as describing the wolf's jaw, either Fenrir's or Garm's. It is also a rune representing the cup that holds the dice in games of chance and in this we see an entire complex of ideas related to chance, Fate, wolves and courage taking place here. It is a rune representing gambling, including Tyr placing his hand in Fenrir's mouth and losing it, just as it is about all the tricks and schemes Loke, Odin and Thor are constantly executing to gain the upper hand in whatever situation. Sometimes they win, other times they lose – this state of giving yourself up to Fate in entertaining active gambling on whatever level appears related to the concept of the wolf. As such this rune would represent any container, what is contained by a hedge and most of all the mouth and the cupped hands. Anything of wolf and dog would fortify this rune that is then used for the purpose of generating boundaries, inviting in chance, generating motion and building courage. Its metal would be fool's gold and its mineral sulfur.

A rune-poem for this rune could be as follows:

Greed and emptiness lies between the wolf's jaw
Just as greed and hope is found in the dice cup of the gambler

ᛉ

For the Nazi occultists the rune **Algiz/Elg** was called die Lebens rune, or the Life rune. The rune was occasionally used on gravestones and as insignia for the Lebensborn society, which was basically a society dedicated to racial hygiene and select breeding of the so-called "Aryan race" or the race of Thule, those being blond, blue-eyed, strong, healthy, etc. This rune is commonly related to victory and chieftaincy and represents both the arms raised in victory and the mighty sword Skirnir, and perhaps Gugnir, the spear of Odin.

Plants sacred to this rune would be silver moss, mistletoe, mullein, *tribulus terrestris*, oak and holly and its minerals would be any stone reputed to give life and victory like bloodstone, fire agate and carnelian. Horns of moose, deer and similar animals would be greatly in harmony with the virtues of Algiz, a rune used for courage, victory and triumph, a celebratory power of life.

A rune-poem for this rune could be:

A good death is what secures victory
A spectacular death will make you immortal amongst the living

ᛋ

Sol is the rune of the goddess Sol, as in the Norse mythology the Sun was viewed as female. As such sunflower and bay laurel would naturally be plants possessing the virtues of this rune, as would solar stones and minerals, like gold, sunstone, tiger-eye and similar. Any feline, it be cat, lynx, lion or leopard would also hold these virtues.

The benevolence and victory found in this rune is of a greater magnitude than what we find in Algiz, which is more about personal victories. Sol is about a victory that spreads across the world and encompasses everything, hence a double Sol with its relationship to increase and domain was adopted by the Nazi occultists.

The Norse rune-poem says the following:

ᛌ Sól er landa ljóme;
lúti ek helgum dóme.

ᛌ Sol
Sun is the light of the world;
I bow to the divine decree.

The Icelandic rune-poem says the following:

ᛋ Sól er skýja skjöldr
ok skínandi röðull
ok ísa aldrtregi.
rota siklingr.

Sól – Sun
Shield of the clouds
and shining ray
and destroyer of ice.

In this way we also find in this rune the true essence of the Æsir, being a solar force aimed towards domain over the ice (associated with the Jotun and the giants, the older Saturnine forces).

This means that there will also be some parts of youthful folly in this rune, seen as a tendency towards hubris and failing to see one's role in the world and the need for others. Sol is the full force of the Sun, pure and simple – and the energizing rays of the Sun can work in vastly different ways from person to person.

The rune can be engraved in amber for protection and victory, and be anointed with honey and blood, preferably on a Sunday during Mass, where the *galdramann* in the shades of the church summon fire spirits like Loke in the same hour, to bestow the wildfire of conquest upon an object, which gives an example of how to simply manipulate such energies for bringing in heresy and Jotunpowers.

ᛏ

With **Tyr** we meet yet another Odin rune, here in reference to his son Tyr, a force representing duty and justice; its shape can suggest the spear or arrowhead and therefore is a reference to Gugnir or arrows in general, as something that points directions, such as the arms of a clock or the arrow on a wind vane.

The Norse rune-poem highlights his sacrifice, namely his hand given to Fenrir to uphold temporary order and so the rune might also represent the hand itself. The rune-poem says the following:

ᛏ Týr er æinendr ása;
opt værðr smiðr blása.

↑ Tyr
Tyr is a one-handed god;
often has the smith to blow

The Icelandic rune-poem highlights the same event in the mysteries of Tyr, but here we see that he is also seen as a personification of Mars and so we can speculate whether the rune can also be seen as Mjölnir, the hammer of Thor, held upright and awaiting the verdict telling it what direction it might beat. The poem is as follows:

↑ Týr er einhendr áss
ok ulfs leifar
ok hofa hilmir.
Mars tiggi.

Tyr
God with one hand
and leavings of the wolf
and prince of temples
Duke of Mars

Tyr is a rune of justice and direction and as such it is an excellent rune to work with prior to any undertaking, as it will ensure that the direction aimed for will be struck.

Metals sacred here would be iron, steel, hematite and in general everything under the domain of Mars – but the impetus of justice will also bring in majestic greenwood like the oak, and herbs like aconite which is known as the "Helm of Tyr". Pennick suggests sage as pertaining to this rune which makes sense in terms of its serenity and active purificative properties.

Mead, beer, blood and honey would also be sacred to this rune and as such we might see here a reference to how Tyr might be the first and last rune carved in a binding rune as these materials are used to consecrate the runes.

Giving up one's blood for the sake of consecration might find its reference in Tyr's self-sacrifice, and speak of the mindset necessary to give direction to any kind of working and summoning.

ᛒ

Bjørk/Bjarkan is a rune said to describe Frigg, mother of the Æsir. The rune represents both the pregnant belly and the full breasts awaiting motherhood. It is also one of the runes clearly representing a given tree, the birch. The birch is a tree that enjoys a lot of water and in this can have some vampyric tendencies insofar as it drains the soil for water with its long roots, allowing little water for other greenwoods, save moss, snowdrops, linen and Forget-Me-Nots, which would be plants typically associated with this rune.

The rune is also associated with the child itself, represented by the young sprouts on the tree, its children. In this way we might see a reference here to the ocean Vanis, Ran and her nine daughters, the waves connecting this rune with the mysteries of womb and origin.

The Norse rune-poem also mentions Loke in relation to this rune in the following way:

ᛒ Bjarkan er laufgrønstr líma;
Loki bar flærða tíma.

ᛒ Bjarkan
Birch has the greenest leaves of any shrub;
Loke was fortunate in his deceit.

There are two matters in this relationship that are interesting, one of which concerns the concept of origin and Frigg being the mother of the Æsir. Frigg herself was not Æsir, but a daughter of Jord, thus a daughter of the womb that made possible all kinds of species, and in this represents kinship across one's progeny. Loke being of Jotun heritage himself was Odin's blood-brother, another one harking from the Jotun. In this way this rune can be seen as a force that consolidates whatever spirits and deities in reverence for its common origin.

The other factor relating this rune to Loke is that birch is a highly praised wood for fire; even the bark is highly flammable and takes fire (Loke) with great ease. In this way it might connect Loke deeply to the female mysteries in Nordic traditions and in particular seidr.

The Icelandic rune-poem highlights the birch's association with spring as when the birches bring forth leaves, spring is properly announced by nature. The poem goes as follows:

ᛒ Bjarkan er laufgat lim
ok lítit tré
ok ungsamligr viðr.
abies buðlungr.

Bjarken – Birch
Leafy twig
and little tree
and fresh young shrub.

The magical use of this rune will consequently be concerned with root, origin and beginnings in general. The rune is protective in nature and holds a great capacity for fire, not strictly the wildfire represented by Loke, but more the fire of the hearth in the kitchen tended by the women of the house. In this mystery we can see how this rune brings in household spirits and land spirits of various forms to work together in unison, the key being to bring attention to Frigg and earth itself as the common cauldron for all earthly life's continuation and existence.

ᛖ

Eihwaz is a royal rune, represented by the horse and in particular Sleipnir. Not only this, it also represents the bond between the horse and its rider. The sanctity of the horse in Nordic cultures is seen in how laws until the 13th century gave harsh penalties for consuming horse meat and how farmers always treated the horse as the king of the stable, as the animal more prized than any other. Whether goat, oxen or whatnot, of all the animals domesticated the horse was in a unique position. We know from the sagas that a mummified horse penis, known as völsi, was at least in one instance used as a magical tool to ensure fertility and stability of a household. It might be that the overarching virtue would be to reinstate the man and woman of the house in their rightful positions or to fortify the natural domain they would hold over their household.

A poem for this rune would be as follows:

A man and his horse, is like a man and his sword
Two souls bound in union, four feet becoming eight
Horse and rider

The horse was also related to the account of the nidstang in the saga of Egil Skallagrímsson, where we learn the following:

King Eirík Bloodaxe wronged Egil and made him an outlaw. The feuding resulted in many dead on both sides. After a battle on the island of Herdla (near Norway), Egil raised a hazelwood pole on the top of this island, and on the top of the pole he placed a severed horse's head, aimed towards Eirik's home. On the pole he carved sacred runes, with a curse upon King Eirík. He also spoke this curse, this "Nid":

> Here I place this Nidstang [curse-pole], and turn it against King Eirík and Queen Gunnhild – turneth I this against all the gnomes and little people of the land, that they may all be lost, not finding their homes, until they drive King Eirík and Queen Gunnhild out of the country.

According to the legend, the curse soon took effect, and King Eirík and his Queen Gunnhild fled to the British Isles.

This might suggest that Eihwaz is the rune of Sleipnir, Odin's eight-legged horse, which some rune experts in turn have suggested is a metaphor for Yggdrasil, encoded in several magical symbols bringing out eight directions from a point. This in turn may reveal something of why the number 9 was considered so sacred, not only as a 3 x 3 (3 being the other sacred number), but also due to its relation to eight directions and the stone and tree planted in the center. Also, Skinfaxi and Hrimfaxi should be mentioned as the horses that bring Sun and Day, and Night and Frost.

Materia magica here would naturally be hazelwood and any other nutty tree and I would suggest a relationship to oak as well, this being a tree that was often planted on the sepulchers of chieftains and kings who in turn often held the horse as a sort of "totem". Hair of horse, horseshoes, gold, ivory and marigold would also be material of use to work with this rune of grace, supremacy, and strength.

ᛗ

Alder tree (*alnus glutinosa*), given its association to memory and wisdom, would be the tree of the rune **Man**. This is the rune of mankind, especially Ask and Embla, the first humans created from driftwood by Odin and his brothers, Vile and Ve, whose names in contemporary Norwegian mean will and suffering. Thus it holds the idea of Fate being predominantly a state of suffering in need conquered with will and direction. Man might also be connected to memory itself, particularly Mime who possessed the well of memory, a well of such great importance that Odin sacrificed his eye to gain access to it – and in this also secured the talking head of Mime upon his decapitation. Viktor Rydberg suggests that Mime was the brother of Bestla, Odin's mother, and as the teacher of nine rune-songs he would then hold a particular importance for Odin and his quest for wisdom. In this way we can see in Man how Odin is bringing forth his ancestral wisdom to embed this in the human being, the wisdom needed to overcome Fate herself.

The shape of the rune is also interesting as it is composed of two Laukr runes and a Gebo suggesting that mankind must view one another as a gift in order to flourish, with a particular focus on marriage or the meeting of man and woman that leads to offspring, a particular fertility pointed out in the next rune, Laukr. The Norse rune-poem highlights the spread of the human race, but also comes with a warning, that the journey of life is not without risks, that there will always be predators out there seeking to hinder our spread and growth:

Maðr er moldar auki;
mikil er græip á hauki.

Man is an augmentation of the dust;
great is the claw of the hawk.

The Icelandic rune-poem speaks of the same things, but with an extra emphasis on the global spread of mankind using ships:

Maðr er manns gaman
ok moldar auki
ok skipa skreytir.
homo mildingr.

Man
Delight of man
and augmentation of the earth
and adorner of ships.

Materia magica for this rune, besides the trees mentioned previously, would be all kinds of fungi and driftwood, and in this salt water, algae, hagstones, amber and crabs.

ᚱ

The rune **Laukr** is an Odin rune representing in particular the leek, a vegetable highly prized in Scandinavia. The willow and the whitethorn would be good candidates for trees representing this rune, and the waters spoken of might refer to the amniotic waters necessary for the gestation of the fused ovum and spermatozoid. Njord and Ran might also be seen in this rune as would all the vaettir associated with freshwater lakes and springs, and the huldre-people, and swamplands.

The association with waters flowing, the mountain creeks, and the richness of both land and hidden treasures locked inside mountains and guarded by trolls is spoken of in the Norse rune-poem:

ᚱ Lǫgr er, fællr ór fjalle
foss; en gull ero nosser.

ᚱ Logr
A waterfall is a river which falls from a mountain-side;
but ornaments are of gold.

The Icelandic rune-poem gives even greater emphasis on the gushing water represented by this rune, and as such it is also a symbol of the waters of wisdom sprouting forth from secret groves and hidden wells:

ᚱ Lögr er vellanda vatn
ok viðr ketill
ok glömmungr grund.
lacus lofðungr.

Lögr – Water
Eddying stream
and broad geyser
and land of the fish.

This rune can be said to represent Odin full of wisdom, upright and content, and is as such an energy that will empower any working with understanding and precise direction. Materia magica here would be rocks and stones found in the river, fern and any plant thriving close to the small rivers and creeks, and berries: blueberry, cloudberry, cranberry, and strawberry in particular.

◇

Ing is another name for Frey and means youth, a reference to virility at its peak. As such the rune might be seen to represent both the head of the penis as well as the womb itself. The tree of this rune would be apple and in this a reference to Freya and Idunn can be found.

It is a rune of stability signifying the commencement and end of coitus and in this a form of completion itself that starts a new cycle. It is a rune of rest and stability, an enclosure and a still point in time. The cycle of the year is represented by Jera/Àr placed together in a way that suggests that the circle has been squared, implying a temporal manifestation. As such, any work in need of something being materialized or secured would benefit from the power of this rune. It is a rune with the vibration of midsummer and so the materia magica for this rune would be whatever tree and flower finds its peak of delight in the summertime, and we can add honey, mead, wheat and rye to what is in the domain of Ing, along with semen and saliva.

A rune-poem for Ing would be:

Celebrate virility when you are young
Because soon enough worry and darkness
Will need reminding of the seedy conquests of youth

ᛟ

Odel is a natural expansion of Ing. Odel signifies inheritance and in particular the inheritance of the farm that was handed down to the eldest sons (who would then represent Frey taking possession of his rightful legacy). The rune also represents the total collection of riches, wisdom and land in a lifetime and is a rune of old age and hopefully satisfaction. Naturally, for men suffering ill Fate in life, this would be a bad rune because the legacy and inheritance spoken of here is replaced by loss and forgetfulness.

Hawthorn and clover would be natural candidates for harnessing the energy of this rune.

A rune-poem for this rune would be:

At the last night of your journey, lay the last brick
Count your blessings and victories
Blessed is he who has land and wealth to give to his children

ᛞ

The rune **Dag** represents the new day, the daybreak and as such it represents both hope and renewal. The man finding peace and contentment in old age will see in this rune the promise of the good death, while those lost in life will see the opportunity of a new beginning in death. There is also an element of peace in this rune. We see how it is basically two Thurs runes turned towards one another in truce, which is also indicative of how life under the sun is ruled by very different orders and spirits than those we find under the moon.

I would say anything peaceful and solar would naturally be turned towards the energies in this rune, like meadowsweet and daisy. Elm might be a proper tree for this rune, as would the mineral flint, and opal.

A proper rune-poem for Dag would be:

Like a new world rose from the waters after destruction
So will the Sun rise after each night
giving us the chance to do well and right
What ugly Fate tried to destroy for us.

A way of "taking the runes"

As we have seen, the first aettir can be understood to represent the human journey, from the spark of life to joy. This journey involves a personal and active use of the runes and it is important to integrate the meaning of the runes in a highly personal way. The runes contain secrets unique to each of us, and so Odin in *Hávamál* ended his presentation of the runes by saying that he could not truly reveal anything to anyone, the runes would always be hidden lest you actively worked them and they started to speak to you. This would suggest that we need to appraise the runes as spirits in their own right, as forces representing the building blocks of creation, being, and the stations of life.

1. You will first carve the first eight runes. You will select a tree that appeals to you and you will from this tree either cut discs or sticks some three inches long, cut flat on one side so you can carve the rune into the wood. The wood should be harvested on a Thursday night, and prior to cutting your branch you will offer to the tree milk and beer at its foot. The place where you cut the branch will be anointed with milk and beer as well. You will call upon the three Norns, Tyr, Thor, Frigg and Odin in your own words and state your purpose and give thanks for the gift you are about to take. In this process you should take care to analyze at each step what action and what thought is represented by any of these first eight runes. You will then find a place where there are trees, preferably in the woods, and you will bring a knife suitable for carving, and one by one you will carve the runes as you whisper their names. All eight being done, you will anoint them with your own blood and some honey. Don't be in a rush, stay attentive, bring cheese, bread, water, wine and beer as food and feed the ground around you with whatever you are eating and drinking. This will appease and attract the vaettir that live where you do your magic.

2. The second task is about understanding how to use the first eight runes in sequences for doing magic.

3. This sequence is then repeated for the other two families with a focus both personal and meaningful for you as well as inviting in the larger dimensions encoded in the aettir.

Chapter Fourteen

Bureus and the Noble Runes

Not much is written about the Swedish linguist (frequently referred to as the father of Swedish grammar) and runologist, teacher of the Swedish King Gustav II Adolf and Queen Kristina, Johannes Bureus (1575-1624). Currently, there is the excellent presentation of Bureus and his runic contemplation by Thomas Karlsson, and the booklet *Johannes Bureus and Adalruna* by Stephen E. Flowers. In the work of Bureus we can see how the runes were truly treated as "cosmic secrets" and represent a unique way of how the runes can be taken and integrated to reveal secrets of a mystical and sorcerous nature in their expansive cosmology. In this chapter we will look at the basic principles of his runic mysteries.

Bureus was a contemporary of John Dee (1527-1609) and the German mystic Jakob Böhme (1575-1624). Seeing these names together and noting that the most active esoteric order available in this span of time was Der Gold und Rosencreuz order, also known as the Asiatic Brethren, we have established the esoteric temperature of Bureus' age and what forms of esoteric knowledge were influencing him as a scholar and royal advisor. A rendering of the same themes as found in these two orders are found within the rites and secrets of the esoteric society, Manhëmsforbundet, that Bureus was a member of. This is revealed for instance in Bureus' focus on theosophy as the crown of royal science; this is not the theosophy of Blavatsky, but rather what is found in its original idea stemming from the Greek theo-sophia, meaning "wisdom of god", "wisdom of the divine" or "wise in divine things".

Bureus' approach to the runes was clearly motivated by Christian soteriosophy, as his realization of the runes came to him when he was confronted with a rune-stone outside a church in 1594. It seems that the runes intoxicated Bureus and after more than a decade of runic studies he saw himself as the Lion rising from the North (Judeah) as a prophet or messenger for a runic path of enlightenment. Judah was the tribe presenting the Davidic dynasty; most of the prominent prophets were from this tribe as well as King Zerubabel, the last Davidic king, who took the Judeans from captivity in Babylon to the promised land. Zerubabel was the heir of a throne long gone but born of the blood of prophets; this was perhaps the point that made Bureus assume himself as the "Lion of Judah", as a prophet and a king with no throne. In the figure of Zerubabel it is easy to see a sort of return to the golden age as Zerubabel lay the foundation for the second temple by taking his people out from captivity. Zerubabel himself is shrouded in much mystery. Even his name, which in various forms replicates a belongingness to Babylon in the form of "seed" or "son" of Babylon, introduces interesting dimensions to the mystery of kingship and prophetic dignity, considering his reputation as one of the wisest men in Persia.

Now, here we must remember that a prophet is not someone who necessarily predicts the future, but is a messenger of God, a *malakihm*, someone with a specific divine message related to life in general, to a nation, and to individuals, or is an upholder of divine law. In other words, the idea of "prophet" indicates someone with a divine vision, whether for a selected few or for a greater congregation of people. Personally, I lean towards the option that Bureus' message was of such personal importance that it is quite impossible to make a finely attuned system from it that will be useful for the many. Actually, it is his varied speculations and permutations that are interesting – and I believe this was his message, to present the creativity inherent in the runes. It is this creative divine element that makes some runes become noble while others not. The noble runes can represent various ways of divine ascent as related to the individual and for a larger group by various reorganizations of the fifteen noble runes.

This idea of divine creativity is a common feature in traditional forms of science and faith, often expressed in erotic language. Modern man with his love for categories and nicely ordered collective systems must therefore discard this profane way of organization in order to grasp the creative playfulness of the noble runes. We feel a sort of safety when we can find a category to place things within, a proper box that generates a form of the order of things. With Bureus this is not so, and I believe this is the key to his runic universe; they mean something specific by themselves and something else according to their permutations and arrangements. The noble runes describe his unique perspective on the mysteries; he tells of life, initiation and godhood, about becoming, and about apocalypse in a highly personal way, so personal that any attempt to present a coherent system in conformity with modern demands will at the least be confusing. This being said, it must be added that Bureus in his calculations of apocalyptic and cataclysmic events by resorting to runes and numerology is quite often speculative and at times too forced. I find this part of Bureus' runology both vague and inaccurate and as such I will discard this part of his teachings.

Bureus was, like so many others of his time, attempting to preserve the mystic and hidden dimensions in Christendom, preserving a belief in one manifestation prefiguring something else to come, and becoming because of other forms prior to it. In other words, Bureus clearly adhered to a cyclical realization of time and existence so prominent in the hermetic and neo-platonic schools of thought where the mystical godhood was clad with layer upon layer of mystery and allegory.

Like the medieval doctors of the Church, like Dante and Böhme, Bureus saw in the runes three dimensions or levels of interpretation. In itself there was a form of Christian exegesis translated into the esoteric dimensions. This also replicated the various dimensions found in cabala, in terms of letters and their constellations and arrangements. He saw the runes as consisting of three dimensions, which are:

1. Revealed Runes or the exoteric dimension.
2. Adulruna/Noble runes or the esoteric dimension
3. Alruna/Runes of the All which is the hidden dimension of the runic mysteries.

The first dimension of the runes is the commonly known runes as they are found in the elder and younger futhark, and so we might see this as the exoteric dimension of the runes. These are the runes used for writing and communication of all sorts of messages related to the mundane and material affairs with added magical – and thus less noble – use. The Noble runes on the other hand are not related to the mysteries of the peasants and country dwellers, but to the esoteric dimensions of the runes as conveyed in several Christian themes that were only the temporal pre-figurations of timeless principles. The third sequence of runes is related to the hidden dimensions of runes. This mystery is simply (albeit with complex consequences) related to the stone: the Philosopher's Stone, the stone the builders rejected, and several other Masonic motifs that are found in the formulae we can refer to as "squaring the circle", i.e., manifestation. We see expressions of the Alruna in the various permutations and geometric arrangements Bureus was making, especially in his diagrams of ascent, his crosses and quintals, which harmonize with the Alruna being more a process of folding and unfolding, typical of cabala as understood by Johann Reuchlin (1455-1522). Bureus certainly knew his work, which provides the connection with Pico della Mirandola and the neo-platonic impetus given to the west by the Florentine Platonic Academy. This is further revealed in the whole orientation of Bureus' mysticism, signified by a detail which symbolizes the whole mystery Bureus wanted to convey, albeit in a hidden fashion, proper to the nature of Alruna. The arrow of Abaris is actually a key to the mystery Bureus tries to impart. In the form of the obscure sage Abaris this all makes sense. He is mentioned by Herodotus and Iamblichus as a sage and priest of Apollo; he is even mentioned by Plato in his dialogue *Charmides* – and it all points toward the same image, a prophet and a priest of Apollo who resided in Hyperborean lands. Hyperborea, the northern land, is where Apollo, the essence of the Sun, the point itself, finds his true home in the time of winter.

For Bureus, Hyperborea, "Beyond the North Winds" was evidently Götaland (Scandinavia) or Sweden, given his nationality and the royal dictate which restricted him from going abroad. Bureus was in the land of the golden age, not realizing that the geographical connotation, Borean, was a spiritual designation and not a mundane one. Personally, I believe the flaws in Bureus' thinking were due to an acceptance of too literal an interpretation of the runes he himself held so sacred – or was it? If we look at the icon, so to speak, of Abaris, he was a modest man who Plato referred to as *epodaikon*, or someone "who heals by resorting to incantations". This fits in well with the articulation of runes in the forms of galdr. Incantations like this are found everywhere in the world, from the recitation of *Kalevala* in Finland to the recitation of certain sequences of sacred scripture in Ifa, what is called *Iyere Ifa* in Yorubaland. Abaris was also worshiped in the temple of Proserpina in Sparta as a figure who provided the way toward the northern lands where he was king during the winter, mimicking the metaphysical role of Proserpina, not because Abaris himself was king, but because the *roi real* Apollo was believed to dwell in the Hyperborea during the time of middle European winter. So, the exile of the king of winter was replicated in the nodes of the Moon where the north node is always representing the pole star, the celestial north, the abode of the perfectii and home of spirit, while the south node represents total materialization and thus complete disintegration and alienation from the source. The north pole or Hyperborea was the golden age, while the south pole was the land of disintegration, a fact further confirmed by the south pole always being opposite of the north node. Bureus saw in this a formula for ascent consisting of the corporeal or lunar realm being motivated by change to reach beauty (which Plato says is truth). The arrow of Abaris (replicated on page 306) is composed of the Noble runes Man, Hagal and Ken. We find man's estate at the bottom signified by the Moon, corporeality, the rune that designates man by its very name, Man. In the center of the arrow we find the rune Hagal, which Bureus assigns the qualities of "mercy" and "cunning".

We lift ourselves from the mundane condition by "grace" and mercy or cunning, where we find ourselves at the crossroad, Ken, the two-horned goat of the womb, being or not being as expressed in Shakespeare's drama *Hamlet*. Here the prince is confronted with apparently dire consequences of equally dire choices which always lead to the same destiny, human ascent. This choice is metaphysically simple: it is about being ruled and controlled by affection and desire or allowing the mind and divine dictate to rule over desire. In this way the mundane condition paves the way for a six-fold condition, where the ordeal of choice is resting. These six points are the quarters of the world plus below and above. After traversing this, another choice is presented, this being whether you choose the left or the right. The same idea of ascent is depicted in the figure below, runes that are denoting an ascent in accordance with Matthew 6: 9-13, known as Our Lord's Prayer, where we find a succession of ascent starting from Our Father (Thor) ending in kingdom, or to use the imagery of hermetical and *merkavah* cabalism, "as above, so below," meaning Kether in Malkuth, Malkuth in Kether.

Tors: Our Father which art in heaven,
Hallowed be thy name.
Kön: Thy kingdom come,
Haghall: Thy will be done in earth,
as it is in heaven.
Man: Give us this day our daily bread.
Is/Idher: And forgive us our debts,
as we forgive our debtors.
Sun: And lead us not into temptation,
Byrghal: but deliver us from evil:

Which gives us the sum of the runic septet and the essence of Byrger Tidesson:
For thine is the kingdom,
and the power, and the glory,
for ever. Amen.

This choice is in turn represented by all three quintets of the Adulruna having a motion that follows the cosmic turn, in other words the same movement as the zodiac, or widdershins if you will, which generate a double pyramidal shape reminiscent of the trine aspects of astrology, said to be aspects of love and friendship.

In addition to the "Abaris arrow" there is also a whole range of cross formations composed of a selected set of Noble runes to express the components of an idea. The formations are recognized by their double meaning, either by splitting or having runes being exactly their mirror conjoined. For instance, Bureus says the sequence of Thor, Odin, Lagher, Idher, Man, Tidher and Frey designate Byrger Tidesson or Christ Crucified. These seven runes are related to the seven planets and the limbs of the body. The right hand and arm are composed of Mars and Mercury, the right hand of Venus and Saturn. This is an unusual representation, a quite odd arrangement that perhaps is rooted in astrological considerations as well, seeing the left hand as the product of Frey and Lagher or Venus and Saturn, Saturn finding his exaltation in the sign of Libra ruled by Venus. On the other side we find Mars and Mercury and so the right side becomes completely malefic, as Mercury is bad and Mars is the lesser malefic, signified by the runes Lagher and Odin and carrying with them the ideas of fate, destiny and the cosmic law, fitting into the apocalyptic visions of Bureus. It can also indicate the dual process of the death of Christ, that on one side ended the old law, while Christ himself was exalted until the day of atonement, where he will be the judge of men, a function of Thor and located at the head, and attributed to Jupiter. Feet are given the rune Idher or Isa, which in both Karlsson and Flowers have been given the attribute of the Sun, which clearly is a misrepresentation of where the attributes to the rune placed in the chest, Man, should have been given. Man, Sun, chest, feet are logically assigned to Idher and the Moon in this context. A philosopher occupied with the sacred center of the world would never assign the center of the human body, the heart, to anything other than the Sun.

But where did Bureus take his correspondences from? He is clear on the fact that these writings found in his "Cabbalistica" and the various editions of the Adulruna are products of vision, a recognition of himself as the prophetic Lion of the north. Clearly his vision was of a remarkably subjective and often exalted level of interpretation, quite frustrating to make sense of at times. However, some clues are readily available. Given his interest in cabala it is fair to assume that the focus on orderings of seven runes which all can contain opposition are inspired by the qualities inherited in the seven double letters in the Hebrew alphabet that express this same duality as in the Adulruna.

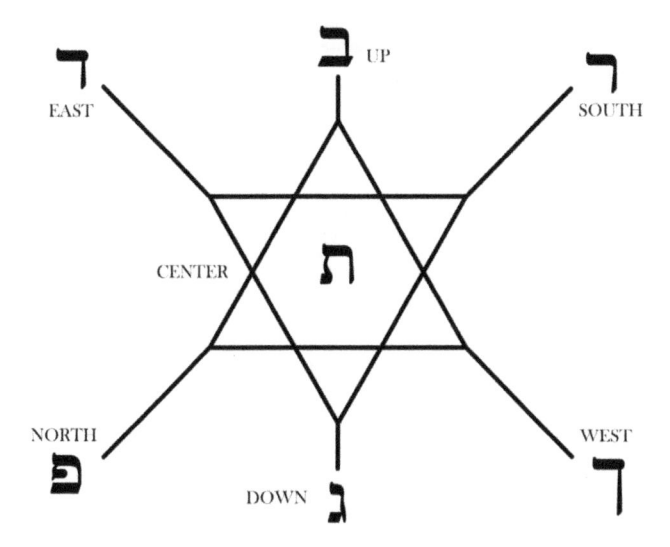

It not possible to present a perfect transliteration by correspondences found in the seven double letters (which are Beth (up/crown), Gimel (below), Daleth (East), Kaf (West), Peh (North), Resh (South), Tau (center), and the Adulruna, but they do express the friction inherited in the human condition, and the *tikkun* or restoration of perfection within the seven double letters are seen as a path of redemption for Bureus.

The *Sheva Kafulot* (7 double letters of prayers) imposed on the hexagram of the seven directions of space is a similar pattern as that found in the three quintets of the Noble runes and also on the cross of Byrger Tidesson. In the septentiary presented here we find a different organization than the one listed, solely in order to demonstrate how various permutations of the letters give a different essence. The model here is the more orthodox presentation of the *Sheva Kafulot*; the one written gives an esoteric significance that diverges from the orthodox, just as Bureus used the various levels of his Noble runes.

The cross of Byrger Tidesson also known as the seventh-changer:

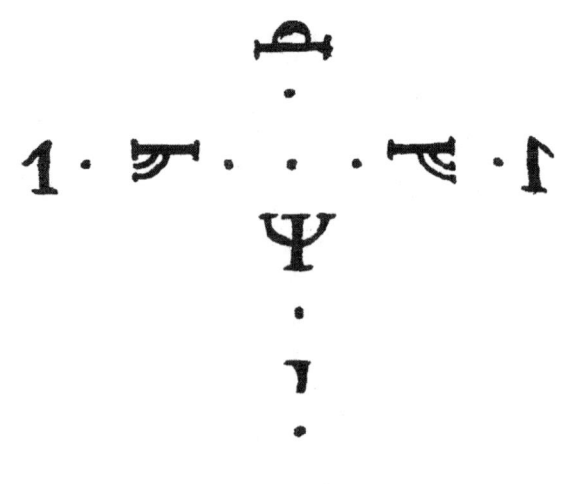

Sjuskiftingen

Bureus' rune-rows look like this and from these fifteen runes he generates three families or quintets relegated to given areas of cosmic, human and social functioning along with their cabbalistic numerical values:

Alphabetum Scanzianum ordine proprio.

ᚠ	*Frey.*	F. ᚠ/v confona.	1
ᚢ	*Vr.*	ᚢ/u.ᚠ/v.ᚠ/y.ᚠ/å.	3
ᚦ	*Tors.*	T / th. þ / dh.	5
ᚬ	*Odhes.*	ᚬ/ð. ᚭ/å. ᛜ/ᛜ/ᛜ/ð.	7
ᚱ	Rydhur.	R/r. ᚱ/r/ er fin.	9
ᚴ	*Kyn.*	ᚴ/ᚴ/c. ᚴ/Y/g.ᚴ/q.	10
ᚼ	Haghall.	H / Gh / Ch.	30
ᚾ	*Nadh.*	N. I/n fin. ᚾ/ån.	50
ᛁ	*Idher.*	I voc. J / j. I'/I/ e.	70
ᛆ	*Æru.*	Æ.. I/a. ᛆ/an.	90
ᛋ	*Sun.*	S pr. I/s. ᛋ/ſ/ ss.	100
ᛏ	*Tidhr.*	T. t/tt. ᛏ/d.	300
ᛒ	Byrghal.	ᛒ/b. ᛒ/B/p.	500
ᛚ	*Lagher.*	L. ᛚ/ll.	700
ᛘ	*Man.*	M. ᛘ/mm.	900

Ordine Latino.

J. ᛁᛚ. ᚠ. ᛏ. J. ᚠ. ᚠY. ᚼ. I. Yᚠ. ᚱ. ᛘ. ᛆ
a b b c d e f g g h i k k l m n

ᛞᚠ. ᛒ B. ᛃ. (Rᚴ. ᛁᛋ. ᛏ. ᛚ ᚼ. ᚠ. ᚠ J.
o o p p q r r r ſſ s t u u y æ ÿ

ᚾᚠ. ᛁᚦ. ᛏ. ᛚᛁᛏ. ᛏ. ᛒ. ᛏ. ᚦ.
v v åå å ö ö ö ch dh gh th

Runorna med sina kabbalistiska talvärden ur Runa ABC

The Triple Quintets of Noble Runes

First quintet or the quintet of fertility

These five runes consist of the following runes, here given in sequence from left to right:

ᚠ ᚢ ᚦ ᛘ ᚱ

Frey: This rune refers to Freya as the womb of waiting and possibility, its root also signifies the fertilized seed that sprouts, as well as referring to cattle, thus providing a link with the Hebrew aleph, meaning ox.

Ur: denoting the primordial powers, what ignites the beginning of manifestation, the bridge over ice, and relates to "work".

Tors: denoting the Æsir Thor and "thora", referring to divine dictate. It also means to turn or re-turn, and it denotes Tyr and other qualities pointing towards celestial command and the godhood.

Odhen: this rune is also called *mercurii litera* and *fata litera*, the Stave of Mercury or the Stave of Fate. It also brings connotations related to inheritance, *Od*, humility (probably in a divine context as accepting destiny). *Odhen* represent man's destiny, the lot Freya gives on her wheel. If we see Freya as the one who turns the wheel, Ur as the measurement and Tors as the divine part ascribed to your lot, Odhen makes this manifest by the hooks and crooks of the path.

Rydhur/Redh: is a rune designating the court of law, the rider of the horse or ship, the captain. Bureus gives to this rune the alternative name of dominion, the ascribed lot of confinement where man is the captain.

We might say that this quintet gives the keys to man's condition, his destiny and allotted estate, as it focuses on the way the Great Law was established in the Greater and Lesser Design of becoming, the lesser being the becoming of the unique individual and the conditions, challenges and blessings each one is born with.

Second quintet or the quintet of birth

Kön/Kyn; is the vagina, the blood and the birth, the pain and generosity of nature. It also brings attention to cunning and king. It truly represents the condition of birth in its format of the Y, the choice of Dexter of Sinister, to go with or against. This rune is the crossroad proper where choices are made.

Haghall: can be seen in many ways, as a sextile cross or as two arrows meeting from opposite ends. The word is derived from *haglek* indicating trickery and cunning in action. Bureus sees in this rune a meeting point between grace and honor which can result in grandeur, from the Latin *grando*, great.

Nådh/Nodher: is the rune of mercy as well as need. You must do what you must do in accordance with divine dictate.

Is/Idher: refers to being completely naked, and also has the name of *poenitentiae litera*, or the Stave of Repentance. It is also related to Idingar, those who are well-versed in law, or wise ones as well as Nidingar, enemies. It carries the message of life being about knowing who is friend and who is foe and reliance on your own inner strength, your nakedness, no matter the pain it might bring.

Ar: is described by a variety of words bringing the mind towards ideas such as honor, eagle, enough and years. As such it denotes the promise of honor coming by accepting one's destiny.

Sun/Sol: can mean both Sun and Son indicating a relationship between the Sun and Salvation by the act of Grace as a consequence of penitence. This rune is according to Bureus called the "hanging sun" contrary to the kneeling sun as is the more common representation of this rune. Bureus was clearly indicating the importance of daybreak here.

Tidher: meaning time and relates to another aspect of Tyr, and also a prefiguration of Byrger Tidesson, the mythical originator of the Noble runes, seen as an anointed one by Bureus. He also ascribes ascent, fire and air to this rune and further it is a reference to Saturn as patience in accordance with the nature of time itself.

Byrghal: is the opposition of Tors, it represents the fall into material manifestation, war and upheaval, all facets of the human condition. Bureus refer to this rune as Binarius Daemon, or the Twin Daemon. It is the world of contrast and the potential for reintegration in man. Bureus sees the unity in Tors' single half circle and duality and the material in the two separated half circles in this rune.

Lagher: is the rune of law and tides, the Laug or colleges of craftsmen. Bureus refers to this rune as descensus or descent; it is the cold waters within the earth, a quiet potentiality within the solid.

Man/Madur: is a rune Bureus says "lost its mouth". In other words, it is the silence of veneration shrouded in the moonlit night, and depicts the acceptance of grace, trial and error as the path of ascent in order to recognize the condition of man, being a dual union of spiritual and material.

In the three quintets Bureus sees man's determined path of ascent, and within each of the quintets there are key runes that according to ordering provide insight into other mysteries according to their organization, as demonstrated in the cross of Byrger Tidesson. The fifteen Noble runes are of a particular importance for man's ascent towards perfection. Bureus saw the material realm as an ocean of chaotic and contradictory forces represented by Byrghal, which represents all challenges inherited in human life, this duality and the powers pulling in opposite directions. He sees Tors as the ideal of unity, because here Thor has warded off the sacred Hyperborean center from the malefic and destructive forces of chaos. Bureus wanted to provide keys to a path of royal and prophetic enlightenment, a reintegration that would make man realize the nature of destiny, the conditioning of birth and then the challenges of life. We see this in the first quintet which provides the more intense powers, and then in the last quintet it all gets gloomier, because here the material reality has become a living reality.

Bureus' thoughts about specific runes representing a path of ascent, as summarized in the Abaris arrow, were also found in the initiatory progress of Manhemsförbundet or The Society of Madur (loosely translated), who chose for their symbol the rune Man/ Madur. We see this is the last rune in Bureus' Adalruna, because here is "hidden the lot of man and the center of the world". Manhemsförbundet had nine degrees depicting an ascent from the darkness of material existence, acquisition of the warrior's powers, respect for women and wife, confrontation with Ragnarök (apocalypse) and then a higher level indicating hope and celestial grace. The ninth and final degree was called "the heart" and here the candidate had to express a perspective of unity. He was as if on the summit of the mountain looking out over material existence without being dragged down into it. Those of the heart were referred to as nobles and the warrior's armor was taken off and the mantle of priesthood vested. In official meetings the brothers of the heart dressed all in black; there was no longer any division, they were one with the essence of Tors and had become living wardens against the powers of darkness, terror and chaos.

The Runecross of Noble runes (Adalruna):

Runkorset

Appendix A

On the Symbolism of the Rune-drum

RUNEBOMMA or the rune-drum used by the Sámi noaids are marked by signs, symbols and figures replicating the noaid worldview in a way that makes it possible to use the drum for divination and for travel, specifying in what region of the world one seeks to venture. Divination would be done by placing a ring on the drum that would then, by chanting and beating, make a path across the world of the drum which would be interpreted.

The priest Thomas von Westen (1682-1727) was instrumental in the gathering of at least 80 rune drums during his mission in the north of Norway. He was clearly a priest with some interest in the spiritual and magical in the world not only due to his interest in the nature religions of the Sámis, but also due to the name given to his pietistic cleric collegium he established in 1710. The collegium of the seven stars connected him and the six other priests in the district into a brotherhood aiming towards unraveling the Sámis through understanding and preaching. Westen was described as a man of mild manner, fond of drink and always curious, but prone to "thunder-talk" when necessary. He confiscated more than 100 rune drums, along with several "gand-flies" kept in small boxes that he delivered to the Waisenhusets library in Copenhagen. The entire collection got lost in the great fire of Copenhagen in 1782.

In spite of the fire, Westen had also his own private collection and the rune-drum he appreciated the most was subject for a dialogue that was later written between him and his friend magister Johan Randulf (1686-1735) in 1723, in what was named *Nærømanuskriptet*. In this text Westen is making a comparative analysis between the Sámi's beliefs mirrored in Greek and Roman mythology and described from the position of a faithful priest trying to mediate the Old Norse faith along with Christendom.

The analysis started with the following dialogue:

"These samís consider their gods in the form of men and in the likeness of man", said father Randulf. "They also call angels and devils by the names of men."
"Indeed they do," Westen confirmed.
"They have the Fridayman, the Saturndayman, the Sundayman, but what does it all mean?"
"They have many gods and even more devils. Soon it is

the noaidegadze and shortly after it is called Gilla-Sparra-Alma – the men adorned with rings of gold and brooches of silver! And then you have Govitter and Passevare Olmai and Passevare Sarva and Lodde and Gili and Rana Neyda – who can keep track of all this?!"

Thomas then got hold of his rune-drum[210] and said; "let me explain..."

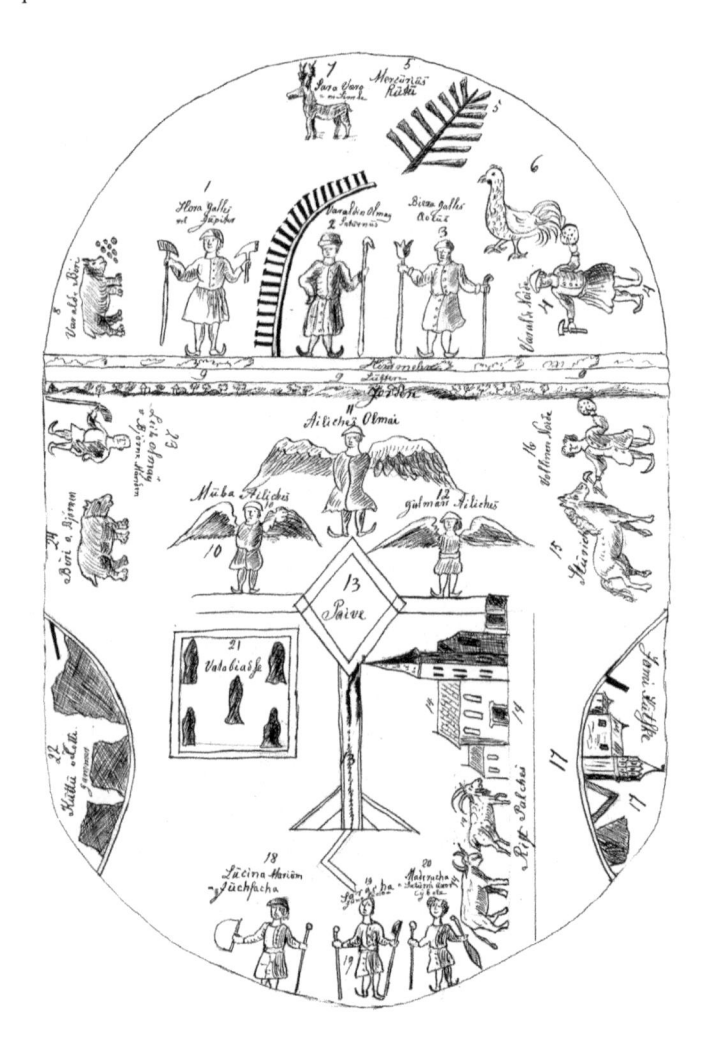

---

210 Drawing by Thomas von Westen 1723, in care of Riksarkivet, the National archives of Norway with the reference number RA/EA-4056/F/L0038: Ms nr. 233.

Appendix A

Hora Galles (Hora Golles/Horagalles), Thor's God, one of the most distinguished of the gods, Thor with his hammer or Jupiter.

Varalden Olmay (Varaldin Olmay), Man of the World, is another one of the mighty gods, he is the same as Saturn.

Biexa Galles (Biegga Galles), the strong man of the wind, he is the third of the mighty gods and is the same as *Aolus* (the keeper of the winds).

Varalde Noide is the heavenly rune-man or prophet. He holds his runedrum in his left hand and stands with a hammer, in the manner of Thor, in his right hand.

Mercurius Rutu, the woods of Mercury. It is depicted as a tree with many branches. It is a governor beneath the three mighty gods, Thor, Man of the World and the Man of the Wind. They execute all of what the Samís desire in heaven as on earth. They sacrifice a rooster to their three most important gods.

Sara or *Sarva Væro* (Særva Wæro), Simle, the reindeer that belongs to the heavens.

Varalde Biri, the heavenly bear. The bears are depicted amongst the Samís as being together with the gods, because they consider them holy and call them 'the dog of God'. A line separating earth from heaven denotes the wind.

Muba Auliches (Ailiches), the Saturdayman, one of the three undergods or angels named after the holiness of his day.

Ailiches Olmai (Ailekes Olmak), the Sundayman, the second of the undergods or mighty angels.

Gulman Ailiches, the Fridayman, the third of the three mighty undergods or mighty angels.

Paive (Beive), the Sun.

Rist Palches or *Paliches,* the Path of the Christians. To express this they have drawn a church, a house, a cow and a ram to make visible what is found amongst the Christian farmers.

Sturich is a horse. It is found on the rune-drum so they can ask it if luck at the end of autumn will provide them with the means to purchase a horse, since they do slaughter and eat the meat of horse when they can afford it.

Vollinere Noide, the prophet of Hell or the Grave. He stands outside the realm of death and will rune-work on his drum with his hammer for those who enter the realm of death, and decides which prayers will be heard, which one of those mortally ill shall live and who shall recover from illness.

Jami Kutske (Jamichukke), the realm of death, where they believe the dead reside and hold power to influence the lives of the living. In the realm of death they have placed a church, a house and a Samí tent (gamme). The thick line symbolizes the dead one whom they will summon in their need.

Juchsacha, the first great goddess, the same as *Lucina Marium.* She will give the women luck to give birth to male children.

Saracha, the second great goddess, whose name is also written *Saragacha.* She is the same as the Roman *Juno Lucina.* They call upon her aid when children are in distress, and she will help women as well as reindeer to give birth.

Maderacha, the third great goddess, she is the same as *Cybele* or *Regis Saturni uxor,* of which both were called *magna mater Deorum.* She possesses the gift of fertility, both for humans and for animals.

Vata biadse or *Vada Baidse* means a water full of fish. It is marked on the drum becasue they can ask *Fonsie God,* which is their Oceanic god and the same as *Neptunus,* if they will have luck fishing in the ocean. If they seek luck in fishing in fresh waters they ask *Harchild,* the god of fresh water and rivers.

Kuttu or *Kotte* illustrates the dwelling of the Samís with their tents.

Leib Olmay, the Bearman, is the god that is protecting the bear but also the one who gives the bear what they need to venerate him. Even if they consider the bear a sacred animal and call it God's dog they do hunt and kill it for consumption. But they have several rules concerning the treatment of the bear. Also, in the hunt one needs to allow the bear to come close; with a few feet between them the hunter will spit tobacco in the ground in front of the bear and exclaim: "shame on you!" and he will shoot.

Biri or *Bini*, is the Bear itself, which is considered sacred. He is also called *Immels*, God's dog. No matter how sacred the bear is, they do prefer the meat of the bear more than anything else, and the skin they do sell. The first to fill their belly, the second to fill their wallet.

Appendix B

The Vargulf and Lycanthropy in the North

There is a fixed time for each Neurian, at which they change, if they like, into wolves, and back again into their former condition. – Pomponius Mela, *Description of the World*

Lycanthropy means a transformation into Wolf. Deities demonstrating a relationship with animals are attested ever since the time of Egypt. When we speak of *canis* and other predatory species, the founders of Rome, Romulus and Remus who were fed by a she wolf (or jackal), should be mentioned, as well Odin who is constantly flanked by two wolves.

Animals also serve as totems and familiars in cultures spread across time and geography everywhere in the world, from the shapeshifting sorcerers of west Africa turning into jaguars to the Nordic berserkers turning into wolves and bears. Furthermore, we have the constant association between witches and their ability to shed their own form and take over the form of their fetch or familiar, whether by possessing the particular animal or physically turning into their fetch.

The act of physical transformation is attested in Lithuania through the *vilkacis*, literally meaning "wolf-eyed". When it comes to turning into a *vilkacis* the stories vary. In one version of the tale it is said that you will at the time of the full moon find a tree whose top branches have grown into the earth, forming an arch. Once you find this tree on the night of a full moon simply stand under the arch and you will be turned into a *vilkacis*. In other myths you need to wear wolf fur and recite some incantations and you become a wolf. These are all themes we find in Scandinavia concerning lycanthropy as well.

We find the same phenomena in Haiti in the form of loup-garou (werewolf), which is said to be created by a secret *pwen* or point given to select people, making them part of the Bizango society. The *pwen* consists of given powders that are cut into the body as well as a pact being made with a *baka*.

In Brazil there are similar stories told related to the spirit Yurupari who can give the gift of transformation into either wolf or wild pig (boar). Given that the Sampwel is transmitting lore and knowledge both from Bantu speaking districts in West Africa and the

Taino Indians of Haiti which in turn originated from the Guarani tribes found in the north of Brazil, we can detect a sort of transition of lore and knowledge with its root in traditional societies, be they from Africa or amongst native nations.

Likewise, in Scandinavia we find much lore speaking about the physical transformation of man into wolf. Quite frequently we find that when such transformation is spoken of, gypsies, Finnish sorcerers or Sámi noaids/shamans are rarely far away.

The most famous story, the one which gave rise to the word lycanthropy, speaks of a total metamorphosis into wolf, an act done by Jupiter to punish King Lycaon, stating that a Jupiterian transgression and curse is at the root of lycanthropy. When we look at wolf ancestry, we find that Apollo figures often as having a particular relationship with wolves and dogs. For instance, his son Asclepius was nursed by a dog and a goat, both sent by Apollo to raise him. Then we have the lesser-known Miletus (Greek for the plant smilax that served as his cradle) who was nursed and protected by she-wolves sent by Apollo. This is the form of Apollo known as Apollo Cunomaglus, "The Hound Lord", where Apollo is connected to Diana and Silvanus, emphasizing the hunt and the wilderness. Apollo, being the son of Zeus and in himself representing all things solar and poetic and prone to prophecy, just like Odin; he was equally lustful for women and nymphs and he also held amazing skills in the sorcerous arts, represented by the wolves that are at his command.

If we look at Greek heroes with connections to wolves we find a host of them. Besides Lykos himself we find Autolykos, son of Hermes and grandfather of Odysseus, who also taught wrestling to Herakles and who lived on Parnassos, Apollo's mountain. We also have a descendant of Autolykos, Harpalykos, another martial arts teacher living on Parnassos; Lykomedes, father of the Atheneas tribe Lykomidai; Lykoreus, son of Apollo by the nymph Korykia; and Lykurgos, a Thracian king, son of Dryas, who was hunting down Dionysos when Boreas the North wind punished him with blindness and strife. Oiolykos is another; Herodotus refers to him as a lone wolf who wanted to make a new colony, but failed in this endeavor.

There are clearly some themes shared in common by Apollo and Odin, besides the association with prophecy and poetry. Apollo and Odin share wolves and serpents, while Odin holds the raven as his own (thought and memory). Hugin and Munin fly out each day and report back to Odin about what they have seen, while Apollo gets the bad news about his lover from a raven. (He turns it from white to black in his rage.) As well as two ravens, Odin has two wolves for his pets, while Apollo had also the epitaph, Lycegenes, Wolf-born and Lycoctonus, Wolf-Killer, attached to him. Odin also turned himself into a snake to get the mead of poetry from Gunnljod, while Apollo's relations with snakes we find at his temple in Delphi as prophetic vehicles.

Apollo was a healer-god, a plague-god who could also cure disease and seems to have merged with another healer-god, Paion, whose cult is amongst the oldest in Greece. Apollo took over the name and passed it to his son, Asklepios.

What we find here is that the werewolf mystery is supported by Jupiter, Apollo, Mars and Faunus and what is interesting here is to see that Odin might be perceived as a composite of these four deities.

The woodpecker also plays into this, due to being a bringer of food, as well as the wolf itself and I would say the snake due to its skin-shedding abilities. In Brazil the woodpecker is a magical bird; its powers are usually harvested to gain entrance through closed doors and thus it might be a matter of transgression encoded as allegory in the practical use of the woodpecker.

This would suggest that the elements of lycanthropy would consist of forging an alliance with the powers in question, in particular Faunus, Faustulus, Apollo and Mars. I would further assume that the fixed star Arcturus is a keyholder to this mystery as well as Ursa Major. Thus it should be possible to bind star and nature by focusing on the wilderness, sojourn and vigil when Arcturus is prominent in the heavens, and hymns and poetry should perhaps be composed in his honor.

A specific diet should be observed consisting of wolf's milk or some sort of simulacra of this food as well as the flesh and blood of wolf. Finally, some act of rebellion should be involved that attracts wrath and in turn a curse. To offer children on the altar of Jupiter is perhaps too drastic, but some sort of dramatic Jupiterian offense would perhaps be a catalyst, as in the story of Lycaeon it is the deliberate breaking of taboo that causes the curse.

NORDIC WEREWOLVES

The accounts of werewolves in the sagas, Eddas and in folktales are rich and have several themes in common with similar legends in the Baltics. In the Icelandic sagas we find werewolves or shapeshifting mentioned in fourteen sagas and poems.

In addition, the motif is found in two Norwegian texts that were both known and read in Iceland: a short episode in *Konungs skuggsjá* and the translation of the *Lai de Bisclavret* (*Bisclaretz ljóð*) in Strengleikar.

The closely related motif of the man-bear is found in *Landnámabók* (12th century), *Hrólfs saga kraka* (14th century) and others. Swedish medieval troubadours ensured the memory in popular culture and it is here we find many accounts of the physical transformation of man into beast, whether wolf or bear. This category of songs was often referred to as troll-songs. One song from the 16th century speaks of how a stepmother transforms her stepson into a needle, then into a knife and then into a scissor, all of them being dull and working against their purpose until she finally transforms him into a wolf. The same song in its 18th century rendering excludes the needle, knife and scissor and enters directly to the transformation being a curse leading to the stepson, now being referred to as a "lost knight", consuming the stepmother's newborn infant. Here it appears that it is the drinking of his stepbrother's blood that ensures the permanence of the curse; other versions place this act as the cause of the curse, and other renderings of the same song present the consummation of the infant's blood as the cure for the curse.

Nevertheless, we have here a few items, real or symbolic, which assist in the transformation. Needle, knife and scissor are all tools made from iron, a metal constantly associated with protection and exorcising or irritating the denizens of the invisible world. In addition, we have the element of blood. Human blood appears to be of some importance in this and whether the reference to the infant brother is an allegory to the blood of a child, the blood of someone unbaptized or of a relative is difficult to ascertain, but the transmission of virtue through the consumption of blood is a mystery fairly well known in legends all over the world, and is particularly related to the vampire legends.

Other troll-songs, in particular "The Fair Maiden in the Wolves Clothing" and "The Power of the Lyre", show another variation, namely that werewolves are made as a woman is impregnated by a werewolf while he is either under the influence of the first stages of transformation or completely transformed. The child being born is in some variations consumed by the werewolf and in others it appears that the child is also a werewolf. In this gathering of songs, we find the occurrence of a tree associated with this mystery, namely linden, also known as Basswood (*Tilia cordata*). In Europe it was considered a sacred tree and was associated with justice and court proceedings and thus matters of court were in the middle ages frequently done under the shade of linden trees. It enjoyed further esteem for being vital for the bees in producing honey from its rich nectar, and was in many songs mentioned together with roses, another plant associated with lycanthropy, although particularly related to vampires. And so, it might be that the flowers that appear as an antidote are the flowers of the linden tree as in the song "Var-Ulfen", where the werewolf is made by the deliberate curse of a witch. Another item that frequently appears is the belt made from the pelt of wolf or bear that aids the transformation into physical form. One of several accounts is typified by the case against Peter Stumpe in Köln, Germany, who was executed in 1590 for the murder of thirteen children and for having ripped out the unborn child of two women by transforming himself into a wolf by using a belt. This belt could be tied to the body circumambulating the belly or be placed across the threshold of the house to cause the metamorphosis. The belt could be used alone or together with a particular ointment composed of wolf's fat and entheogenic herbs. There is also an interesting account from Hamdal, Norway, dating to 1660 in which a wise woman called Karenn Erichsdaatter said that by using the belt at night the vord, or *vardyvle* (were-animal), which was the term used for *vorden* taking on animal shape, would go out in the shape of a wolf, and she also gave a "belt-prayer" as follows:[211]

> I bless my belt
> Beneath Queen God's Sun
> My vord is in the vaettir
> My soul in the heavenly kingdom

Speaking of auto-transformations which do not need a belt, we find for instance in Qvigstad's *Lappiska eventyr og sagn* a formula which repeats itself in other sources. The person that seeks to gain this mystery will need to sleep at the foot of a given tree on a full moon night; this tree had to have a part of its branches bending naturally towards the ground and form a shelter. The person undertaking this would then state their intention to sleep at the tree and will then be shown in dreams how to proceed with effectuating the transformation. This tree might very well have been a linden tree.

In another work, Jon Johansson's *Signerier och besvärjelser*, we find two other formulas for werewolf transformation.

The first one says that you need to go to the cemetery on a Thursday night – preferably close to Christmas/Winter Solstice, Easter or Summer solstice, and between midnight and one o'clock you will dig up a fresh male corpse and strip the skin from it, which will then be used as a belt. In some versions this belt is worn, but more commonly this belt should be large enough to make an opening to crawl through on another Thursday night in the same hour.

---

211 Lid 1950: 87.

The second formula says to identify the grave of a murderer or someone who took his own life and dig up the corpse. From this corpse the tendons from the left arm should be removed and tied together by spinning the tendons as if they were threads, and again a ring is made that is then used to crawl through. The act of crawling through this ring of skin or tendons is repeatedly done against the sun, i.e. from west to east. Some accounts given to us by Ella Odstedt speak of this crawling needing to be repeated several times and that bit by bit the transformation spreads and becomes more and more violent, on each Thursday night close to the full moon when this is done.

In other districts, like Dalarna and Värmland in Sweden, we don't encounter the use of the belt, but instead we find the skin of the wolf being used. The accounts we have are sparse in details and give attention to the dressing of the wolf skin at the proper time as what ensures the transformation. Certainly, there must be more to this than just dressing the skin; in one account by Odstedt we find the detail of a belt attached to the fur and so from this we might conclude that a belt or similar made from human skin which was taken from a corpse is actually a vital part of the mystery.

In the cases of metamorphosis being caused by a curse or an enchantment it is always uttered by a cunning one, who simply states the name of the person and their intent and in that moment the process is begun. The antidote is often to call the name of the person when he or she is wolf, thereby bringing forth the human form again and breaking the charm/curse. The werewolves turned into such by an enchantment are frequently said to run on three legs, with one leg standing out in the shape of an erect tail. Also, in the many accounts given, the appearance varies from full transformation into wolf to partial, yet when someone is fully wolf there is still some compassion or reason gleaned through its eyes. In the cases of a transformation not being notably physical, it is common to find comments about how the eyes changed into the eyes of a wolf along with the person behaving more savagely than usual. In this specter we find accounts speaking of the werewolf being unusually hairy or having slightly bestial forms; sometimes the changes of the features are less dramatic, and it is possible to see the human form beneath the changed form. In other instances, not.

The key term in this context is hamr. One finds references to men changing into wolves by taking upon themselves a *vargshamr* (a wolf's shape) and becoming *vargar* (wolves). The Icelandic terms for wolf are *vargr* and *úlfr* – terms that are also used for what we now call *vargúlfur* (werewolf). Other related terms connected to werewolves or shapeshifting beings are *vargstakkr* (wolf coat), *úlfhamr* (wolf skin), *úlfheðinn* (wolf skin/pelt) and *berserkr* (bear coat). This means that both *úlfheðnar* and *berserkr* are two kinds of animal-warriors, first mentioned in *Haraldskvæði* (*Hrafnsmál*), where they are constantly close to King Harald.

One of the most recognizable attributes of the berserkers is that they fall into a "berserk frenzy". They run wild in battle, become crazed, and roar or howl. No weapons can harm them, and they are not easily affected by wounds. The berserk frenzy appears closely related to shapeshifting, for in both cases men acquire the attributes of animals. The main difference resides, perhaps, in the fact that with shapeshifting it is assumed that the vord is cloaking itself in a different shape or pelt (hamr). The condition is therefore psychological in the case of the berserker, but physical in the case of werewolves and other shape-shifters according to the sublime studies by Aðalheiður Guðmundsdóttir.[212]

Guðmundsdóttir also points out that people who had power over their souls by being able to shapeshift were called *hamrammir* or *eigi einhamir*. She refers to the works by the 18th century historian and teacher Finnur Jónsson, who wrote about seidr and argued that most sorcerers and shamans had the ability to change themselves into the shape of any living creature. It is clear that the animal into which a person is transformed has a symbolic value. This can be seen in shapeshifting stories from around the world, including those from Iceland, or in tales in which beautiful maidens turn into attractive birds such as swans or cranes. Wolves were beasts of battle, with strongly negative associations, as we see with *vargr* also being used as a reference to outlaws.

By all accounts it appears that the transition into werewolf was accomplished by moving one's vord into a different form by the aid of a vaettir. The transformation would be aided by the full moon and the possession of specific materia magica, such as a wolf pelt and herbs, along with enchantments. The transformation could be oneiric as well as physical but also it would appear that an element of possession was a part of this mystery, as in the case of the berserker.

---

212 2007.

Appendix C

Correspondences between Runes and Trees of the North

This list is a suggestive correspondence between trees and runes in relation to similarity of virtue, in this case giving particular focus to trees and bushes that stand out in a particular way and mirror runes in ways that have been useful for me.

Fé	Ask/Ash (*Fraxinus excelsior*)
Ur	Osp (*Populus tremula*)
Thurs	Slåpetorn/Blackthorn (*Prunus spinosa*)
Às	Gran/Pine (*Picea abies*)
Raid	Spisslønn/Maple (*Acer platanoides*)
Ken	Rogn/Rowan (*Sorbus aucuparia*)
Gebo	Kirsebær/Cherry (*Prunus cerasus*)
Wunja	Eple/Apple (*Malus pumila*)
Hagal	Trollhegg/Alder buckthorn (*Frangula alnus*)
Is	Furu/Scots Pine (*Pinus sylvestris*) /Kastanjetre/Chestnut (*Castanea sp.*)
Ar/Jera	Selje/Goat willow (*Salix caprea*)
Yr/Eihwaz	Barlind/Yew (*Taxus baccata*)
Pert	Sølvlind/Linden (*Tilia tomentosa*)
Algiz	Einebær/Juniper *Juniperus communis*)
Sol	Tinved/Buckthorn (*Hippophae rhamnoides*)
Tyr	Eik/Oak (*Quercus sp.*)
Bjørk	Bjørk/Birch (*Betula sp.*)
Ehwaz	Svartor/Alder (*Alnus glutinosa*)
Man	Hassel/Hazel (*Corylus avellana*)
Laukr	Hagtorn/Hawthorn (*Crataegus monogyna*)
Ing	Pors/Myrica (*Myrica alba*)
Odel	Bøk/Beech (*Fagus sylvatica*)
Dag	Alm/Elm (*Ulmus glabra*)

BIBLIOGRAPHY

Allen, R. H. (1899). *Star Names: Their Lore and Meaning*. Dover: US
Alver, B. G. (1971). *Heksetro og Trolldom*. Universitetsforlaget: Oslo
Amundsen, A. B. & Laugerud, H. (eds.) (2010). *Religiøs tro og praksis i den dansk-norske helstat fra reformasjonen til opplysningstid ca 1500 - 1814*. University of Bergen: Norway
Andrén, A., Jennbert, K., Raudvere, C. (eds) (2006). *Old Norse Religion in long-term Perspectives*. Nordic Academic Press: Stockholm
Andrén, A. (2014). *Tracing Old Norse Cosmology*. Nordic Academic Press. Lund: Sweden
Asbjørnsen, P Chr. (1949). *Norske huldreeventyr og folkesagn*. Johan Grundt Tanum: Oslo
Bang, A. Chr. (2005). *Norske Hexeformularer og magiske oppskrifter*. Ka forlag: Norway
Bilardi, C. (2009). *The Red Church*. Pendraig Publishing: US
Birkeli, E. (1944). *Huskult og Hinsidighetstro. Nye studier over fedrekult i Norge*. Det Norske Videnskaps-Akademi i Oslo/Jacob Dybwad: Oslo
Bæksted, A. (2002). *Nordiske guder og helter*. Aschehoug forlag: Oslo
Bø, O. (1987). *Trollmakter og godvette*. Det Norske Samlaget: Oslo
Carshult, B.G. (1941) *Undenäsbygden genom tiderna*. Skövde: Stockholm
Cucina, C. (2011). *Traces of Runic Lore in Italy: The Wooden Calendar 'Book' in Bologna and Its Medieval Connections*. Classiconorroena 29 pp. 95-181: Italy
DuBois, T. (1999). *Nordic Religions in the Viking Age*. University of Pennsylvania Press: US
Dumézil, G (1973). *Gods of the Ancient Northmen*. UCLA: US
Eggertson, J. M. /'Skuggi'. (2013) *Sorcerer's Screed*. Lesstofan: Iceland
Ellis Davidson, H. R. (1964). *Gods and Myths of Northern Europe*. Penguin: US
Enoksen, L. M. (1998). *Runor*. Historiska media: Sweden
Eytzinger, F. (2013). *Solomonic Magical Arts*. Three Hands Press: US
Ficino, M (1989). *Three Books on Life*. Mrts; New edition edition: UK
Flatin, K.A. (1991). *Tussar og Trolldom*. Lokalhistorisk forlag. Espa: Norway
Flowers, S. (1989). *The Galdrabók*. Weiser: US
Flowers, S. (1998). *Johannes Bureus and Adalruna*. Runa-Raven Press: US

Flowers, S. (2016). *Icelandic Magic*. Inner Traditions. Vermont: US
Fries, J. (1993). *Helrunar*. Mandrake of Oxford: UK
Gorsleben, R. J. (1930). *Hoch-Zeit der Menschheit*. Koehler u. Amelang: Leinen
Grambo, R (1979). *Norske trollformler og magiske ritualer*. Universitetsforlaget: Oslo
Grambo, R. (1990). *Djevelens livshistorie*. Ex Libris. Oslo: Norway
Guðmundsdóttir, A. (2007). The Werewolf in Medieval Icelandic Literature. In *Journal of English and Germanic Philology*, July. The University of Illinois: US
Guènon, R. (1925/2001). *Man & His Becoming According to the Vedanta*. Sophia Perennis: US
Guénon, R. (1945/2001). *The Reign of Quantity & the Signs of the Times*. Sophia Perennis: US
Guénon, R. (1962/2004). *Symbols of Sacred Science*. Sophia Perennis: US
Häll, M. (2013). *Skogsrået, näcken och djävulen*. Malört förlag: Sweden
Hagen, R.B. (2015). *Ved porten til helvete*. Cappelen Damm: Oslo
Heide, E (2006). *Gand, seid og åndevind*. Dr. Art. Dissertation. University of Bergen: Norway
Heide, E. (2011). "Loki, the Vätte, and the Ash Lad: A Study Combining Old Scandinavian and Late Material." *Viking and Medieval Scandinavia*, Vol. 7 pp. 63–106.
Hesse, H. (1963). *Steppenwolf*. Bantam: US
Hodne, Ø. (1995). *Vetter og skrømt i norsk folketro*. Cappelen forlag. Oslo: Norway
Hodne, Ø. (2008). *Trolldom i Norge*. Cappelen Damm: Oslo
Hodne, Ø. (2011). *Mystikk og magi i norsk folketro*. Cappelen Damm Faktum: Oslo
Hultcrantz, Å. (1983). "Current Anthropology." In *A World Journal of the Sciences of Man*, Vol. 24 No. 5. University of Chicago Press: US
Jakobsson, Á. (2003). *The Trollish acts of Þorgrímr the Witch: The Meanings of troll and ergi in Medieval Iceland*. Saga Book – Viking Society for Northern Research 27, 5-24.
Johnson, T. (2013). *The Graveyard Wanderers*. S.E.E: UK
Karlson, T. (2005). *Adulrunan och den götiska kabbalan*. Ouroboros: Sweden
King, G. (2016). *The British Book of Spells and Charms*. Troy Books: UK
Kjeldstadli, K. (1999). *Fortida er ikke hva den en gang var*. University of Oslo Press: Oslo: Norway

Kristiansen, R. (2005). *Samisk religion og læstadianisme*. Fagbokforlaget: Norway
Lecoutoux, C. (2003). *Witches, Werewolves and Fairies*. Inner Traditions: Vermont
Lecouteux, C. (2013). *The Tradition of Household Spirits*. Inner Traditions: Vermont
Lecouteux, C. (2015). *Demons and Spirits of the Land*. Inner Traditions: Vermont
Le Goff, J. (1988). *The Medieval Imagination*. University of Chicago Press: US
Lid, N. (1935). *Folketro*. H. Aschehoug & Co forlag: Oslo
Lid, N. (1950). *Trolldom*. Nordiske studiar: Oslo
Lindbohm, D. (1998). *Magi*. Replik: Sweden
List, G. Von. (1908). *Das Geheimnis der Runen*. Verlag Guido von List Gesllschaft: Wien
Lorenzen, M. (1872). *Signeformularer og Trylleråd*. Marinus M. Schultz: Aalborg, Denmark
Lorie, P. (1992). *Overtro*. C. Huitfeldt forlag: Oslo
Løkka, N. (2010). *Steder og landskap i norrøn mytologi*. University of Oslo, PhD dissertation: Oslo
McKinnell, J., Simek, R. & Düwel, K. (2004). *Runes, Magic and Religion*. Fassbaender. Wien: Austria
Mitchell, S. A. (2011). *Witchcraft and Magic in the Nordic Middle Ages*. Penn: US
Noonan, G. (1990). *Fixed Stars and Judicial Astrology*. American Federation of Astrologers: US
Odstedt, E. (1943/2012). *Varulven i svensk folktradisjon*. Malört förlag: Sweden
Ögren, K. (2005). *På jordfast grund*. Logia: Sweden
Ohrvik, A. (2012). *Conceptualizing Knowledge in Early Modern Norway: A Study of Paratexts in Norwegian Black Books*. Ph. D. Dissertation. University of Oslo: Norway
Olsen, M. (1917). *Om Troldruner*. Uppsala: Sweden
Orchard, A. (1997). *Dictionary of Norse Myth and Legend*. Cassell: US
Pennick, N. (1989). *Practical Magic in the Northern Tradition*. The Aquarian Press: UK
Pennick, N. (1992). *Runemagic*. Aquarian: US
Pennick, N. (1995). *Runic Astrology*. Capall Bann
Pollan, B. (2002). *Noaidier*. Den Norske Bokklubben: Norway
Price, N. (2013). *The Viking Way: Religion and War in Late Iron Age Scandinavia*. Oxbow: UK

Raudvere, C. (2002). *Trolldomr in Early Medieval Scandinavia*. In Ankarloo & Clark (ed.) Witchcraft and Magic in Europe. Penn: US
Raudvere, C. & Schjødt, J.P. (eds.) (2012). *More than Mythology*. Nordic Academic Press. Lund: Sweden
Reichborn Kjennerud, I. (1927). *Vår gamle trolldomsmedisin*. Det Norske Videnskaps-Akademi: Oslo
Ross, C. (2010). *The Cambridge Introduction to the Old Norse-Icelandic Saga* Cambridge University Press: UK
Rustad, M. (1993). *Vinjeboka*. Solum Forlag: Norway
Simek, R. (2007). *Dictionary of Northern Mythology*. D.S. Brewer: US
Solli, B. (2002). *Seid*. Pax forlag: Oslo
Spiesberger, K. (1954). *Runenmagie*. Richard Schikowski Verlag: Berlin
Spiesberger, K. (1982). *Runenpraxis der Eingeweihten*. Richard Schikowski Verlag: Berlin
Ström, F. (1961). *Nordisk hedendom*. Akademiförlaget: Sweden
Steinsland, G. (2005). *Norrøn religion*. Pax forlag: Oslo
Stokker, K. (2007). *Remedies and Rituals: Folk Medicine in Norway and the New Land*. Minnesota Historical Society Press: US
Sturlason, S. (2002). *Edda*. Det Norske Samlaget. Oslo: Norway
Taylor, C. (2007). *A Secular Age*. Harvard University Press: US
Taylor, T. (1981). *The Hymns of Orpheus*. The Philosophical Research Society: California
Tillhagen, C-H. (1962). *Folklig Läkekonst*. LTs Förlag: Stockholm
Tillhagen, C-H. (1968). *Folkelig Spådomskonst*. Fabel: Sweden
Tolley, C. (1993). *A Comparative Study of some Germanic and Finnic Myths*. Dr. Phil thesis. University of Oxford: UK
Vexior 218. (2010). *Gullveigarbók*. Fall of Man: EU
White, G (2016). *Star.Ships*. Scarlet Imprint: UK
Wilby, E. (2006). *Cunning-Folk and Familiar Spirits*. Sussex Academic Press: UK

Index

Symbols

3 (importance of number) 40, 42-43, 67, 71, 235, 250, 296
9 (importance of number) 122, 235, 250, 260

A

Æsir 18, 19, 39, 40-41, 43, 46-47, 54, 56, 103, 119, 121-124, 126-127, 129-130,
   133-136, 139-140, 143-144, 150, 152, 153, 168, 172, 177-178, 180, 191,
   193, 208, 213-214, 245, 261, 271, 274, 292, 294
Achemilla vulgaris 89
Adam of Bremen 63, 124-126, 143, 151, 152, 201, 202
Aegir 105-106, 112, 122, 128, 254
Aeneid 17
Alcyone 180, 182
Aldebaran 168, 174, 180, 182
ale 38, 41, 67, 69, 86, 104, 114, 116, 146, 148, 150, 155, 157, 163, 182, 214, 244,
   245-246, 247, 260, 261, 263, 264
Alfar. *See* elves
Alfheim 46, 105, 106, 134, 208
Algol 179, 183
Algorab 183
Alphecca 183
alveblót 106, 149, 150
amber 69, 285, 286, 292, 297
Amma 147
Ananke 48, 49, 171
Anaximander 40
ancestors 30, 47, 49, 79, 98, 105, 113, 123, 146, 149, 153, 154, 162, 208
Angrboda 43, 47-48, 51-52, 138, 202. *See also* Heid
Antares 180, 182
Apollo 53-54, 169-170, 173, 176, 192, 207, 306
apple 136, 177, 179, 247
Arcturus 182
Aristotle 17, 36
arrow of Abaris 306-307
Åsatrulaget 18
Åsgardsreia 102, 109, 116
Ask 37, 120, 122, 130, 168, 247, 274, 296
aspen 114, 247, 281
åsynje 101, 102, 129, 150, 164, 177
Audhumla 36, 38, 39, 121, 270, 272
Aurboda 134, 150
Aurgjelmir. *See* Ymir
Austri 106, 178
axis mundi 43, 46, 53, 55, 130, 167, 169, 170-171, 174, 176, 276

B

Balder 32, 51, 55, 56, 127, 131, 132, 139
barley 247
Battle of Hastings 31
bear 45, 68, 79, 94, 162-163, 179

Bed of Ran 49
belladonna 162
Berghjelmir 36, 38, 193
berserkers 62, 94, 148, 234
Bestla 36, 38, 121, 260, 274, 297
Betelgeuse 176, 179, 182
Bible 64, 66, 67, 68, 156, 218, 219
Bibliothèque bleue 20
Bifrost 37-38, 55, 177, 286
Bilskirne 131
birch 114, 246, 247, 294-295
black 117, 156, 197, 198
Black Books 19, 20, 59, 64-66, 192, 253, 275
black dwarves 47
black magic 22-23
blood 67-68, 69, 72, 85, 88, 117, 146, 147, 150, 153, 244, 246, 263, 264
blood-pact 67, 68, 121
blót 29-30, 114, 116, 144, 146-147, 148, 149-150, 151, 164, 166
blue 117, 216
boar 45, 178
Bolthorn 36, 121, 260
bones 69, 72, 117
   human 67, 81, 83, 87, 110, 117, 160
Borr 36, 121, 274
Brage 132, 136
breath. *See* önd
Brisingamen 107, 178, 262, 285
Bryhild 102
buckthorn 248
Bugge, Sophus 231, 232
Bureus, Johannes 231-232
Buri 36, 38, 121, 272

C

Cancer 54, 169, 182
Capella 168, 174, 180, 182
Capricorn 54, 177, 183
Cassiopeia 174, 175, 179
Castor 168, 177, 178
Catholicism 19-21, 29, 32-33, 64, 79, 165, 218, 222-224
Cepheus 175, 178
changeling 70-71
charm (general) 25, 117, 150, 204
charms (and prayers) 64–65, 69–71, 70–71, 82–87, 91–92, 158–159, 216–217, 220–222
Christianity 20-21, 29-33, 51, 64, 107, 126, 132, 136, 143, 145, 148-149, 165, 184, 209
Christmas Eve 66, 73, 79, 164, 165, 220
clover 23, 73, 299
constellations 174-176, 178-179, 180-181
crossroad 67, 74, 82, 111, 117, 150, 155, 176, 207
crows 72, 73, 155, 162
Crue Christi Clavis est Paradisi 84
Crusades 33
cult of the house 98, 110, 146, 173. *See also* farmstead
curse-poems 250
Cygnus 176, 177, 179

D

Dáinn 109, 178, 179
Darradarljód 76
Darwin, Charles 40
death rites 156-157
Deneb Algedi 177, 179, 182
Deutsche Mythologie 60. *See also* Grimm, Jacob & Wilhelm
devil 53, 63, 67, 89, 110-111, 114, 165-166, 218, 223, 248, 250
diabolism 22, 63-64, 224
Diodorus 30
disablót 103, 173, 288
Disir 98, 99, 101, 102-104, 147, 173, 185, 208, 213, 288
distaff 77, 89, 131, 171, 173, 179, 181, 189
divination 23, 38, 79, 195, 317
Draco 53, 174, 175, 176, 179
dragon 43, 81, 104, 113, 172, 173-174, 176, 177, 278
draugr 67, 71, 80, 87, 98, 106, 109-110, 112, 117, 154, 155
Draupnir 107, 131, 278
dream-porridge 73
dreams 22-23, 72-73, 113, 154, 186
Duneyrr 178, 179
Durathrór 178, 179
Dvalin 173, 178-179, 262
dwarves 43, 47, 87, 98, 99, 106-107, 109, 120, 150, 172, 178, 263, 278, 279

E

Easter 165, 166, 220
Eddas 17, 29, 30, 144
Egil Skallagrímsson 25-26, 150, 196, 250, 296
Egil's saga 113, 117, 160
Eikthyrnir 168, 178, 182
Eir 101
Eiríks saga rauda 69, 117, 191, 194, 207
elderberry 248
Elder futhark 229, 231, 235, 250, 269, 270
elves 47, 98, 99, 105-106, 112, 113, 115, 116, 119, 130, 135, 146, 149-150, 153, 162, 247, 248, 250, 263, 268
　black elves 43, 106, 197
　bright elves 46
Embla 37, 120, 122, 168, 247, 296
enchantments 22, 63, 64, 65, 69, 71, 72, 80, 81, 83, 84, 89, 95, 126, 132, 153, 177, 190, 194, 195, 201, 203, 206, 211, 212, 213, 215, 218, 260, 267
Enlightenment 18, 34
Erda. *See* Fjörgyn
ergi 60, 189, 197-201, 205
Eyrbyggja saga 60, 61, 105

F

Fafnir 172, 278
Fáfnismál 172
fairies 37, 45, 72, 109, 115, 119
fairytales 60, 70, 138
familiar (spirits) 66, 71
Fárbaute 138
farmstead 29, 43, 44, 97, 100, 102, 114-115, 133, 135, 144-146, 153, 160, 165, 167
fate 26, 49, 50, 79, 81, 94, 97, 99, 100, 101, 102, 20, 157-158, 165, 169-170, 171-

173, 181, 186-187, 190, 193, 214, 245, 272-273, 283, 287, 296-297
Faustbooks 20, 59, 219-220
Fenrir 47, 48, 61, 133, 134, 138, 139, 140, 182, 183, 203, 245, 280, 285, 290, 292
fetch 66, 68, 76, 78, 99, 103, 185, 193. *See also* fylgja
fingernails 38, 87, 90, 101, 110, 156
Finns 63, 66, 77, 209, 212
fire 36, 38-39, 45, 51, 55-56, 115-116, 127-128, 136, 138, 167, 217, 280, 285-286, 288
Fjolsvinnsmál 101, 201
Fjörgyn 48-49, 103, 113, 121-122, 127, 136, 245, 274. *See also* Jord
Flamel, Nicolas 269
Folkvang 46, 135
fool's gold 69, 290
Fornalder saga 80
Fornjot 128, 130
Forsete 132
Fossegrimen 110
Fóstbraedra saga 110
Freki 81, 122, 199
Frey 105, 106, 114, 121, 122, 124, 126, 127, 133, 134-135, 146-147, 149-150, 162, 180, 182, 183, 194, 247, 287-288, 299, 308, 312
Freya 52, 61, 76, 101-102, 103, 117, 121, 126, 131, 134, 135-136, 147, 162, 173, 178, 180, 182, 183, 191, 193-194, 197, 199-201, 208, 214, 247, 248, 249, 262, 288, 299, 312
Freya's bracelet. *See* Brisingamen
Friday 89, 131, 165
 Holy Friday 66
Frigg 48, 94, 103, 113, 114, 121, 122, 126, 131, 132, 162, 163, 164, 172, 173, 176, 179, 181, 182, 183, 190, 200, 214, 246, 247, 248, 249, 269, 274, 294-295
fylgja 75-76, 98, 101, 103, 122, 129, 147, 172, 185-187, 205, 207, 208, 214, 288

G

galdr 25, 63, 76, 117, 190, 195, 196, 202, 203-204, 206, 207, 211, 212-213, 280, 306
galdralag 25, 204
gandfly 77, 78
gandr 63, 76-81, 90, 112, 116, 117, 131, 149, 190, 199, 212-214
gandreid 75, 76, 78, 212
gardsvord 104, 105, 110
Garm 133, 245, 290
Gemini 168, 174, 178, 182
genii loci 104, 207, 278
Gerd 134, 135, 150
Geri 81, 122, 199
ghosts 108-110, 117, 155, 158, 173
giants 36, 39, 43, 56, 121, 138, 171, 193, 256, 273, 274, 275, 292
Ginnungagap 36, 37, 38, 81, 139
Glitne 132
Gnipahulen 47
Goths 232, 234
graveyard 66, 69, 71, 81, 87, 88, 109, 110, 117, 153, 157, 159, 161
graveyard dirt 69, 81
Grid 134
Grimm, Jacob & Wilhelm 18, 60, 207
Grimnismál 44, 102, 169, 212
Gulating law code 20, 146, 204
Gulltopp 130
Gullveig 51, 52, 192, 197, 202. *See also* Heid

Index

Gungnir 107, 131
Gylfaginning 119, 120, 171, 178
Gyllenbust 131
Gyme 134, 150

H

Hades 47, 48
Hálfs saga ok Hálfsrekka 102
ham 75-76, 105, 106, 208, 276
hamferd 44-45, 50, 185, 209
hamingja 101, 163, 172, 173, 185, 187, 208, 276
hamr 185-187, 196, 208-209
Hárbardsljód 154
haugbu 153, 155
Hávamál 24, 26, 85, 100, 116, 148, 149, 157, 186, 203, 204, 235, 240, 255, 300
heart
  eating 69
  of animals 84
  of humans 160, 184
heathenism 18, 29, 31
Heid 47, 48, 51-52, 61, 102, 122, 132, 138, 147, 191-193, 197, 202, 209, 214
Heimdal 40, 56, 122-123, 128, 130-131, 140, 180, 183, 287. *See also* Rig
Heimskringla 144, 207
heiti 51
Hekate 161, 197
Hel 43, 47-49, 101, 117, 137, 138, 168, 203, 256, 285, 286, 287
Helgafjell 49
Helheimen 43, 47, 48, 49, 117
Hella. *See* Hel
Helsblinde 138
henbane 250, 260
Heqt 161
Heraclitus 39
Herodotus 30, 33, 261, 306
Heruli 233, 234, 250
Hervarar saga 208
Hesiod 48
Hildsvini 135
hollow people. *See* huldre
Homer 17, 33, 207
homosexuality 199-200. *See also* ergi
Hönir 55, 120-121, 122, 177, 274
Hrólfs saga kraka 62, 191, 206, 207
Hugin 50, 74-75, 81, 122, 182, 185, 191, 199, 246, 324
hugr 49-50, 69, 73, 74-76, 81, 85, 101, 116, 184-186, 190, 191-192, 209, 211, 213, 214, 276
huldra 50, 61, 68, 102, 107, 109
huldre 44, 50, 70, 71, 79, 80, 98, 105, 106, 107-108, 113, 114, 115, 117, 135, 154-155, 248, 249, 250, 298
Hymiskvida 147, 245
Hyperborean North 49, 55, 169, 170, 181, 306, 314

I

ice 36, 119, 128, 171, 199, 264, 270-271, 272, 273, 275, 286-287
Iceland 20, 29, 60, 104, 149, 172, 219, 234
Idunn 132, 136, 177, 183, 247, 299

Inquisition 33, 222
Ironforest 47, 51, 138

J

Janus 54
Jesus Christ 32, 65, 147
Jómsvíkinga saga 62
Jord 48, 113-115, 119, 121, 127, 132, 133, 134, 135-136, 139, 142, 147, 182, 245, 247, 294
Jormundgandr 43, 47, 48, 111, 138, 140, 182, 189, 194, 203, 212, 271. *See also* Nidhöggr
Jotun 23, 24, 26, 36-37, 38, 40-41, 47, 51, 54, 55, 56, 61, 68, 108, 119, 121, 129, 133, 139, 150, 171-172, 190, 203, 207, 261, 273-274, 292
Jotunheimen 43, 44, 47, 61, 115, 168, 176
juniper 248

K

kennings 30, 51, 95, 150, 239
Ketils saga hængs 61
kveldrida 75, 108, 205, 208

L

Lady of the House 94, 103-104, 113, 131, 149-150, 165. *See also* Thora
Laestadians 68
Lance of Tyr 106
Landnámabók 112, 167, 326
Laxdaela saga 76, 160, 204, 206
Lethe 48
Lilith 107, 161
linden 249, 276
linseed 249
ljódahattr 25, 204
lodestone 53, 181
Lodfafnismál 110
Lokasenna Loke 106
Loke 38, 52, 55, 136-139, 177-178, 180, 182, 183, 198-199, 202-203, 285, 289, 290, 294-295
Loketretta 131, 135, 136, 139
Lopt 115. *See also* Loke
Lord's Prayer 67, 218, 307
Lothur 120, 122
Lutheranism 21, 29, 63-64, 127, 218, 222-224
lycanthropy 190, 323, 324, 325, 326

M

Macbeth 99
Magnus, Olaus 64, 77, 112, 143, 229, 231
magpies 72, 155
mandrake 182, 183, 247, 275, 284
Manhëmsforbundet 303
mara 75, 107, 108, 117, 205, 248
mararida 75. *See also* mara
marmaele 112
Mary (Virgin) 163, 215
Mass (Christian) 82, 84, 90, 292

Index 343

of the dead 161
Mass of Trolls 209-210
materia magica 89, 155, 244, 246
matrimony 131, 155, 164
Maundy Thursday 67
memory 49-50, 72-73, 75, 77, 99, 104, 121, 170, 185, 191-192, 209, 296-297
mermen. *See* marmaele
meter (poetic) 30-31, 204, 245, 250, 255
Midgard 23, 37, 43, 47, 51, 56, 106, 113, 120, 123, 167, 203, 276
Midgardsormen. *See* Jormundgandr
midsummer 145, 166, 183, 288, 299
milk 38, 74, 114, 116, 155, 165, 301
Milky Way 177
Mimir 120-121, 170, 176, 183, 244, 246, 262, 276
  wells of 130, 168, 173, 193, 261
minne 73, 104. *See also* memory
mistletoe 54-55, 132, 249
Mjölnir 107, 132, 149, 164, 274, 293
Moirai 171
moon 54, 61, 79, 80, 105, 133, 146, 166, 171, 174, 202, 306, 307, 308
moss 87, 110, 113, 247
Munin 50, 74-75, 81, 122, 182, 185, 191, 199, 246
Muspellheimen 36-37, 47, 48, 54
myrkaridur 61, 107, 108, 166, 205
myrkrida 61, 75, 208, 212

N

Naglfare 38, 136, 156
Nál 138
naming 97
Nanna 127, 132, 136
Nennir 94
Nep 127, 136
níd 25, 195
Nidavellir 47
Nidhöggr 43, 53, 56, 111, 113, 131, 138, 140, 168, 169, 170, 171, 173, 176, 179, 181, 183, 184, 206, 270, 271. *See also* Draco
nidstang 150, 195, 296
Nifelheimen 36, 37-38, 43, 47, 48, 54, 256
nine woods 38, 88, 153, 247, 248, 249, 250
nine worlds 43, 44-45
nixen. *See* nøkken
Njord 122, 134-135, 298
noaids 59, 63, 66, 78-79, 198, 209-210, 212, 213
nøkken 94, 98
Nordri 106, 178
Norns 24, 26, 48, 81, 98-102, 111, 158, 162, 169, 171-173, 181, 190, 208, 214, 235, 245-246, 251, 256, 272, 283, 286
north 38, 45, 48, 49, 53, 54-55, 71, 83, 93, 169-170, 173, 309. *See also* Hyperborean North

O

oak 69, 168, 178, 248, 263
Ód 120-121. *See also* Odr
Odin 23, 26, 36, 38, 48, 49-50, 54-55, 72, 76, 95, 97, 110-111, 119-124, 126, 128-129, 131, 132, 133, 134, 136, 138, 146, 154, 166, 168, 170, 173, 176,

177-179, 182, 183, 191, 193, 197-202, 204, 205, 212, 235, 240, 245, 248, 255-256, 260-263, 264, 269, 274, 276-277, 283, 285, 297, 308
Odin's ring. *See* Draupnir
Odin's spear. *See* Gungnir
Odr 120, 135-136, 260, 261
Odyssey 17, 207
offerings 91, 93, 104, 111, 115, 144, 146, 153, 155, 214, 246, 263
Olavs saga 112
omens 22-23, 72-73, 155-156
önd 77, 116, 120, 186
Ondurdis. *See* Skade
Order of the Knights Templar 32
Orion 170, 174, 176, 179, 181, 183, 262-263
örlög 99, 100, 102, 120, 186, 187, 283
oroboros 53, 180
Orphic Hymns 49
Örvar-Odds saga 61, 191, 194, 197

P

pact 66-67, 111, 164, 264
Papaver somniferum 159, 162
Pennick, Nigel 180, 281, 283, 290, 293
Perseus 174, 175, 179
Philosopher's Stone 269, 305
pixies 43, 50, 150
Plato 306
Pleiades 176, 180, 182
Pliny the Elder 54, 234
Polaris 53, 174, 176, 179, 181
Pollux 168, 178
pregnancy 103, 161-164
private cult 20, 29-30, 98, 143, 144-145, 150
Procopius 106, 234
Procyon 182, 183
Protestantism 34, 35, 223
Ptolemy 180
public cult 18, 29-30, 31, 143-144, 146-147, 197

Q

queer theory 199

R

Raesvelg 37, 169, 171, 173, 177, 182
Ragnarök 37, 38, 51, 133-134, 139-140, 156, 180-181, 202-203, 271, 280,
Ran 49, 112, 122, 128, 204, 254, 294, 298
Ratatosk 169, 179
ravens 54, 69, 72, 155, 170
red 117
Reformation 21, 63, 212, 222
Regulus 180, 183
resurrection 32, 51, 132
Rig. *See* Heimdal
Rigstula 40, 122, 123, 130
Rindr 121, 133
rowan 69, 249, 285
Rúnatal 240, 255

runebomma 78
runes 19, 24, 26, 101, 117, 126, 133, 162-163, 173, 180, 181, 203
  ale-runes 148, 244
  biargrúnar 244, 245
  bótrúnar 244
  brimrúnar 241, 244
  hook runes 253
  hugrúnar 242, 244
  limrúnar 241, 244
  málrunar 244
  meginrúnar 243, 244
  ǫlrúnar 244
  sigrúnar 244
  twig runes 235, 253-254
runic *aettir* 235, 250, 253, 254, 270, 300
runic symbols
  Algiz 181, 291
  Ansu 182
  Àr *See* runic symbols: Jera
  As 276-277
  Björk 183, 294-295
  Dag 182, 300
  Eihwaz 182-183, 289, 295-296
  Fé 181, 182, 233, 270-272
  Gebo 182, 280-281, 297
  Hagal 182, 282-285, 287, 307
  Ing 135, 182, 299
  Is 183, 273, 285, 286-287, 307, 313
  Jera 182, 183, 287-288, 299
  Ken 182, 183, 273, 279-280, 288, 307
  Laug 182, 183, 314
  Laukr 297, 298-299
  Man 296-297, 307, 308, 314, 315
  Naud 182, 183, 244-246, 284-285, 287, 288
  Odel 135, 183, 299
  Perth 182, 183, 290
  Raid 183, 277, 279
  Sol 182, 291-292, 313
  Thurs 182, 183, 273-276, 300
  Tyr 133, 182, 183, 244-246, 247, 292-293
  Ur 182, 272-273, 312
  Wunja 182, 183, 281-282
rye 114, 247

S

sacrifice 54, 80, 114, 116, 124, 146, 155, 280, 288
  self-sacrifice 170, 200, 245, 263, 292-293
saliva 69, 156, 244, 246
Sámis 59, 66, 77-78, 198, 209
SATOR square 244
Saturn 53-54, 133, 274-275, 308, 314
scrying 70, 86
seidr 22-25, 52-53, 59, 61, 63, 76-78, 80-81, 108, 153, 269, 294
seidseat 207
serpent 55, 139, 173
shamanism 61, 189, 198, 209
shapeshifting 75, 107, 185, 204, 289

shit-eye 90
sieidi 78-79
Sigerdrifamál 110, 126, 127, 148, 162, 240, 244, 255
Sigyn 138, 139
silence 74, 116, 117, 152, 153, 196, 217, 260, 314
silver 67, 70, 71, 83, 107, 156, 211, 212, 273, 277, 281, 291
Simon Magus 218
Sirius 169, 182, 183
sitting-out 154, 195, 207, 213, 214, 263, 281
Siv 131
Sixth and Seventh Book of Moses 68
Skade 94, 103, 104, 134, 139, 147, 178
skalds 30-31
Skuld 99, 100, 102, 171, 172, 236, 256, 272
Sleipnir 138, 183, 198, 205, 276, 285, 295, 296
social order 40, 56, 103, 113, 122-123, 130, 139-140
Socrates 208
soul 74-75, 76-77, 81, 93, 97-98, 110, 156, 172, 184-186, 202, 208-209
Spare, Austin O. 256
Spica 183
spindle 77, 103, 171
stang 101, 196. *See also* nidstang
St. Cyprian 218-219, 220. *See also* Black Books
St. Elmo's Fire 156
St. John's Eve 165, 166
St. Lucy 102
Sturlasson, Snorre 17, 29-31, 35-36, 44, 125, 136, 143-144, 168, 190, 207, 261
Styx 48
Sudri 106
Summa Theologica 32
summer solstice 54, 166, 169, 171
sun 53-56, 79-80, 127, 130, 133, 146, 149, 166, 171, 174, 278-279, 291-292, 306, 308, 313
Sunday 89-90, 164, 166, 292
Surt 37-38
Svartalfheim 43, 47, 106
Synagogue of Satan 21, 63

T

Tacitus 123, 133, 232, 236, 261
Tartarus 48
The Golden Legend 33
Thora 94, 113, 149, 165
Thor's hammer. *See* Mjölnir
Thule 17, 53, 55, 234, 270
thunderstone 163
thursar 119
Thursday 66, 67, 70, 71, 73, 74, 81, 83, 84, 87, 88, 89, 105, 117, 152, 163, 239, 246, 275. *See also* Maundy Thursday
Tjatse 134, 136, 177-178
toad 72, 114
Toad Bone ritual 72
toenails 51, 89, 90
troll 23, 60-63
trollblót 152
troll-cat 89
Trollchurch 151

Index

trolldom 13, 17, 18, 19, 22, 23, 24, 25, 38, 57, 59, 60, 61, 63, 64, 65, 66, 67, 71, 81, 85, 89, 91, 92, 93, 94, 95, 98, 108, 112, 116, 117, 122, 126, 174, 189, 190, 191, 193, 198, 199, 201, 203, 204, 205, 214, 224, 247, 250
troll-knife 87-88
troll-letters 90-91, 217
troll-pouch 69, 87
trollrida 60, 75
troll-shot 60, 82-83
troll-songs 76, 117, 268. *See also* galdr
troubadours 24, 25, 30, 132, 136, 143, 204, 260
Trudgjelmir 38, 128, 173, 193
Trudvang 46, 131, 148
Tryggvasonar 62
Trymheimen 134, 177
Tyr 133, 152, 180, 214, 245, 246, 250, 280, 290, 293. *See also* runic symbols: Tyr
tyre 80-81

U

Ullr 122, 134
Uppsala 103, 123-124, 135, 147, 151-153, 201-202
Urd 99, 100, 172, 235-236, 272, 283
   well of 149, 171, 193, 256
Urdabrunnir. *See* well of Urd
Ursa Major 53, 55, 174-176, 179
Ursa Minor 53, 174-176, 179
utesitta 154, 207, 213, 263, 281. *See also* sitting-out
Utgard 23, 36, 43, 45, 47, 121, 131, 167, 203

V

vaettir 24, 47, 50, 80, 97, 98, 100, 101, 110-116, 138-139, 144-145, 153-155, 167, 186-187, 195, 206, 207-208, 213-214, 247, 248, 249
Vaftrudnesmál 131, 142, 171, 172
Vále 121, 133, 138-139
Valhalla 49, 102, 168-169, 204, 276, 277
valkyries 76, 99, 101-102, 103, 180, 288
Vanadis 103, 135, 147, 208. *See also* Freya
Vanaheim 43, 46
Vanir 41, 50, 65, 99, 100, 103, 105, 106, 119, 120-121, 122, 126-127, 135, 190, 208, 211, 213-214
vard 75-76, 207
vardlokkur 63, 75, 194, 206, 207, 208
vargulfr 107, 249
Ve 36, 38, 122, 260, 296
Vedrfölnir 169, 177
Vega 178-179, 183
Verdande 99, 100, 171, 172, 235-236, 256, 272, 286
Vergil 17
Vestri 106, 178
Vidar 120, 134
Vile 36, 38, 120, 131, 260
völsi 150, 194, 295
Voluspá 40, 43, 44, 47, 52, 61, 80, 98, 101, 113, 120, 131, 140, 171, 190-192, 196, 197, 203, 271, 283
volva 61, 69, 101-102, 117, 131, 134, 135, 150, 186, 190-191, 193-194, 196, 198, 206, 207, 211
vord 76, 101-102, 110, 172, 186-187, 208

Vuokko 78

W

ward-tree 100, 113, 144, 164, 167, 169, 207
whirlwind 77, 83, 209
white 23, 54, 55, 71, 74, 82, 101, 112, 117, 122, 130, 131, 132, 133, 134, 135, 156, 169, 183, 194, 197, 216, 236, 268, 287
Wild Hunt. *See* Åsgardsreia
winter solstice 54, 173
witchcraft 22, 52, 59, 60-61, 63, 194, 209, 217, 222, 223
witch craze 31
wolves 45, 51, 54, 61, 76, 81, 139, 162, 170, 181, 186, 245, 271, 290
Worm, Ole 231
wormwood 168, 182

Y

Yggdrasil 37, 43, 53, 56, 113, 124, 130, 196, 201, 214, 276, 289, 296
Ymir 36-37, 38, 119, 130, 256, 272, 274
Ynglinga saga 76, 108, 109, 110, 123, 126, 128, 135, 148, 185, 189, 191, 193-194, 197, 204
Ynglingatal 30, 128
Younger futhark 229, 235

Z

Zeus 176

Lightning Source UK Ltd.
Milton Keynes UK
UKHW040620190122
397355UK00001B/8